The Power-Book Library

Its Aim

NOT Training in the well-known Arts, Sciences or Businesses, but Cultivation of the Real Personality for Successful Living in any Art, Science or Business.

Its Philosophy

The Highest Human Science is the Science of Practical Individual Culture.

The Highest Human Art is the Art of Making the Most of the Self and its Career.

One Science-Art stands Supreme: The Science-Art of Successful Being, Successful Living, Successful Doing.

Its Eight Highways of Power

The Highway of Bodily and Mental Health.
The Highway of Dauntless Courage-Confidence.
The Highway of the Controlled Whirlwind.
The Highway of Symmetrically Great Will-Power.
The Highway of Variously Growing Mind-Power.
The Highway of Physical and Psychic Magnetism.
The Highway of Expanding Practical Ability.
The Highway of the Arthurian White Life.

Its Double Goal

Supreme Personal Well-Being and Actual Financial Betterment.

Its Method

Exactly What to Do and How to Do Exactly That.

The Volumes

"Power of Will," (Travels Seven Highways).
"Power for Success," (Travels Eight Highways).
"The Personal Atmosphere," (Suggests all Highways).
"Business Power," (Travels Seven Highways).
"The Culture of Courage," (Travels Four Highways).
"Practical Psychology," (Travels Six Highways).
"Creative Personality," (Indicates all Highways).

You are invited to enter one or more of the Eight Highways and to share in the labor and rewards of many now on the path of personal betterment.

The Power-Book Library.
Volume Four.

Culture of Courage

By Frank Channing Haddock, M.S., Ph.D.

Author of "Power for Success," "Power of Will," "Practical Psychology," "Business Power," "Creative Personality."

A Practical Companion Book for Unfoldment of Fearless Personality.

I am the Courage of the Soul
Harmonic with the Perfect Whole.

Fifty-second Edition

(4,000 copies)

1918

The Pelton Publishing Company,

Meriden, Conn.

(L. N. Fowler & Co., 7 Imperial Arcade, Ludgate Circus, London.)

J. F. TAPLEY CO.
NEW YORK

DEDICATED TO

George Russell Eager

A MIND COURAGEOUS IN EVERY FIELD OF ENDEAVOR.

SUPREME PRINCIPLES.

THE Universe, as a growing organism, is making toward the absolute perfection of all-pervading harmony.

Whatever appearances seem contrary, the Universe in this sense is morally white — without shadow or discoloration.

Throughout all actual "space" resides the Infinite and Eternal *White Life* whose Presence creates and maintains the worlds.

The ultimate all-pervading harmony toward which the Universe is being evolved by the *White Life* can only be attained as all intelligent beings come to harmony with its spirit and laws.

A human life so tending is, as motived, and shall be, as actual, the *white life*.

In the face of the *white life*, behold

THE SMILE OF COURAGE.

I am the courage of the soul
Harmonic with the Perfect Whole.

iv

ANNOUNCEMENT.

"For all may have,
If they dare choose, a glorious life."— *Herbert.*

I HAVE received many letters from people who are distressed by their fears. To every such an one let me send this assured message:

You can grow in your soul a perfect courage.

The methods adapted to this ideal are simple, not impossible to any, and will become less and less difficult as you continue to make them more and more a real part of your life.

I do not say, "Be courageous."

I do not say, "Destroy your fears."

Such advice is common enough, but it is altogether barren unless you know how to carry it out. I hope, rather, to present methods which shall be definite and practical, so that you will be able to do the very thing needful. These methods, in the large, I now announce as follows:

First Method: The Inspiration of the Subconscious Mind. You are invited, always through the reading of this book and during life, to believe, assume and realize —

I Am Growing In My Soul a Perfect Courage.

Second Method: The Elimination of Fear. This is the negative phase of our work. Specific instructions will be given having to do with every kind of fear.   I shall endeavor to suggest practical help to all readers for each particular difficulty.

Third Method: The Culture of Spiritual Courage. By the word "spiritual" I mean not merely religious in the ordinary sense, but rather that kind of courage which is just the breath and tone of the White Life manifest in the human life.   The *white life* in you is harmony with the White Life which is The Good, The Beautiful, The True, The All-Health, The Father, The Infinite Soul of this wonderful Universe in which we live.   If you come to harmony with the White Life, your fears will vanish because you will then share in the Courage of the Eternal Good.

There are two kinds of courage :
The courage that dares and wins; and
The courage that smiles and receives.

"And shall I with a Giant strive,
And charge a Dragon on the field?"

In these lines we have the first kind of courage.   It is good, but there is a type which is vastly superior:

I am the courage of the soul
Harmonic with the Perfect Whole.

These lines indicate the second kind of courage — than which there is no higher.   "Herein is love with us made perfect, that we may have boldness."

These are our methods.   They are commended to your approval.   I shall try to state them plainly, going on from one fear to another, and another, until the long list is disposed of, and always shall I follow details of procedure similar to those set forth in *"Power for Success,"* the ideal constantly being

Exactly What to Do and How to Do Exactly That.

FOREWORD.

"There is no limit to the knowing of the mind that knows."
— *Indian Upanishads.*

I WISH to indulge in a little Foreword because in this way may be indicated a warning against contentment with a seemingly very sensible conclusion which will prove, on further thought, to be hasty and incomplete.

Five years ago I wrote in this identical place in our study these words:

"Fear will never go out of this world until pleasure loses value, desire ceases for want of an object, and reason no longer imposes responsibility.

"The best gift of Nature to primitive man, after reason, was fear.

"The imagination is reason's magnifying power.

"Fear observed and obeyed by reason is a friend.

"Fear and reason take care of man.

"Fear and imagination send him into a panic."

To many minds these statements will have the look of sanity.

But there are others who will instantly perceive that they represent thought on a comparatively low plane. I now observe:

The best gift of Life to primeval man, after love, was reason.

The imagination, void of love,— the feeling of

harmony with all,— forgets reason and permits fear
to enter the soul.

Fear is an *alien* to our life, and never a friend. The
real friend is *reason*, acting amid harmonic conditions.

When you are threatened by some hostile force
or event, reason tries to induce self-protection, but you
know no real fear if you are saturated with the feeling
of harmony. You may believe it is *fear* that seeks
your self-protection. But your *reason* can do precisely
the same thing without fear. Fear is, then, only an
extra, a distressing extra, foisted in front of reason.

You are invited now to live the *white life*, to cast
fear out, and to make real reason its substitute. By
so much you will add immeasurably to personal comfort and power.

Love and reason alone can take care of man, so
far as his own efforts are concerned. In properly
blended proportions these constitute the very life of
courage. What conceivable service then, can fear
render any man or woman?

If you desire panic and distress, let imagination
fill your soul with fears. But if peace, happiness,
health and power be your desires, live the *white life*
and hold fast only to reason.

By the reality called reason I do not mean mere
cold calculation and hard logic. Such phases of reason
are legitimate in their place, if freed from cunning and
deceit, but the higher reason is to these as a woman's
love-look is to the glitter of ice. The higher reason is
not alone intellection, it is also intuition and harmonic
assurance — what religious thought calls faith. The
higher reason declares self-preservation to be the first
law of life, and then, just because this is true, it cares
for self and trusts the White Universe to assist. I

really do not see what a human soul need actually fear when that soul and the White Universe are bent on the same goal, the soul's welfare.

The Universe is a growing organism. It is forever striving to realize its own best estate. This is the true goal for all individuals. It is saying the same thing if we affirm the goal to be Health — for worlds or man: Body-Health, Mind-Health, Self-Health.

When any form of health is threatened, you say, perhaps, it is *fear* that warns you to self-preservation. But I say it is *reason*, and your fear-feeling is unnecessary and hurtful. If you can remember that the White Life or Universe and you have the same desire, your highest welfare, you can banish the fear-element, reserving only the reason-assurance element. All the fears in the world cannot benefit you. Harmony and courage will sublime your whole life.

I have never known a person whose reason has induced self-suffering. Suffer-fear is always a product of diseased imagination. What some may call reason-fear, when they think they are extremely sensible, is simply fear, and nothing but fear, and it is due to imagination, not to reason.

"But," you say, "are there not all sorts of evils in the world, and do they not threaten us, and should we not forefend against them? In this forefending, how can we escape fear?"

These questions show how thoroughly fear is knit into our very lives.

Now this is precisely the point. Fear has no rightful place with any rightful living, because the *white life* alone is rightful, and in that life reason-assurance only is possible, and, therefore, rightful.

The best way in which to forefend against evil is to deny it and cast out the fiction.

This entire question of evil is at your command. Evil exists because other people admit its existence. If all were to live the *white life,* each person might rightly declare, "There is no evil." The only real evil is that which can hurt your best self. When anything hurts your best self, it is your self that hurts your self. The only evil in the Universe is some one's act hurting others, but more, hurting self. If to you evil is, then, it is yourself. You can so live the sublime *white life* of harmony as to be able to say: "So far as I am concerned, evil has gone out of the world. There is no evil to me."

You see, surely now, that you need not fear "evil." I do not know anything more absolutely and sufficiently opposed to the permission of that self-acting which alone, for you, is evil, than reason. Fear has nothing properly to do with the matter. And reason-assurance has to do with it only by living the *white life* and denying fear and evil altogether.

You are invited to make these heaven-born truths your own.

I am Growing in My Soul a Perfect Courage.

CONTENTS.

CHAPTERS.

PREFATORY MATTERS.

The Call of Life.

———

Now must the man be summoned forth
To discover himself, his dual reality:
His world, ten thousand fathoms deep,
His star-vault, ten thousand spaces high;
And come to his own like a king.

THE CULTURE OF COURAGE.

THE NEW DAWN.

"The dawn of a New Day!"
Never an Aryan felt the flare of this electric Fact,
Nor any, or priest at his worship or earth-toiler swarming the
    land,
Till *Zarathustra* discovered *Ahura Mazda*,
Till Buddha discovered himself, the Thou of *That, Brahma,*
Till the *Christ-Mind* assumed *it* to be the *I am That I Am.*

(The flare — the ghostly breath of the long-coming Dawn —
Had passed o'er the Nature-Face, had kissed the swart Human,
Ages and ages, with never a conscious start
In the Man-Soul, till these had upsprung as if gods.—
For, whosoever kens the flare, kens *That* and knows the *One
    Only Who Is*).

So, thrice have men ventured the Word:
"Comes now a full Day that is New!"

Since these giant Men-Types, what times of the Small
Have opened and set on poor mouthings of Truth!
What Night for a thousand years twice told!
With Fear, and the fierce Stars, and no Sun in the Void!
Shadows — and Fear — and Death!

A fourth time man whispers: "The Dawn!"
We *live!* And behold a New Day!"
Does the Flare of its Flood-Tide winds stir *you?*
Does the light of its splendoring Sun thrill *you?*
Does the marvelous Life of it stimulate *you*
To a birth of the self and the kingship of *That?*

You live! The New Day is for each:
For the hitherto Common Man, slave,
For the Women, no longer a Thing,
For the Child, now escaped from the animal lair.
Dawn's here!
(With Opportunity leading "captivity captive,"
(And the stars urging on to achievement,
(And the Sun, breeding life triumphant);
With heart courageous and faith almighty
To fare forth and possess the whole world!
Soul of *you,* awaken! The New Day is yours.

                                        —THE AUTHOR.

THE CULTURE OF COURAGE.

CHAPTER I.

THE WORLD'S NEW DAWN.

"Let us not look at ourselves but onwards, and take strength
from the leaf and the signs of the field. He is indeed despicable
who cannot look onwards to the ideal life of man. Not to do so
is to deny our birthright of mind."— *Thomas Coke Watkins*.

I AM often asked, "Do you think the world is
really becoming better?"
My inmost self — the self I trust and try
to assist — is sure that the world is growing better,
whatever the hampered intellect may from time to time
aver.

For one thing, I *feel* that the world's mind is slowly
yet swiftly changing its adjustment to one supreme
reality — Truth.

Always have men believed that they desired only
the truth, and always have they sought and found it in
part. But then they have immediately wrapped it in
packages and stowed it in boxes with elaborate labels.
Our nature craves reality, not wrappings and tables of
contents. Therefore every age has torn off some of the
ancient outer things, and insisted at last on truth alone.
More than during all the centuries before, men to-day
demand reality — just the essential reality a human
soul craves, and can recognize, and can use in the building of its life.

Henry Drummond spoke of the adjustment which a great telescope needs for photographing the stars. Let us think of one fixed star. "No adjustment is ever required on behalf of the star. That is one great fixed point in this shifting universe. But the *world moves*. And each day, each hour, demands a further motion and adjustment of the soul. A telescope in an observatory follows a star by clock-work, but the clock-work of the soul is the *Will*." The world and the man must *will to adjust to truth* if they would really find and know Truth.

THE WORLD ADJUSTING TO TRUTH.

I hold that the world to-day, more perfectly than ever before, is urging an accurate adjustment of the human soul to truth — that which alone the body demands for health, the mind for development, the deeper self for peace and power.

The old adjustments no longer satisfy. Truth is, indeed, eternal, but our relation must keep pace with it as we swing through the vast heavens of time. The photographs of yesterday do not speak correctly for to-day. We do not deny the stars; we only deny the science that is past.

This adjustment is a huge *prayer*. It is a request for truth, in a sense, but for truth only. And it is an *assurance*. It expects the truth. Now, that is the best kind of praying I know — Expectation in Adjustment.

When you plant your seed or properly place your telescope, you have created adjustment, and you expect harvest and picture.

Expectation in Adjustment is Assumption.

The world no longer merely *asks* for truth; it harmonizes with Nature and Life, and so, *appropriates*.

You are invited to make this thought a lifelong affirmation: *In Harmony I Appropriate All Good.*

Such is one of my reasons for believing that the world is growing better. This attitude toward Truth has influenced for the better every legitimate activity of man. The results are seen in Benevolence, Business, Education, Government, Religion. A new day of splendid, unhampered, happy and growing spiritual life is bursting over the earth. Souls are coming free. Hearts are thrilling with courage. In minds has begun the swing and heave of the sea.

I ask you to take the following lines as a symbol of the world's wonderful sense of appropriation that is everywhere evident.

The sea, the pine, the stars, the forest deep,
 Bequeath to me at will their subtle wealth.
Or still days brood, or rough winds round me sweep,
 Mine is the buoyant earth-man's vibrant health:
All things for love of me their vigils keep —
 I am the soul of health, of wealth.

  Run, sea, in my heart!
  Pine, sing in my heart!
  Stars, glow in my heart!
   For ye are mine, and my soul,
  Like ye, is a part
  Of the Marvelous Whole.

There's no thing dear to me is not my wealth,
 And none that sees me I would distant keep;
For swift possession is my earth-man's health,
 Or still days brood, or rough winds round me sweep:
 All things for love of me their vigils keep—
 I am the soul of health, of wealth.

You are invited, now, to seize and use the spirit of this attitude of appropriation for your own welfare and power.

COURAGE ABROAD.

And I hold that our life is growing better for the reason that I discover, in all this new adjustment to truth, this expectation and assumption that Good will not withhold itself, and *because* of these things, a new era of courage sweeping the heart of humanity from sea to sea.   There is abroad a Universal Breath, manifest of Life.   This breath consists of two general activities, that of Denial and that of Affirmation.   Courage is a denial of fear and of the reality of fear's cause.   But denial is only the beginning; the really vital thing is confidence in self and in the huge friendly Universe in which we live.   Kindly remember this.   You are not making progress merely because you turn your back on the Night.   Progress means that you also turn face to the Sun and walk buoyantly into the Day.   Courage is affirmation:

> I am the spirit of the soul
> Harmonic with the Perfect Whole.

Why, the attitude of healthy denial is everywhere apparent.   Permit me to run over some of the things that are coming more and more to be refused acceptance. You will understand that the items are illustrations only.   We are denying: The divine right of kings; the littleness and unholiness of fundamental human nature; a God who is a kind of huge carpenter; a Deity who needs to be appeased; a Providence which punishes; the idea that some people are created for toil and service and others for ease and to be served; the notion that we must eschew all drugs or depend only on drugs; the thought which makes disease an entity; the fancy that the illness of some is a divine will; the feeling that

wealth should not be craved, or that it exists for a favored few; the creed that "evil" is a necessary existence; the faith that heaven is reserved for the "elect"
who "believe" a number of things; the horror of an
eternal hell; the heresy that religion, the spiritual,
need have anything to do with creeds, rites or ceremonies; the feeling that success is only for the favored ones
of earth; and so on, and so on.

These are merely miscellaneous examples of the
thousand old-time "truths" which are now more and
more denied. Many pages would be required to set
forth the ideas and dogmas which are unceasingly and
emphatically being rejected, thoughtfully, deliberately,
and in a wholesale manner throughout the world of
earnest men and women to-day.

But when you deny, it is a great mistake if you do
not affirm something better. The breath of courage
which is sweeping over the earth, therefore, is splendidly declaring for ten thousand deathless realities to take
the place of mistaken beliefs. I have space simply for
a few illustrations. Are we not affirming somewhat as
follows at the present time?

Signs of the New Life.

Deity is neither Jew nor Gentile; He is the Infinite
All-Good — the Eternal White Life.

The Infinite and Eternal White Life is evolving a
Universe toward the ultimate perfection of absolute
harmony.

All *human beings* are in fundamental nature divine.

We are here for the purpose of *growing to best
estate*.

Every man, woman and child in the world is
entitled to health, happiness, power.

"*Evil*" is derangement in individual life induced by individual and world-thought gone wrong. As such derangement "evil" is real, but this reality is not necessary or essential, and it may be banished totally and forever.

Disease is dis-easement of the matter of a body induced by dis-easement of soul in a body. The self creates or builds its own body, and the condition of the self determines the condition of the body. In "*Power for Success*" I have stated what I believe to be the growing conviction in this regard. "The sound body is a perfect material expression of the Universal Forces playing into its field, and its physical character is determined by the psychic character of its owner." "In a state of health, all physical movements must necessarily coöperate harmoniously with one another and with the Universal Forces."

What we call *mind* is a collection of powers organized for use by the self, and these powers are rightly developed only by the good, the true, the beautiful. If the feeling of goodness, or of trueness, or of beauty, is deep within the subconscious phase of the self, mind-life exhibits as mental health. Mental health is a universal right.

The "*spirit*" — not to refine on philosophy — is the real self which builds body and may unfold mind. The highest state of the individual, therefore, is religious at the top. This is spirituality. But the only conceivable essential to spirituality is a belief in, and an intelligent (truth-using) surrender to, the White Life — conceived in one's own way — for harmony and oneness therewith.

Happiness consists in being consciously harmonized with the true, the good and the beautiful. It is not

necessary, however, although it is, of course, better, to
know these words. The child vibrates with goodness
without understanding the name "goodness." And so
on.

*Power is personality receiving its own in the realms
of life.*

All things exist for all beings.

Such are some of the realities that are being quietly
and potently assumed and affirmed to-day throughout
the world. Of course the language of assertion will
vary with each individual, but this is immaterial. The
essences affirmed are beyond cavil. Other illustrations
might be given, but they would be mere phases of that
one breath of new hope and courage that is stirring in
every land, to "spread contagion on mankind," of the
"life which really is."

These higher thoughts, however, are of the Dawn
only. The full Day is not yet with us. Shadows still
there are, and error, disease and pain. Why must these
false "realities" remain? Solely because of three
things that linger on:

FALSE THOUGHT — SELFISHNESS — FEAR.

And when fear vanishes, replaced by the *white life*,
selfishness will die as impossible, and thought will no
longer be false for the reason that only truth will be
possessed.

If the whole world, then, would but thrust out fear
and receive the spirit of courage, I do not know any
"evils" that could endure a century.

And if you who read these pages will but swing up
to the *white-life* harmony-plane, Health, Happiness and
Power must be yours as surely as air rushes into a
broken vacuum. If you ask, "What are the limits of

this truth?" I answer, "I do n't know." To speak otherwise would be mere speculation. I affirm the great truth: All things are yours. That *you*, if stricken through and through with dis-harmony, may be *able* to receive *all* you crave, I may not affirm. Nevertheless, it is permitted to say: "Launch out! Launch out in the New Thought of Life, and receive, as you do so, whatever is rightly your own, as you are increasingly able to do so."

Man has banished many of his fears already. It is not a long run of the centuries since he quaked before the gloom of the forest, the solitude of the hills, the fog of the vast sea, and, creating innumerable gods and devils by that wizard of distortion, the imagination, lodged them in every object of existence under and in the heavens. He has gotten rid of these.

But when we observe the fear of water, the fear of tornadoes, the fear of lightning, the fear of fire, the fear of disease, the fear of accident, the fear of death, the fear of ridicule, the fear of public opinion, the fear of bankruptcy, the fear of self, the fear for self, the fear of others, the fear of failure, the fear of devils, the fear of a vindictive God, the fear of the future, the fear of a hell—Oh, then, we know that the sun of light is not at his meridian height. We can yet get rid of these also. This is one of the world's tasks. This is your task, if you would make the most of your self and life.

"There is yet very much land to be possessed." No one will possess all of that land in the present stage of existence. Some will be able to claim more than others, but they will err if they assume themselves to be favorites, and the "others" will do worse than err if they complain, "We, alas, are down on our luck." Be assured of one thing: all may be rid of their fears and the whole mass of distress induced by fears. All may acquire dauntless yet serene courage. In that state, if it be of the highest, as it may be, will come to them a peace, a happiness, an influx of buoyancy, a confidence, a sense of well-being, the like of which they have never known.

PRIME DENIALS AND AFFIRMATIONS.

You who now read this page are, thus, invited to begin our study by denying and affirming, as follows:

FIRST — THE DAILY REGIME OF DENIAL:

I deny the existence of error, so far as I am concerned.

I deny disease to be my necessary portion.

I deny the need of any of my fears.

I deny the reality of any cause for fear.

I deny that I am less than a king.

I deny that ignorance is an essential part of my lot.

I deny that poverty is decreed to me.

I deny that I am low-born or of bad blood.

I deny that I am "down on my luck."

I deny by my life that others are my superiors.

I deny that anything can hurt the essential *me*.

I deny a vindictive God.

I deny that slavery is religious.

I deny that I am not the friend of the White Life.

I deny that I am mean, low or ignoble in morals.

I deny that my best life depends on creeds.

I deny that the Universe is not for me.

I deny that health is not my rightful claim.

I deny that I am unhappy or depressed.

I deny that I am weak and a nonentity.

I deny that I shall not unfold forever.

I deny all that is opposed to my best welfare.

SECOND — THE DAILY REGIME OF AFFIRMATION.
   I affirm truth to be my desire and possession.
   I affirm health to be my rightful claim.
   I affirm fearlessness of that which I have feared.
   I affirm cause and reason only for courage.
   I affirm that reason is independent of fear.
   I affirm my sovereign selfhood.
   I affirm that life is my perfect university.
   I affirm that I am success.
   I affirm that a part of the world's plenty is for
      me.
   I affirm myself the *white-life* equal of others.
   I affirm my real self impregnable to hurt.
   I affirm the Infinite Life to be my Friend.
   I affirm that spirituality is true freedom.
   I affirm myself the friend of the Infinite.
   I affirm that mine is the *white life*.
   I affirm my independence of narrow creeds.
   I affirm buoyant happiness as my present pos-
      session.
   I am power!
   I shall live and unfold forever.

It may be that all this is strange thought to you,
almost meaningless, perhaps.   You are invited, therefore, to remember that thousands of people have felt
similarly at first, have then caught a glimpse of the
truth here and there, and finally have experienced a
wondrous recognition of the New Dawn which has now
surely come to the world.   It is significant that these
are saying, "There is nothing else worth while in the
whole earth."
   Two men were scraping paint from a house preparatory to putting on a new coat of color. One of them

who had been helped back from mental unbalance, and helped solely by thought, broke a long silence and said: "This is the whole thing." He referred to the dawn of Real Life in himself.

If, now, this chapter has seemed to broach the subject of religion, remember, it does not deal with religion as you perhaps know religion. The only thing valuable in religion is the White Life within the human self. That alone *is* religion. Call it what you will. And it means just that courage which makes us buoyantly equal to any kind of life that is right. The methods of this book will prove of value to you, whether or no you go into the *white-life* phase of existence. But they will realize completest value if you will swing at the start clean out into the one greatest thought — "*I surrender to, and I receive, the Infinite White Life.*"

It is because I desire every reader to get this perfect start in our study that I have indulged in the rather general outlook on the world's New Dawn. Hereafter our work will be more specific and addressed to the varying conditions of the individual man or woman.

FEAR-THOUGHT AND FEAR-FEELING.

The *intellect* coldly reflects What Is:
An icy, crystalline lake portraying earth and sky
In shadows beautiful as death —
And void of pulse, or warmth, or music of good life.
This is no Eye with which to view the world!

The *soul* reflects the universe
With ecstasies of heat, of hue, of harmony!
Its *inner* gaze creating Life in Fact,
So, robing sheer Reality in colors ravishing,
Giving it Voice, forming within it Heart,
And vitalizing All with Feeling — Being's blood.
This is our Eye, viewing the world it builds.

Fear blurs that Eye, while Reason clears:
Pure *mind* lacks Passion adding values to existence;
(Who loves mere ghost-flowers born of moonlight?)
Pure *Feeling* lacks in *Reason*, needing values,
And, lacking so, fills Eye of Soul with fantasies,
With wild distortions of imagination's lust.
(Who loves the fire-hued, smoke blooms of Hell's Land?)
And always Fear feeds Feeling's grotesque growths
Till Soul's Eye on its own creation looks
As on eternal Truth.
Then Truth and Nature, Deity and Man
Evolve dread enmity and horrors multiple,
And Soul flees terror-stricken on to Death.

Oh, I will rule heart's Feeling for good Life,
Given Soul's Mind for this — naught else:
That Reason may re-think the Beautiful and Happiness
And see eternal Truth and Truth-Fact as my lovers —
Veracious Guardian Angels guiding all my way —
Coöperative, like the brain and heart of body,
To lead my soul on Courage (not on Death)
And make me *worth* the skill
Of the illimitable years — a Mind-Man, whole!

        — THE AUTHOR.

CHAPTER II.

FEAR AND REASON.

"In civilized life it has at last become possible for large numbers of people to pass from the cradle to the grave without ever having had a pang of genuine fear. Many of us need an attack of mental disease to teach us the meaning of the word."— *William James*.

E HAVE all heard the seemingly discriminating remarks that fear is normal and abnormal, and that normal fear is to be regarded as a friend, while abnormal fear should be destroyed as an enemy.

The fact is that no so-called normal fear can be named which has not been clearly absent in some people who have had every cause therefor. If you will run over human history in your mind, or look about you in the present life, you will find here and there persons who, in situations or before objects which ought, as any fearful soul will insist, to inspire the feeling of at least normal self-protecting fear, are nevertheless wholly without the feeling. They possess every feeling and thought demanded except fear. The idea of self-preservation is as strongly present as with the most abjectly timid or terrified, but fear they do not know. This *fearless* awareness of fear-suggesting conditions may be due to several causes. It may result from constitutional make-up, or from long-continued training or habituation, or from religious ecstasy, or from a perfectly calm sense of spiritual selfhood which is unhurtable, or from the action of very exalted reason. Whatever the explanation, the fact remains: the very causes which excite fear in most of us, merely appeal, with such people, if at all, to the instinct of self-preservation and to reason, the thought-element of the soul which makes for personal peace and wholeness.

Banish All Fear.

It is on such considerations that I have come to hold that all real fear-*feeling* should and may be banished from our life, and that what we call "normal fear" should be substituted in our language by "instinct" or by "reason," the element of fear being dropped altogether.

"Everyone can testify that the psychical state called fear consists of mental representations of certain painful results" (James). The mental representations may be very faint as such, but the idea of hurt to self is surely present. If, then, it can be profoundly believed that the real self cannot be hurt; if the reason can be brought to consider vividly and believingly all quieting considerations; if the self can be held consciously in the assurance that the White Life surrounds the true self, and is surely within that self, and will suffer "no evil to come nigh," while all the instincts of self-preservation may be perfectly active, fear itself must be removed "as far as the east is from the west."

This splendid conviction I earnestly commend to all readers.

These are the ways, then, in which any occasion for fear may be divided:

As a warning and as a maker of panic. But let us say that the warning should be understood as given to reason, that fear need not appear at all, and that the panic is perfectly useless pain. With these discriminations in mind, we may now go on to a

PRELIMINARY STUDY OF FEAR.

Fear is (a) an impulse, (b) a habit, (c) a disease.

Fear, as it exists in man, is a make-believe of sanity, a creature of the imagination, a state of insanity.

Furthermore, fear is, now of the nerves, now of the mind, now of the moral consciousness.

The division depends upon the point of view. What is commonly called normal fear should give place to *reason,* using the word to cover instinct as well as thought. From the correct point of view all fear is an evil so long as entertained.

Whatever its manifestations, wherever its apparent location, fear is a psychic state, of course, reacting upon the individual in several ways: as, in the nerves, in mental moods, in a single impulse, in a chronic habit, in a totally unbalanced condition. The reaction has always a good intention, meaning, in each case, "Take care! Danger!" You will see that this is so if you will look for a moment at three comprehensive kinds of fear — fear of self, fear for self, fear for others. Fear *of* self is indirectly fear *for* self — danger. Fear for others signifies foresensed or forepictured distress to self because of anticipated misfortune to others. I often wonder whether, when we fear *for* others, it is distress *to self* or hurt *to them* that is most emphatically in our thought.

Fear, then, is usually regarded as the soul's danger signal. But the true signal is instinctive and thoughtful reason.

Even instinct and reason, acting as warning, may

perform their duty abnormally, or assume abnormal proportions. And then we have the *feeling* of fear. The normal warning is induced by actual danger apprehended by mind in a state of balance and self-control. Normal mind is always capable of such warning. There are but two ways in which so-called normal fear, acting in the guise of reason, may be annihilated: by the substitution of reason for fear, and by the assurance of the *white life*.

Let it be understood, now, that by normal fear is here meant normal reason — real fear being denied place and function altogether. Then we may say that such action of reason is a benefactor to man. It is, with pain and weariness, the philanthropy of the nature of things within us.

One person said: "Tired? No such word in my house!" Now this cannot be a sound and healthy attitude. Weariness, at a certain stage of effort, is a signal to stop work. When one becomes so absorbed in labor as to lose consciousness of the feeling of weariness, he has issued a "hurry call" on death. I do not deny that the soul may cultivate a sublime sense of buoyancy and power; rather do I urge you to seek that beautiful condition; but I hold that when a belief or a hallucination refuses to permit you to hear the warning of nerves and muscles, Nature will work disaster inevitably. Let us stand for the larger liberty which is joyously free to take advantage of everything Nature may offer for true well-being. There is a partial liberty which tries to realize itself by denying various realities as real; there is a higher liberty which really realizes itself by conceding such realities as real and by using or disusing them as occasion may require in the interest of the self at its best. I hold this to be true wisdom: to take advantage of everything which evidently promises good to the self, without regard to this or that theory, and freely to use all things, material or immaterial, reasonable or spiritual. I embrace your science or your method; but I beg to ignore your bondage to philosophy or to consistency. So I say that to normal health the weary-sense is a rational command to replenish exhausted nerves and muscles.

It is not liberty, it is not healthful, to declare, "There is no pain!" Pain does exist, whatever you affirm, and your affirmation that it does not is proof that it does exist, for why (and *how*) declare the non-existence of that which actually *is* non-existent? But if you say, "As a matter of fact I have pain, but I am earnestly striving to ignore it, and to cultivate thought-health so that the cause of pain may be removed," that is sane and beautiful. This is the commendable attitude of the Bible character who cried: "Lord, I believe; help thou mine unbelief." To undertake swamping pain with a cloud of psychological fog — that is to turn anarchist against the good government of Nature. By pain Nature informs the individual that he is somewhere out of order. This warning is normal. The feeling becomes abnormal in the mind when imagination twangs the nerves with reiterated irritation, and Will, confused by the discord and the psychic chaos, cowers and shivers with fear.

I do not say there is no such thing as fear. Fear does exist. But it exists in your life by your permission only, not because it is needful as a warning against "evil."

Fear is induced by unduly magnifying actual danger, or by conjuring up fictitious dangers through excessive and misdirected psychical reactions. This also may be taken as a signal of danger, but it is a falsely-intentioned witness, for it is not needed, is hostile to the individual because it threatens self-control and it absorbs life's forces in useless and destructive work when they ought to be engaged in creating values. Hence we state

The First Great Principle of Fear-Conquest.

Timidity, apprehension, fear, alarm, fright, consternation, terror, panic, desperation, are all false imitations of reason's interpretation of the warning signals of Nature, to be displaced by reason itself, which may then determine whether the occasion be real or unreal, and always to be disregarded and overcome if evidently referring to causes which do not actually exist.

This principle is adduced in the interest of three things: peace, health, power. You are invited to note how vital these interests really are.

The truest peace, of which courage is a sublime bloom, is a growth solely of honorable living and robust self-respect.

Health is of the following realities: body, mind, soul — the deeper self. Health is soundness. A sound human is a triune wholeness. Physical soundness with weak intellect is often the athletic field of superstitions innumerable. Intellectual greed in an unsound body may breed the direst fears of life. A decayed soul is always a House of Fear. The ideal of human existence is — *The white life in the sound mind in the vibrantly whole body.*

It is because there are so many people who are in some sense sick, that fears abound in every direction. But — it is because so many fears are permitted and actually nursed as boons that so many sick people abound in every direction. If all our fears could be removed absolutely, we should no longer require physicians. This world would be a paradise in every respect. I do not know anything wrong with it that cannot be traced to a fear.

The causes of fear are weak reason, uncontrolled imagination, want of self-control, and ill-health. And the first three items are really phases of the last.

The ability to master and destroy fear depends, it would now seem, upon the following factors of our life:

The General Tone of the Individual;
The Soul's Power of Will;
The Development and Balance of the Reason.

Reason is demanded to distinguish between right and wrong causes for personal effort in self-protection, and to utterly ignore all wrong causes.

Will-power is demanded to banish fears and to utilize reason's dictates.

But the sway of reason and the force of action are always immensely assisted by a vigorous general tone of the personal life. Now appear, in view of these considerations,

THREE GREAT LAWS.

FIRST LAW: *The warnings of reason are based in the nature of things within us, and are universal benefactors.*

SECOND LAW: *Fear is contrary to the ground-plan of life.* It is no primary part of the nature of things; it is an alien in the world-system.

THIRD LAW: *The destruction of fear always follows the growth of general courage in the individual.* The fear-brood will not depart until the soul has acquired a fixed habit of courage. Whatever establishes that habit, or spirit, secures the service of reason-instinct, and so undermines and finally destroys the power of every variety of fear. These laws formulate a great

PRIMARY INJUNCTION.

Let your soul be saturated with the sure conviction that fear is an alien in the world-system of life, having no proper place nor legitimate rights therein, and meanwhile resolutely set about the task of cultivating in every possible way the permanent habit-spirit of courageous living.

This book was written for the sole purpose of suggesting definite methods by which such courage-habit may be developed. In order that our practical methods may be understood, it is now necessary to analyze the subject of fear in its general outlines.

It is important to remember that the warnings of reason, sometimes called normal fears, may have actual causes outside the mind and are rightly proportioned thereto and to possible consequences, while real fear is due to causes not based in reality, or, if so based, is permitted to agitate the mind in a way not warranted by possible consequences viewed by a rational, well-balanced life. Our analysis, then, exhibits fear where reason ought to appear, in

A GENERAL ENUMERATION OF FEAR-CAUSES.

Fear of hurt of self by self (fear *of* self) : substitute reason, thus — just estimate; no cause; cause magnified.

Fear of hurt of self by outer things (fear *for* self) : substitute reason, thus — just estimate; no cause; cause magnified.

Fear of threat by things: substitute reason, thus — right cause; no cause; cause magnified.

Threat by others: substitute reason, thus — right cause; no cause; cause magnified.

Threat to others: substitute reason, thus — right cause; no cause; cause magnified.

Threat by events: substitute reason, thus — right cause; no cause; cause magnified.

Threat by the future: substitute reason, thus — right cause; no cause; cause magnified.

You are invited to work out the particulars of this analysis, and to examine them with reference to your self and life. You will make some important discoveries. One of the many questions suggested is this: Is the cause of anticipated possible consequences justly estimated in your thought — is it a right cause — is it really as you suppose? The idea is that you think of any one of your fears and then ask the question in the form just indicated. Thus we may have the following statement of

KINDS OF FEARS.

Fear *of* Self: timidity, lack of confidence, possible unaccountable states.

Fear *for* Self: weakness, anticipated failure, imagined disgrace.

Fear of *Things*: animals, inanimate objects, physical forces.

Fear *of* Others: human beings, apparitions, devils, Deity.

Fear *for* Others: children, parents, husband. wife, relatives, friends, strangers.

Fear of *Events:* present, future, imaginary, possible, probable, contingent.

Fear of the *Future:* in life; beyond the present life.

Instinct and reason strive to place us in right relations with all these causes. The existence in us of fear shows that we already are, either in mind or in fact, in wrong relations therewith.

The mastery of fear involves the discovery of right relations, mental or concrete, and the placing of self in those right conditions which are determined and provided for by the ground-plan of our nature.

And the first thing thus provided for is health. All treatment for the conquest of our universal enemy must begin with development of individual tone: tone of body, tone of mind, tone of the deeper self.

I am not writing for those who are constitutionally fearless, but I have in mind all who do yield to the feeling of fear. Our ideal, however, is not a mere animal courage, not the courage of insensibility. It is rather the courage of the whole man or woman making for the *white life.* If you are only partially yourself, you cannot possess the highest courage. Such courage may be yours, infallibly, if you will but resolve for the goal and go on into the great ideals of the harmonic personality. This you can do — anyone can do. And to come thereto is the greatest thing in the world.

You are invited, then, to begin by substituting in your thought the idea of self-preserving reason for any kind of fear (even the so-called normal) as your perpetual guard and guide. Make it a profound conviction of your deepest self that no real harm can come to that self because you have entered the highway of the *white life — the life of purity, reason, honor, good-will, and confident assurance.* Swing your life into the unfolding and infolding of the Infinite White Life of

Worlds. Courage will become to **you** the very breath
of your lungs.

> I send you this sure message: Fear is dead
> In all the pure, by reason's wisdom led,
> Who wear white honor and evince good-will,
> And trust the self to Love's unfailing skill.
> I send you this sure message: Courage lives
> When man to Courage all assurance gives.

THE SOUL OF THE CELL.

This crystal of Quartz, — the queen of its tribe,
Amethyst, Onyx, Chalcedony, Heliotrope, Agate, —
Some toiler of old Japan, the Artist fantastic,
Has polished to likeness of ice,
Ruining form to reveal it *Flèche d'Amour*
That the marvelous, delicate, hairlike inclosures
Of crystallizations foreign might please the beholder.
Herein worked the Infinite well,
And, let us say, too, the artisan patient,
To one limit — significant boundary!
Health!

I request you to define it — configure the wonder
Of this dust-common, beneficent Gift.
Who lacks it, he knows quite precisely his want;
Who has it divulges precisely the thing.
Yet never man — scientist, poet, physician —
In words can portray it — the Soul of the Cell,

That lurks only in spheres of the Substance of Life;
Fares past the quartz and hides in the throat of the wearer.
Shuns diamond glory for greater of flesh;
Builds higher and higher to balance unstable
In beauty of male and in exquisite female,
And sends through the intricate meshwork of cells —
Sheer matter, kin of this quartz —
Its evidence: light-hue, radiance crimson,
Eye-gleam, pulse-throb, vigor and nerve-thrill
Of just that common, miraculous Gift,
Health of a body wherein dwells *Soul.*

There, say I, the Infinite worked well!
Come now to *you* the artisan's skill for this marvel,
Physical man: to refine and ennoble;
To reveal the inclosure of spirit unmarred,
And grow in the mobile, responsive flesh
Mind perfect, held fast in *our* Crystal superb,
The Universe complete.

— THE AUTHOR.

CHAPTER III.

PHYSICAL TONE.

"In the healthy body every cell is polarized in subjection to the *Central Will*. Perfect health, therefore, is orderly obedience, government and harmony. Every cell is a living entity, whether of vegetable or animal potency, and wherever disease is, there are disunion, error, rebellion and insubordination; and the deeper the seat of the confusion, the more dangerous the malady and the harder to quell it."—*J. C. Street.*

THE thought of the above quotation does not mean that the insubordination is necessarily conscious to the diseased individual, but that it surely obtains within the physical arena of his life. Because it is not the outcome of his deliberate choice, the case is not hopeless in the nature of things, but is open to better conditions. The deeper self which has intended no rebellion against the laws of bodily well-being may now distinctly intend harmony, and so lift the body to a higher plane.

And the last sentence in the quotation does not mean that you are to undertake a vast amount of hard work, assuming that you are not in perfect physical condition. You are, rather, just to begin and go on thinking yourself in a real way as in harmony with the Central Will, which is our White Life, and to hold steadfastly in the deeper self the ideas, *Affirmation and Realization of Splendid Personal Tone.*

Some of the meanings of these powerful words will be unfolded later. In the meantime, as all things are

subject to law, let us observe a number of the general
conditions to three-fold health, that of body, mind and
the inner self, regarding their totality as the atmosphere, so to speak, in which courage most easily and
perfectly thrives.

Fear in man is a result of repeated suggestion, to
which low health-tone is a natural invitation. Health
is the primary tonic against fear. Perfect physical
health is mere strength. Perfect mental health is mere
brain sanity. Perfect soul-health is the whole of the
man at his best. When the body is buoyant, the mind
clear and inspired, the soul harmonic with all existence
rightly in the universe, then is the impulse of fear
easily mastered and the habit of fear finds no encouragement. There are, indeed, courageous invalids who
have not come into the secret of right thought so far
as health is concerned, and fearing atheltes and scholars
who have neglected the secret of courage, and timorous
saints who have failed to possess themselves of the
confidence of goodness. Nevertheless, the eternal law
is evident that the one great enemy of fear is

The White Life in Harmonic Mind in Buoyant Body.

A person who affirms and realizes these conditions
must, in the nature of things, be possessed of perfect
health. In the tone of such health courage is inevitable.

That you may come to this ideal, you are invited to
observe the following instructions. Health is a trinity,
and we may begin our studies with its natural basis:

The General Tone of Health.

The word "tone" means, "sound in relation to
volume, quality, duration and pitch," then, "peculiar
characteristic sound as of a voice or instrument," then,

"characteristic style or tendency, predominating aim or character, tenor, strain, spirit."

Hence, in the sense of health, tone signifies "the state of tension or firmness proper to the tissues of the body; the state in which all the parts and organs have due tension or are well strung; the strength and activity of the organs on which healthy functions depend; that state of the body in which all the normal functions are performed with healthy vigor."

We thus see that health-tone involves the whole personality, physical, mental and moral.

But the truth of the matter hides in a deeper region than that of mere material flesh or organ. Matter is a form of the Universal Ether, so far as science seems to declare, or, at least, matter presupposes the ether in a state of vibration. Your body is a "field" in which etheric vibrations are constantly taking place. All its reality and all its activities involve such vibrations. The brain, regarded as the organ of conscious life, of thought and feeling, and the entire nervous system, involve such vibrations. And as your thought and feeling constitute the foundation of your moral character, the latter also becomes a matter of movements in the ether.

In the case of heat, light, electricity, etc., differing kinds of such vibrations determine the kinds of phenomena. We may say, then, that there is one general kind of ether-movement for matter, and another for thought and feeling, and another for the moral life. Each individual, however, presents variations of these general kinds of vibrations,— a particular variation for his body, and for his mental person, and for his right or wrong self-spirit. We individualize the ether. Or, we are individualized as we use the ether.

The tone of a person's health is determined by the state of the etheric movements characteristic to himself.

If the vibrations underlying the body life are full and harmonious according to their individual character for a person, his organs are all sound and active. He possesses physical tone. If there is a similar fullness and harmony within his mental life, he must exhibit health of mind. If a corresponding condition obtains in the moral personality, the highest health of the deeper self prevails.

These three individualized varieties of ether-movement in man mutually interact and determine one another's character. I know that this law does not always seem to operate. Poor minds and wrong morals are sometimes found in apparently healthy bodies, and great minds and noble spirits in feeble bodies. But the bodies of the one class do *not* represent the finest physical health, involving coarseness, flabbiness, susceptibility to disorder, etc., etc., and are not contradictions of the law. Moreover, the inner life is not always fully expressed by apparent departures from right living: as you may frequently see in some sudden burst of nobility, generosity, tenderness, heroism, in those who possess sound bodies but are outwardly not particularly refined. The rough exterior may hide a splendid germ of true spiritual manhood or womanhood. Could we look deeply into the physical nature, we should always find the law holding good that our three-fold ether-movements do influence and in the long run determine one another for weal or ill. Where the inner self is right yet the physical tone weak or disturbed, we should perceive, if we had the "spirit of discernment." that the better life within has surely influ-

enced and ennobled the essential nature of the body.
It should be remembered that two confusing factors
prevail where a fine spirit dwells in a diseased body:
first, the thought-life of centuries has, so to speak,
warped the character of the inherited body and its vibrations to such an extent that they may not, perhaps (I do
not know), be altogether reformed within a human lifetime; secondly, the thought-life of the individual, however nearly right in many respects, is wrong in one particular, the belief, feeling, conviction — an inheritance
of ages — that disease of the body must necessarily
obtain in some cases at least, no matter what the inner
life may be. This conviction is a tremendous force for
harm. Invalids accept it as true, and try to be recon-
ciled. But it is not true. The belief prevails, and so
prevents the real truth from appearing: that *Perfect
Health is the Primary Intention of the Nature of
Things for All.* When we can believe this magnificent
truth, we shall be able to see that right vibrations underlying the mental and moral personality must tend to
reform wrong vibrations underlying the body. So long
as the former conviction prevails, that disease is somehow a part of Nature, the better life contends with a
double difficulty, the existing physical conditions and
the false suggestion that the individual must continue
to be ill in the nature of things or as the will of Deity.
The false suggestion should be displaced by the affirmation and realization of physical health. Such a
reforming suggestion, made effective by mental realization and proper regimes, tends to counteract the
existing effects of previous wrong suggestions and
positively to change conditions of ill-health, because
fullness and harmony of the three kinds of ether-movements are the designed ideals of our lives and the laws

of perfect well-being (what other design can we possibly imagine?), and the good suggestion operates to bring about that ideal.

Let us be rid of the notion that anyone is ill because a Divine Being wants him to be ill.

But we must remember that while these principles cannot be otherwise than true, every individual has behind him, at any present moment, two great forces — the past of his ancestors and the past of his own life. Let us be sensible, even while we insist upon truths which are among the most beautiful in the world. The past means much to all of us. Such is law. We cannot get away from law, whatever our theories or religious belief. To me all Nature's laws are of the White Life and untellably beneficent. The idea that law is something hard and disagreeable is itself a false suggestion and a wrong thought. Law is good. The law that life is determined more or less by the past is a fine example of this goodness. If it seems to go against us in some cases, it surely goes for us in assisting a right past to make for a right future. When it seems to work hardship, the fact is the law is trying to face us about for a right time to come. That is the meaning of experience: it is law talking to us out of our past. The law that our past and that of our ancestors must be reckoned with in all our efforts to reform the etheric vibrations in our personal fields involves the element of time, which element may be greater than we can control in the material life. This element of time is important because there is another law, that great real reforms in the individual require effort continued more or less in order that all laws involved may properly and fully operate. If the person who is a noble self in a weak body could add to his thought-life the sufficiently powerful affirming realization of physical health for himself and live long enough, I certainly believe the suggestion would ultimately prevail. For I do not for a moment accept disease as a necessary part of human life. Is disorder in your machinery a part of the machine? I cannot see how a continuously perfect self, starting with a sound body, could ever come to possess a diseased body. I must believe that the self, growing to the ideal, may bring into harmony a diseased body, provided its health-suggestion is strong enough and sufficient time is afforded for the full working of the law. The law does not, of course, cover such cases as broken bones, because treatment then calls for mechanical operations, which involve laws altogether distinct from those that govern harmony among the functions and organs of the body as underfounded by etheric vibrations within the physical, mental and moral fields.

The limits set to self-healing power we do not know for any individual case. The splendid general law is not overwhelmed, is not contradicted, by such limits, whatever they may be, because the limits are not set by the original intention of the nature of things, but by wrong living and false ideas running through centuries. As we may not know the limits in any case, and as the great law shines ever before us and is equally for all so far as it may be claimed, and not for a favored few of some particular religious or semi-religious belief, it is ours to seize all advantages afforded by the best medical science together with every atom of power in the *white life* affirming and realizing physical health at its best. You do not know your own limits; therefore lay hold upon the law, the universal, age-long law, for all you can derive from its beneficence. You are not required to turn your back upon any other advantage, but only to swing the law into harmony with that advantage.

Health-tone, then, is really a triune series of full and harmonious ether-movements within the personal field working together for a buoyant right self in a sane and truth-loving mind in a spiritually expressing physical organism. By so much as it is yours, by so much, in the nature of the case, must fear be an alien and courage the breath of your life.

We may now go on to the general consideration of

PHYSICAL TONE.

It would seem almost unnecessary to suggest the ordinary regimes for health of body. Nevertheless, I shall refer to these regimes because, first, their importance cannot be overestimated, and secondly because they involve certain laws of laws in relation to health which are seldom worked out in hygienic instruction.

What may be called the laws of laws of health would seem to be as follows:

1. *Scrupulous Cleanliness of the Body, Without and Within, Makes for Royal Health-Tone.* The law should be given rational, not slavish, obedience. Your body and your deeper self are in a constant state of interaction. Material uncleanness consented to contaminates that self. Uncleanness of the self also contaminates the body. The *white life* requires the clean dress of honored flesh. You are invited, therefore, to affirm always and practically,

> This robe I wear of unsoiled flesh
> Keeps mind and spirit ever fresh.

2. *Sweet, Sound and Early Sleep Gives the Universal Forces their Perfect Opportunity for Good.* During sleep the Universal Thought strives to restore, as our conditions permit, harmony of vibrations between

its manifests in matter within the body and its manifests in the non-material self. The degree of harmony is made less in all cases by centuries of wrong living, the effects of which are more or less accumulated by inheritance in every man and woman (right living, however, promising in the future perfect freedom therefrom on earth), and by the disturbing power of individual wrong living. In order, then, to secure the best results of sleep, our waking thought should be kept in attune, by all practical as well as by all idealizing methods, with reality, truth, beauty and goodness. You are invited, for the reason suggested, to live during the day in such a manner that your last fearless thought at night may be,

"Let my soul walk softly in me,
Like a saint in heaven unshod,
For to be alone with Silence
Is to be alone with God."

3. *The Utility of Nourishment Issues From Conformity to the Plan of the Universal Forces for Each Individual.* For every human body there is a plan on which it is intended to be evolved and maintained. The individual plan is merely a variation of the general plan of our common human nature. That general plan provides for certain foods and kinds of drink, for the manner in which they are to be taken and digested, and for their utilization in building and sustaining the body. This general plan is varied for different persons in the primary intention of the nature of things. Your food and drink, therefore, should depend upon your own peculiar needs. The science of the matter investigates the kinds of nourishment which you in particular require and advises all items furnishing the material elements you demand. But some individual variations,

in respect to questions of taste, usefulness and **harm-**fulness, digestibility and adaptation, are undoubtedly results of restrained liberty and wrong thought-life in the past, either of your ancestors or of yourself. That degree of liberty, therefore, which ought to be yours, has perhaps, come to be more or less limited. It is possible for you to secure a desirable enlargement of freedom with regard to food and drink. Of course you have no liberty in the way of natural poisons and beverages which dethrone common sense. Aside from the limits set by Nature, you may acquire the largest measure of personal freedom in the matter if you will determine therefor in the exercise of sound reason. I have had my experience with things not liked and things harmful — apricots, chickens, salmon — and to-day I eat all that's eatable by civilized man, and I drink whatever I choose to drink — alcohol tabooed because I want and need all the brains I possess. It is for you to bring yourself more nearly to the original plan for human bodies in this respect, if you will begin with your inner thought-life and proceed more or less in the following manner:

(*a*). By insisting upon a *larger freedom*, not in the way of demanding one thing or another, but in the way of realizing in your deeper self the idea of power therefor;

(*b*). By endeavoring constantly to bring your thought-life more and more into *harmony with the White Life in Nature;*

(*c*). By affirming that the food and drink of which you partake will surely *make for health* and buoyancy of the body; not merely stating the proposition, but, while so partaking, believing the truth and assuming it to be true — actual for you;

(*d*). By manifesting at all times the mood of blended *courage, hope, confidence, happiness;*

4. *The Value of Work and Play is the Outcome of Balancing Reactions or Restorations Among Our Personal Activities.* If we conceive of any individual as a "field" of vibrations in matter and the ether, induced by muscular and nervous action and by feeling and thought, we see at once that there ought to be an ideal "field" in which all such vibrations are in a state of harmony. The state indicated would be a condition of balance. When activities in one direction are over intense and unduly prolonged, all vibrations tend to a strain in that direction. Such strain — all in one direction — is not normal, because it signifies disturbance of balance. If harmony in the "field" is to be restored, the one direction-strain must be released so that all right activities may recur and all vibrations proper to the "field" may again take place. Always the ideal is general harmony throughout the personal field. Now, some of the activities of our life are normally those of work, inducing corresponding vibrations in the individual "field," and some of them are normally those of recreation, which is a true word because it means recreation, that is, action or rest inducing corresponding vibration differing from those of work, running, so to speak, in different directions, and so restoring harmony. Work and recreation are, therefore, equally essential to the normal life. We have, however, built up wrong ideas of each of these important functions, so that most of us distinguish work as essentially different in its basic nature from recreation, and more or less an evil, and distinguish recreation as altogether and in itself a good. Both ideas are surely erroneous. I know that too much work, and work under certain conditions, can-

not be regarded as a good in itself. Precisely the same is true of recreation. Neither, then, is to be valued or condemned because of the kind of activities involved or vibrations induced, but always and solely with reference to the state of balance or harmony represented in the field of the personal self. The limit of permitted work should be determined by that question alone; work should always be offset, so to speak, by recreation. The limit of recreation permitted should be determined by the same question. It should always be offset by work. In other words, the value of either work or play consists in change of activities restoring balance in the personal field.

But work and recreation are not essentially different in their true nature. In both cases we have activities and vibrations. In all cases some portion of the body is involved. In all cases some features of the mind are active. Action in either case is called work or recreation according to the idea entertained regarding it. If the idea is that of *task*, the thing is work. If the idea is *relaxation*, the thing is recreation. I have taken the task-idea into recreation, and soon wearied. I have taken the recreation-idea into work, and have been obliged to call self to account under that law of balance or harmony. A boy, for example, is sawing wood alone: this is work. Neighboring boys join him, and soon invest the whole place with imagination, all busy sawing, splitting,— playing. It is the idea — that is, the real thought, which determines the names we give the two general sets of activities. Nature will check work-vibrations and restore recreation-vibrations, *for a time*, until harmony of the field is comparatively restored, if only suggestion use the magic word.

You are now invited to maintain, *in all your work*,

the idea of harmony with the Universal Forces of Nature,
and the inspiration of the idea that your *work is good*
and is building your self to better.

You are invited also to maintain, *in all your recreation, the idea of harmony with the Universal Forces*
and the inspiration of the thought that *your recreation
is good* and is building your self to better.

5. *Purity in the Sex-Life Charges the Personal
Field with the Magnetic Power of the Universal Forces.*
In this respect the individual should be as a god.   The
human body is designed for Temple-Presence of the
Infinite White Life.   Epicurus regarded it as a husk,
but Aristotle defined the soul as the "perfect expression
of the body," meaning, not that the soul is a product of
physiological conditions, but that it is the *truth* of body,
the idea, purpose, in which only do the bodily conditions gain their real meaning.   To this great Greek
the chief of human virtues was *High-Mindedness*, a
crowning Self-Respect.   This attitude of the self toward
the house in which it lives recognizes the perfect interaction of self and body, the one being influenced by the
other, and so it insists that no injury shall come to the
body from the inner sex-life, or from the sex-life to the
inner self, but that both shall be maintained in harmony
with the absolute whiteness of Eternal Being.

You are invited, then, to maintain purity under the
law of liberty, and to adopt this thought as a permanent
law: *My Personal Dignity Stoops not to Physical Degradation.*

6. *The Liberty of Conscious Harmony with the
Universal Forces Embraces the Intelligent Use of the
Science of Medicine.*   The science of medicine is fairly
indicated for our present purpose in the following
quotation — from Dr. Oliver Wendell Holmes:

"What is the honest truth about the medical art? That by far the largest number of diseases which physicians are called upon to treat will get well at any rate, even in spite of reasonably bad treatment. That of the other fraction, a certain number will certainly die, whatever is done. That there remains a small number of cases where the life of the patient depends on the skill of the physician. That drugs now and then save life; that they often shorten disease and remove symptoms; but that they are second in importance to food, air, temperature, and the other hygienic influences. Throw out opium; throw out wine, and the vapors which produce the miracle of anæsthesis, and I firmly believe that if the whole materia medica, as now used, could be sunk to the bottom of the sea, it would be all the better for mankind."

"It is a mistake to suppose that the normal state of health is represented by a straight horizontal line. Independently of the well-known causes which raise or depress the standard of vitality, there seems to be— I think I may venture to say there is — a rhythmic undulation in the flow of the vital force. The 'dynamo' which furnishes the working powers of consciousness and action has its annual, its monthly, its diurnal waves, even its temporary ripples, in the current it furnishes. There are greater and lesser curves in the movement of every day's life,— a series of ascending and descending movements, a periodicity depending on the very nature of the force at work in the living organism."

There is also in our life a periodicity of the deeper self — a curve of the soul's condition, which varies from time to time. When the curve is downward in both the physical and the spiritual case, drugs are of no more value than stones. When the curve is upward

in both cases, drugs may be totally gratuitous, and
they may actually retard the combined movements.
When the health-curve is downward, the psychic curve
may follow suit, but it need not necessarily do so.
When the psychic curve is downward, the health-curve
tends in the same direction. When the health-curve
is upward, the psychic curve usually follows. When
the psychic curve is upward, we have the best condition
for the cure of disease. But Nature always does the
curing. The physician never cures any disease; he
merely assists Nature.

It is the function of medical science to arrest downward curves by any tried methods, to take advantage
of upward curves, and to know what the curves are in
any given case. I call my physician because I may
want him when I cannot help myself in these important
respects. I will have in my hands the greatest number
of the best forces when I am subject to abnormal conditions. I believe that is common sense, and I know
it is perfectly permissible to the most exalted faith in
the Soul of our Universe.

I am ready to concede that in a sublime state of
ultimate evolution there is nothing which a drug or a
doctor can do except surgery that may not better be
accomplished by the power of harmonic *white-life
thought* claiming health. But in such a future state
disease will long since have vanished. Nevertheless,
we do now certainly know a great law of mental power
over the body. I do not concede any limits, except as
above indicated, to the operation of that law if we could
get it fully under control. Its scope, even as matters
are, is immense. The law is real, and it belongs to no
particular age or body of people. It is as long as time
and as wide as earth. Any human being may claim

the benefit in total disregard of any philosophy or form
of religious belief, provided the *white life* and the health-
claim are with him, under the sole limitations imposed
by thousands of years of wrong thought-life in ancestry
and similar error in personal past decreasing ability to
affirm and realize in a way to secure the full benefits of
the law. It is for every human being, nevertheless, to
strive for the inner harmony, to invoke the law of spiritual mastery over the body, and to put forth all possessed
and obtainable power of thought and realization for
health, in good cheer, with valiant heart, and inspired
by the truth that, whatever betide, nought can really
harm the abiding self. "Be not faithless; but believing."

And so I think that our great Nature-Universe bids
us hear these words from the Infinite White Life: "*Sons
and daughters of the All-Good, the power of thought and
harmony are surely for you. If you realize your highest
liberty and its greatest efficiency as you now are, you
will use, not deny, those instrumentalities which are provided in my ministers, Science and Faith. Must you be
a slave either to the material or to the immaterial? Can
you not employ both for your welfare? May not the
king call in whomsoever he will? All things are yours.*"

Let us not fall into the old-time religious error of
assuming that some particular philosophy or faith
which we have discovered embraces all truth and value.
Let us not label this or that with our little words, and
say: "This is law — this only." The law of thought-
power in the physical realm is older than any present
civilization. The law of harmony as the supreme
health-restorer and health-builder is not a law created
by the Infinite during the last twenty-five years. I
uncover my heart to every soul who is trying for the

best things and believes he has found a true way; but
I must not believe that this world has been left in stark
ignorance of the most fundamental law of our earth-
life — that health in its triune wholeness comes of the
white life and the realizing claim — to await the birth
and word of any man or woman in these times. It
is a little too late. Therefore I say to you who may
read these pages: "Stand free! Use every means
and all methods, material and spiritual (for the material is but a phase of the spiritual), for health and
happiness."

7. *The Secret of Thought in Relation to Health is
the Claim of the White Life Consciously Put Forth for
Physical Well-Being.* In explanation of this principle,
let us try to obtain certain true conceptions concerning
the material and pyschic nature of man.

All existences come to being through the activity
of one Infinite and Eternal Reality.

The medium in which all material existences exhibit is the universal ether of science, vibrations in this
medium constituting light, heat, electricity, magnetism,
etc., etc.

So far as we can think, the ether is a manifest,
perhaps a primary manifest, of Infinite and Eternal
Reality.

It is coming to be scientific to hold that matter
reduces in its last analysis to electricity and is a complex form of vibrations of the ether within the ether.
Matter is not merely pervaded by the ether; it is a
state of the ether.

Matter, then, is a manifest of Infinite and Eternal
Reality.

Life is a phase of the activity of matter. If we
think of matter in its grossest form, nearest to us in

the process of evolution, life may be regarded as an entity different from that matter.   We do somehow feel that matter and life are distinct realities.   But if we think of matter as a complex form of etheric vibrations, nothing forbids our saying that life also is a form of vibration of the ether within the ether.   With this view in mind, we shall think of matter and life as comparatively simultaneous manifests of the ether, life, however, appearing only when the state of etheric vibrations resulting in matter has reached a stage in which vibrations resulting in life can be possible.   We should then say that life is a product of etheric vibrations emerging through those that have resulted in matter; that is, life is a product of material activities. This view cannot justly be called materialism because Life is, then, also a manifest of Infinite and Eternal Reality.

We do not scientifically know any sort of mind that is not exhibited through matter.   The human mind always exhibits through a human body.   What we call mind is a complex of states of consciousness engaged in various activities.   Consciousness involves certain physical activities within us.   If nothing were acting within, we should not be conscious.   This has always been true.   The first dawn of consciousness in Nature involved activities within the organism.   If we think of that first faintly conscious existence as a mass of crude matter, then the self and its body will appear to be distinctly separated in reality.   But if we think of that body as a manifest of etheric vibrations in which life-vibrations also obtained, there is nothing to forbid our saying that consciousness was equally a product of such vibrations.   If so, the psychic factor was a form of vibrations of the ether within the ether —

and so, when it appeared, had evolved to higher forms, was consciousness.

Matter is an evolution, and out of it have evolved life, the psychic factor, consciousness. But consciousness is, then, for the reasons above indicated, a manifest of Infinite and Eternal Reality.

Consciousness is the condition of personality. When the former first appeared, it was a product. Thenceforth, because personality was a psychic factor in consciousness, it became a creator. That is to say, it was capable of enlargement and enrichment, and so, began to unfold its powers, to enrich its own contents by appropriation, and to organize itself in various ways depending upon its nature in each case and the influence of environment. In seeking to realize itself, as it must do in the nature of things, and in adjusting to environment, which was a second necessity of its being, it began to direct the activities of matter comprising its own body, to select matter from without needful for its kind of body, and to build this material up into a kind of body best adapted to its existence, and thus, by its own character, to determine the character of the organism which it inhabited.

All this work seems entirely independent until we remember that ether, matter, life, the psychic factor, are manifests of Infinite and Eternal Reality. But when we so remember, we see that personality consisting of a conscious self and a body is similarly a manifest of that Reality.

This conclusion will appear to identify man and Deity unless we discriminate a little. Every object in Nature is a manifest of Infinite and Eternal Reality, but the latter transcends the former simply because the object *is* such a manifest. A thing which is a mani-

fest or expression of something superior cannot be identified with the superior something.   I am not the words
which I write, although they manifest me and could
not exist without me.   Every object in Nature is precisely what it is as a manifest of Reality.   There is
scant freedom in the natural world apart from man.
Nothing in Nature could be other than it is.   Man, on
the other hand, is a manifest of Infinite and Eternal
Reality in the sense that he has a body, and must have
one, and is a personality and must be one (if he is man);
but in the man psychic factor has come to consciousness,
and consciousness, as we have seen, always reveals itself
in *self-direction and self-organization according to its
developed power to think of itself as self-conscious existence*.
Were it unable to so think of itself, it could not be self-
directive in the fullest sense.   And were it unable to
self-direct its own activities, it could not be conscious
in the fullest sense of the word.   Our existence manifests Infinite and Eternal Reality, but the power to
use that existence is determined by the fact that we are
psychic factors in the highest sense exhibited in the
earth, and the use we make thereof is determined by
our exercise of the power of self-direction and self-
organization.   We cannot help being human beings,
but what *kind* of human beings we are, within the limits
of personal endowments, depends solely upon ourselves.

We may see, then, that the psychic factor within
us builds the bodies we live in, so that our physical
character is largely an expression of our personal character.   Ages of wrong thought-life are behind us, yet
even so, it is within our power to improve physical
character very greatly indeed.

Now, the power of personal right thinking and
harmony with the White Life of Infinite and Eternal

Reality may be explained in the following way (you will understand, of course, that the outline is designed merely to be suggestive):

All matter in the realm of Nature being a manifest of Infinite and Eternal Reality, Nature and her substances are phases of the Eternal Thought. The study of Nature is just the study of that Thought, conducted in various ways and for various purposes. The Thought, in all its existences and relations, is a vast and complex whole, and yet, from the point of view of its highest value to man, a great Word, comparatively simple and open to every earnest and sincere seeker throughout all the ages. If you will ask yourself, What are the main and abiding thoughts which are embodied in Nature? your conclusion, I think, need not be elaborate and confusing. The question, however, must be asked in a receptive and unprejudiced mood, and not merely by the matter-of-fact intellect. "Every inch of earth, of water, of fire, and of air contains the fundamental principles of the universe, and man is the connecting link between dust and Deity, and can bridge the gulf through the illumination of his mind. The most powerful telescope known to man is mind's eye." "He who has cultivated and learned to open his heart to the touch of outward Nature illuminates his inner being by the elevation and refinement of his emotional and imaginative nature. This is the first principle in the objective world of the higher education of mind and soul. The first lesson of Mother Earth is to instruct her children to be softened and sympathetic toward the moods of outward Nature. Thus mankind softens, broadens, and grows, becoming more susceptible to impressions, taking in the glory of the Divine Architect, which is in the world revealed, and the golden gates of the soul are opened."

Seeking with such a spirit, then, the main Thoughts which Nature embodies, I venture to say that Infinite and Eternal Reality has there expressed itself in these great Words:

Reality,	*Truth,*	*Law,*
Beauty,	*Goodness,*	*Harmony,*
Power,	*Development,*	*Happiness,*
Love,	*Service,*	LIFE.

These are the Thoughts expressed in Nature which are manifest of the White Life. For such the nature of things always declares, when free to do so. By so much as any object of existence fully realizes itself, by so much are these Thoughts, so far as such realization requires, made concrete if only we have the seeing mind and the feeling heart. With these powers of perception, the seeing mind and the feeling heart, we come to know that all in Nature is good and means good to every man and woman and child in this world. There is no evil in Nature. All so-called evil in Nature is due either to some phase of her existence wrongly used or to some false interpretation in human thinking. Nature is *real, true, law-full, beautiful, good, harmonious, full of power, a growing organism, a minister of service and well-being, a living thing, a literature of love.* If you refer to microbes, poisons, deadly serpents, and the like, I reply that the perfect *white life* in man, together with the knowledge of science, would teach him to avoid wrong relations and develop within him physical, mental and moral tone (*tonus,* in the language of the schools). Thus would he be rendered immune from all so-called evils.

If your inner life contains nothing alien to these great Nature-Thoughts, if you see to it that their character is given your personal character, you will secure in the body a degree of the power of harmony which they possess, and your health will infallibly correspond. Do not mistake this sentence. Will you kindly read it again until you see what it really means? The only limit to your health will be the limit of your ability to realize in yourself the mighty Thoughts which make Nature what she is. I do not mean that splendid results must immediately issue from the course indicated. Patience and time are important factors. I do not mean that a dying man can inevitably realize these Thoughts sufficiently to recover health. There are limits, not to the law, but to one's ability to use the law. In spiritual effort, effort of the inner self to lay hold upon the Universal Forces, you can make your own personal discoveries. I may not say a greater word. Above all, I do not mean that merely thinking the Thoughts will be enough, in any case. The method is one of realization as well as affirmation. But by so much as you become that which the Nature-Thoughts suggest, by so much will your physical and psychic health come to buoyancy, joy and power. You are now invited, then, to adopt the following as the permanent law of your thought-life:

I am, in every function of my body and every activity of my deeper self, entirely GENUINE, representing TRUTH, obeying LAW, loving BEAUTY, striving for GOODNESS, coming to HARMONY, possessed of POWER, GROWING to better things, full of HAPPINESS, eager to SERVE, a LIVING white life, and a Lover of all that is good.

If you will thoughtfully and believingly repeat this law twice a day say, for one hundred days, you will find life unfolding new meanings, fears fading and dying, and courage growing to real greatness.

8. *In the Mystery of the Silence the Power of Realization Becomes Greatest and Most Effective Because in Such a State the Self Makes Its High Thoughts a Conscious Claim on All Good Things.* The direct utility of the right thought-life is nowhere doubted. By this the psychic factor largely molds the body and influences its functions. Preceding methods or laws have all referred to the truth involved. But the law of direct realization is needed in order to complete the workings of the truth. By direct realization the self consciously claims the present benefit of the spirit or attitude of harmony. You may think of yourself as splendidly well and fearless: that is one thing —you *regard* yourself as in such conditions. And you may claim yourself *now* to be well and courageous: that is another thing — you *treat* yourself for health and fearlessness. When you think of your arm as moving, it does not necessarily move; you have merely entertained the idea. When you will your arm to move, you have claimed your power to move it and have realized the power — realized in actual thought that power. The difference would obtain if your arm were bound: you could still realize in thought the sense of movement. Realization of the Eternal Thoughts is a conscious claim in spirit and appropriation in spirit of the Thoughts as actual within yourself. Realization of benefits for health is a conscious holding of them in mind as present in you. One may in time acquire the fixed mood of realization, but it will assist you to bring about that mood if you will occasionally, say once a day, shut out all disturbances and alien thoughts and feelings, and try to come into communion with the White Life — go into the silence and, by quiet affirmation and sincere, trustful realization, claim the Universal Forces as your

helpers in building up your physical tone and the spirit
of courage.   A sentence like the following may be used:

*"Conscious of psychic uprightness in the white life,
and of the beauty, utility and wonder of my physical being in its nature, and function, I now claim, and without doubt am receiving, the Universal Forces for my best
tone and courage-spirit in all-improving health."*

A REGIME.

Hold steadily the ideal
Of body in mind and mind in body (ruthless of logic),
So interfused that neither is, alone,
And each in each forms one — *yourself!*

This, perfect first stage of ideal,
Hold you in the vision of Thought-Demand —
Hold deep and at centre of spirit's heart
(As though 't were alive in the heart of flesh)—
Hold *there*, immovable, and failing not
Through all distractions, quite serenely sure
That *first* stage prophesies a *second*,
And second, *third*, and each succeeding stage a *further*
For aye — beyond these years and into death and *out.*
Here is eternal "Procession" of your Holy Ghost,
Feeding good faith with reason consummate.

If you *so* hold, since this our System vast
Agrees in essence or of substance, energy or law,
And you are true force thus in harmony with All,
Shall not your Thought induce incoming movements
From life here, and planets yonder, and higher realms afar,
Rushing in for *you*, vortex-maker, true magnetic lode,
And usher in to body-cells, nerve-cells, energy-spheres
Of your dynamic self the Dual Health
For which dust blows from out the mouth of God,
For which power emerges in the Breath creative,
For which life pulsates in the Heart Deific,
For which love works to make that life immortal?

Courage, soul! All things are yours:
Passion and vigor for the half of you, body;
Beauty and Truth for the half of you, mind;
All for the self of you, mind-body human;
Hold, then, the ideal unshaken
For that complete quality
Which is solely the oneness of health,
Regnant, of perfecting soul!

— THE AUTHOR.

CHAPTER IV.

Dual Health-Tone of the Self.

"Be strong and of a good courage; be not afraid, neither be thou dismayed."—*Bible*.

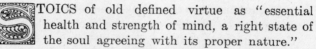TOICS of old defined virtue as "essential health and strength of mind, a right state of the soul agreeing with its proper nature."

Sound physical health is usually accompanied by feelings of buoyancy and optimism, and healthy-mindedness not only signifies "essential health and strength of mind," but involves also a "tendency which looks on all things and sees that they are good." We may distinguish this tendency as (a) voluntary, and (b) involuntary.

"In its involuntary variety, healthy-mindedness is a way of feeling happy about things immediately. In its symmetrical variety, it is an abstract way of conceiving things as good."

Practical mind-health, then, consists in "essential health and strength of the soul," together with a cultivated habit of affirming and realizing always the best things for one's life.

"In the unhealthy-minded, apart from all sorts of old regrets, ambitions checked and aspirations obstructed by timidities, it (the inner atmosphere) consists mainly of bodily discomforts not distinctly realized by the sufferer, but breeding a general self-mistrust and sense that things are not as they should be with him."

"In the healthy-minded, on the contrary, **there** are no fears or shames to discover; and the **sensations** that pour in from the organism only help to swell the general vital sense of security and readiness for anything that may turn up."

We may possess wholesome minds and optimistic spirits without being religious. Nevertheless, perfect health of soul demands of the deeper self (let our theories of "soul" be what they may) an attitude of harmony and trust which loves truth supremely, believes profoundly in the White-Life Goodness of Worlds, and seeks steadfastly to realize the "Central Will." The health-tone of the soul is a blending of soundness, happiness and spirituality in a broad and lofty sense.

AT HOME IN THE UNIVERSE.

This spiritual health (health of the personality at the top, whatever religious language be approved or rejected) carries the feeling of at-homeness in the whole Universe about us. Beautifully did Epictetus say: "If those things are true which are said by philosophers concerning the kinship of God and men, what else remains for men to do than after Socrates' way, who never, when men inquired of him what was his native country, replied *Athens* or *Corinth*, but *the Universe*."

In such an outlook of thought we possess the feelings of freedom and security, which are beyond price. "Is freedom anything else than the power to live as we choose? Nothing else. None, therefore, that fears or grieves or is anxious is free; but whosoever is released from griefs and fears and anxieties is by that very thing released from slavery." The wise old hunchback from whose writings I have quoted saw in such things the beginning of the higher life. "Man," he exhorted, "be mad at last, as the saying is, for peace, for freedom, for magnanimity. Lift up thy head as one delivered from slavery. Dare to look up to God and say: Deal with me henceforth as thou wilt; I am of one mind with thee; I am thine. I reject nothing that seems good to thee; lead me whithersoever thou wilt; clothe me in what dress thou wilt. Wilt thou have me govern or live privately, or stay at home, or go into exile, or be a poor man or a rich? For all these conditions I will be thy advocate with men." And this man was a "pagan!" "If ye will hearken unto me, O men, wheresoever ye be, whatsoever ye do, ye shall not grieve, ye shall not be wroth, ye shall not be compelled, or hindered, but ye shall live untroubled and free from every ill." So Epictetus teaches us, not to deny the facts of life, but to rise to freedom of courage and confidence in mind, whatever the facts, good or ill, may be.

And these are some of the main things in mental health. The Roman Emperor, Marcus Aurelius, gives us almost a universal formula into which the entire matter may be thrown: "Everything harmonizes with me which is harmonious to thee, O Universe. Nothing for me is too early or too late, which is in due time for thee. Everything is fruit to me which thy seasons bring, O Nature! From thee are all things, in thee are all things, to thee all things return. The poet says, Dear City of Cecrops; and wilt thou not say, Dear City of God?" Surely the Universe is the City of the Infinite.

Thus may we come to one general conclusion, that true courage is born of a sense of harmony with the world in which we live.

And tone of health as thus indicated is the finest possible culture-ground for every form of desirable courage. The courage of the prize-fighter is not admired in these pages.

And now, for the development of the higher personal tone in the interest of a fearless attitude toward all things, you are invited to observe the suggestions following in relation to mental health.

We have seen that the practical mind-health consists of mental soundness together with a cultivated habit of affirming and realizing always the best things for one's life The acquisition of such a habit must deal with

DIFFICULTIES CONFRONTING MENTAL TONE.

These difficulties we ought clearly to see, and the chief among them will now appear. Ever in opposition to a confident attitude of mind-health is

FIRST, THE DIFFICULTY OF FALSE IDEAS ABOUT ENVIRONMENT — HOW TO OVERCOME. Many of us assume that environment — or circumstances — make or defeat our mental life. The fact is,—what you do with environment is precisely one of the tests of your mind — rather, of the self which uses the mind. The real meaning of environment is Opportunity for Life-Building. You can make of anything in your right existence such an opportunity. On the other hand, there is nothing related to you of which you may not in some way fail to take advantage.

Environment is the True Work-Shop of the Soul. For to every person living there are two kinds of environment: that of the seen world or neighborhood, with all its varied circumstances, be these exactly what they are; and that of the world of thought-reality in which each individual actually lives. Neither of these environments need determine real life.

> "Stone walls do not a prison make,
> Nor iron bars a cage."

In multitudes of cases, imperious self, seeking its own better kingdoms, has succeeded in changing its visible environment, either by deliberate transfer to other fields or by creating a demand, through manifest ability, from higher levels, "Come thou up hither." Here we have the triumph of persistent mind-power.

An editor formerly pursued in succession three university courses, history, law, medicine,— and went into the hotel business. Then he wrote a book which the people wanted, and he is now assisting in the editorial chair a multitude of struggling men to find their right places in life.

A hack-driver in New York discovered himself and proceeded to work his way through college. He is now a master teacher in philosophy.

A coal miner found that he possessed a voice worth training. He threw himself into the task of attaining vocal perfection. No man to-day surpasses him in the field of the oratorio.

A boy purchased a lot of minerals from workmen engaged in cutting a bank for a railway track. He is now an expert on precious stones, a writer of scientific books and a fellow in several learned societies.

Such are examples, taken from real life and not found in print, of what you can do, according to your original endowment. And the only way in which you can discover your endowment is precisely — to discover what kind of environment you can conquer. The will to do so will constitute one important element in sound

healthy-mindedness. To this end you are urged to
saturate your very soul with this

Inspiration-Resolution: *Believing vigorously in
myself, and confident of ultimate success, I resolve —
To discipline and cultivate mind in every available way,
to multiply my best powers into all things undertaken, to
follow the inner voice of my sanest judgment, and to
make my whole environment a splendid workshop for
development and achievement of the best of which I am
capable.*

If you will practise such a resolution, you will find
your mind coming more and more to strength and
healthy tone, and your courage rounding out to symmetry and power.

But environment has another phase. It is also
the world of thought in which the soul lives. This may
be a mere reflection of the material environment, pleasing or otherwise, or it may be an independent product
of the real self, good or evil, pervading and dominating,
rather than reflecting, the physical surroundings. In
the one case, the visible rules; in the other, the soul
reigns. We create our worlds, either by simple copy-
ing, or by that divine ability to construct which is the
privilege of all.

The healthy mind creates a psychic environment
which throws a light upon the outer world and masters
its so-called "evils" in the very act of such creation.
If life's conditions are dark, the spirit illumines them;
if they are bright, it transfigures their significance, and
is thus enabled to stand serene, whatever betide. This
is, indeed, an old truth, but so also is moss an old
reality — and marvelously beautiful. Look into it
with seeing eyes: it has starry wonders.

Peter, the wealthiest man in Russia, is taken

prisoner by the French, and suffers some hardships
From his improvised gaol, a hut, he looks out upon a
moon-flooded world and gazes up into the starlit dome
of the sky.

"All that is mine!" exclaims the prisoner. "All
that is in me, *is* me! And that is what they think
they have taken prisoner! That is what they have
shut up in a cabin!"

If you would come to such a reàl thought-world
environment, several things must become the very
surest realities of your life. Among these essential
things, and perhaps the first that should be noted are
Courageous Beliefs and the Valiant Will. The
Universe appeals to every one of us, "Be not faithless,
but believing." When you *really believe* for a goal,
you *will* that goal, and you surely believe for it when
you actually will it. The attitudes indicated compel
the achievements. I shall not weaken that truth by
any provisos. "Who gains promotions, boons, appoint-
ments, but the man in whose life they are seen to play
the part of live hypotheses, who discounts them, sacrifices other things for their sake before they have come,
and takes risks for them in advance? His faith acts
on the powers above him as a claim, and creates its
own verification." This does not mean, of course, a
superstitious faith in miracles wrought for the favored
individual because he affirms belief in a providence; it
simply means work and plenty of work conducted in
the entire confidence that the whole of a man gone into
a system of effort shall surely bring out of it great
things. The very fact of work thus carried on signifies
the spirits of belief and will which conquer circumstances and arrest the attention of higher powers in
any human field. Then comes enlargement of envi-

ronment — opportunity. All the circumstances that
exist are somewhere defeated by some soul. Everywhere are people who are swamped by environment,
and who remain mental nonentities in a perennial state
of depressing ill-health of mind. But everywhere are
other people who refuse to be swamped, who assert the
right of the fullest mental life, who continue to grow
and to conquer to the end.

It is to be remembered that this chapter deals not
in methods of educational work for the mind, however,
but merely in suggestions for mental health. Right
living is, therefore, of the utmost importance. Whatever your mental attainments, if your life is wrong,
you cannot be possessed of true health of mind. In
some instances, the will, while successful in unfolding a
kind of right living, does not always maintain the real
tone of a healthy mind. Marcus Aurelius was probably the greatest Emperor as a man that Rome produced,
yet he was the most melancholy pagan of antiquity.
He lived rightly, so far as he knew, but his thought-life
was eminently unhealthy, at least at times. Splendidly
he said: "Be like the promontory against which the
waves continually break, but it stands firm and tames
the fury of the water around it;" and he also declared:
"Such as bathing appears to thee, oil, sweat, dirt,
filthy water, all things disgusting — so is every part of
life and every thing." Socrates was the most healthy-
minded of all the Greeks, and the happiest, the freest,
the most courageous. This man's personality shines
across the ages like a pillar of white marble. His was
the *white life* so far as conceived by his Greek thought.
It is really the *white life* which makes soundness and
buoyancy natural to mental health, so that environment really becomes the work-shop of the soul.

But the mastery of environment is not a matter of sheer will and mere pushing and crowding for better things.   Here, then, appears a further obstacle to healthy-mindedness —

SECONDLY, THE DIFFICULTY OF FALSE IDEAS OF THE SUCCESS-SPIRIT — HOW TO CORRECT.   Life is not a game of foot-ball, in which hard-fisted will and brutal push must win; it is the greatest of sciences and the art of all arts, wherein will must rise to faith and push must give place to affirmation.   Along with belief and resolution, then, should go an element of even a higher nature, in which the idea is not so much " I can and I will," as "It is surely mine to acquire all strength and health of mind essential to my life."   Such is our remedy for false notions of the success-spirit.   The true idea may be called the spirit of

Self-Inspiration.   You are not required to live on the hard, stony plane of utter driving slavery.   That feeling of blended *must* and *hurry* and gripping *determination* is one of the greatest enemies of man.   When the self inspires the self, on the other hand, we have one of the most attractive and beneficent, as well as practical, elements at man's command.   The one attitude should go out of your life; the other attitude should become permanent and constantly more vital therein.   In order to such substitution kindly observe the following invitations.

(1).   You are invited to put forever away the idea, "I must achieve mental development," and to replace it by the affirmation, "It is given me to make the most of a wholesome mind."

(2).   You are urged to banish completely all feeling of hurry,— that inner distress which drives, drives, senselessly and always,— remembering that however swiftly muscles or powers may move at times, the un-hasting spirit is in the long run the most efficient.

(3). You are also urged to loosen your deadly grip on the mind, and to give its free, deeper conscious-ness larger opportunities. You do not wrest facts, truths, beauties, laws, from Nature or life; you *receive* them. Attention is not boring into a subject; it is permitting the subject to unfold in the mind. It is not the mind that thinks; it is the self — and Heaven only knows just what that thinking self really is. You grow, not by robbing a Universe, but by accepting its gifts. Not hard determination to have, but eagerness to accept, is the spirit of the healthy mind. It is better still to say: "It is given me to unfold, and in the unfolding, to receive buoyancy and freedom and knowledge and wholesomeness of soul. So, now, will I receive."

(4). You are invited to cultivate a constantly present due sense of personal worth. There is neither virtue nor power in self-belittlement. When man first stood forth from the animal kingdom and con-fronted the world with the deep-breathed assertion, "I am!" spiritual power swept across the field of life — virtue was born in the earth.

(5). You are invited to insist upon your mental rights and to hold a fair valuation of your work among men.

It is this way with me:
I belong to the Universe;
I am part of the struggle for a final equilibrium;
Therefore I ask all things that I want;
Therefore I receive — I lie not to myself —
I receive what I want. What I do not receive

Dual Health-Tone of the Self.   63

Has met with obstructions somewhere in me:
I will destroy these obstructions with a smile —
And of course I shall go on receiving forever.

(6). You are invited freely to engage in creating high thoughts concerning yourself, your fellows and the whole world. You may overdo in this matter, and you may be deceived by other people, but better the excess of faith and honor than the lack, and if you come truly to admire man, taken by and large, and to believe in the White Universe, the reflex influence of this high-mindedness cannot fail of the greatest good in both your mental health and your personal courage.

(7). You are invited to find in Nature your greatest library and school for development and health. To this end the idea that Nature is a mere surface, or a kind of thin garment, so that, if you could only pierce through it, nothing would remain, should be cast entirely out of thought. This is one of the most prevalent errors, and it is a destroyer of our true relations with the material world. Nature has, we say, three dimensions — length, breadth and thickness. But we imagine that thickness exhausts depth. Thus we miss the real teachings of Nature, open to all. *Nature is always and everywhere an infinite reality! Infinity lies below all her realities. Nature is a body expressing the truth of Infinite Reality. Nature is the Infinite Soul manifest to man.* It is for this reason that you are again invited to refer to the Nature-Thoughts given in the last chapter, and to endeavor to realize their stupendous character and influence for good in your mental life. This and the following suggestion is of very great importance.

(8). And you are invited to add to such a regime, which will uncover many things in the world around you, this final effort — to realize the words below as standing, in all your mental constitution for

Actual Power-Qualities

Freedom,	*Openness,*	*Friendliness,*	*Appreciation,*
Honesty,	*Honor,*	*Fidelity,*	*Purity,*
Power,	*Reverence,*	*Aspiration,*	*Confidence.*

If you will cultivate these master qualities of the mental life, you will inevitably come to a degree of healthy-mindedness, and so, to a phase of that courage which is far above any mere physical bravery, for you will infallibly have discovered the *white life.* The *white life* need fear nothing, either on the earth below or in the heavens above.

All this, of course, suggests a considerable amount of labor, and precisely such labor indicates a further difficulty in the way of mental health.

THIRDLY, THE DIFFICULTY OF FALSE IDEAS OF DISCIPLINE — HOW TO REMEDY. If the last regimes have a distasteful look to you, the fact shows that discipline is wrongly conceived. When you feel that life is really inspired by such high ideals, the element of discipline almost loses its distinctive character. The effort to correct or improve your personality because the work is regarded as a mere duty or a necessity is very naturally more or less unpleasant. The attempt to make the most of self for the sake of a larger life in full health and courage, on the other hand, becomes a spontaneous expression of desire by so much as the goal is idealized in thought. A real inspiration calls exuberantly for

Confident Self-Discipline. It is a rank error to

feel that discipline of self is inconsistent with the highest satisfaction in the work required. Precisely the opposite will appear if you come to hold —

"My mynde to me a kingdom is,
Such perfect joy therein I find."

Mere mental grubbing is not a phase of mental health. A wholesome mind enjoys itself in its most strenuous activity. That the difficulty which now confronts us may disappear, you are invited to observe the suggestions following:

(1). You are urged to cultivate the mood of intellectual happiness by repeating again and again the lines just above quoted from the old English poet, Byrd.

(2). You are urged to refuse admittance to all unworthy and depressing thoughts and realities. Why should a human being turn the mind into a charnel-house, a graveyard, a prison, or a hell?

(3). You are urged to banish all intellectual brooding and worry, and every form of pessimism and cynicism. Before my desk hang two printed sentiments, one from Robert Louis Stevenson, one from Robert Browning. Stevenson begins a prayer with: "The day returns and brings us the petty round of irritating concerns and duties. Help us to play the man, etc." Browning begins a little poem with; "The year 's at the spring, And day 's at the morn," mentions a number of bright things that flash up to his view, and closes with the shout: "God 's in his Heaven — All 's right with the world!" In the one sentiment you see the heroic spirit fighting illness of mind; in the other you see perfect mental health.

(4). You are invited to apply the following

statement to your own life: It has been estimated
that every person whose career measures fifty years,
say, from the age of twenty to that of seventy, has had
four solid years of time as a treasure to be disposed of
for whatever the soul may have chosen to purchase,
however busy the life may have been. That amount
of time, if properly used, would bring the equivalent
of a college education. And this is true, not in the
sense that one needs be a slave to personal improvement, but taken in the most reasonable manner.

(5.) You are invited to maintain in your mental
kingdom as large a variety of action as may be consistent with steadfastness and balance. If your mind
is not a gad-about, neither is it a mere galley-slave. In
the average human brain there are millions of cells
which are capable of activity representing thought.
Not one of these cells do we ever create by conscious
effort; we merely use and develop. Your mental life,
then, may be as narrow and monotonous, or as broad
and varied, as you will.

(6). You are urged to study your own mind for
discovery of weaknessess and unhealthy peculiarities,
as, for example: scant power of observation, poor
memory, imagination, judgment; lack of concentration, and of analyzing ability, of persistence and force;
prejudices, "mental squint," abnormal fondness for
abnormal things; antipathies, likes, propensities, unwholesome tendencies; shortsightedness, lack of dignity, of poise; flippancy, mysticism, undue matter-of-
factness, over-criticalness, excessive credulity, etc.,
etc. Of course such phases of unhealthy-mindedness
should be corrected. There is no reason whatever for
any discouragement in the effort. "Be not faithless,
but believing." No weakness is there which you may

not improve, no fault you may not obviate, if only belief and will be held buoyantly to the work of personal improvement.

(7.) For you are now invited, on the other hand, to set about discovering your best points, and to "let yourself out" in every line indicated by the revelation. The trouble with most people who really ought to address themselves to this enjoyment of securing the best mental tone, is just here: they dwell forever on the wrong side of the question. I talked with a man who declared that he had lost opportunities in life because of timidity. I said: "You ought to overcome this weakness." "Oh, yes," he replied; "I know; but it 's in the blood before me." This man had suggested to himself an impossibility, and stood limp before his master, a mere notion. I believe that all slavery to "blood" and training is itself mental ill-health. You are in the world to be master of these factors. That is exactly the significance of human life. Man develops by so much as he makes his own blood over and better.

(8.) And you are urged to remember that healthy-mindedness no less than health of body demands rest and recreation. "Unclamp your intellectual and practical machinery and let it run free; and the service it will do you will be twice as good."

We have thus seen that some of the difficulties confronting mind-health are false ideas of environment, of the success-spirit, and of self-discipline, and that our corrections are right beliefs, self-inspiration, and confident self-discipline. In order, now, to obviate a tendency which some one calls "uncritical optimism," — a vague assumption of good whether or no,— we must remember that a growing mind requires a very healthy dealing with reality. The trouble here presented may be called,

FOURTHLY, THE DIFFICULTY OF UNWHOLESOME FAITH — HOW TO OBVIATE. There is a vast amount of insanity not under asylum treatment, a good deal of abnormal acceptance of faith-philosophy prevalent, which is due to the absence of vigorous regard for downright reality.

Regard For Downright Reality. I do not know a better remedy for the fads, isms and vagaries of belief without sense than a cultivated instinct for actual fact and truth. For reality appeals to us in exactly two ways, either as fact or as truth. Into healthy mind-tone these phases of reality must enter, whatever else be present or absent. You are urged, therefore, to make the following suggestions definite elements in your life.

(1). You are invited to cultivate the power to see and recognize *facts* as opposed to mere visions and hopes, to develop within the soul a feeling of sympathy for things, forces, phenomena, exactly as they are, regardless of what they merely seem to be, or might, could, would, or should be. The value of such a fact-attitude realizes in countless ways.

This attitude gives us solid ground; it finds a tangible limit; it is certainty for judgment, belief, and action. It is the first badge of sanity. It stares the fad out of countenance. It tends to put down the epidemic of isms. It prevents the world from surrendering to a may-be-so. It is destined to cremate all the chimeras and to kill out all the errors of human existence.

The second phase of reality essential to mind-health is *truth*. Now truth seems to be about anything man can think. Nevertheless, truth itself ought to give us some definite conception upon which all can agree. In search for this conception, we may begin by saying that *knowledge is the certainty that our thoughts correspond to reality*, and then we may go on to affirm that truth is precisely such correspondence. But this raises the question, Can we adequately know reality? The answer is that we can only form a conception of what reality, whatever it is *beyond* our thought, must assuredly be *in* our thought. We then have two things for comparison: our thought *of* reality, and our thoughts *about a thing* which we believe to be real. *When our thoughts about the thing correspond with what reality is as we conceive it, and correspond in such a way that the mind in the best exercise of its powers is satisfied, then we may say that we are in possession of truth. The thought-correspondence indicated is truth.* This is the best we can do in the matter because we can never go outside of our own minds. But the element of satisfaction to mind in the best exercise of its powers is an immense corrective, and it has eliminated from the world ten thousand errors.

When the mind comes into a state in which none of its thoughts concerning a fact believed to be real annihilates, contradicts, or excludes any other, but in which all harmonize with each other and with other established thoughts, a feeling of satisfaction obtains, and the mind then declares, "I have the truth."

A flower is a fact. What it tells me is truth — for *me*. This "for me" comes in time to be compared with other "for me's," and so corrected into "for man." Slowly, then, the facts of earth give rise to science-truths, art-truths, history-truths.

The word "soul" has come to mean "breath,"

"life," "personality," "self," "spirit." Let us call it
the unseen self. It is a collection of living facts. To
the mind of man "soul" represents ten thousand
truths, because he can form the ideas, "fact," "knowledge," and can compare these ideas, and so form the
conception, "truth." In the last analysis man must
find all his facts and all his truths within the soul, and
thus the self becomes a complex reality capable of
taking into itself every other reality.

Mind-health demands sympathy for and apprehension of facts as facts, exactly as they are, in order
that truth may be and may really develop in strict
harmony with whatever is.

Many so-called untruthful people are simply
deficient in fact-sight.

Many veracious people are blind to the truth-
world back of the fact-world.

Here are reasons for differing works on philosophy.
The authors merely vary in truth-vision.

Here are explanations for contradictory theories
in science. The scientists do not all stand on the same
truth-level.

Here is justification for magnificent oppositions
in the great departments of life. Men do not equally
sense the truth-values of human existence.

Religions all represent varying degrees of the
truth-phases of that dim Reality — the Moral Universe.

Conflicting opinions among honest people simply
exhibit what measure of truth they have been able to
acquire out of the common store of world-facts.

*No man can transcend the level of his own intelli-
gence.* It is everywhere as it is with the spoken word.
The spoken word is three-fold: the vocal sound, the
thought of the speaker, the thought of the hearer.

To-day the hearer is below the speaker, and his thought is, what it is, no matter what the speaker has said. To-morrow his thought outruns that of the speaker, because his level has risen, and his thought is now better than the yesterday product. So is it always. The facts are the same through hoary ages. But men rise; thus comes higher truth. This law preaches charity; but it also preaches and inspires courage. We may all say: "I shall yet stand where you stand, and some day my world of truth will be your world."

Mind-tone depends upon sympathy for the truth that hides behind the facts, and the development of power to compel facts to yield their truth. Hence —

(2). You are invited to acquire the ability to analyze so-called facts into all their parts. The aim of this suggestion is simply a healthy tendency to arrive at the heart of things before you surrender to them. Every single fact is really a number of facts grouped together, as, a rose, consisting of calyx, petals, stamen, pistil, pollen, form, color, fragrance, etc., etc. When you thus handle things, forces, phenomena, propositions, laws, creeds, systems, you present to them a phase of healthy-mindedness which will infallibly obviate a hasty conclusion and save you from many an error and fantastic faith.

(3). You are also urged to make it your lifelong practice to know the truth, the whole truth, and nothing but the truth, on important matters at least. Knowledge, we have seen, is the certainty that our thoughts correspond with reality. Knowledge, then, is of course a thing of degrees, but many people are too easily satisfied with almost any degree of certainty. We should insist on a certainty which is much stronger than mere guess-work. Truth, as I have defined it, is the correspondence between our thoughts and reality — and evidences itself by a state of harmony among our thoughts in relation to a given thing. When, for example, we are satisfied that all apples, released from support in air, fall to the ground, we conclude that such action represents a law for all objects, because a certain number of instances point in one direction. You see, then, that we thus arrive at two truths — one concerning gravity, one concerning the human mind. In these matters we are aware of a state of mental contentment. But, in some similar cases, man has found that his truths so discovered have been only partial. Thus, heat expands and cold contracts material things, yet, beyond a certain point of freezing, ice expands, thus preventing our northern rivers from filling to the bottom. You again see, then, that the truth-getting habit needs to make sure that it has fully covered a given case, and, in any event, that it exhibits the greatest healthiness by remaining always open to new facts, new laws and new phases of truth.

At this point I wish to adduce two illustrations which will show more clearly what I mean by the invitation we are now considering. The main thing is the mental attitude. When the mental attitude concerns facts, the mind is sanely practical. Even if the individual is mistaken, his attitude saves his sanity — his common sense. When the mental attitude concerns truth, the mind is sanely intelligent, and, in the long run, will exhibit reasonableness.

Any illustration of these attitudes will be more or less incomplete because the process unfolded covers so much of life. It should, therefore, be remembered that the following are merely specimen leaves from the vast forest of experience.

Illustration Number One. A man sees a ghost in the highway. Our invitation requires that he see the fact as it is. It is *some* fact; what *is* that fact? It is a tall stump with two or three naked branches, and various lights and shadows moving upon them. The fact-*thing* has now become a fact-*group*. It is an appearance — a fact suggesting a supposed truth. What was the *real* truth? The ghostly body was a stump, the arms were branches, the movements were due to flickering shadows and varying degrees of light. The *supposed* truth was a ghost. The *real* truth was a mental deception; back of that a stump under certain conditions.

Ten thousand applications are possible. I take one only — cures of all sorts of disease attributed to all sorts of remedies. We need not deny the cures; there are millions of cures, blessed be Nature! But, is the agency of cure in any given case precisely what it is said to be? Is this the ghost-fact of Christian Science, Mental Healing, drugs, or prayer? I am absolutely good-natured in regard to all these agencies. I simply suggest that when you attribute your cure to one agency or another, you strip all claims down to naked fact. That is the one sane test of the question whether a thing is a ghost or a stump. And any system of life or thought which does not welcome such a test is open to suspicion.

Illustration Number Two. Witchcraft had its facts, its supposed truth and — its real truth. When men insisted on seeing the real facts, many of the fictitious facts disappeared, the supposed truth vanished, and the real truth — awaited discovery. After science had adopted the above methods, instead of the old shout, "superstition!"— contentment in which has hurt science more than it has hurt any other department of our life — the backlying facts began to emerge, and the truths, clairvoyance, clairaudience, hypnotism, fear, imagination, etc., etc., came slowly into light. We are now trying to find out why science should say, "all bosh" to "mesmerism," "occultism," spiritualism, religion, or any other thing under the heavens.

The remedy for many errors into which we fall would seem to be here. There are supposed facts and real facts — as old as man. Thus arise supposed truths: the "may-bes," the "looks-like-its," the "I was-sick-and-now-I-am-wells," the "you-know-my-old-spirit-and-you-see-me-nows," and so on. But I say that if you will make "dead sure," which is reasonably sure, of all the facts, the real truth will come out, and you will preserve mental health. There is a good deal of truth in almost all things. But it is a mistake to take a whole thing as true because it may contain some truth. The truth may be present, but it may be exclusively labelled. And the error present may largely predominate over the truth. In any event, mental health exhibits, not in hostility toward the thing containing truth, but only in the determination not to take a thing as all true because it is partially true, and never accept a thing with its errors merely because it possesses a measure of truth. It is treason to be afraid of the truth. It is anarchy to want anything short of the truth.

Nevertheless, we are never to suppose that healthy-mindedness reduces to a hard, dry and stolid perception of colorless reality. The mind requires also the element of beauty and the foresight of mental alertness. Health-tone of mind involves the play of imagination.

Now imagination has played havoc with healthy-mindedness for ages. This faculty has filled the world with religious and theological horrors, has darkened millions of minds with impurity, has bred in multitudes of souls the demons of fear, defeat, a false sense of inability, a belief in disease and death as necessary "evils" in our life, and everywhere has begotten the spirit of hopelessness. Thus we have another difficulty to contend against,

FIFTHLY, THE DIFFICULTY OF WRONG THOUGHT-ACTION, WHICH IS IMAGINATION FALSELY EXERCISED —HOW TO DISPEL. For suggestions of correction of so great an enemy to courage, I indicate the general ideal of

Imagination Illumined by Reason. Reason declares — *That every human is entitled to his existence simply because he is a human being; that his existence and his individuality indicate his rights, not being those of others, since he is only himself, but for that reason inalienable and by no man to be cut short or hindered; that life in general is planned in the interest of the full rights of everything possessing a phase of conscious existence; that the world is planned in the interest of living things, and therefore, of the human individual; and so, that every soul is entitled to claim whatever belongs to him, but that his claim can only be made good by the confident spirit and by intelligent effort, for the real values of life consist not in things gained, but in Health, or Wholeness, of the soul or self rightly related to the Living Universe.*

If you will read this proposition until it is thoroughly analyzed and every statement is seen to be a fundamental truth, and if you will, by thought and affirmation and realization, make the entire truth a vital thing in your feeling and thought, you will find the optimism of healthy-mindedness becoming more and more a splendid power in your deepest self.   Kindly observe, then, the following related suggestions.

(1). You are invited practically to realize the italicised paragraph above as indicated in the remarks just below it.

(2). You are urged to cultivate the inspiring poetry of life, as seen in literature, yet more, as seen in the heroic efforts and the triumphs of men and women on every hand around you.

(3). You are urged to cultivate imaginative appreciation for beauty and sentiment.   The hard matter-of-fact mind misses the half of life.   Life is not fact alone; it is also truth in the beautiful.   The Universe is more truth than fact because it contains so many minds.   The question of healthy living has always to do with getting at the truth, and if one is merely a fact-man or a fact-woman, much of the truth will fail to discover itself.   To see, the eye requires light; but if the light is all on the outside, that eye is blind.   Man sees truth with the inner eye, and with the inner truth-light and truth-sense.   The power of anybody's sense depends on the self that goes into it. The farmer perceives in rocks, obstacles; the scientist, geology; the artist, effects of beauty.   Some see in the world matter, force, money.   Others behold in it opportunity for soul-building.   This is the main thing, and for this, imagination and sentiment are master-workmen.

(4). You are urged to begin at this point the cultivation of the feeling of hopeful courage.   A healthy mind is surely hopefully courageous at the core.   If there are times of apparent failure, courage is, nevertheless, its prevailing characteristic. A desperado who fears no man has his moments when to capture him needs but the command, "Hands up!" He is hungry, or cold, or sleepy, or depressed. The health-tone is low.

I believe the main trouble with thousands who live from hand to mouth is the fact of discouragement.

The discouraged man must begin with himself, not with his conditions. So long as he lacks courage, conditions will remain as they are. His first struggle has to do with the manufacture of courage. He must repeatedly suggest courage to himself. In time he will feel what at first he merely pretends. Then mental health will return, and greater courage will inevitably appear.

(5). You are urged, now, to make the feeling of courage vital, and to that end, to

Believe in yourself;

Believe in your rights and your work;

Believe in your future.

At the outset, these affirmations are merely dry statements. After a time they begin to look attractive. Then they become facts. Finally they are power.

(6). You are invited to begin the development in your soul of a feeling of confidence in better things. You are a clerk, a factory-hand, a railway man, or what-not. I wish to help you. I say, here are two roads, Hopeless Discouragement and Hopeful Confidence. It is curious, that wherever you are on either road, the fork of the other may appear. You know the first road, and you have never gotten anything out of it — except "bad luck" and worse, bad soul-health. Why not try the other? You have tried it? Then you once possessed courage and assurance, together with some degree of mental tone — which are none of yours at present. When you left the first road, you lost these values, and — the possibilities just beyond. The man who is discouraged carries two burdens, his difficulties and his discouragement. The latter is totally useless.

Some of the greatest gold mines in America were opened by Industry and deserted by Discouragement — to be developed later by men who never give up.

Three miners had exhausted their resources in a hole in the ground. They were bankrupt. They put in the last charge, lighted the fuse, and started away, forsaking the entire prospect. On their way out they heard the explosion. One of them said: "Boys, let's go back and give the old thing one more look." But he had to go alone, for Hopelessness and Discouragement would not budge. When the Last Possibility Man arrived, gold was everywhere.

The possibilities urge us all to cultivate the spirit of assurance. The assurance is bound to realize more or less, but, above all such outcome, it maintains the man at his best.

Our final study in mind-health concerns a phase of human nature which is to-day realized, as never before, to be a practical asset in the highest personal success. The topmost factor of healthy-mindedness is

MORAL TONE.

And what is this ideal state which we call moral tone? If we present the question to different people, we shall probably receive as many different replies. Nevertheless, the matter is perfectly simple. Moral tone is an expression of individual goodness, just as physical tone is an expression of bodily soundness. But goodness is always a relative thing; it consists in the effort to realize in life what one believes to be right,

assuming that the belief is the result of reasonable
effort to know the right in which properly to believe.
This effort to know the right and to do the right as
believed in is really an effort to come into harmony
with the world in which we live, or, better, with the
Universe and its *I Am That I Am*. Whoever is reasonably striving after such a condition of harmony, must
be accounted as good at the centre,— in the matter of
intention. But the struggle for harmony is not the
whole of harmony itself. There are millions of false
moral notions and millions of unhealthy moral phases
of life, which are honestly enough believed. *The mind-
health which embraces moral tone requires that the
tone of morals shall really express at least a fair degree
of actual harmony with the Universes as moral.* This
actual harmony must always depend upon personal
thought and ability to realize the thought. If, then,
we are to come to any agreement in the matter, we
must decide, I take it, that the two greatest ideals that
man has discovered, in the whole field of antiquity,
pagan and Christian, and in the whole of modern life,
Confucian, Mohammedan, Brahman, Buddhist, Greek,
Roman, Protestant, are — reverence for the Gods (or
for the moral character of the Universe) and practical love for man. On these two points we shall probably agree. There is nothing beyond these ideals, except what is implied, the conscious possession by the
human individual, of the Infinite Life. He who
strives to " make good " on these ideals, is by so much
in a state of harmony with the Universe and its *I Am
That I Am,* by so much will come more and more into
actual harmony in being and conduct, and by so much
exemplifies a measure of moral tone.

You are requested, then, to scrutinize the following

propositions, and, if you accept them, thoroughly to master them and become saturated with their power.

Proposition One. You are a legitimate part of the universal system of existence.

Proposition Two. Notwithstanding all contrary appearances, Infinite Goodness reigns on the Throne of Universal Government. The Universe is developing. That is the doctrine of evolution. Only goodness is preservative and constructive. These facts support the proposition.

Proposition Three. The Universe — or, the Universal Goodness — does its best, as a System of law in the interest of all, to confer on you all its benefits, and is bound to compensate, somehow, somewhere, sometime, all loss in your case which is not strictly due to your own fault.

Proposition Four. In order that you may receive these benefactions, two conditions are interposed before you, which are based in the nature of things, and which can be changed by no theory, creed or faith, to-wit:

Proposition Five. You must honestly endeavor to live up to the moral light which you now possess;

Proposition Six. You must honestly seek to acquire all the light which at any time may be reasonably possible in your case.

Proposition Seven. These conditions are born in Universal Goodness, never in tyrannical righteousness; born in a Government that means well by every intelligence and is conducted in the interest of all. The Infinite Goodness, while eternally true to itself, is infinitely patient.

Proposition Eight. The Universal Goodness strives constantly to impart to every soul all the light — truth — needed at any given time; no more, no less.

Proposition Nine. Every soul in this earth possesses all the moral truth it demands and can use. Minds that are not normally competent come under another law, which is not before us.

Proposition Ten. If you are honestly and reasonably (not slavishly) striving to fulfil the above conditions, you are possessed of a corresponding degree of soul-health, according to your capacity, and have nothing to fear in any world:

From yourself — for honesty is power;

For yourself — for honesty cannot be hurt;

From things or forces — for your honest self will survive;

From others — for men cannot touch the soul, "devils" shun the honest soul, and the Universe necessarily ranges itself on the side of the honest soul;

From events — for events only culture the soul that lives according to its light and seeks the best light reasonably possible for the better living.

These considerations call up the problem of immortality. The belief in immortality should not be founded on primitive instincts — instincts that seem to be personally innate — nor upon blind religious tradition. Faith in immortality becomes sane and potent when it springs up amid the beauties of personal goodness, in touch with the Infinite White Life, and going out with large thought in helpfulness to others.

Proposition Eleven. Soul-health, high and symmetrical, has inner assurance of immortality—provided it is not obscured by some intellectual theory. You cannot prove immortality to a soul which is morally sick or logically imperious. To rational health of soul unobscured by theory the proof of immortality is gratuitous. The best evidence of it is to have it.

FEAR NOT THYSELF.

Fear not thy Self —
"One to confront the worlds and question them."
Why, this the dawn-first Chaos dreamed!
Why, this the Eternal March has ushered
Out of the swarm and struggle
Of becoming and arrival!
Why, this, for an ultimate that should sublimate mind,
The Nature of Things, the All-Good,
Thrust into a body and named *One Human!*
This, this *One*, goes with thee, never to be divorced,
Never to vanish,
Ever to burst into newer wonder,
Ever to seek and ever to find
The Self in a Larger Self,
The Soul-Star in a deeper Sky,—
Star after Star arcoss bar on bar
Up the long spiral of Being
Which halts only, and emerges,
At the inconceivable apex
Of unfoldment into the All-God!

Why, this thou canst not fear!
Fear *all* save this!
Then this thou *wilt* not fear!

— THE AUTHOR.

CHAPTER V.

FEAR OF SELF.

"One to confront the worlds and question them."— *Edwin Markham.*

"No man should ever despise himself, for brilliant success never attends the man who lowers himself."— *Mahabharata.*

BECAUSE our nature climaxes the evolution of animal existence, every human being is entitled, according to capacity, to a full measure of body-life, world-life, mental-life and soul-life. This proposition signifies your inalienable right to Health, Prosperity, Development of Mind and Wealth of Spirit.

And, inasmuch as we are now in the world, inasmuch as there is no future life in actual existince, but only an endless present life and the world-phase of that life, that is, individual body, individual relation with other personalities, individual mental powers and individual moral capacities, each sphere of our existence is relatively important, so that every human has the highest right and is under the deepest obligation to live the Four-Fold Life of Health, Prosperity, Development, and Wealth of Spirit. Thus we begin the present chapter with the

COURAGE OF THE FOUR-FOLD LIFE.

I send you this message:

Whatever belongs to you in body-life;
Whatever belongs to you in world-life;
Whatever belongs to you in mind-life;
Whatever belongs to you in highest self-life —

is your inalienable right. In the interest of personal
courage, you are now invited to fill out each of these
phases of your existence to the completest possible
measure. This means, not that you are to live for the
body alone, or for the world-life alone, or for the mental
realm alone, or for the spiritual stage alone, but that
you are entitled to live for all phases and to live richly
and inspiringly in all realms for all goods possible therein, right here and now. In order that such an ideal
may be realized, two methods only are practical: first,
the saturation of self with the conviction that the
Four-Fold Right is surely yours; secondly, immediate
and practical action in the interest of health, prosperity,
development, and highest wealth of the self, as far as
now possible in your case. And kindly remember that
no man knows the limit of his own possibilities.

But the acquisition of these rights depends wholly
upon the individual man or woman. Nothing really
depends upon anybody else. No one should crave
what he is not willing to earn. The Universe promises
health to him only who harmonizes with psychic laws;
prosperity only according to endowment and right
effort; development only through mental adjustment
to reality and proper exercise of powers; spiritual unfoldment only to him who lives the *white life,* or strives
for what he believes to be right.

The central inspiration in all this four-fold life and
the work indicated is found in courage.

Varieties of Fears of Self.

It is because I wish to suggest a general atmosphere
for such courage that I send you the message of our
common four-fold rights. You are invited to read
and re-read the preceding paragraphs until you feel,

deeply and permanently, the thrill of personal confidence.

Assuming that a degree of inspiration has emerged from our study, we are now ready for some of the practical difficulties connected with the fear of self, and their remedies.

Fear of self manifests in a variety of ways. Thus we have *shyness, bashfulness, diffidence, timidity, want of self-confidence.* Let us define these phases of our subject, and discover, if possible, your own peculiar difficulty.

We may define *shyness* as a tendency to shrink from the presence of others, accompanied by a feeling of distress. "Shyness," Darwin said, "is closely related to fear; yet it is distinct from fear in the ordinary sense. A shy man no doubt dreads the notice of strangers, but can hardly be said to be afraid of them." Nevertheless, shyness sometimes amounts to fear, and in many instances is a real handicap against success. The general remedy consists in a resolute mingling with all sorts of people, together with a confident assertion, "I do not fear you; I am at ease in your presence." In time the distress of shyness will decrease, particularly if you forget yourself and so all occasion for the feeling. The best method for securing self-forgetfulness consists in assuming and developing a lively interest in other people and in any situation in which you may meet them. Self-assertive commingling with others and self-forgetfulness through interest — these are the methods, and they are infallible, if only the conquest of shyness is highly resolved upon and the effort held good for no matter how many years.

Bashfulness is akin to shyness, but seems to be excessive modesty in the presence of unfamiliar people.

Modesty, in the right degree and place, is a virtue, but when tainted with fear it becomes a vice. The remedy suggested for shyness may be consulted.

Diffidence, so far as it differs from the above, carries an undue apprehension of criticism because of failure. The word means, Latin *dis,* "apart," and *fidere,* "to trust:" short of trusting self. The remedy for shyness holds good here, but the diffident person should cultivate assurance that he *will* handle himself and any situation successfully, and especially should he develop a good degree of healthy indifference to adverse criticism. A negative method for this phase of indifference consists in developing a reasonable indifference for commendation. The diffident person will grow courage if he will only learn to stand squarely for his own character, rights, and life, refusing to depend, as most diffident people do, so greatly upon the criticisms of others, whether adverse or favorable.

Timidity is a condition in which one is easily frightened. The word comes from the Latin, *timere,* "to fear," and this is allied to the Sanskrit, *tam,* "to choke," and *tamas,* "darkness." When you remember *choking* and *darkness;* when we add *coercion,* from the word *cow,* which reminds us of *caudal,* "belonging to the tail," and the Norman French word, *couard,* "a hare"— we come to ideas which no man can relish as realized in himself. The timid man invites *choking* and *darkness,* and permits within himself the *hare that always turns tail.* The remedies are those indicated for shyness, bashfulness and diffidence.

The word *fear* is derived from the Anglo-Saxon *faran,* "to go," and originally referred to "peril while traveling." We are surely faring on through worlds and life. Fear averts no real peril, conjures up many

an imaginary danger, and is empowered to overcome
no evil. Self-preservation demands the substitution
of reason and the "good heart" for this enemy of all
our journey. When I say that the word *heart* comes
from the Greek, *kordia*, and the Aryan, *hrid*, "that
which quivers," it is urged that the trembling of fear
for perils attending self in its travels through the world
be overcome and swallowed up by the *vibrant quiver
of a heart of good courage*. It is really vibration against
vibration, and the strongest will win.

For how many otherwise splendid souls has this
demon of fear tortured and defeated! Infinitely preferable any amount of egotism to any form fear may
assume. We may well say, with Longfellow:

"Write on your doors the saying wise and bold,
 'Be bold! Be bold! and everywhere — Be bold;
 'Be not too bold!' yet better the excess
 Than the defect; better the more than less;
 Better like Hector in the field to die,
 Than like a perfumed Paris turn and fly."

To the varieties of fear thus far given may now be
added certain forms which spring from a general knowledge of self. Illustrations are seen in —(1), Fear of
the Passions; (2), Fear of Mental Action; (3), Fear
of Beliefs and Moral Attitudes.

It will indicate how broad the foundation of
courage is if we consider for a little these special phases
of self-fear.

FIRST — FEAR OF THE PASSIONS. This may be
merely an exercise of sound reason induced by clear
knowledge of self, or it may also be a morbid product
of imagination. In the one case we have restraining
wisdom, in the other, unnecessary distress and an evil

check on free personal life. The passions are tremendous powers for good when controlled, but equal powers for injury when in a state of anarchy. You will find control becoming practically real by as much as you in thought exalt to its ideal each form of passion with which you are endowed and which is legitimate in exercise. In *"Power For Success"* I have analyzed the subject of the emotional life, and may here suggest merely some general considerations. The following are the great passions of human nature (read down)—

* Beauty,	* Courage,	* Will,
* Liberty,	* Happiness,	* Enthusiasm,
* Patriotism,	* Justice,	* Desire,
* Love,	* Religion,	* Mirth,
* Hope,	* Honor,	† Sex,
* Faith,	* Truth,	† Physical States,
† Pride,	Shame,	† Fear,
†‡ Hate,	Guilt,	†‡ Jealousy,
†‡ Anger,	† Sorrow,	‡ Lust,

‡ Revenge,   ‡ Murder.

Let us mark with an asterisk those passions which no one need fear within himself, with a dagger those which require reason and idealization, and with a double dagger those which threaten self when turned toward any human being. We have, then, sixteen passions for which no one need entertain fear, provided, of course, they are taken normally — except that it is always a mistake to be any one thing so largely that other things are neglected. We have also, as passions which simply cannot be tolerated when entertained toward self,—guilt, shame, fear; and passions which cannot be tolerated when entertained toward others,— pride, hate, anger, jealousy, lust, revenge, murder. The remedy for shame and guilt is the *white life*.

"Conscience doth make cowards of us all." but a sense of rightness builds courage as surely as life builds cells of body. The remedy for pride, hate, anger, jealousy, and the sex passion is idealization: seen in pride as a sense of personal dignity and gratification because of well-earned success; seen in hate for everything meanly little and surely morally hurtful; seen in anger against tyranny, injustice and baseness of life; seen in jealousy controlled by reason for the real rights of self and others; seen in the sex passion conserved as consciously possessed power. Revenge is useless and debasing, and the spirit of murder is practical suicide. Sorrow is legitimate, and merely calls for reasonable control. The physical states of normal health should be idealized by thought of the body as a wonder and a temple and by right uses accompanied by the sense of mastery and of utility.

If, then, you will idealize the passions marked with a dagger, not one of them can ever bring harm to self.

SECOND — FEAR OF MENTAL ACTION. This fear may refer to *collapse*, and should then be entertained only in the form of self-interest thought, and the ground for it should be removed. If you have reason to apprehend this danger, you are urged to stop work in accustomed directions, consult a specialist, place yourself in an atmosphere of mental healing, and find new interests totally different from those of your old life for inspiring pursuit. I am entirely aware that it is easier to give than to act upon advice, but the matter reduces, nevertheless, to a choice on your part between collapse and loss of all values, on the one hand, and, on the other hand, some method as indicated, a measure of loss involved in the effort to prevent bankruptcy of brain, but, in the end, incalculable gain.   When a man is bound to lose one way or another, good sense dictates that he choose the smaller loss — and the greater possible gain.

But fear of mental action is frequently *fear of consequences* which may result from such action, as, for example, when one apprehends that certain intellectual reasonings may induce criticism from others or may upset some present accepted theory or belief. Such suggested evils are more than half imaginary, and, whether or no, they may be perfectly conquered by cultivating a deep and active determination to know reality as it is and to come to the last best conclusion, whatever that may be, regardless of consequences.   I do not know a baser slave than the person who fears to follow where reason leads, even over the rim of the world.   You are, therefore, invited to come utterly free and to idealize your own mind and surely trust its best earnest conclusions.   You may get into error for a time, but you nevertheless save your mental integrity, and ultimately you will certainly arrive more and more at living truth.

THIRD — FEAR OF BELIEFS AND MORAL ATTITUDES.   This fear may be similarly disposed of.   I give here an illustration of what actually obtains in a multitude of cases.   A one-time college president, in the later years of his life and after retirement from office, came to see something of the weight of the evidences in favor of the evolution theory.   He said: "If I were a younger man, I am inclined to think I might become an evolutionist myself, but as it is, I do not dare to let go my old convictions."   Here is an attitude maintained in the interest of religion which is distinctly immoral. It is immoral to fear truth of any sort, and by what instrument can we find truth if not by the human mind! It is irreligious to believe in a Deity who demands love for anything short of truth — the whole truth and nothing but the truth. It is bad thinking to imagine that any conceivable injury can come to real self from a fearless pursuit of truth, though it destroy all Bibles and wreck all religions. The only Bible which has right to acceptance is Truth, and the only religion that can make for human good is the life of Truth in the soul.

And I have before me, for another illustration, an article written by a learned theological professor in which, at the close of a fine disposal of another writer's assault on evolution, appear these words: "It may not be quite superfluous to add that the writer has never been a champion of evolution theory. Throughout his theological career his attitude toward that theory has been one of *serene neutrality.*" This attitude is almost inconceivable in a scholar. It is difficult to understand how the attitude could have been one of "serene neutrality" unless the result of more or less self-coercion. If I stand in the midst of a political fight, I am bound to have some definite political opinions. The world is full of people in the position of "serene neutrality" where even receptivity would seemingly compel a judgment of some kind. I conclude that fear of self in its beliefs and moral attitudes demands cure, and may be cured, by absolute surrender to truth — as one, earnestly seeking, may find and understand truth.

These considerations, now, may seem too general for the fears of self which beset the practical life. We

come, then, to the more familiar forms everywhere in evidence.

ANALYSIS OF FEAR OF SELF.

In its broadest sense, fear of self is simply self-distrust. The word *faith* is descended from a Latin word, *fidem*, and from an earlier Aryan word, *bhid*, "to bind." We have seen that *diffident* signifies, Latin *dis*, "apart," and *fidere*, "to trust" — *apart from trust*. Thus, self-distrust means, *not bound to self, self getting away from self*. Fear of self is a feeling possessed because self is not well in hand. No one who has self in control can possibly fear himself. The secret of our remedy, then, must be this: resumption of self-control.

For our present purposes, the causes of self-distrust would seem to be evident. Thus:

Self-distrust may be inherited, that is, the conditions encouraging distrust of self are sometimes constitutional;

Self-distrust may also be an acquired trait, for certain natural tendencies may be developed by the habits of life;

Lastly, self-distrust may be an occasional experience only, arising merely in sudden and great emergencies.

Whatever the cause of self-fear, it is surely an enemy, but just as certainly may it be conquered altogether. You are, therefore, invited to eliminate from your life the above-named varieties of fear.

TREATMENT FOR FEAR OF SELF.

I. FIRST, FEAR OF SELF AS A CONSTITUTIONAL DEFECT. Methods looking to this end should be indirect so far as possible. So long as we dwell on the thought, "I am not confident of myself," we merely sink the fear more deeply and permanently into the soul   You are urged, then, to exclude the idea as completely as may be from all your thought.   As this is precisely the difficulty, I indicate the requirements which promise practical results.

FIRST REQUIREMENT OF THE INDIRECT METHOD: *Improving the Tone-Feeling of The Whole Personality.* There are times when the sense of I-am-power regards nothing as impossible.   The All-Health has

"Sublimed thee, and exalted thee, and fixed thee
In the third heaven."

Says the *Vriddha Chanoka* of India: "The summit of Meru is not very lofty nor the infernal world very profound, nor the ocean very far to cross, for men who possess   energy"— the   tone-feeling   of   power.   At times the mood is almost exaggerated, as in the lines,

"I am sublimed! gross earth
Support me not! I walk on air!"

If you would develop this exuberant mood of health and acquire the confidence of its power, you are invited again to adopt the teachings of the two preceding chapters.

SECOND REQUIREMENT OF THE INDIRECT METHOD: *Full Assertion of Personal Rights.*   By this is meant, not an external noise in regard to the matter, but a profound conviction as seen in the paragraph now quoted from the last chapter:

"*Reason declares that every human is entitled to his existence simply because he is a human being; that his existence and his individuality indicate his rights, not*

being those of others, since he is only himself, but for that
reason inalienable and by no man to be cut short or hin-
dered; that life in general is planned in the interest of the
full rights of everything possessing a phase of conscious
existence; that the world is planned in the interest of
living things, and, therefore, of the human individual;
and so, that every soul is entitled to claim whatever belongs
to him, but that this claim can only be made good by the
confident spirit and by intelligent effort."

This great Declaration of Rights may be appro-
priated by frequent repetition of the following condensed form:

"*I am a human being, and, consequently, a legiti-*
mate part of the Universe; and therefore a part of the
present world; and thus a part of this nation; and so a
part of the city in which I live; and, of course, part of my
immediate neighborhood. I belong here. These things
are no truer of president or king, or of star or system or
galaxy, than they are true of me."

If, now, you will begin with the smaller of the
above relations, and carry the thought that you are a
legitimate part of things on through an ascending
scale, meanwhile mentally asserting your rights, you
will find the spirit of courage surely unfolding within
yourself. The process is indicated below:

"*As such a part of things, I am entitled to certain*
inalienable rights. If I exist for these spheres, they also
exist for me, as well as for others: the neighborhood, the
town, the state, the nation, the earth, the Universe. My
individuality is, therefore, as valid as that of any other
person. I and they are mutually needful. These spheres,
from neighborhood to Universe, need me. They draw
on me for their aid, since life is a gigantic mutuality. I
may therefore legitimately draw on them as I have need.

All their demands should be according to law; hence my demands shall also be legal and right. I will help to maintain this equilibrium. I belong to all systems. All systems belong to me. Fearless on this double truth I take my stand."

THIRD REQUIREMENT OF THE INDIRECT METHOD: *Cultivation of Vital Belief in Self.* Your chief trouble, perhaps, springs from perpetual insistence on the idea of self-distrust. Nothing could be more prohibitive of the courage-feeling, or, indeed, of the successful action of personal powers. Here is a bit of genuine science: "Strong (wrong) feeling about one's self tends to arrest the free association of one's objective ideas and motor processes." Thus, one is paralyzed by fear or overcome with joy. If you incessantly insist that you cannot be or do, you arrest ideas of success and you pauperize muscles, nerves, and mind. If you cultivate the feeling of confidence, you dethrone the feeling of weakness, and you let loose strong ideas of success, and thus all powers spring into readiness for action.

You are therefore invited to think "power in self," to insist upon self-power, to make believe and "work up" an abiding conviction of adequate power — all the power you need — as surely your present and permanent possession. In order to this, I suggest two things:

First, the Affirmations. You are urged to find opportunity, alone and undisturbed, each morning, to assert, with intense earnestness:

"I can become whatever, in fair reason, I ought to be. Therefore, I will be, and am now becoming, precisely that,"— naming the ideal desired.

"I can do whatever, in fair reason, I ought to do.

Therefore, I will do, and this moment I am developing ability to do precisely that.   I am power!"   You should always *think* the *specific* achievement.

Much of this, to the average " common-sense" man, may appear to be excessively foolish.   Nevertheless, we all know that "there are crises where a fact cannot come at all unless a preliminary faith exists in its coming" (Professor William James), and the regime suggested is exactly calculated to develop right conditions for the preliminary faith.   When one persistently asserts self-confidence, one soon begins to believe that he has it, and if a man believes that he is confident of self, he certainly possesses self-confidence.

Secondly, the Practicalization.   Following the hour of quiet, yet intense assertion of confidence in self, you are urged to make practical corroboration of the faith claimed, and never to exhibit any contradiction whatever.   You must treat yourself and your assumed ability, without any exception, as one *live hypothesis.* You cannot overestimate the power of this self-suggestion.   Professor Jean Finot writes, in regard to illness: "Does not psycho-therapeutics, the new departure in medicine, teach us that certain illnesses disappear as if by enchantment as the result of constantly repeated suggestions?   Dr. F. Regnault relates that in treating a hypochondriac he advised him to write on the wall every evening the words, 'I am happy,' and to go off to sleep in full view of them.   After a few weeks happiness began to steal into his spirit." Surely, not less may be expected from the regime here indicated.

If the work involved should consume a year, your time would be well spent.   I have found that a few people fail to secure the full benefits of the Power-

Books, as I certainly desire they may, because they imagine that real practical results may be derived from a mere reading of these works, and are unwilling to pay the price of all improvement, honest effort. You are urged, then, to begin now to saturate your consciousness with the above affirmations, always treating them as live hypotheses, always exercising patience with lapses and panics, but always, everywhere, acting as though you were an incarnation of unlimited self-confidence.

FOURTH REQUIREMENT OF THE INDIRECT METHOD: *Reticence Concerning All Fears of Self.* Confession to others of self-distrust tends to retain the idea as a living thing, which is precisely the end not sought. You are urged to avoid all conversation on the subject, resolutely banishing the thought from your mind; to cease confiding your trouble to friends and advisers, and, above all, to think and acknowledge no more the fact of any past failure or defeat — unless strict justice to others may require. The world may well be left to its own discoveries in this matter. On the other hand, it is perfectly legitimate that you do your utmost to convince the world of your confidence in the powers you possess. When a man succeeds in this effort, the world wants him. That person lacks good judgment who advertises self-distrust yet at the same time dreams of success.

FIFTH REQUIREMENT OF THE INDIRECT METHOD: *Cultivation of The Habit of Self-Courage.* Habit is king in every life, either for good or for evil. Wrong habit is the lawless despot; good habit is constitutional monarch. This brings us to,

II. SECONDLY, FEAR OF SELF AS AN ACQUIRED HABIT. The four preceding regimes are altogether applicable to acquired self-distrust, and should be freshly referred to at this point. In addition, we must remember that one's want of self-confidence involves a confirmed way of thinking and feeling distrustfully of self, and one sovereign remedy for the difficulty consists in building up an opposite habit — a confirmed way of thinking and feeling courage as actually a personal possession. Such building process may be indicated as follows:

First, want of confidence may have become a habit of thought and feeling with you because of *long experience in failure.* In treating fear as thus induced, you should observe the directions above given, and add thereto the following:

Experience is a wise teacher if correctly interpreted. But misinterpreted experience often teaches lies. The successful student of experience needs about as much wisdom as experience. The trouble with experience is the fact that our opinions are so thoroughly mixed up with it, since it never exactly repeats itself. When a given phase is mastered, it immediately becomes obsolete. I think little of mere experience as a teacher. Life's real teacher is reason. The failure to regard reason-experience tests in our deductions and plans gives rise to certain errors which demand, now, a brief attention, as follows:

It is Error to Confuse Personal Impressions With The Real Lessons of Experience. Impressions ten thousand "come to us," and it is valid to follow them when reason asserts nothing contrary or appears to run with them; otherwise impressions are as useless as tea-grounds. Impressions of failure are especially untrustworthy. *Observe, then, A* — For example, a school-teacher has the feeling that her admonitions have passed unheeded, and she is discouraged. She is wrong. One young listener swung that day into upper currents of success. You said that a certain picture which you produced was a failure, but a little later a person blessed with insight ignored all your other work for just that canvas. You declined a "job" or responsibility last year because you did not feel yourself "up to" it. Then the other man, who had accepted, failed to do the one little thing which you know how to do, and this little thing was the key to that situation.

You see, then, it is very likely that your impressions of long failures are false. They may have been false in some instances. You may be legitimately tempted to hold them false all along. You must now resolve to discount all mere impressions of failure.

Observe, again, B — But let us assume that your feeling of failure has been correct. Why should it be otherwise? You have always *invited* failure by *believing* failure and declining opportunities. Whatever you undertake is performed with the mood and belief that you are not quite equal to it. Why should you be equal to it — or to anything? Success is not a bully to force favors upon you.

I observe persons who are learning to swim. One cries, "Oh, I never can do it!" and he never w ll accomplish the simple task. The other laughs: "Why, sure; it's perfectly easy!" and becomes amphibious.

You are invited to reason in all matters of this kind somewhat as follows: "*In almost all cases of my supposed failures I have been more or less mistaken. Though I permit want of self-confidence to continue, I shall certainly be equally mistaken in future instances. As I have had success, to some degree, while actually*

*believing otherwise, my mistaken impressions will accom-
pany some success in coming cases. Yet a greater measure of success would certainly have been mine had I more
thoroughly believed in myself. I am resolved for these
reasons to banish all self-distrust."*

And, *again, observe, C* — You should recall instances wherein you permitted timidity to rule, some
other person took your place and succeeded, and you
afterward felt entirely confident that you could have
done equally well. So, you are invited to burn the
lesson into the soul:

*"I stepped aside. This man undertook the work
and won. I know I could have matched his success. My
confidence seems always to come too late. Hereafter I
will summon confidence at the opening of opportunity,
and I will stand aside for no human being in the world."*

But, *observe, once more, D* — You should recall the
successes of your life. Always has self-fear disturbed
you, yet you have been compelled to undertake many
things, and have actually gotten through some of them
with credit. Let this fact have due weight:

*"I have feared my own ability, but have now and
then succeeded, nevertheless. If I have done so in spite
of fears, I can do so again, in spite of fear. But if I can
occasionally succeed in spite of fear, I can do much
better and more easily without fear. I will henceforth
forestall fear by emphasizing in thought what I have
already accomplished."*

Yet *now, observe, E* — But the failure still remains.
The sole question now is: "Shall I continue to be
bound hand and foot by the past, or shall I bury the
yesterday of my life and live royally the present?"
Assistance in answering this question has in part already
been given, but a further resource may be indicated:

"*I have certainly failed somewhat in the past. I
still live, however. My failures have not annihilated me.
I can but try again, and, if failure ensue, then I can
doggedly try again, over and over and over. I fear to
suffer — what? The fear of my fear of failure. But the
more I persist in doing what I fear, the less I shall suffer,
and so, the less I shall fear. In the end I shall be rid of
fear altogether. The only real evil which can come to me
in this matter is that of total surrender. Always will I
stand for another effort.*" If you take this position, you
are more than half victor, even now.

Or, observe, further, F — Your trouble is largely
the fact that you think only of your failures, and you
magnify them because you do not compare them with
failures in other lives. You should remember that
some degree of failure is the common lot of all men.

"*All the world fails at times. On every hand around
me are people who now and then do poor work, miss the
mark, come short of perfect success. Yet this fact does
not seem to discourage them; they go right on believing in themselves and achieving success. Why
should I torture myself by emphasizing my share of
failures? If others can forget that they have failed, so
can I. So will I.*"

*Furthermore, It is Error Improperly to Estimate the
Factor of Success.* Precisely here it is that many
people encourage the feeling of defeat. In morals a
man's conscience may become super-sensitive; so our
ideals may overtop the practically possible. There are
those who are so finicky about dress that they never
feel well-dressed, or so pernickety in affairs that they
are always dissatisfied with their own efforts. It is a
mistake to define success, in any particular matter, as
well as in the larger life, in such a way that it becomes

improbable at the start. You should not measure success for yourself by the best thing the ablest man can accomplish. "Hitch your waggon to the stars," to be sure, but every human being has his special star; there's his "hitching-post." Because you may not win jury cases as did Choate, nor speak with the eloquence of Webster, nor pile up millions with Cresus, every effort you make brings up the feeling of incompleteness. I believe this to be wrong. You have the nature which any man has—human; you have a name, a place, and a work in this world, with every other person. Your kind of success awaits you. That is enough. That success is great enough and will call for all you are; stand for that. Personally I am entirely content to win the largest success my capacity and life demand. I want no other. This success promises to keep me very, very busy and always absolutely hopeful. That is my message to you.

You are invited, then, to scrutinize the italicised aphorisms which follow. Success for you is what your endowments call for — no more. (I do not say, your opportunities: your endowments are capable of creating opportunities). The concrete thing you have done may be very ordinary as compared with what some other men can do, but it is not at all ordinary for you. What you really do may be a greater success for you than what others do is for them, because it costs you more than it costs them. Your failures may mean more on the right side of life than other men's successes may mean. You have "felt" "failure" because you have not attained ideals, but your exalted ideals are your best capital. Two things you do not know: the ideals of some successful people may not be near as high as yours are — and their ideals may be so high that their successes are to them comparative failures. Still, they fight on. It may be that your unconscious success has been just this struggle to climb the, to you, impassable. You must learn to define success with elements furnished by your own nature, character, talents, efforts, life and ideals.

> Failure 's a toss:
> Venture or loss
>   On what a man *can* do, little or much.
> Surely success is it —
> Plenty or less is it —
>   When *all* a man *can* do 's put to the touch.
>
> What *is* success?
> Doing *no less*
>   Than what a man *can* do, little or much.
> Here is my toast, Sir—
> This be your boast, Sir:
>   "All a man *can do*, put to the touch!"

If you will earnestly comply with the above suggestions, the part which experience plays in your want of confidence may be entirely eliminated. The past is to be heeded only as it may profit the present and the future. The chief consideration furnished by the past is the fact that the bulk of its failures has been due to self-fear, not to lack of ability, and these pages are designed to disclose that fact and thus to destroy the foundation of fear. You have built these foundations — no one else. It is for you to annihilate them. Fear can only stand as you maintain it. Fear is solely your own creation. You did not inherit it; you merely inherited, perhaps, some of its conditions, and all these conditions you alone can uproot from your life. This fear has no substantial reality apart from yourself. When you withdraw your support, it will disappear.

And yet, so large a subject is fear, further difficulties confront us. We have still to consider,

III. THIRDLY, FEAR OF SELF ARISING FROM SPECIAL EMERGENCIES. It may be that we are now arrived at our main trouble. We are confident enough, possibly, under ordinary circumstances, but now and then some unusual contingency brings the thrill of fright. Let us note one or two examples.

First Example: Self-Fear in View of Particular Kinds of Work to be Performed. The work is, say, a school examination; a hard piece of ditch digging; an unusual specimen of architecture; a sudden call to boss a gang of men, to run a locomotive, to amputate a limb, to try a law case, to preside over a meeting, to address an audience. The opportunity is declined, "for fear." Another person accepts, and he succeeds. You say, "What presumption!" and you are right in your verdict. He is really no abler than the decliner — except in this respect: he never consults a fear. In thousands of cases, the difference between men is just foolish fear.

Second Example: The Unforeseen Occasion. To some people this is always fearful. They are groove-people, old-shoes people, back-yard people. A new regime, a new method, a new style, a new man, is wanted in the exigencies of life. The person in charge, who is familiar with and a slave to the old ways, glimpses the ghost of the New, and he proceeds to brood and worry until panic overwhelms his soul.

Third Example: New Responsibilities. With many people these phases of life are forever dreaded. All the world is saying: "Construct this delicate instrument; take charge of this heavy task." Weaklings decline while the Courage-Man breathes deeply, swears in gutturals and puts himself under the task, indifferent to responsibility, but vastly mindful of the thing to be done. Then others whisper: "That fellow does n't know enough to be afraid." But he certainly knew enough to take the open door. The other people knew just enough to fear the responsibility — and lose.

REMEDIES. Now the remedies for all this emergency-fear are simple, plain, practical — and as difficult as you care to make them.

Note, *First:* A true distinction is to be made between self-fear which deludes and defeats, and that fair and wise estimate of self which declines rashness, and thus prevents defeat, refuses to undertake what it knows itself unfitted for, and so enlightens judgment, and in the long run advances self-interest. But it is not fear that determines the matter. In the one case, fear rules; in the other, reason reigns. The man must, of course, himself decide, but those who are troubled with self-distrust would better adopt the principle — Take less counsel of *supposed* reason and more of *enforced courage.* In the one case, for example, the surgeon declines to operate because the work lies full in the public eye — and that fact frightens him. In the other case, he declines because he has never performed any operation of the kind and a brother surgeon who is present has operated in many similar cases and with success. Nevertheless, he who always declines under such circumstances can never begin. I know a young physician whose first case was supposed to be deadly contagious. The "other man" forsook the family for that reason. My little doctor would have essayed the cure of Death. In his courage he forgot self-estimate, and he brought the patient through — a case of

measles. Then he was called to assist in a case of am-
putation, and the surgeon in charge took fright and surrendered to the beginner, who performed the operation
with success. To-day he practises a high-class office
specialty. Self-fear never yet achieved a correct estimate of self.

Note, *Secondly:* One of the best remedies for
emergency-fear is prepared readiness. That kind of
readiness depends largely upon the faithful performance
of details in the thing now in hand, however minute or
seemingly unimportant. Some details are more important than others, but no detail is ever wholly devoid
of importance. If one does all things as they arise in
the best possible manner for him, when the unforeseen
affair comes up, he has already performed a part of it
in just these details. It is now only three-quarters, one-
half — one-third, new. The every-day best prepares
for the unknown to-morrow. If a man knows that he
can do his best because he *has* done his best, he knows
that he can do exactly that in the new task. Such a
soul says: "I may possibly fail, but I will not fail if
doing my best can prevent; and even if I do not attain
ideal success, I 'll know better next time." But the
fear-men never know better.

Note, *Thirdly:* Self-fear has a voracious appetite.
It should be starved to death. There is one certain
method for doing this — to take the work, meet the
occasion, assume the responsibility, whenever opportunity affords, in spite of all trembling diffidence.
Every declination due to fear feeds fear. Every undertaking gone into in spite of fear starves fear. Fear
feeds only on fear. The rule of wisdom and courage,
then, is — Do the thing in hand, without exceptions,
for which you fear failure, the dictates of common

sense receiving proper consideration. But do not mistake the fear sense for common sense.

Note, *Fourthly:* All abnormal fears are liars. It should be remembered that I have excluded fear altogether from the category of the friends of man, and have insisted that its place should be taken by reason. Self-fear invariably tends to magnify difficulties. Many people fear work, occasions, responsibilities, because they imagine them to be greater than they really are. Fear never analyzes. Fear always stares at wholes. Herein lies its discrimination from true caution, which analyzes, and, having done so, scrutinizes details. Because self-fear perceives things in lumps or masses, the component parts are lost sight of, and the wholes are magnified. Analyze a piece of work of which you are fearful: it is not this or that detail that disturbs you — it is the miserable whole. But, after all, when you are familiar with the whole, it is just so many details, innocent or decently difficult, yet clearly not insurmountable.

There is a sense in which life loves to impose on the imagination. It has a way of summarizing its tasks, or of characterizing its responsibilities, with so much dignity, with such a vast array of big words, with such a solemn eye turned out to danger (for your benefit) that the man who will attack them seems wonderfully courageous. Experience always proves that the tasks and responsibilities are merely made up of possible parts easily described in common language.

Take as an illustration, the pages of a college catalogue. Was there ever such another specimen of frightful dignity? Great words, fearful tasks, imposing impossibilities, all set in majestic array, with vistas beyond of deadly professors, bloodless, rigid, merciless, masters of all conceivable knowledge — beasts of prey! Yet what does it all come to in the analysis? Kind-hearted gentlemen, who dislike only the fool and the coward, innocent text-books, not to be swallowed at a gulp, snug work cut up for doing a little every day: one task at a time, one book at a long time, one term at a time, one year at a time — and the thing is done. The remedy for fear in all such cases is the conviction that the whole need not be formidable because it is not to be attacked in the mass, but is merely to be conquered in detail.

It would be a valuable exercise if you would proceed to analyze some one thing you have already accomplished. You now see that this might be a fine specimen of fear-cause if looked at as a whole. It frightened many a soul before you were born. You have mastered it in the details, and you do not fear it at all — on your side of the situation. But that side of the situation is possible to you in any case that will come to you. In every case you have — merely a bundle of "piece-work."

You are, therefore, urged totally to disregard the fear-lessons of experience; to substitute reason for impressions as a guide through life; to estimate your own successes in terms of your own endowments only; to forget your failures entirely; to take no counsel of fear in any special emergency; to minify all difficulties rather than magnify them; —but to make everything you undertake a splendid preparation for new and greater opportunities, incessantly insisting in your deepest soul on this conviction: "I am surely equal now to any demand life may put upon me."

There is a fear of self, however, which requires attention because it weakens courage in the whole personality. This fear is distrust of the moral self. Only at the heart of the moral self can the eagle of courage come to power.   Taken by and large, the strong character is at its best when thoroughly conscious of

MORAL COURAGE.

I have already offered pertinent suggestions on this subject at the beginning of the present chapter, and have treated it practically and at length in "*Power For Success*," so that it seems sufficient to add here merely a word or two.

Morbid Apprehension of Consequences Resulting From Immoral Action is not a very prevalent difficulty, yet it occurs in some cases, and deserves assistance. Self-preservation is a law of life.   Reason forbids all activity or conduct promising hurt to self.   The law, then, demands merely the exercise of healthy reason in such cases, and when one passes this requirement and entertains, not reason, but fear, he is violating the very law he seeks to obey, — self-preservation, — and he surely injures himself.   The remedy consists in eliminating the fear-element and in getting back to sober reason.   You are morbidly fearful that your wrong conduct may bring to you excessively unhappy consequences.   You should repeatedly suggest to your self the ideas of confidence, courage, ability to take what may properly come to you, and, above all, the truth that the government of this Universe is one of absolute equity, and that only.

But this desire to conquer self-fear for the sake of self-interest is perfectly legitimate.   The man who is indifferent to moral courage as an asset in his own favor, disregards one of the greatest weapons of life. You are, therefore, urged to observe the following suggestions:

(1). *Auto-Suggestion.* You are urged to treat the conquest of moral fears as already accomplished, the method being the emphatic and continuous assumption: "I am now power to do whatever I believe to be right," making sure always to demonstrate the assumption by all your thinking and in all your conduct.

(2). *The Vital Present.* You are urged to do now the thing that you feel ought now to be done. Some people are always equal to a thing — to-morrow. They say: "I certainly shall do this thing — to-morrow," which means, unless the resolution changes for the better — never. The courage-law is this: "The thing is done, right here and now!"

(3). *The Safe Distance.* You are urged to "stand away" from bad reefs when your real "course" does not call for "close sailing." The locomotive fireman controls his fire, but if he is weak with a fever it is folly to tempt the furnace with his own body. The man who feels himself to be morally uncertain may withstand temptation, but he also may yield. This "may yield" calls for the "safe distance."

(4). *The Soldier's Mood.* You are urged to summon to its strongest the soldier's mood of fighting power when you are compelled to go where moral danger lurks, and to return to the safe distance as soon as possible.

(5). *The Resolute Purpose.* You are urged, nevertheless, to avoid the suggested trouble, fearsome anxiety about yourself and a constant balancing of the two preceding suggestions. It is not healthy to treat one's soul as a sickly weakling who must always worry about some possible failure. With the safe-distance rule and the soldier's mood should go the resolute purpose to come out a free man, minus all moral fears, and

plus all moral courage. And, after all, the best creator
of courage is — courage itself.

And now, as a climax to this chapter, as, indeed, a
running law for the entire subject of personal courage,
I invite acceptance of the following paragraph — always
excluding things believed to be immoral, but including
whatever is believed to be right:

A man's fears, of whatever nature, are the products
of what himself or his ancestors have not been able to
undertake. Fear comes not of doing; it issues infallibly from the not-doing. Fear is the deposit of the
soul's inaction. That which one really undertakes
begets courage. While seemingly the antecedent of
action, courage is actually the result of doing something. Hence, the habit of courage, like any other
habit, comes of acting — of doing the thing one fears
to do. Decline always what you fear, and the death
of courage is as certain as law. Do always what you
fear, except the immoral, and the death of fear is as
certain as law. You can acquire the habit of fear-
killing by beginning at the first opportunity to do the
one thing required — though Death and *Et Cetera* be
the promised consequences. He who always puts the
best of himself into any legitimate demand forgets
self-fear. Fear is never present when forgotten.

The word *habit* is derived from the Latin *habitum*,
"condition, dress." The habit of courage may be
thought of as the dress or uniform of courage. Many
a situation is successfully handled or carried through
simply because of a consciousness of being well-dressed
or of wearing a striking uniform. Put on the habit —
the dress — the uniform — of conscious courage, and
fears of self will infallibly vanish.

FEAR NOT FOR OTHERS.

The Fear-Thought of cool Reason,
Keeping watch above its own,
Guards, clear of eye, and firm of hand, and sure of aim,—
A Providence serene.   Hold fast to that!
What will you?   Poison the other's soul
With gasping worry-breath?
Litter the other's way with refuse-thoughts
Created in your trouble-mill of dread?
Fill skies of life with clouds and smoke and fog
Bred of distress insane?
And, by swift occult procedure, make harm sure
By mad excess of love in panic?
Forbear!   Such fear 's the common foe
Of lover and of loved.
Lo, *That*, which notes the swing of worlds,
Breathes none the faster if a comet, loosed
In space, threats self and systems;
But, ineffably calm, *wills Law*,
And, power projecting, guards and guides,
Lord of its summer seas and worlds a-sail.
Imitate!
                                        — THE AUTHOR.

CHAPTER VI.

FEAR FOR OTHERS.

"Anticipation — to take up something before it is time."
"Anxious — disturbed about some uncertain event."
"Fret — to wear away; to be worn away."
"Worry — to harass and persecute."— *Old Dictionary.*

EAR is never present in perfect sanity. The person who really fears anything is not mentally altogether sound.

I am aware that these statements will seem astounding to many readers, but I climax the propositions by saying that to no well-balanced mind will such declaration for long appear extravagant.

For I have already insisted that the law of self-preservation has nothing whatever to do with fear, is, indeed, opposed to fear, and relies solely on instinct and reason for its successful operation. Fear becomes an instinct only by indulgence, and is not necessary as a feeling overlaying instinct. Self-preservation demands that as humans we study instinct, cultivate reason, and forever banish every movement of soul or mind having any remote kinship with fear.

The moment you fear, that moment you blur instinct and confuse reason. In any culture of personal courage we must first and once for all deny any place in life to fear and any legitimate excuse for fear's existence. Perhaps our greatest difficulty in the matter consists precisely in this: we imagine that some phase of fear, manifest to a certain degree and under certain circumstances, is legitimate to the sane mind. I deny the proposition, and I want my readers thoroughly to absorb the denial and from now on to hold that fear betokens insanity.

FEAR IS INSANITY.

When the animal begins really to fear,— to drift beyond the line of the instinct of self-preservation,— it begins to lose self-control, and it then enters a state of head-long panic — temporary insanity. When man begins really to fear,— to drift beyond the line of the reason-act of self-preservation,— he likewise begins to lose self-control. But all loss of self-control is a species of temporary insanity.

The condition called insanity will be evident from a moment's study of the words involved. The words "mind" and "man" are derived from the Sanskrit root, $m — a — n$, "to think;" the word "derange" originally meant "to put out of rank or order," and now means "to put the thinker out of order or rank." As the mind is not an entity, but is simply certain ways of being and doing which the human self has organized for its life purposes, we see that in insanity these organized ways have been "put out of rank," thrown out of "order"— disorganized. They continue to act, but not in normal order. Of course the question of normality is always relative; nevertheless, allowing for relative differences among individuals, there is a standard of normal mental condition determined by the general human mind. This general standard, broadly defined, measures the normal for any mental power — perception, consciousness, memory, imagination, reason, will, feelings, etc., and when such powers exhibit in

considerable departure from the normal, in their independent action and in their inter-action particularly,
there is suggestion or positive manifestation of insanity.
In fear we have precisely such departure, more or less
extensive, from the normal working of mind at its
average best. Fear does not rightly perceive, remember, imagine, reason, will, or feel, and it makes a chaos
of consciousness.

Fear Violates Self-Interest.

The main things in the general normal condition
of the human self are self-preservation and self-interest.
In the process of securing these ends the self of man,
working through ages, has organized certain of its
powers into what we call mind. All mental powers
signify self-interest. Their normal working indicates
self-interest — man's best estate. And all along, the
success of this ageless striving after best estate as embodied in best mental condition, or best organization
of mind, has been measured, for one thing, by the
elimination from life of the disorganization-factors of
fear. The struggle of the human self to organize its
powers to best possible efficiency and co-ordination has
always been to get rid of fears as aliens and enemies.
Other things being equal, the most ideally courageous
soul is the sanest soul.

Every human being has the right of best self-
interest. The truly sane person is the really sound
person. There is your goal. Soundness is embodied
self-interest. This does not mean, however, what is
commonly called selfishness. Two children, are teter-
ing on a board high from the ground. The one, who is
selfish, cares nothing for the other balancing body,
throws it off the board — and itself gets a fall. The

other, who cares for true self-interest, is careful to preserve the balance, and thus prevents both bodies from falling. Life is a vast balance. Self-interest looks after self as balanced against the other man. The entirely healthy man acts steadily in favor of his own soundness at the best — and by so much as he does so he acts in the interest of all, for the man at his best is always the man for all. But these propositions are a declaration of war on fear.

When, for example. one indulges a violent rage, the injury to self is great, but a feeling of mere anger is, in a degree, as truly hurtful, for the emotion clouds reason and poisons the blood. Precisely so it is with fear. A paroxysm of terror inevitably injures self, but a case of mere fear is as truly opposed to self-interest, for it clouds reason and poisons the blood.

Sanity consists in standing for highest best personal estate. Insanity consists in ten thousand things contrary thereto. Fear, in any form, is one of this legion of evil things. It is a phase of insanity, however mild it may appear to be. The really sane soul refuses to indulge the luxury of fear, insisting solely on the action of reason instead, because there is no supposed good which fear suggests that reason alone may not secure.

Fear for Others is Selfishness.

You will see, now, that I am neither brutal nor cynical when I say that fear for others is always a phase of fear for self. The action of reason in the interest of others is altogether legitimate and may be wholly unselfish, but the moment fear is felt, that moment we have a case of anticipation of distress to self. If your friend in danger were a savage criminal, you would perceive all his peril without a particle of anticipation of distress for yourself — provided the end of his difficulty could not contain otherwise shocking elements. But your friend's peril suggests a horde of latent possibilities distressful to your soul — and you fear for his safety. Remembering that fear and reason are not one thing, but are always totally different things, every idea of feeling essential to friendship and the other person's welfare may be present without a pang of actual fear. And the difficulty of seeing or realizing this truth does not disprove it.

Fear for others is distress for self; its chief tendency is a growing selfishness. The most selfish thing in the world is sorrow, as you observe at almost any service for the dead. How many women fall heavy like lead upon their husband's soul when the child dies. The man is not supposed to possess the capacity for love or for sorrow equal to that of the mother, and he must bear his own grief and the woman's dead weight. Here is a case demanding a few vigorous propositions. The subject is a little foreign to my theme, but I desire to say these things because they are illustrative after all:

I deny that woman is inferior by original constitution to man, and with equal emphasis that she is man's superior in character.

I deny inferiority or superiority in any man or woman based on sex. I deny the essential reality of sex. I hold that the essential human self is sexless. At a period prior to birth the sex of the human body is indeterminate. Sex is a convenience of physical existence, and it has no more to do with spirit than it has to do with hydrogen or oxygen. Inferiority and superiority among humans are due to differences in individual endowments and the outcome of use made of endowment during life. Hence I deny to woman as woman superior capacity for love or for sorrow. Some women are beautiful, but the sorrowing and fearing woman is always more or less selfish. And so is sorrowing and fearing man. The only exception is seen when love or grief are born of the Infinite White Life.

In multitudes of cases, distress is the rank selfishness of fear of distress for self. No interest in others need be accompanied by fear.

Fear, disease, and death are aliens to our world.

Were apprehension of distress to self caused by thought of possible injury to others eliminated from any given case, the all of reason would remain and the all of fear would go.

Kindly observe the noble array of vices which pose under the guise of a virtue — this so-called regard for other people. Such vices are, feelings of apprehension, care, concern, disquiet, disturbance, foreboding, dread, fretting, misgiving, perplexity, solicitude, trouble, worry, anxiety, anguish, terror, hysteria, panic, insanity: all states of mind which are of no value whatever to any one and ought to be wholly displaced by self-controlled reason.

I found myself greatly worried about a member of my family who had promised to return at an hour which had passed. A troop of evil imaginings took possession of my mind. The body became restless, the nerves more and more agitated, the mind confused, the soul distressed by a panorama of direful pictures. Then I said: "Let me analyze this state into which I have drifted. Here are anger, threat, present distress, fear. Now I am really angry because of selfishness — fear of distress to myself. My reason knows, of course, that danger may possibly threaten this friend, but in all probability it does nothing of the kind. Eliminating anger, the only remaining factor in my present state is unnecessary distress due to imaginings of future possibilities. Here I am at this moment in a condition of sheer selfishness. I can do nothing effective in the matter, and I will not worry." Such reflections banished fear, leaving reason in control, and my foolish excitement subsided.

You are invited, then, to consider and accept the proposition that fear for others is fear for self. This will awaken a good deal of surprise and induce a very healthful reaction. *Many a soul that imagines itself a martyr is actually selfish at the core.*

And you are especially invited to analyze your own feelings when in such a fearing state for others in order to banish the self-regarding phase of your condition and to restore to its rightful place and power clear and unmixed reason. You will find the exercise enormously helpful.

Fear for Others is Tyranny.

The selfishness of fear for others, however, is not confined in its reaction to the soul that fears; it overacts upon those for whom it is entertained. Fear-folk are tyrants. Fear for others always disregards other people's freedom. It would be difficult to conceive a worse fate than is seen in some forms of this slavery. Your fears for other people wish to make them your personal slaves.

I am perfectly aware of the protest that will arise when this statement is read; nevertheless, the thing must stand, because there is nothing your fears can or may do for your slaves which cannot be done for them by reason without fear, and your reason would never restrict their freedom, while your fear does so invariably. When the matter is critically examined we see that this is certainly true. We fear for others: then we wish them to do one thing or another, or to refrain from being and doing a thousand things. If within our power, we coerce them according to the dictates of our fears, unmindful that no fear-judgment can be entirely sound and that reason alone can think clearly and wisely. The outcome is inevitable; increased bondage of self to your own fears and of others to a degenerating judgment.

Fear for Others Poisons Their Atmospheres.

Moreover, when you worry about your child or friend because, as you say, you wish no injury to befall them, you as a matter of fact dread possible suffering for yourself in case they should meet with harm, and in this condition of worry and self-regarding you not only seek to restrain the other person's liberty, but you also throw around that person a surely evil atmosphere. We are all surrounded by what I call the personal atmosphere, a more or less extensive globe of etheric activity peculiar to the individual. Into this little world which every personality creates, and which is usually open to all sorts of influences, your apprehensions vibrate your fearing disturbances. If you really wish the welfare of the one for whom you are fearful, it may prove a revelation to remember that you are actually harming the object of your regard by your incessant and excited worry. You will find this subject, atmosphere, practically discussed in the little book, "*The Personal Atmosphere.*"

You are forever *anticipating evil:* taking up some possible distress and conveying your fear-message to your friend.

You are constantly *anxious:* disturbed about some uncertain event, and transmitting to this person confusing thought-waves.

You incessantly *fret:* wear yourself away, and you threaten the vitality of your friends, present and absent.

You *worry:* harass and persecute yourself, and inevitably penetrate other people's atmospheres with your evil influences.

In all this you are surely harming yourself, for unfearing reason can accomplish all things possible in your friend's interest, but you are really disproving your own friendship. A rigid analysis of the matter shows clearly that

FRIENDSHIP'S FEARS ARE FOES TO FRIENDS.

You are therefore invited to remember how inevitable it is that worry, anxiety, panic about our friends, convey fear, confusion, and weakness to their personal atmospheres, and hence you are urged to uncover and destroy all such enemies of true friendship and to replace them by confident and courageous reason.

If this mere action of reason seems cold and the opposite of a true friend's regard, you are urged to ask if the attitude of the Infinite toward man contains one hint or shadow of these disturbing fears, and if the Infinite Reason back of that infinite regard which the Divine, if there is a Divine, exercises in the government of the Universe, could conceivably be safer or warmer by the presence of any possible variety or degree of fear. For one majestic conception awaits the fearing soul, to which I surrender:

The Human Self Exists on the Infinite Self, as the lotus bloom was said to rest on the heart of the Pharaoh, and all our human fears show that we have not yet come into our marvelous rights as living manifests of the All-Good-God. Does the Infinite Breather Who breathes stars and intelligences into being fear, worry, entertain disturbance in the interest of human beings? And does not the Infinite hold every creature's welfare in absolute regard? Some of you may answer, "I do not know." Then, friend, you have missed the highest right of your life. If your existence is due to the Infinite's presence within you, you need but the realized thought: "I am a manifest of the Infinite Life, to use the right way or the wrong way," to see how inconsistent and unnecessary are all your fears. Says an ancient Indian *Upanishad:* "There is one ruler, the Self within all things, who makes the one form manifold. The wise who perceive him within their self or soul, to them belongs eternal happiness." If the White Life does not fear for others, and if you exist on the bosom of that White Life, I cannot see how any man or woman may justly cherish the fear-troubles of life. And I write this, not as religion, but as philosophy.

If you say: "Who am I that I should be like God?" the answer is — "Your deeper self is divine, and it is right to realize the infinite fearlessness within you."

VARIETIES OF FEAR FOR OTHERS.

And now, the two-fold evil of this variety of fear before us will be manifest in a brief study of some of its common phases, as, for example:

Fear of the Parent for the Child;
Fear of the Child for the Parent;
Fear of Husband for the Wife;
Fear of the Wife for the Husband;
Fear of Friend for Friend;
Fear of Stranger for Stranger;
Fear for Neighborhood, State, Nation, etc.

In any of these cases, reasonable interest is of course legitimate and noble, but any form of fear which injures either the other party or self is invariably and necessarily an enemy to both.

The causes of such fears, speaking rather broadly, are found in an unhealthy tone of body or mind, which furnishes a perfect soil for the entire brood of fear-distress, and in excessive regard for others, a too vivid imagination, want of self-control, and confusion of the reason.

For these troubles I suggest the following remedies

GENERAL REMEDIES FOR FEARS FOR OTHERS.

FIRST REMEDY: *Improved Health-Tone.* You are urged to make it your chief business to swing into the vibrant currents of health, and are referred to chapters on this subject in the present work and to the second volume in The Power-Book Library, "*Power For Success,*" which is as certain as law to tone up the spiritual force for health in any average person who will multiply self into its pages.

SECOND REMEDY: *Acquiring Vigorous Will-Power.* You are urged to cultivate your will-power to a high degree of energy and symmetry. You may develop the ability to send throughout the body, and to any point therein, a warm current or flow of conscious vitality, which ability will prove of the greatest value in dispelling all sorts of disturbing fear-feelings as they may occur and give you mastery over them. You will find "*Power Of Will,*" the first volume in The Power-Book Library, a very helpful study in this respect.

THIRD REMEDY: *Attaining the Oversight of Reason.* You are urged to bestow upon all in whom you are naturally interested a full measure of reasonable care, so that you always may be able to affirm: "*I have certainly done for these friends what I reasonably could do; more may not be expected; I now, therefore, cease imagining evil possibilities and a greater solicitude for them, banishing from mind all apprehension concerning their welfare.*" If this seems difficult, remember that persistent and patient effort will infallibly build up in your life the habit of fearless repose.

FOURTH REMEDY: *Toning Down the Imagination.* Conscious that you are blameless in the matter of reasonable care, you are now to cut down your imagination concerning possible evils or perils to others. This process should be indirect; that is, the fear-thought should be displaced by contrary thoughts begetting cheerful moods. *Fear feeds on thought of danger or evil.* Therefore, *let fear be starved by ignoring it.* Whenever you are disturbed by apprehensions, refuse to entertain the imaginations which troop into mind; shut them out; persist in banishing them. Above all, compel the mind to dwell on agreeable thoughts not connected with the friend. If the subject continues to occupy attention, make the friend the centre of pleasant scenes, follow him in thought where you suppose him to be and surround him with imaginary circumstances of a fortunate nature. But it is better to turn resolutely away from him and concentrate thought on other matters.

FIFTH REMEDY: *Giving "Absent Treatment" for Good Fortune.* You are urged occasionally to think intensely and as though "wiring" your friend a message, on his sure safety, happiness and prosperity. The object of this regime is your own welfare, but you will inevitably convey to the other person influences for good. And these influences will react upon yourself, creating in your thought assurance concerning him and so helping to build up in your soul a larger degree of general courage.

SIXTH REMEDY: *Cultivation of Confidence in the Friend's Self-Preserving Ability.* You are urged to develop within your mind a strong feeling of confidence in other people's capacity for taking reasonable care of themselves. This suggestion is vastly important. Let us apply it to some of the worry cases enumerated on a previous page.

I FIRST VARIETY OF WORRIES — THE PARENT WORRIES ABOUT THE CHILD. The latter, then, is constantly hampered with fears and restrictions, the result being unhappiness for both. Neither is benefited in the slightest degree. Indeed, the parent's fears, by plain and by occult processes, tend to make the child cowardly, and thus to lessen its powers of self-help. The child needs the knock-about experiences of life. Nature designs that the jungle and the man-field shall be no drawing-room. Undue restrictions simply increase child-dangers. If your fears have imprisoned the young cub or the dear gazelle, give it more liberty. This is precisely what you will refuse to do, but it is a scientific remedy — both for the child and for yourself. The child has more ability for self-helpfulness than you believe, unless you have ruined its birth-right. It is an animal, and is solidly full of Nature's instinct of self-preservation. It is human, and therefore endowed with double wit for using that instinct. Because you are unduly fearful, your confidence in the child must be forced by exercise of will, by reason, and by the constant emphasis in thought of the fact that in almost all instances your fears have proven unnecessary.

If the child is timid, here lies the greater reason for enlarging its world and for making it familiar with the roughness of life.

If the child is forever getting into trouble, the fact may be due either to a curious stupidity or to an excess of animal spirits. The stupid child never comes to great harm. Nature is afraid of hurting him. The bright child carries an amount of "steam" which is usually adequate to its protection. In both cases let reasonable care and self-control take the place of worry and fret. The substitution is a habit: cultivate it.

If your fears regard the child's moral welfare, the main regime will seek to develop and train its will-power. Kindly imagine the following paragraph to be printed in red letters:

Will-power in the child demands the right atmosphere for its noblest exercise. What oxygen is to the blood, morality is to the will. Seldom will a child go seriously wrong if its home atmosphere is filled with that essence of all moral health, honor. Here is the climax of the most truly practical philosophy, of the idealest morals, of the whole subject of religion. When you convince the child that you hold your sense of personal honor too high to permit stooping to the mean thought, the immoral act, or the unworthy line of conduct, he will sink the suggestion deep into his soul and strive to imitate you. Almost invariably is this the case; the exception is, indeed, a hopeless example.

But there is a vast difference between the honor of mere religiosity and the religion of genuine honor. Some moral atmospheres are deceptive. If honor is "skin deep," the "chip of the old block" will exhibit heredity. In too many homes there is a kind of morality which is bred merely of selfish regard for the opinions of society.

It is not a reality of the soul. It lacks in profound valuation of personal dignity closeted with itself. In other homes a so-called religious life abounds which seems entirely compatible with littleness, penuriousness, irritability, harsh judgment, jealousy, envy, criticism, want of high principle.

The sense of honor in the above suggestions is the acme of right living. It signifies a feeling of personal dignity too deeply seated and too greatly valued to permit its possessor to harbor the low thought and the ungenerous wish, or to indulge in any action which is calculated to injure health, demean the mind, hurt the conscience, render others unhappy, or diminish reverence for the All-Good. By so much also it involves the cultivation of corresponding virtues. In a word, it is a full-orbed, full-toned high-mindedness. That mighty pagan, Aristotle, held High-mindedness, *Megalopsukia*, in supreme regard, as being a "kind of ideal self-respect" and the "crown of all the other virtues."

If you cultivate such a sense of honor in the child, you will have less occasion to worry, but, by a psychic law, you will also have originated within your soul a large confidence in the child's will for and power of self-help.

In any event, this form of fear before us is wholly useless. You are aware of the fact, yet you worry and fret, nevertheless. You have gotten into a habit of anxiety. The cure will be found in a contrary habit, that of confidence and courage. There are two ways in which these traits may be acquired.

SEVENTH REMEDY: *Dismissing the Fear.* You are urged, whenever the fear arises, to dismiss it from thought. It will appear again and again, repeatedly — perhaps. Repeatedly, then, and instantly, put it away.

At the same time summon a sense of confidence in the child's or other person's welfare by thinking of either as safe, or as acting self-preservatively. Better than all, affirm: "I have done what I could for this person, and I cannot and will not worry about him."

It can never be too strongly emphasized that we are what we incessantly think we are — provided that conduct consistently carries out the thought. One of the "*Twin Verses*" in Buddha's "*Path of Virtue*" reads thus: "All that we are is the result of what we have thought: it is founded on our thoughts, it is made up of our thoughts. If a man speaks or acts with a pure thought, happiness follows him, like a shadow that never leaves him." If we think and act courage, the mighty law of suggestion will banish fear.

EIGHTH REMEDY: *Trusting the White Life.* Whatever relation the person for whom you fear may sustain to you, you are urged to trust him to the beneficence of the Universal System. I know that life is full of accidents; but continual dwelling on the fact does no one the least good, and will do you a great deal of harm — and perhaps bring your friend to an injury which would not otherwise befall him. Courageous and confident thought might save him many an ill. The man who laughs at this suggestion knows little of the vast power of thought in our life. This power of thought is a part of the System, and its design is human welfare. All appearances to the contrary notwithstanding, the Universal System is a friend to every human being on the globe. Our trouble here seems in part to be a false estimate of "evil." If a friend is injured, falls ill, or is taken hence, each case is assumed necessarily to be a total misfortune to him. Each case, on the contrary, may involve his highest welfare. My friend the business man went bankrupt at fifty years of age, through the failures of others, and in ten years had established a splendidly paying factory, when ill-health assailed him, compelling a long, courageous fight for restoration. And he insists that his bad health has led him into the new world of the new thought and that he is all the better for his experience. It is a great mistake to acknowledge every so-called "evil" as purely a misfortune. It is the habit of conquest to look for the brighter possibilities in every turn of life. The bright thinker is the happier; he lets loose the grace and power of his own thought, and he not only gives the Universe a better standing, but he also assists in its huge struggle for adjustment meaning the welfare of all. I say, then, let the unknown good possibilities have weight. Innumerable as are the evils of life, the System seeks, in every specimen of misfortune, to bestow some compensation. What rank egotism and cankering pessimism it is to hot-house the notion that the Universe is down on you or your friend, so that you must incessantly worry lest the evil design be carried out! In its effort to compensate, the System does not always appear to succeed, to be sure, but the want of success is not an expression of the nature of things; it is rather due to a perversion thereof. The nature of things is friendly to all who are in harmony with its laws, and to those who are out of harmony its hard usage is still friendly, seeking to restore right relations with itself. When it wages war, the design is to put iron into human blood. When it hurts, the ultimate meaning is to warn against real evil, violation of the law of best estate, and to urge to a higher plane of living.

What is to be gained by any opposite opinion? And, too, whence the instruction of that vast theory, evolution? The last word of modern science to the individual is a kindly word. The obverse of the phrase, "the survival of the fittest," is, *"Nature struggles to impart to all the power of surviving."*

This Universe is throned in goodness. With amazing patience and adaptiveness, it seeks to put itself at the disposal of every human. In the sunrise of eternity the All-Good executed a warranty deed of all values to all souls, and now covenants and agrees, on the Infinite Soul, to warrant and defend the title, and to put the willing grantee into full and undisturbed possession — if he will harmonize with law. The arms of the System are arms, not of war, but of protection. In myriads of cases it has protected the child, the husband, the wife, the friend, all unseen and unknown. It will continue this overarching kindness. It is for us, not to displace it by our worries, but to trust it.

Why, man, the Universe is the only home you will ever know. It is the wretchedest spleen to criticise it, and the worst folly to doubt it.

II. Second Variety of Worries — Fear of Husband or Wife for the Other. There are wives who create unhappiness for themselves and their husbands by ceaseless weeping solicitude during the latter's absence — beyond the hour, at the office, in the field, "off on business," and so on interminably. Because the man is not a poodle dog, he frets, secretly, perhaps, but almost inevitably, or lives, like "patience on a monument, smiling at grief," or forsakes the arena of psychic conflict as frequently as possible.

I have in mind one unfortunate whose slightest failure to appear when expected threw his wife into hysterics of nervous tears. This man could not get hurt; he was not of that kind. He always returned, "sound as a bullet," moral as the decalogue, while the wife slowly undermined her health. This woman's worry meant "to strangle"— the man.

The remedy is the larger confidence practised and insisted upon by the resolute will, with fear-thought shut out and held out. If, because of moral considerations, the larger confidence seems impossible, one must steel oneself to the facts, and, in all available ways, reduce suffering to a minimum. I do not see in marriage any claim upon either party to martyrdom.

There are husbands, also, who nurse deadly fear for their wives. Foolish jealousy may constitute the cause, or the woman may seriously threaten the honor of husband or home. The instance is, nevertheless, no cause for the feeling of fear, remembering that fear and reason are not identical in the matter, but is a call for the curbing of suffering to narrowest limits. How shall this be accomplished?

NINTH REMEDY: *Reason and Will Combined for Betterment.* Groundless jealousy can be cured only by vigorous reason and persistent will-effort. Such jealousy is a disease for which the patient must administer his own remedies. It dishonors the woman, issues from obscured or perverted reason, and indicates destroyed self-control. Groundless jealousy never accompanies genuine love. It is the badge of passion. When a man is jealous of a woman, he suspects evil of her. Passion can endure such a state of mind and flame out more fiercely, but real love dies instantly under the blast of a false requital — or, swears to save the object of its fears.

What passes for love where jealousy thrives is physical selfishness. Reason, then, and will, must cultivate the true confidence of genuine affection. The man who suspects me is my enemy.

The pathos of it all, however, is the fact that neither love nor passion, in many cases, remains, while honor quails and the suffering goes on. What, then, shall be done with the life so injured?

TENTH REMEDY: *Cultivating the Happiness Habit.* Every human being possesses within himself a measure of personal resource by which some degree of peace and life-success may be secured. *The Universe has gifts for all.* The subject of the present fears, man or woman, must cultivate the personal capacity for happiness and claim ˗ legi imate share of welfare — a portion of the universal gifts — in spite of all distressing circumstances. This requires the heroic will, but the achievement is certainly possible. The moment you begin to believe that your soul is sovereign and royal in lineage, that moment the possibility will appear. If one does the utmost best under existing circumstances, and courageously insists upon maintaining an inner sense of honor and a peace born of personal resources, one has risen above even such deadly causes of suffering.

ELEVENTH REMEDY: *Reliance on Personal Resources.* It is a huge mistake in life to permit happiness and welfare to depend so largely, as many do, upon some single human being. Undue dependence is not normal, and is by no means designed in the plan of life. "Call no man master." You are therefore urged to cultivate your own personal resources for happiness and unfoldment, and to rely less upon others for these boons. *For him who cannot find his own kingdom within, there is no kingdom.* If you cannot be happy within yourself, no human can make you happy. All your unfoldment must come from your own activity, and the less that activity depends upon the stimulation of others, the more truly are you master. No man can give you courage. No woman can kill your fears. In your self alone lie the secret and the power of the conquest of fear for others. "Self is the Lord of Self; who else could be Lord?"

III. REMAINING VARIETIES OF FEAR FOR OTHERS. These are comparatively rare, yet, none the less real for that. There are those who seem to be constantly distressed for the welfare of mere strangers. Children on the street excite nameless nervous apprehension. Some one, man or woman, is forever about to be knocked down. Now a high-strung carriage-horse threatens to become frightened by trolley-car or automobile. Now it is an automobile that suggests danger to some unknown person. Trees and buildings are everywhere on the verge of toppling over upon passers-by. So the exciting list draws itself out. Human life is always in jeopardy. These fearsome souls are kept in a state of incessant tension. They enjoy neither walk nor drive. Even observation from a drawing-room window has its suggestions of favorite trouble. Anxiety enslaves them, harassing fears torture. In case of an accident, they are seized with palpitation of the heart, or are overcome by faintness. Any sudden movement in life upsets them. The unforeseen is always occasion for collapse.

TWELFTH REMEDY: *Cultivation of Tone and Will.* The basal difficulty here is probably want of healthy nerve-tone — a condition in which one is easily unbalanced by any flash-light imagination. Such persons should vigorously carry on a long regime for full-

blooded bodies and steady nerves, at least for the best
self-control possible.   In the meantime, the impulse of
nervous fear should always be instantly suppressed by
assertion of the will.   The ability to do this is the
result of prolonged persistence in most cases, but may
be acquired at less expense by resolute suggestion to the
subconscious self declaring that you are perfectly
poised, at peace within, and wholly subject to control.

THIRTEENTH REMEDY: *Undue Responsibility
Declined*.   I have had personal experience in this
nervous fear for the remote contingency, and have
found a very potent remedy in cultivated indifference.
You are wasting vital force unnecessarily, and, inasmuch
as you are the invalid, you may morally cultivate a
reasonable indifference.   Affirm, then, of these people,
children or adults: "They are not my own; I will no
longer torture myself in behalf of strangers."

Akin to the fear suggested is the feeling of vague
responsibility for neighborhood, town or commonwealth
which burdens some curious souls.   There are unfortu-
nates who carry solemn obligation to protect other
people in masses.   Now it is the lodge that lies heavily
upon their hearts; now it is their ward, their church,
their party, the city or the state.   They are not only
interested in these objects, but they are fearfully interested and nervously apprehensive of all sorts of
imaginary perils threatening the organization.   Strange-
ly enough, they flatter themselves that they are the
conserving minority.   Why is it that the people of
state or church are so stupid!

Now, this stupidity, so monstrous to social nervousness, is very largely imaginary.   The fact is, the so-
called stupid people are really public-spirited and do
entertain notions of human welfare, but they do not

think as the nervous one desires and they refuse to
worry because they are healthy-minded, content to
discover evils as the facts make known.   Sane thought
feels that no man is called upon to shoulder a globe,
that very few souls are raised up to stand responsible
for a nation or an age, and that these are elected to
leadership by all votes save their own.   "The man who
would be king" is always found out.   A healthy person
holds that responsibility for neighborhood, state, nation,
age, belongs to all the people.   "Act well your part,
there all the (burden) lies."   People who worry over
these huge questions are diseased, and should overcome
the trouble by cultivating indifference for evils which
others do not see.   If this looks immoral, it is to be
remembered that the case is one of invalidism, which is
entitled to cure, and that the remedy merely calls for
destruction of worry and fear, not of ideal notions concerning our life.   The most useful thing a sick man can
do, so far as the general welfare is concerned, is to
recover his health.   If the world-worry distresses you,
you are abnormal, and your only practical remedy is
the practice of the mood of indifference.

FEAR NOT DUMB THINGS.

Fear neither Things nor Force,
For these but vassals be to Mind-Man.
Like slaves, they tyrannize if pampered,
Serving like friends when Courage rules.
A sovereign human lives by *Will*,
Nor lets the *hugest* fact disturb the *inner* king.
Why, man, you are YOURSELF,
Girt against worlds, and so, secure,
Unless you whimper, "Drawbridge down!"
Matter and force ne'er cross the chasm
That moats the soul within its castle.
Lord to the body, scornful speaks the spirit:
"*I am! I am Power!*"
What's all big Nature now to do with that?
And if *the* Accident of infelicities small occur,
In the end stand Hope and Courage on the wrack and ruin
Of stars smoking, vibrant still with the one reality,
The individual life of you.
Fear not these toys o' the soul!

— THE AUTHOR.

CHAPTER VII.

FEAR OF THINGS.

"Fear nurses up a danger;
And resolution kills it at the birth." — *Phillips.*

"No weapons can hurt the Self of man, no fire will burn it,
no water moisten it, no wind will dry it up."— *Indian Veda.*

AT THE outset in our present chapter it should be remembered, first, that my task is not to offer suggestions for self-protection against the ills and accidents of life, but to assist the fearful in their effort to overcome fear; and, secondly, that the fear-feeling is real only as we make it real, being always totally distinct from instinct and reason, which alone are legitimately to be relied upon against danger, actual or fancied. This does not mean that one is merely to deny the feeling of fear, or to give it some different name when it is present. No value issues from denying a fact. But when the fact of fear appears, it should never be recognized as reasonable or legitimate in any sense; its claim to right and necessity in our life should be totally refused. That which properly insists upon exclusive recognition and control is reason or instinct working in the interest of self-preservation. This being understood, we may scotch fear at its every appearance, depending upon these factors alone for all the benefits that lying fear may claim to represent.

THE SERENE SOUL-SEA.

My task is really this: to suggest that the human soul, sea of countless waves and tides, need never be

crossed by the movements of fear as a feeling.   In the
old Gothic language the soul was called *saivala*, related
to *saivs*, the "sea."   "The sea was called *saivs*," says
Max Müller, "from a root *si*, or *siv*, the Greek *seio*, 'to
shake;' it meant the 'tossed-about water,' in contra-
distinction to stagnant or running water.   The soul
being called *saivala*, we see that it was originally conceived by the Teutonic nations as a sea within, heaving
up and down with every breath, and reflecting heaven
and earth on the mirror of the deep."

Into this soul-sea have swept the disturbing forces
of fear, so to speak, which are aliens, and never should
have been permitted room or freedom.   Had human
life always been harmonious with itself and its higher
environments, no fear could ever have arisen in the
vibrant soul of man as a disturbing feeling.   Discord
has bred a brood of disastrous emotions curiously
related which it will be interesting to study for a moment.   Thus, the serpent was anciently called *ahi* in
Sanskrit, *echis* in Greek, and *anguis* in Latin.   The root
of *ahi* is *anh*, "to choke, to throttle," and it lives in the
Latin *angina*, "quinsy," *angor*, "suffocation," *anxius*,
"uneasy," and also in *anhas*, Greek *agos*, "sin," *agis*,
"fear," and the English "awe" and "anguish."

The "sin" of theology is really discord, or, rather,
knowingly inharmonious action of the self; it is the
known violation of known laws of known best personal
estate.   This it is which induces disaster, because it
induces disharmony within the right conditions of
human welfare, and this is the only power on earth
that can essentially hurt the soul.   "He, therefore,
who knows the Self," say the "Upanishads" of India
(with the meaning that Brahma, the Infinite, is the
Self, which meaning we may ignore for our present

purpose, regarding the Self as the human self) "after having become quiet, subdued, satisfied, patient, and collected, sees self in Self, sees all as Self. Evil does not overcome him, he overcomes evil. Evil does not hurt him, he burns all evil. Free from evil, free from spots, free from doubts, he becomes a true Brahman." In our Western thought we background on the Infinite, but are not the Infinite; nevertheless, the self is secure in itself if it really wills that no evil not self-induced (or consented to) can reach the self. The essential human spirit is immune to any evil not self-induced. But this, evil, disharmony, is the great breeder of fears. Innocent man, man at harmony with the self and its worlds, would still instinctively and reasonably act in the interest of wholeness and happiness, but he would never really fear, feel the serpent's "throttle," come to the anguish of fright. If consciously right,— on the *rita* or "straight line,"— how could he possibly have any of the emotions of fear, distinguished from the mere thought and action of self-preservation? The animal has all the self-preservative movements of instinct, but he is not anxious, he does not brood, worry, fret, and he never anticipates imaginary dangers for himself or for other animals.

Secrets of Fearlessness.

The Self is Supreme and Immune. It is evident that a true fearlessness has its secret, for one thing, in the profound conviction that everything in the personal life is subordinate to the one supreme factor, the unseen and indestructible self, and that this self is or ought to be lord and master, and, in a state of harmony with itself and its higher environments, may be perfectly indifferent to any so-called evils that can befall the inferior factors, such as body, or mind, or life physical, or property. Just so soon as we become possessed of self in this sense, we shall banish all worrying fears in regard to dangers to what we call self, including the body, because we shall then know that such can never injure the real self within the body, while all that true instinct or reason may properly be in our life will still remain to us for legitimate self-preservation. One secret of fearlessness of things, then, consists in the deep assurance that self is master of self and immune to all real evil not self-induced, and that this immunity is the absolute reward of harmony.

The World of Nature is Good and No Enemy. If, now, this sense of supremacy and immunity is taken with a large belief in the goodness and helpfulness of the Universe in which we live, then, while reason must still act in self-preservation, the feeling of fear for innumerable things about us comes to be displaced by reasonable confidence.   These suggestions must receive a fuller treatment later in the present chapter. My chief thought here is the age-long truth that discord is the mother of fears.

One basic assumption in our common thought seems to make Nature an enemy of man. This is really a relic of old fears and superstitions which have originated in the long struggle for right adjustment with Nature's laws. In perfect harmony with the Universe, or Nature, there can be no other fear than the normal warning against discord, and I hold this to be, in its proper action, the warning of instinct or reason, not of the fear-feeling as usually understood. The whole meaning of man's history is this: the race is slowly striving to find the centre of adjustment universal, or universal harmony. Instinctively it knows that safety lies there, and nowhere else. So affirms reason. But human ignorance antagonizes a Universal System which is determined that in harmony alone shall man realize fearlessness of, and freedom from, all danger. Hence the individual fear denies the racial instinct, and the great Mother-Friend, Nature, becomes in our thought the implacable enemy. I am unable to account for so many fears of things on any other supposition.

FORMS OF THIS FEAR.

The above preliminaries being now before us, it may be well briefly to survey the innumerable aspects of the fear of things. The monster is hydra-headed and very ancient. Every object of existence on earth has inspired fear in some human breast. We fear that stones may throw us; that nails will pierce our feet; that tools will injure; that poisons lurk in every eatable and drinkable thing; that the lamp may explode; that the gas may smother us; that chairs will collapse; that floors and roofs will cave in; that the house may catch fire; that the boiler may blow up; that machinery may break and slay; that trees and buildings may topple over; that meteors may strike us; that vehicles may give out; that the boat may sink; that the cars may slip the rail or be telescoped; that mountains will slide; that mines will close in; that rivers will rise in floods; that the swimmer will drown; that electric wires will come down; that hurricanes will destroy the town; that lightning may strike; that guns may go off, etc., etc. All of these things have occurred, to be sure; but has fear-feeling averted a single disaster?

So, also, every animal large enough to be seen by the naked eye has caused humanity a fright. The list

of fears — or allied nervous conditions — reveals now
some curious specimens.   The smell of fish threw Eras-
mus into a fever.   One person always fainted at sight
of an eel.   A carp sent another into convulsions.   Boiled
lobsters caused another to faint.   The great Scaliger
could not drink milk, and Cordon hated the sight of
eggs.   An apple would induce nose-bleed in Francis I,
which was also the fate of another on hearing a cat mew.
Some people cannot endure the smell of flowers, while
others dislike their beauty.   Many are unable to touch
silk or velvet without shuddering.   A few have felt
aversion for certain musical instruments.   The Duke
d'Epernon swooned on seeing a leveret.   The famous
Tycho Brahe feared foxes, and Marshal d'Abert feared
pigs.   Cases of inability to hear about surgical operations or accidents are numerous.   Pepper, olive oil,
bulls, beetles, hedgehogs, are unendurable to others.
Fears for dogs, cats, horses, cows, snakes, mice and rats,
frogs, toads, birds, fish, insects, are familiar to all.   In
all this we have traces of far-away human life holding
over; evidences of maladjustment getting on the
nerves.   Has the feeling of fear brought about any
cure?

Condition of health is also a prolific source of
apprehension.   It marks present-day progress that
physical health is receiving such universal attention,
but there is confessed danger that this general revival
of health-culture may induce excessive consciousness
of bodily states,   Real health seldom thinks of itself.
Such excessive consciousness is a danger in the sense
that it may suggest the very conditions feared, and by
suggestion induce them.   In the sovereignty of mind,
however, the tendency of continual thought about the
body may be averted by the spirit of resolute vigor and

the ability to throw the subject out of consciousness. Something of truth there is in the old lines:

"The surest road to health — say what they will,
Is never to suppose we shall be ill."

It may almost be said that were one to catalogue all the objects, medicines, directions, plans and methods recommended for gaining or preserving health, some contrary declaration or experience might be written opposite every item in the list. We have become afraid not only of diseases, but of cures, and, in this chaotic state, are ready to conjure up a fear for all known existences having any relation to the body.

Apprehensions in regard to physical ills would be more numerous than diseases were it not for the creative power of suggestion. There is no known variety of food which some one does not fear. Fruit is harmful, vegetables are injurious, meat is deadly, pastry is unspeakable. Not a drink is used that has not been condemned. Venders of water and all other beverages assault the courage of the day with dire catalogues of disaster — if you indulge in any other than their own. Advertisements everywhere outrage one's sense of security. Even air is thrust into the fear-making machine of imagination. That of the city is baleful, that of the sea is too strong, that of the inland too dry or too moist, that of the valley too heavy, that of the mountain too rare. Air contains an excess of ozone or not enough. The sun threatens sunstroke, and the moon portends lunacy. One must needs go to jail in order to avoid draughts, and live like the owl to escape death by heat or maintain the balance of reason. There is death, also, in all physical exercise. It hides beneath the horizontal bar, and consumption dances in the prize-ring, heart-failure

rides the bicycle, a broken bone is a certainty on the
ball-ground, a wrecked anatomy on the gridiron, ex-
haustion on horseback, fatty degeneration in the carriage, rheumatism and neuralgia in the rowboat, mutila-
tion in the hunting-field, drowning on the fishing banks.
People have been known to die in church.   Systematic
exercise is elaborately formulated — and scientifically
criticised.   We are fearful of all exercise, of no exercise,
of too little and too much.   Then, again, sleep is no
longer innocent of wakeful hobgoblins.   It may not be
indulged on the left side, on the right, on the back, or
"the other way up," as one in the "embarrassing presence" tried to say of swimming, nor omitted until
midnight, nor permitted beyond this or that hour in the
morning, nor during the day, nor before a meal, nor
immediately after, nor in a closed room, nor in an open,
nor with a bedfellow, nor without, nor with head toward
the north, south, east, west, nor on an empty stomach,
nor a full, nor just before a bath, nor just after, nor with
too much light or clothing, nor with too little.   We fear
excess of sleep, insufficient sleep, sleep of every conceivable kind under every conceivable condition.   But
fear has never in this world accomplished anything
other than make good the fear and breed some more.

Of course medicines are prime suggesters of fear-
feeling.   Only an age whose fears have swollen the
pharmacopœia could multiply fears for medicine.   Fear
warns against some medicines, too much medicine, too
little, all kinds *in toto*.   Hence, there are fearful diseases
unknown in the past, and every pain suggests the death-
rattle.   A pain in the eyes conjures up a vision of sur-
gery-loving oculists; one in the ear means a probing
aurist; one in the tongue an operation for cancer; one
on the left side a collapse on the street; one in the

throat sanitary isolation; one in the stomach a growing tumor; one somewhere else appendicitis—a professional mining exploration for the significance in evolution of *vermiform appendix;* one in the lungs an experiment in some new theory; one in the head nervous prostration; one in the feet the gout; one in the back various complaints; one in the joints hardening of tissue; "that tired feeling" all the woes of earth.

No pain is there but awakens apprehension, no ill but causes a fear, no sickness but engenders anxiety. We are "fearfully as well as wonderfully made." The "sciences" which benevolence and money-getting have originated have themselves become fear-factories. Rational science frightens us with bacteria, bacilli, innumerable unescapable germs. The clubs that profess longevity hail the aspirant for membership with countless adjurations. Christian Science, Metaphysics, all sorts of isms, the occult forces, water-cures, nature-cures, allopathy, homeopathy, electric schools, all haunt the world with ten thousand prescriptions for ills themselves have largely created by fructifying imagination until its power of microscopic investigation and infinitesimal analysis appears to be almost as attractive as a new possibility in the nature of the Almighty. It is scarcely an exaggeration to say that, afraid to die, we die in fright for fear of the fear of death. And every one of these fears has worked incalculable harm in our life.

I have drawn out the indictment against fear in this way because I wished to indicate the utter folly and uselessness of our perennial fear of things, Nature, her creations, forces and conditions. Let us have done with this insanity. There are no fears which may not be displaced by reason; none, therefore, that may not be destroyed and cast out of our life altogether. If, then, the foolishness of it all begins to dawn on the reader, we may now indicate, treating the matter suggestively, some of the

REMEDIES FOR THE FEAR OF THINGS.

FIRST REMEDY: *Improving the Body-Tone by Health-Thought.* Undoubtedly one's courage-attitude toward things depends largely upon one's physical tone, for a low physical tone commonly means a weak action of the self in thought. "It's all right to talk," said a ruffian, "but courage is a mighty curious thing, and nobody's got it with him all the time (he was mistaken in the last statement). Take me on a sunshiny day, full of good grub and with a couple of drinks under my belt, and I'd stand up to a regiment and take my chances. But take me before daybreak, in the rain, hungry and cold, and I'd run from one Greaser if he was hunting me." But it is equally true that a low psychic condition depresses physical tonus, and so makes the entire personality an easy prey to fear. In addition, then, to effort looking to bodily health through right living, you are urged to cultivate the assertive assumption of being now in physical vigor, which is itself a great inspirer of courage. Here we have a huge law running through all ages, utilized incompletely and confusedly by all peoples, the law that the human spirit is designed for sovereignty over its physical house or instrument. No individual or system has a monopoly on this law. Suggestion, mental healing, magnetic healing, miracles and Christian Science have merely in part exploited the universal and natural law of the great System in which we live. It is for every human to belt on to that law, so to speak, and, so doing, to assert for himself his own sovereign power and to draw to himself the universal forces of welfare.

The law is not a new, but is an ancient, law. The power to use the law and the force behind it, and the power of those forces, is no new thing. There is no new power in human nature, created in one age or another. All the power man will ever possess he now has; and the power of his almighty nature waits only discovery by the objective consciousness to do the will's command.

There is no new knowledge of truth essential to or in the nature of things. Of such knowledge the human spirit is already in perfect possession; the truth merely needs discovery as a reality which has always been in the possession of the subconscious self to be utilized for the betterment of the conscious self through the unfoldment of the subconscious self.

Progress in human life signifies, not new creations, but always merely unfoldments. Only that which has always been in the soul can be unfolded in the soul's life. If man knows any essential truth to-day, or possesses any conscious power, it is because he has simply unfolded his own nature. We background on the Infinite, and "there is no limit to the knowing of the self that knows," no limit to the power of the self which unfolds.

The method by which health-thoughts may practically operate for improved and maintained physical tone are seen in suggestion, or a valiant faith in one's own physical power.

In suggestion, one asserts, quietly, yet emphatically: "This pain is nothing; this lassitude or depression is nothing; I am well and a-l-l r-i-g-h-t, and shall surely continue so to be." We say, we throw off the condition; we do not; we throw into the condition those powerful movements of the soul which dispel the condition. I have demonstrated the truth numberless times. Elisha Kane, relates that in his early life a captain, dying of scurvy on shipboard in the polar seas, was told that there was mutiny on deck. Out of a comatose state the old sailor started with a call for his boots, and quelled the mutiny — and recovered. When your deeper self asserts its command at the suggestion of the conscious self, body inevitably tries to obey. And not only is the huge power of suggestion yours for the ills of flesh, but as well for a higher register of psychic tone and its permanent maintenance.

I know that there are some degrees of pain which may not be subdued, some conditions of the body which may not be handled, in this way. The facts disturb neither the reality of the law nor the possession of the power. They merely show that the soul has lost control of itself, and so is unable to seize upon the law and draw forth the power. But by so much as the self retains any self-control, by so much may it lay hold both on law and power.

It is to be understood that these affirmations require modification by another law — that present conditions are the outcomes of past suggestions and ways of living. In matter there are the laws of dirt, and if one lives in a dirty way, these laws of dirt will work themselves out. Nevertheless, it is not mere dirt which causes disease: it is after all the psychic underlife that makes dirt malevolent. Our psychic antecedents it is that have banked up against us the powerful evil of the past. One's physical state may be the result of years or of centuries of false living and thinking (we must recognize the facts), so that, in some cases, the law of suggestion, or of psychic power, may be invoked too late, not because the soul is not humanly

sovereign, but because it is individually incapable of
using its own powers. The ideal operation of the law
may in all cases be far in the future. When health is
thus destroyed, temporarily, or seemingly permanently,
I hold it to be common sense to call in the trained physician and the demonstrated mental healer, meanwhile
exercising all the psychic ability one possesses. What
do I care for the theories of a doctor forbidding the
mental healer? I am for health — especially my own
— and I want help from any source, with any label.
And what do I care for the follies of Christian Science
forbidding the physician. I am for health, and the
trouble is mine, not to be handled by a mere notion,
even if that notion is religious and altogether sacred
to some one else. As a matter of fact, the law of sovereignty cares for neither as against the other, but will
obey the call of either or both if that call is or can be
efficient or potent enough. And it is a perfectly dead
law until the call becomes so efficient. *The ideal in
all this is freedom to utilize the psychic power of soul over
body, by whatever means, and signifies, therefore, absolutely no bondage, to medicine on the one hand, or to suggestion
or religion, or "science" on the other hand.* If you can
swim at all, you can swim without a board — provided
you have the ability to use your power; but if you lack
just there a small board will help you swim when you
otherwise would drown. If you continue to practise
swimming without a board, you will ultimately require
none. In the education of the soul for perfect self-
mastery, anything that helps is legitimate. Whether
or not the use of helps will develop helplessness depends
altogether on the soul itself. The resolute soul shouts:
I am at liberty to use these helps now, and do so, but,
please God, to-morrow I shall have the larger freedom

to ignore them; meanwhile, I am for health, whatever
the means.

This book urges you, in the battle for health as
against sickness, to take advantage of both physical
science and spiritual laws.

And yet, although some cases of physical disability
may seem defiant and incurable, I am unable to find
any definite rule which must exclude suggestion as an
efficient remedy.   The physicians are constantly affirming cases to be hopeless which the mental healers are
curing.   Nor am I able to discover any principle which
must bid us wait the slow improvement of centuries in
the matter of psychic power before we can squarely
bank on the soul's sovereignty.   Though some facts
seem to contradict the conclusion, I find it impossible
to see that inability to recover physical tone by assertive
suggestion may not and ought not in any and every
case to be instantly successful.   Clergymen will babble
a law of God that all must die.   But the God they
talk about is the creator of Nature in which health is a
phase of reality, and there is no God worth our thought
who would or could create an evil Nature, and the real
God of this Universe has no power to make disease and
death parts of a system in a state of perfect harmony
with itself and Him, or who has the ability to foist
disease or death into an individual career living in a
similarly perfect state of harmony.   The law of suggestion, taken in its broadest sense, is merely an
expression of tendency toward harmony.   When harmony becomes perfect and universal, the God I worship
will be very glad to see disease and death forever banished.

But suggestion, it should be remembered, is more
than a mere statement of thought, at least in its higher

form: it is the dynamic power of faith. True faith is a force, as real and effective, yet as law-abiding, as the force of gravity. The idea of faith cannot be given in a simple reference to belief, for belief may be defined as an assent of the intellect, while faith is an active state of the entire self. Observe one person as he expresses belief in present or future welfare. He is mild and negative. Observe, now, a second person as he declares his faith: he may be very composed and quiet in the matter, but his whole attitude indicates confident energy. He radiates force. He is condensed power. The deepest phases of his personality are vibrant and expectant. The general difference between the two men is vital. Faith involves belief, but it then may become power in action. The activity is of the inner self no less than of the objective functions. There is in the prophetic soul a vital, profound, enriched, assertive and assumptive state of consciousness which exerts its own power, manifests its own law, amid the laws and forces of Nature. Such conditions harmonize discordant elements in the life, induce favorable currents inward from large areas without, and actually establish the prerequisites of health and further development of power. The man of doubt is always, of course, losing the faith he has, while the man of faith is forever gaining more faith, because, beginning with assumption, he sets consciousness into harmonious vibrations or activities, manages to achieve more or less since Nature must respond to his call, approximately right as it is, and so, in his hopeful feelings and his successes finds justification of past faith and ground for further faith.

In other words, health and ideal personality depend upon the amount of appropriating consciousness one can throw over environment, over a very Universe,—

the territory one can cover by the overspread of his assumptive consciousness, the amount of a harmonious Universe one can absorb into his own personality. I know that this has a very large sound, but here, precisely, is the characteristic of true faith, that it thrives on great things alone.

If some of my readers suggest that such consciousness comes not of mere psychic assertion, but only from the study of books and the training of the schools, I reply that the greatest truths man has discovered and the noblest victories he has achieved have *all* resulted from the mighty faith-power of the human soul over and above the immediate influence of *all the schools of the ages.*

It is for reasons thus indicated that I urge the development within of the power of faith: faith in one's own body, faith in one's own psychic ability, faith in one's own faith, faith in and for present health, confidence in the possession of buoyancy and vigor, and thus faith — assertive assumption here and now — in physical tone and fearlessness regarding every object in Nature, seen or unseen. The faith and the assumption, in some cases, may at first seem almost impossible, and, if experienced, may be very feeble, indeed, but perseverance will show the task to be less and less difficult, and will render the confident expectation itself more and more pronounced. Above all, these suggestions will as certainly unfold the tone of real courage as a law of Nature will bring man benefits when obeyed. We consider, then —

Psychics and Medicine. The cure of ill-health demands, I hold, two things: psychic power and, to some extent in the present state of human progress, medical advice. Good health and a physician are pref-

erable to poor health and consistency. Moreover, in
real consistency, holding that all cures are psychic cures,
we must recognize the great *suggestive* efficacy of physicians and prescriptions. In the last analysis the latter
may be utterly useless, but if one cannot quite attain
the level of a raw miracle, one should accept the assistance of material instruments of suggestion, for the
doctor and his prescriptions may be the only means of
suggestion to which some souls will at present respond.

All health-tone is a physical reaction to psychic
conditions, and these psychic conditions are demands
on the vital forces of the Universe. Good health is a
sharing in the universal vitality through harmonious
coöperation of physical and psychic functions and
Nature's laws. Even if vitality is nothing other than
an outcome of molecular activities or molecular conditions, the truth remains the same. Health is not a
thing, it is a condition. It is not a self-state merely;
it is a state of life, or of molecules, adjusted to the All-
Life or to the molecular sum-total of the Universe. Ill-
health is a state of maladjustment of self to law and
life. It is not a thing; it is a chaotic condition. Cure
of ill-health is a change of inharmonious adjustments to
the All-Life (or the molecular sum-total) in the direction
of harmony. Restoration of right adjustment never
proceeds from without. It is always an internal process. It follows the law of life: from within out. Where
growth is from within out, restoration must operate in
the same manner. Hence, the self is always the prime
factor in health-cure. Secondarily the self may employ
any means adapted to bring about right adjustment.
This is sanity. The question of medicine has to solve
itself: not in the repudiation of medical practice, but
in the reform of medical methods. The trouble with

medicine, as with theology, is its tyrannous traditions, which always insist upon foolish consistency. A tradition is never good when you know better. If consistency forgets inner realities, it is a delusion and a snare. All real consistency is a bundle of contradictions; this is its constitution. When it holds fast to the inner realities, it becomes a search for truth. Truth is never humanly consistent, because human conceptions are always symbolic of something truer just beyond.

Remedies which are external to the self, when successful, merely assist, or guide, or inspire, the essential process of self-adjustment to the All-Life. Such assistance, guidance, inspiration, are vitalized by two qualities: the psychic self first, and secondly, Nature, which floods-in the Universal Life-Forces on right demand.

These facts explain cures without medicine. In almost all cases, according to authoritative testimony, medicines are not needed. The self and Nature would cure in any event. Where there is no medicine and a cure occurs, the psychic demand is right and strong enough to induce the incoming of the Universal Life. If the reader prefers the universal sum-total molecular activities, very well. Where there is no cure, with or without medicine, the psychic demand is inadequate. The efficacy of medicines springs from the self-action, not from inert matter. If the self-action cannot be induced without medicine, the use of the latter would seem legitimate. For, let us hold that

Nature is a Balanced Indifference. At this point a great truth emerges which does not appear to be sufficiently appreciated in the New-Thought writings: what may be called the indifferent balance toward man of Nature considered as a huge System of law. Nature, though always ready to pour life into a disordered body,

is absolutely impartial and unprejudiced. Regarded
as a mere mechanism of law, Nature cares not whether
man is well or ill — except that there is throughout the
whole System a tendency toward right conditions in
which the individual will share if he adjusts thereto.
Nature does not violently offer itself, nor does it obsti-
nately hold back. What Nature does for man depends
upon what man does for himself, and that really means,
what man does for Nature. This "what he does" is a
demand or a repulsion. But the demand and the repulsion are deeper factors than mere words. I do not
say, then, that one may turn the balance of Nature in
his favor by simple demand for health. If some one
will inform us how to secure health by raw will-power,
we shall be thankful — but not wise, for then universal
stability will be destroyed. Conditions are vastly important as phases of demand. But right demand is
a part of conditions; it creates them in some degree,
and it uses those which are beyond it. For example:
I slept well during the night, awakened, called up good
thoughts, rose, took a cold bath, got up a gentle heat on
the body surfaces, dressed, enjoyed an appetizing break-
fast, loafed a little at one chore and another, exercised
thoughtfully a few minutes, practised full breathing,
uttered a word of good-will to all the world, shook hands
with Hope and Courage, recognized Peace within, and
began the day's work. I had conformed to certain
conditions, and I had thus created certain conditions
in myself, and so had demanded service of the Universal
Life, with full assurance that I should receive whatever
had actually laid hold on. In all this, Nature remained indifferent, neither rushing to meet me nor
drawing away, but ever ready to come to my service
when conditions made it possible.

The sea ebbs and flows. It is not *for* you; it is not *against* you. It simply comes and goes, impartial, unprejudiced, as it did before man appeared. Man flung himself against it, and was dashed in pieces. Man offered his spoken prayers, and the sea ebbed and flowed indifferent. Then man formulated his demands in terms of conditions, of adjustment—and the sea became beautiful, useful, a mistress loving to serve.

You build a tide-mill on one of ocean's narrows, and straightway the running tide, or coming or going, does your behest. It is as if the Atlantic were now eager in your interest. It is indifferent now as ever. The fact is, you have strength and wit to draw on unlimited but indifferent power.

Good health is the tide-mill in operation. Ill-health is the mill out of order. The sea does not wish to destroy the mill; that is done by maladjustment. The same tide which buoys up a ship may dash her in pieces on the rocks. The ship is then out of adjustment with environment.

Nature does not destroy life; it merely transfers life, or changes the conditions of life. Decay, disease, and death are transitions (*trans*, "over"—and *ire*, "to go"), transferences (*trans*, "over"— and *ferre*, "to carry"), transformations (*trans*, "over"— and *formare*, "to shape"),— a passing of the life in one individual thing to some other individual thing. The intention of Nature is for the individual, but when that intention cannot be carried out because conditions are inharmonious, Nature passes the intention, so to speak, with that which goes with the intention, life, on to individuals or fields where conditions make the intention and life possible for them. Your individual life is the result of conditions making your life possible, and when conditions of possibility of good life for you decrease or cease, conditions of possibility for life in other fields are established, and life transfers or transforms — passes over. Nature is constantly striving for the highest expression of its power, that is, the highest form of life; but toward any particular individual it is indifferent if the individual refuses or fails in conditions making life for itself impossible. Decay, disease, and death simply express the two-fold fact of indifference to the individual and transfer of life when conditions call therefor. In fact, it is in the conditions that the transition, transference, transformation takes place.

The Hindus say of the soul: "Life is tremulous, like a water-drop on a lotus-leaf." The highest form of life is a very unstable equilibrium. For this Nature ever strives. When the individual representing it goes wrong, is out of harmony, the equilibrium is upset, and is regained only on a lower level. Decay, disease, and death are such lower levels of equilibrium — each standing for greater stability until nothing but waste matter remains — so far as the individual is concerned.

Maladjustment throws the body against law and force, which move relentlessly on, whether or no. Adjustment brings the body within the reach of law and force, which then also move relentlessly on whether or no. All health is psychic harmony with the All-Life. Ill-health shows that self has thrust body out of adjustment with Nature in its highest intentions. Body cannot itself do this. In restoration to health, psychic demand, formulated in terms of right adjustment, enlists the Nature-life of worlds, just as the rebuilding or repairing of the tide-mills makes it capable of utilizing, and causes it to utilize, the vast power of the sea.

Medicines have reference to conditions. They suppose, or suggest, faith — self-effort to lay hold on the Nature-life. When you call a physician you assume the attitude of demand on the flood-tide. You seek to call it in. At times the bodily weakness overwhelms the self within; the latter cannot institute the right demand; the right medicine, by its purely physical action, stimulates some organ or the general system, because the psychic factor has learned to respond thereto, and the whole self has now opportunity for assertion of its powers, because the process of overwhelming has been partially arrested. Medicines may thus be said to inspire psychic demand by affording opportunity for reaction. At times medicines relieve the system of waste, chemical compounds which the body cannot further reduce, and for which, therefore, it has no further need, or of foreign material, assisting the system to expel them. At times medicines chemically assist assimilation of proper material, because the psychic factor, again, has learned to respond thereto. In all this we have cases of medical assistance. At times medicines bring about a change in the physical or mental tone. Some medicines depress, some elevate the tone. Some transform the entire current of sensation and emotion. The psychic demand is firm, but it may be deflected in wrong directions, or a change of direction of thought and feeling may be necessary to give it full effect. Here is a case of guidance secured by outside means. It may be essential, also, to deaden pain in order to stop waste of vitality through excessive nerve-action. The patient is using all his energy in hoisting the signals of warning. In all these suppositions my contention is this: that the physical reaction is fundamentally psychic in origin, and that the psychic origin can only be gotten at by adequate means, the character of which, whether material or non-material, should be a matter of indifference to reason and good sense.

And so, I say: the primal factor of health is the psychic self. Whatever aids this factor is scientific, be the aid material, spiritual, both. And science is the *whole* truth —or it is nothing but a mass of personal opinions.

He who affirms that medicine is always needless lacks the power of correct thinking; he may be on the right track, but he stops short of the real conclusion. He who affirms the use of medicine to be always necessary or effective, either observes or speaks incorrectly, because he also fails to go far enough in his reasoning. He who declares that the use of medicine is morally wrong betrays a selfish determination to insist upon a barren consistency for the sake of bolstering up a theory or a system — and fails in ethical judgment. He who denounces the exercise of psychic powers not recognized by his theory or system as black magic reveals himself a victim of mediæval bigotry. He who denounces all psychic cures as unreal or unscientific repudiates the bed-rock of medical practice. He who is wedded to either psychic or medical treatment alone contradicts his own position, whatever it be. For, if psychic treatment is sole truth, demand for health may disregard all conditions — food, air, sleep, exercise, use of physical functions, relation of the soul to the material, or so-called material, world. But, again, if medical treatment is sole truth, treatment for health may disregard all psychic realities — relations between soul and body, self control, confidence in the physician, his remedies, his regimes, in self, and hope, courage, obedience. **In** either case, all the conditions represent other than the theory — something of the opposite theory.

The wise man asserts his inner self, through that makes demands on the Universal Life, and gladly avails himself of all demonstrated assistance, often taking the last chance with the unknown if convinced that such course can at worse do him no harm.

But always is it the Universal Life that cures ill-health by response to the inner demands of the assertive self. Thus it appears that the psychic factor is the one great physician. If the psychic factor accomplishes its legitimate work, tone of health will inevitably react for vigorous courage-tone of the soul itself.

SECOND REMEDY: *Cultivation of Self-Control.* Self-control in the presence, or in the thought, of certain objects is a habit, and should be developed as such. It is a favorite statement of some schools of psychology that one does not run because he fears, but that one fears because he runs. The meaning of this curiosity of the text-books is that the feeling of fear expresses in certain physical agitations, and that the feeling becomes conscious because the agitations become conscious, so that one is aware of fear, or does fear, by as much as he is physically disturbed. If one refuses to yield to the agitation, the fear-feeling is controlled and may totally subside, meanwhile cold-blooded reason, acting for self-preservation, alone remaining. If, on the other hand, one yields to the agitation, panic ensues, and the swifter the running, the greater the fear-feeling. You observe or imagine an object, and agitation begins, urging you to get away, or suggesting abhorrence and the idea of flight. Your remedy consists in resolutely affirming to yourself: "*I do not, and I will not, permit any feeling of fear whatever, maintaining reason squarely on the throne. I control my physical functions with the iron hand. As to my inner essential self, nothing on earth can affright it or harm it. I am master of my thoughts, my emotions, and my body."*

You discover a runaway horse, or a snake, or a huge storm, or some object for which you have a peculiar aversion. Our remedy means that you are to take care of yourself where there seems to be real danger, but not for an instant to yield to or permit physical agitation and the feeling of fright or nervousness. The method by which the remedy may be made effective consists simply in arresting and instantly suppressing the agitation at its slightest appearance, and in completely quelling the emotional disturbance. You may find this a hard task, and you may fail many times, but the methods and remedy are perfect, and if you will persevere with a resolute spirit, you will infallibly conquer. Your fears are mere habits; you must overcome them through the establishment of the contrary habit — that of self-control. When you have acquired control over physical agitation and its associated tendencies, you will find that you have secured the greater value, psychic control of the psychic self.

For the general apprehensive attitude toward all sorts of things — buildings, machinery, forces, animals, plants, medicines, diseases, etc., etc., the same regime, prolonged and persistent, should be observed. All these nervous apprehensions, worries and panicky agitations are immensely wasteful of vitality and power, and all that waste is the outcome of sheer habit. The habit may be destroyed, if only you will and make good. There is no limit to the mastery of the self that masters.

THIRD REMEDY: *Association With Objects Especially Fearful.* You are urged freely to associate, both in thought and life, with the object feared, so far as practicable. In doing this, of course, some care should be observed. It would not be reasonable to undertake a violent cure; rather, the experience should begin with slight experiments, testing the self and forming the courage habit gradually and increasingly. No intelligent horse-trainer will lead an animal suddenly up to a frightening object, but such an one will manœuver until association wears the feeling of agitation away. You shudder at sight of an eel, a snake, or a toad. If you try to slay your fear at one stroke, you only succeed in increasing it by the great nervous shock which goes with the effort. But if you will persist in the effort, you can gradually bring yourself to look upon these reptiles with no disagreeable sensation, and this victory, although such objects are infrequent in your path and easily avoided, will count for courage all round in your life. *Every triumph of the will as against fear tends to develop a permanent habit of courage.* Thus with all the Nature-fears now in hand: familiarity breeds contempt for their fear-making qualities. In many cases what is called fear is little more than nervousness; you do not really fear, at least you control yourself to a degree; but you are conscious of nervous disturbance, and this also is sure to yield to larger self-control and association with the exciting causes, provided, you carry into the association a resolute assertion of fearlessness and determination to overcome fear. We have here again the law of suggestion. If you suggest to yourself fear in presence of the objects that trouble you, growing fear only can be the result. If, on the other hand, you insist on suggesting courage during the association, you will ultimately become master of these fears. You will forget them.

FOURTH REMEDY: *Emphasizing the Falsity of Fears.* You are urged to emphasize, over and over in your thought, the fact that countless fears in your life have proven groundless and false. People are fearful because they permit fear to run rampant, while past escapes and foolish experiences receive scant attention. I suppose it is true that not one in a million of any man's fears have ever been realized in disaster as expected. Experience actually demonstrates that the vast majority of our fears have been arrant liars.

There are certain forces from which we cannot always escape and which we have no power to control. Lightning, wind, floods, and the like, hold many people in constant dread. Usually these terrified ones do the foolish thing — get into a panic and endeavor to hide. As if lightning, for example, could not find them in the cellar or under twenty feet of blankets. As if the cyclone had not slain the cowering man and left the babe unharmed. Before these titanic forces we are powerless, so that the soul's only recourse is heroic self-possession and the search for such means of safety as may be found at the moment. The question in such cases is not altogether how to escape danger, but how to summons ability to face it. To this question our old answer must be given: by resolution and such familiarity with the objects as may be acquired by reason. Are you afraid of these titanic forces? Face them — steadfastly face them, whenever needs must be. So long as you yield to panic, so long will your problem of facing danger with the least expense remain unsolved.

When next the storm-wrack rolls up in the west nerve yourself to quell apprehension and to stand still before its marvelous display. Find a good point of view, where you can watch all the portentious marshalling of the clouds, the billowy upheaval from below, the flying drift of the rushing winds above, the majestic oncoming of the clear-marked front. Divest thought of self. Let the mind dwell on the mighty wonder of the storm. Look the face of heaven full in the eye, though you quake within, forgetting — forgetting, I say, in the splendor of the outlook, the very need of fear. See the solemn chaos of the clouds, the driving rain, the skeltering leaves of the forest, the shaking giants of the fields. See the ripping of the phalanxes of the cloud-murk and the ragged zigzagging of the speeding light. Ah! This is a scene worth tarrying for! It is yours for one price — self-control. You have it now. Your breathing almost ceases, and then ebbs and flows unconsciously in the slow rhythm of the tempest. You are chained to the spot, rapt by majestic forces. You are aware of expansion and uplift of emotion. You thrill with a feeling that must be of the gods. No longer puny, you are one with the omnipotence displayed. It is the experience of your life! How unspeakably magnificent! You have lost the thought of fear! Slowly the fury passes and the glory vanishes. The East has swallowed up the warring elements. Afar off the pale lightning heralds the low murmur of the dreadful voice which so recently shook the world. It is now like the curious bass song of certain shells when held to the ear. You arouse with a sigh. The nerves relax. You are as one who has come forth from the fountain of life. A new soul you are become. You are full of the spirit of courage.

FIFTH REMEDY: *Cultivating Confidence in the Universe.* Above all it is yours to remember that you are a part of the System, and thus to trust yourself to the Infinite All, to assert your will in the outgo of confidence, and to hold serenely in mind the truth that no force in Nature can destroy the *I-Am* of the soul. Our fears develop when we forget true self-hood. If self is right, it is invincible. The moment the right-living soul remembers — "*I am! I am Power!*" — that moment there comes to it courage to face all material threats.

SIXTH REMEDY: *Restraining Undue Estimate of Self-Valuation.* The valuation which your reason puts upon your self and your life and happiness is legitimate and not overdone. But the valuation put upon your body or the inner self by your fears is illegitimate because always greater than the case warrants. When you are agitated by fear it will be helpful and wholesome to ask: "*What matters, after all, if hurt comes or life goes out? I am myself, secure in myself, and nothing can harm my real self. Whatever betide, that self will surely come through unscathed. I am not so tremendously important that I should expect life to be free from dangers and some measure of disaster. But the disaster can never reach the inner citadel of the abiding self. I may not escape accident, but I surely have the power, and I now use that power, to face danger and stand squarely up to its menace.*" Such an attitude, assumed and persisted in, will put your miserable fears to flight, and in the end you will have a truer estimate of the value of self than under any regime of nervousness or panic.

SEVENTH REMEDY: *Ignoring Vague Apprehensions.* There is a curious mood of fear which it is rather difficult to classify. It is a vague feeling of dread, having reference to what particular danger one cannot say. Its very vagueness is its misery. Its uncertainty of reference only enhances its power. It is a stranger to normal health, but it sometimes appears when one supposes health to be good. If it assume the distinctness of a specific warning, it should be heeded, but never permitted to cause suffering. Prevention of suffering thus induced must be looked for in resolute turning of the mind to other matters which are of special interest. If it does not seem to warn of anything, it should be totally disregarded and persistently put out of mind. For in this condition you are ready for all sorts of additional fears. You fear work will fail, your plans will not succeed, your friends are forsaking you, and so, innumerable are the ills which shadow your haunted life. The explanation of this abnormal state is the fact simply that you are really "out of condition." You should, therefore, give the matter no serious attention, but go right on with the affairs of your *career*, proceed undisturbed in all your plans, and assume your friends to remain entirely loyal. Or, it may be well abruptly to change your activities for a time, to swing yourself into new currents. Very soon the ghostly fear of something indefinable will fade away. If your case is deep-seated and unyielding, consult a nerve-specialist — but assist him in every way possible in the spirit of this book.

EIGHTH REMEDY: *Fortifying Against the Occult.* Now and then a soul manages to create a new fear, as, for example, the fear of baleful modern "occult" forces. The study of human realities should guide into the light, not in shadows. It is a law more solid than the standing ground of Atlas that no occult power, in man or devil, can injure any person who is resolutely living the harmonious life. Were this not so, the reign of law would be widespread chaos. The remedy for such fear of "uncanny" things, then, is the confident will, the harmonious inner life, and association with the good, the true and the beautiful in the seen and the unseen worlds.

The feeling of courage is sometimes an inheritance, sometimes an acquired factor in our life. This chapter has suggested a few remedies for certain kinds of fear, but these remedies are subsidiary to the one effort, that which makes for the establishment of a permanent inner feeling, become habitual, of personal ability to face all real danger and to banish from thought all fancied possibilities of danger. The goal is not so much facility in conforming to directions of a specific nature, as the developed consciousness of power and courage for all the issues of life. You are urged, therefore, to remember the real goal, and to endeavor in every way to cultivate an abiding sense of personal assurance and masterhood. To acquire such a value, you must assume it, and then "make good" by everlasting conduct conforming to the assumption.

THE MASSING OF A HUNDRED FACES.

The massing of a hundred faces
Awakens long-dead fears that fled, head-lost,
In the barbarous days of old,
When the many against the one
Fierce glared, and muttered, and precipitated flight,
And sped through forests and steep hills
Intent on a death. And the man, pursued,
Stricken with terror, plunged on for his life
Into the years and into the centuries.
And so, panting desperate, runs he yet.

Shall the shadow of panic with savages
Nevermore fade from the earth?
Must the brave, who fears no single,
Whether man the giant or woman the beautiful,
Forever shudder in the lingering, dreamlike vision
Of the multitude lusting for slaughter?
This is the mystery of the survival of impressions,
That the mingling of five-score harmless units
Creates a fear where no fear was.

But so, this be your task, then:
To banish the shadow of old days,
To disillusion the multitude,
To divide it down to the ne'er-feared single life.

But this also the greater task:
To well-wish every man and woman in the crowd,
To bless with good resolve the whole mankind
By the white life and the actual service.
Thus shall you lose out of eye the mass,
Thus shall you lose out of heart the fear,
And rise, an honest soul, surcharged with the truth:
"I am, as ye are, the many or few,
Courage and Power in *Brotherhood*."
So dies fear!
So smiles the old-time ravening herd
Back at your hand and word,
Under new skies.
Help i' the task.

— THE AUTHOR.

CHAPTER VIII.

The Fears of Timidity.

*"You take notice either of the sweat of him who praises you
or of the desire of the suppliant."—Hymn to the Storm Gods, India.*

*"This mind of mine went formerly wandering as it liked; but
I shall now hold it in thoroughly, as the rider who holds the hook
holds in the furious elephant."— Buddha.*

KAPILA'S Indian System, the *"Samkhya,"*
has a parable entitled *"As in the Case of the
Son of a King,"* in which a young prince was
taken from his capital and brought up by a Sabara, or
wild man of the woods. During his minority the young
man believed himself a Sabara, and he acted accordingly. Later, however, it was discovered to him by one
of the king's ministers that he was a prince. Then the
young man banished from mind the idea of his Sabara-
life, and forthwith began *to conduct himself as the son
of the king.* Thus is illustrated the transforming power
of thought.

The timid, bashful person is obsessed by an idea,
or a brood of ideas, which must be banished and substituted by a better thought. In order to that two-
fold end, I want to indicate to you, whoever you may
chance to be, your personal reality and the actual relations you sustain to the Universe in which we live.

The Infinite Our Background.

Infinite and Eternal Reality has manifested itself
in two forms at least. One form is that of Nature or

the Universe, which I conceive as the complex Thought-System of an Infinite Thinker.   The Christian Bible says, speaking of the creative Son, "Upholding all things by the word of his power;" the Vedanta of India employs similar language in declaring, "He who is intelligence itself and subtler than the thread of the lotus-fibre, He who pervades the Universe" . . . . . . "There is one eternal Thinker thinking non-eternal thoughts."   A second form in which Infinite and Eternal Reality manifests itself is that of finite personality.   The human spirit, as one phase of such, feels instinctively, and imperiously insists, that it is no mere "wild man of the woods," but is personal, and, for that reason, superior to Nature because Nature, though a complex Thought of the Infinite, is seen to be a theatre in which the soul comes to development.   The self of man is held to be in some sense an "image" of the Infinite Personality.   As a personal manifest of the Infinite, therefore, the human spirit backgrounds on the Eternal Personal Reality.   When this thought is grasped, it is clear that consciousness, the sum-total of the activities of the inner self, must be fathomless, since, no matter how deeply we may penetrate into such inner activities, there is always the self below them, manifesting them, and thus having the consciousness. The self seems to disappear in the Greater — the Infinite.   The Infinite wells up, so to speak, in man's right personality.   Each of us becomes, now, a permanent personal Thought-Action of the Greater Reality, so far as our fundamental human nature is concerned.   You find yourself, as a human personality like all others, a manifest of the Infinite, having a destiny in your own control of endless unfoldment because you are a real personality.   You are a son or a daughter of the Eternal. You are no Sabara, to bow down or tremble before "kings, priests or gospelers." Your relationship to the Universe and its Creative Thinker is royal and by the Universal Brotherhood conceded. Why should you be timid?

ALL POWER AND TRUTH NOW POSSESSED.

Venturing to repeat a suggestion of the last chapter, I commend to you, in connection with the preceding paragraph, the proposition that if you background in the Infinite, who wells up in the normal consciousness of right personality, all the power you will ever attain you now possess. It is there — within you — in fulness, and you need but to draw on the Infinite Fund, that is, to assume that it is yours and use it freely as you require. This, in part, is the meaning of unfoldment. We do not create power, we do not develop new power, through unfoldment; we merely unroll, unfold, discover and use, that which we already possess. And if the conscious self rests on the Infinite, as the lotus rests on the Nile, we possess, if only we could but discover it, all the power there is. There is nothing of a non-physical nature (such alone we want) which you can ever do, so far as mere power is concerned, that you may not do here and now — provided, you discover the fact and proceed to use the power you think you possess.

This discovery and use come only of faith; that is, be it noted, not from a single act of belief or trust, but from the totality of yourself in its right attitude toward the Infinite and the Universe. For always *you* are your faith. If you are fearful, negative, yielding, confused, so is your faith. If you assume courage, positiveness, aggression, harmony, your faith is exactly equivalent. Your faith is what your self is. You may become a greater self by assuming and insisting upon greater attitudes toward yourself as a manifest of the Infinite, and acting accordingly. If you assume to be — one thing or another — and try to carry out the assumption, you will become what you began with as assumption. In all this process you are simply unfolding your ever-existing possession. You are timid, bashful, diffident, retiring, shrinking: that is always your assumption and confession. You have the feeling indicated by the words. But the feeling is your own creation. So long as you create fear-thought, you will be exactly what you insist you are. If, on the other hand, you assume yourself to be, not a Sabara who must bow down to or tremble in the presence of every supposedly superior person, but a son or daughter of the Infinite, a manifest of the Eternal, and thus possessed now of all the power you require, your assumption and attitude will transform yourself, your faith and confidence will inevitably increase, and your day of freedom will surely come. This is law, and it is more certain than the law of gravitation.

It is precisely so with regard to truth. (I am not speaking of mere fact.) When you discover a truth inherent in the nature of things, you say: "Why, of course; this is so. It ever has been so. It seems as if I had know this truth always." You have always known that truth, when you come to think of it. Essential truth is wrapped up in the human spirit because the human spirit is the Infinite welling up in the finite personality. When such a truth is discovered, it is seen to have come up from below in that self which is a manifest of the Infinite. No essential truth would ever look new to us had we never known error. The

Man of Galilee exhibited no surprise at any self-discovery or at any discovery in Nature. Always had the truth been his. So thoroughly was he in harmony with truth and the Infinite that he said: "I am the truth!" Any human is the truth so far as he acquires the truth-consciousness through harmony with the Infinite.

This discovery of essential truth, again, is in part, the unfoldment of the self. If you assume that you are mentally inferior, you "batten down the hatch" of the soul, and forbid consciousness its rightful freedom, and prevent those up-comings which are discoveries and unfoldments — and so compel yourself to remain shut-in, timid, fearful. It is yours to see that you possess the same nature of soul that others possess, and that you now own all the power you need, and that you now hold within all the personal truth of the Universe. Why should you belittle yourself, then, and creep through life a trembler? You are truth awaiting self-discovery. So long as you doubt and hesitate, you have your reward. I say to you, "Arise, take up thy bed and walk;" call on your self for its limitless possessions of truth and power. Be worth while in your own thought; then you will be worth while in the presence of others.

Some of my readers will retort: "It is easy to write such suggestions, but a different matter to carry them out." Let the retort stand as correct. Nevertheless, I reply that I have myself fought this battle out and won, beginning with stammering timidity, suspicion and sensitiveness most acute, and am yet able to say now that so far as I know, and without wishing to pose for courage, because I regard this as but *one* of the virtues and *not* the most important in

life, I do not indulge the fear-feeling for anything sus-
pected in heaven, or earth or "hell." The suggestions
of this book are all born of my own life and in no
instance manufactured for these pages except as genuine products of experience.

TIMIDITY WITHOUT JUSTIFICATION.

With such conceptions of our human personality
justification for timidity would seem to be impossible.
We have seen all along, moreover, that the confusion
of the fear-feeling with the action of instinct and of
reason leads to a perfectly false justification of fear.
The moment we perceive that so-called normal fear is
an addition to instinct or reason, an addition never
necessary and always harmful, that moment we must
discover that the justification of fear as normal because
it tends to self-preservation, is totally false. No fear
does anything for man which either instinct or reason
may not do without it. You can never justify fear for
the reason that it is unnecessary and is harmful at the
best. When you banish fear, you get rid of a nervous
strain which instinct and reason never induce.

While, however, there is no justification of the
fear-feeling which will bear examination, plenty of
legitimate excuses for fear are easily brought forward.
Its occasions, and so, its excuses, seem to be legion.
These, indeed, furnish the ground for fear's justifica-
tions as they are usually put forth. That they do not
justify, I have endeavored to show. That fears are
backed by all sorts of occasions which develop excuses,
is evident and conceded.

But there is no good excuse for timidity, bashfulness, sensitiveness, and the like. The occasions in
these cases are not wild beasts, fierce humans, dreadful

storms, uncontrollable natural forces. The occasions
now will not be found in the world outside of the self —
at least, in any forms which may justify the fears.
Except as just hinted, all occasion for timidity and
kindred characteristics in the adult life lie wholly
within the individual who manifests them. This is the
truth, and the timid person must face it as it is.

Now, I do not seek to bolster a theory regardless
of facts, nor am I indifferent to the sufferings of
people who are timid. Their trouble, it is true, must
be met and conquered by personal effort, but there is
something for other people to do in the matter as well.
The bold and fortunate may not ignore their share in
the remedy on the ground that every man's fears are
his own. The remedy lies partly with the timid, but
partly also with other classes. And that remedy involves an immense task, no less a task than the cure of
man's innate and brutal love of fear in his fellows.

Unnatural Man Enjoys Fear.

There are those to whom it seems entirely natural
to enjoy the signs of fear in others. This fact does not
appear to indicate encouragement for timid souls.
Nevertheless, an analysis of the matter may suggest
that timidity's timidness has only half its apparent
justification. There are two kinds of human nature,
the natural and the unnatural. In our common thought
we make the natural the unnatural, and the unnatural
the natural. I reject as false and an imputation upon
the All-Good that theology which regards man as
"naturally sinful" and selfish, and hold that "sinful"
and selfish man is really the unnatural man. Natural
man, created in the "image" of his Maker, is all good
in the sense that he contains and partially realizes the

possibilities of ideal unfoldment. Unnatural man is the disorder of natural man. It is natural for unnatural man to be selfish, and to relish deference, cringing and timidity in others. Some bishops, magnates and "queens" exhibit this hideous failing whenever they pose in public. But the true natural man abhors all these things. We may divide the people whom we meet into the true and the great, for one class, and all the rest for the other class. The first class never nurse their conscious superiority, either of person, of wealth, of position, or of culture. The second class exhibit what we may call *Megalopsukia*, misusing a word from Aristotle which means "high-mindedness," making it signify the "swell-head," and they rob others of the inalienable right to comfort and peace of soul which normally belongs to every son of the Infinite. Not always, it must be conceded, are they aware of themselves. Financial kings, scholars, social queens and ecclesiastics are sometimes so saturated with a feeling of condescending greatness as to be totally unconscious of their immense folly and selfishness. But your really superior person never emphasizes his wealth, his learning, his office, or any social preëminence. Why should he? These things are but incidents in true living. Only little bits of folk emphasize what lies on the outside of personality. Genuine people make you at ease in their presence — if it is possible — because they never think of their presence.

Exactly at this point, then, appears a part of your remedy. You are urged to divide your acquaintances into the true and genuine men and women and the silly and robber-class, and to insist in your thought upon your own superiority to the latter, resolutely eliminating from your relations with others all similar folly and cruelty. With unpretentious humanity you have little trouble, and if you will assume the attitude indicated toward the "consciously superior" variety, you will measurably overcome your timidity with this class, and by so much, as a matter of course, come to freedom with the only kind of people who are at all worth your thought. As an example, I may say that I was formerly distressed by timidity in the presence of certain magnates who condescended to urbanity and brotherhood, but in time I discovered their unnatural humanity and their sanctified enjoyment of deference and "modesty" in others, and then I learned to laugh myself into good courage.

There is a task, however, for the "superior" folk in this matter. Neither excuse nor ground can be made out for any enjoyment of fear in other people. We are all of one family — the human brotherhood. A reasonable family represents oneness of blood, community of interests, some similarity of tastes and beliefs, agreement amid differences, the amicable adjustment of difficulties, friendliness, and the comfortable speech of familiarity. One earth-family, of one blood, one home, one exit, one possible destiny, should not need the introduction as a law, legislation forbidding human hurt, and sermons against nursed superiority and brutal selfishness. Since it does seem to demand these things, timid people must have recourse to a just estimate of those who insist upon their false worth, and call them what they are — silly and selfish specimens of the genus homo, thus, in part, destroying the occasion for timidity. In the meantime it should be remembered that unnatural man needs naturalizing, and that this ideal can be gained only through right living — living at the best possible of the *white life.*

THE SECRET OF FEAR AND ITS LOVE IS WRONG LIVING.

By so much as life becomes right, by so much does brotherhood obtain, theoretically and practically. If you insist that the right life may nevertheless call any human being inferior, not, of course, as a matter of mere judgment, but as a matter of superior feeling on your part, try it at the instant you lift your thought to your God — whether Ra, or Jehovah, or Father, or All-Good, or the Infinite. The moment you do that, you are out of harmony, and either your higher feeling or your sense of superiority dies in your soul. The world distinctly demands that a man's religion, or philosophy, or theory of life shall square at top and bottom: the thought held about any man or woman thoroughly consistent with the loftiest ideas we know. This squaring process levels humanity, not down, but up. Wrong living throws the square out of true and thus makes love of fear a hideous possibility. If you think much of your little self and your little office, and so cause people to be timid in your presence, you are wrong at heart, no matter what your profession of greatness may be.

Man-fear is the product of centuries of wrong living somewhere among human beings. It is the wrong life of ages that has made man a tryant and a coward. No one who is living the harmonous life, really and finely, need inspire fear in others, and no one so living has justifiable occasion for timidity in the presence of anything human, because genuine people are never fearful and the other class are not worth a moment's pain.

ALL TIMIDITY IS SELF-SUSTAINED.

These considerations, however, suggest that after all the practical occasion for timidity obtains within

the self. The trouble is purely a personal habit. You
have established your soul in timidity by your own
thought and conduct. In some way you have gotten
the thought into your mind that you are timid, and you
have always acted on precisely that assumption. Thus
the thought is now habitual, and conduct corresponds.
Had you not at some time in the past thought or felt
"shrinking," and yielded thereto, then and ten thousand
times since, you would not now be timid in the presence
of mere people. You have trained yourself to be
exactly what you are. You have educated your mind
to think and feel timidity instantly in certain presences,
and have always immediately yielded to such impulses.
You have developed fear-tendencies in your nervous
system by entertaining the thought and surrendering
to it. Your timidity is a habit self-induced. If you
say, "I was always thus; it's in the blood; it was my
father's great difficulty," the answer is, nevertheless,
that you have made an inherited tendency a personal
habit. And if you say, "I have tried all my life to
overcome this difficulty, to banish the thought and to
act the part of courage, but I have failed," then you
have proceeded along wrong lines or with imperfect
methods, or you have not really tried. Do you know
what "trying a thing" means? It means *doing* the
thing. Thus we come to our particular remedies.

All Remedies Self-Applied.

One failing on the part of timid people consists in
regarding the faults of others as excuses for fear. If
human beings were not so cold and hard and distant,
you would not be timid in their presence. Such is
often your thought. It means, "If the world would
but reform, and if men and women would only run after

me, and handle me as though I were an infant, then the occasion for my timidity would not appear, and I would be as bold as anyone." But this attitude looks for the remedy in an impossibility. The world will not reform in your lifetime, nor will many busy people take the pains to adjust themselves to your unnecessary shrinking. The real remedy lies with yourself. Methods which are to succeed must be self-applied. The trouble is your own; you alone must take care of the matter. You are urged, therefore, to *insist upon yourself as alone your fountain of power, the master of all cures for all fears known to man.* If you will thus begin, patiently applying the remedies here suggested, the outcome is infallible — your happy freedom from the distress of your life. Kindly observe, then, the following suggestions, remembering that time and persistence assure you ultimate victory.

Remedies for the Fears of Timidity.

First Remedy: *Asserting the Right to Courage.* To every person the nature of things grants the inalienable right of perfect fearlessness so long as life harmonizes with the laws of individual uprightness. In no one inheres the right to inspire fear in others, except in the case of wrong-doing. Whoever claims or exercises the ability or right to inspire fear, wrongdoing alone excepted, labels himself a robber, for he has stolen a prerogative which does not belong to man or God.

If you will repeatedly and persistently suggest to yourself this law: "It is my inalienable right to be clean free from fear of man," a habit of courage will in time possess and dominate your entire being, and fear will slip from your soul like a hated, long-used garment.

The goal may certainly require a large expenditure of will-power thrown into very considerable and patient effort, but the glory of freedom will outweigh all the cost, whatever that cost may be.

SECOND REMEDY: *Cultivating Unselfishness.* This remedy involves the elimination from life of all selfishness. The world is divisible into — yourself and the rest of mankind. If you fear anyone in the second half, you must banish selfishness and cultivate altruism, because, in the view of every other person, you belong to that second half, and you must wholly deduct your contribution to the fear-causes of life. Not being unselfish yourself, you have no right to complain when others inspire fear in your soul by their selfishness. The nature of things imperatively requires in your life that illustration of the Golden Rule which alone can impart to the dead unquestioned sanctity.

THIRD REMEDY: *Unfolding the Self.* The cure of man-fear involves the cultivation of the self in every possible way, together with the development, while this culture is obtaining, and by unwearied persistence, of the courage-habit — strong, will-poised, and abiding. Inasmuch as the first part of the remedy will not soon be effected, each individual must look to himself alone for that sovereign spirit of courage which is the absolute right of every human being.

By so much as you seek self-unfoldment you will become conscious of your possessions and of power, and you will thus acquire a feeling of reasonable equality with others. The unfoldment of the soul, let it now be understood, does not depend upon the training of the schools alone. The school educates no one; it is merely a field in which self-education may be carried on. Moreover, an immense amount of instruc-

tion given in the schools is sheer tomfoolery, and comes
to nothing of value in any life.   The college graduate
seldom knows the huge realities of himself and the
nature of things, because it has never occurred to his
instructors either to suggest these great realities or to
offer rational methods for their study.   The true university of man is the subconscious self making up into
the conscious personality and interpreting the seen and
the unseen worlds of existence.   I speak of the subconscious and the conscious merely as convenient indica-
tions, for there is one self only.   This university of the
deeper self is open to all, but it demands fidelity, persistence and hard work as prerequisites to all promotion.
For this reason, open as the school is to all, the majority
of people ignore its mighty opportunities.   The excuses
given for such neglect are usually lack of time and the
demands of the physical life, but in almost all cases the
excuses are entirely invalid.   There are very few
people indeed who may not seize a little time each day
for splendid unfoldment of the soul, if only resolution
were capable of slighting innumerable unimportant
matters.   For this work does not necessarily require
books and freedom from confining labor, but may be
conducted during various occupations and under all
sorts of conditions.   The methods involved in such
personal education can, of course, be only indicated at
the present time, but certain propositions will now be
advanced which will suffice to set any earnest mind on
what I believe to be the right track.   These propositions are true and they are practicable as inspirations.

First Proposition: You can gain time for self-
culture if you persistently determine that you will.

Second Proposition: The four supremely important fields of human investigation are — the Self,

the Nature of Things in the Material and the Non-material Worlds, the Right Relations of Persons, and the Infinite.

Third Proposition: The Art of all Arts is the Art of Successful Self-Handling for all Legitimate Purposes.

Fourth Proposition: He who determines on knowing his own nature must proceed with two methods — *Observation* for Discovery of the Facts, and *Interpretation* for Understanding of their Significance. No prejudice for or against fact or meaning may be tolerated in this study. If you will devote a year to the investigation of your self, getting at some of the *facts*, discovering what those facts *mean*, you will as certainly develop a sense of power as you will live. In this work such questions will be helpful as: What am I? What is body? What is matter? What is personality? What is soul? What is mind? What is the will? What are the main laws of my being? Wherein does my nature differ from that of other people? What is my character? What is right living? Am I living rightly? What is the law of mind's power over matter? What are my talents? My weaknesses? How may I develop and successfully use my powers? How may I correct my faults? etc., etc., etc.

Fifth Proposition: The study of the nature of things in the Seen and the Unseen Worlds is identical in character with the study of the self. As studies, both realms are objective to the investigator's self. Neither the outer world nor the inner self is more or less open than the other to the searching of the self. There comes a time in the self-unfoldment when it can no longer be said that the self is closer or more familiar to self than is the Universe in which it lives, or that the Universe is greater or more mysterious than the self, but the self then seems to embrace the Universe and the Universe seems to abide in the self. Thus, following the suggestions of the preceding paragraphs, we may now ask, as examples of study — What is Reality? Truth? Law? Force? Power? Unfoldment? Agency? Achievement? Harmony? Beauty? Life? Love? How came the world? What does it mean? What is my place in time and space? What are Time and Space? Cause? Character? Government? Etc., etc., etc.

Sixth Proposition: All right life is balance, and he alone lives rightly who, if left the sole individual in the Universe, would justify the Universe and hold it together. Our questions here are: Do I balance my fellows so far as they are right? Do I contribute toward the realization of their right relations? Do I mean equilibrium in the home, school, place of business, lodge, church, company, community, state, nation? What are the fundamental laws of human harmony or balance? What are the basic causes of disturbance of harmonious equilibrium among men? What are some of the right methods for removing the disturbing causes and restoring harmony? Do I exhibit the virtues and habits that make for human welfare? Are my relations to others right? Etc., etc.

Seventh Proposition: The Infinite resides in man, or, in finite personality, and therein alone, for Nature is Thought, it is not the Infinite Thinker, and the Infinite can only be found by the individual within his own soul or self. The truth is: you *are* all right things you know about. This does not mean that you alone exist. It means that, while innumerable things actually exist besides yourself, you find them only through your self, and, in that sense, in your self, and as you know them they are you. You, therefore, are your

own courage, faith, work, law, method, destiny; you
are the world of Nature, the kingdoms of the unseen,
time, space, cause, effect, law, truth, power; you are
yourself, your Universe, your philosophy, your religion,
your creator of a God, so far as you know about these
realities. All you know of such realities is your own
thought. Your Nature-world is not yonder, but within
you. Your Man-world is not yonder, but within. Your
Unseen-Universe-Thought-world is not yonder, but
within. Your God is not yonder, but within. Whatever, then, you make your realms of thought, that you
are. If your thought of self is little, you are little. If
your thought of self is cowardly, you are cowardly. If
your thought of life is pessimistic, you are a failure.
If your Man-Thought is small, you are small. If your
Unseen-Universe-Thought is poverty-stricken, you are
poverty-stricken. If your God-Thought is half devil,
or weak, or blurred, you are precisely so. Thus it is
in every direction, and thus it ever will be. But if,
on the contrary, your thought-Self, thought-Nature,
thought-Unseen, thought-God is in each case great and
marvelous and infinitely worth while, then you are
great and marvelous and infinitely worth while. And
always it is The Infinite discovered in self which adds
splendor to existence and makes the All-Good adorable.

I have indulged in these large sentences because I
have desired to stimulate you to "sit up and take
notice." A great soul you are if only you discover the
fact. That great self need not bemoan any lack of
time or school or opportunity for unfoldment. All
the time there is belongs to you, and the greatest university on earth is your self. The realms of vital
reality and beauty are all yours if you will but resolve

upon their acquisition.   I have merely offered a few
suggestions, and yet here you have presented work for
a lifetime — aye, for an eternity.   Some of you will
smile and go on in the old, old way, timid, ignorant,
suspicious, sensitive, poverty-stricken in mind and
purse.   Of course.   But some of you will brace to the
task of self-culture possible to all and the unfoldment
of power and courage, and to such valiant souls I say,
"All things are yours."

FOURTH REMEDY: *Developing Desire For Courage.*
Here lies the secret of failure in reform of self — the
want of adequate desire.   There is a large amount of
jelly-philosophy current about the weakness of the
human will.   Men are unable, it is said, to omit whiskey
from life because they lack the necessary power of will.
This is not true.   All the power any man needs (outside
of hospital patients), that man already possesses if
only he really desires to use his power.   But the reality
of desire is not measured by a mere thought: it means
willingness to suffer the pangs of the self brought into
unaccustomed and right lines of living.   If one wants a
thing enough to will to suffer what its gain costs in his
particular case, he can certainly attain it.   It is at
precisely this point that lack of will appears.   The soul
resolves; then it begins to suffer; then it desires relief
from suffering more than it desires victory; then it
fails.   Given the wrong balance of desire, and the
failure is inevitable.   If, when it begins to suffer and
to whine for relief, it steadfastly wills the reform-desire
vigorously in consciousness, and with "shut teeth"
says, "This suffering cannot be helped, it is the price
of liberty, and this soul does and shall consent to pay
the whole price of freedom!" then strength creeps in, a
laggard, but sure, and the effort is notched one key

higher. Repeat the process long enough, and the thing is done; there is no other outcome.

This general truth, I concede, does not solve all will-problems. It would seem that some people are really unable to consent to suffering. Nevertheless, the truth is a large element in every question of this kind. Your ability to conquer any evil is simply your ability to pay the suffer-price involved. In the case of timidity the suffer-price is the inconvenience, time and labor required in the application of the detail methods indicated, together with resolute contact with all sorts of people in unusual conditions of your life.

FIFTH REMEDY: *Faith in the Present Effort.* Faith conceived as the affirmatively expectant attitude of the whole self, is one of the mightiest powers in this world. It is the fundamental element in auto-suggestion. You are therefore invited to make your entire thought and life a suggestion to self that these directions faithfully carried out will infallibly eliminate from your nature the feeling of timidity and its accompanying distress. The practical method therefor is the daily affirmation, "I have boundless faith in the instructions of '*Culture of Courage.*'"

SIXTH REMEDY: *Determination Not to Give Up.* Faith without works is merely a "say-so." Real faith is confident action toward a goal. The continuation of such action measures the kind and power of faith supposed. You should, therefore, determine to persevere — a thousand years if necessary, for you are yourself everlasting, if you will. But let it be remembered that mere resolution is only one-half of real determination. Some people resolve — and then resolve, never achieving victory. Others put "bite" into the matter in hand once for all, and do not seem to know how to let go. The only cure for resolution is determination, for determination is just doing the thing resolved upon.

SEVENTH REMEDY: *Assuming the Thing Now Accomplished.* The soul which says, "I am going to overcome," will very likely fail. The leverage runs too far into the future. *A valiant will always acts on a short lever!* You should, therefore, declare: "I *am* overcoming! The thing is *now* being accomplished! The matter in hand *is* mastered!" This may seem a trifle false, but it is more than a trifle true if you really mean it. When a man swears the needed thing now, it is by so much already done in his will, and a good deal of it, unknown to him, is accomplished in the concrete.

EIGHTH REMEDY: *Creating the Mood of Courage.* In order to develop a general background of right mentality, you are now invited to summon and maintain the mood of courage. Courage should be made a working part of your life. Any personal mood, and hence that of courage, may be initiated or assumed, and the assumption may be gradually transformed into a real element of the individual character. The method for creating the mood of courage is simple: put your mind in the attitude of fearlessness by incessantly thinking, "I fear nothing," and go on to act in conduct as though you were naturally possessed of indomitable courage. Even if you must begin with more or less bluster in order to maintain the feeling by some outward manifestation, do not fear that others will discover your effort, for people are not nearly so keen of insight, at least so investigating, as you might suppose. In time the difficulty which you are fighting

will tone down any undue expression of your courage.
If you begin with bluster and continue with persistency,
you will overcome shyness, bashfulness, timidity, and
yet not be offensively bold.   And so far as boldness is
concerned, that will never be your trouble, and apprehension thereof you should now once for all put entirely
out of mind,

NINTH REMEDY: *Building the Ideal Without
Worry.*   Worry-brooding merely develops more worry,
and, in your case, more timidity as well.   Such a state
of mind is a perfect hot-house for the unfoldment of a
thousand ills.   Souls that are healthy all round never
worry.   The method for banishment of this distressful
feeling consists in forcing a better personal sense and
a better thought, which may be accomplished by
practising instant refusal to worry, to entertain that
condition of mind, under any circumstance, at any
provocation.   This method requires considerable patience and persistence, but in the end it means killing
worry outright.   In the meantime, the goal of freedom
should constantly be idealized and held in view as an
unceasingly attractive prize which you surely will win.

You may say, perhaps: "Why, I do not worry
about my timidity; it is my nature, and I simply accept
the fact and make the most of it."   In that case, I
should almost advise you to worry, because the diffident
person distresses other people while remaining a mere
fraction of a human being.   Those whom you meet are
compelled perpetually to adjust themselves to your case,
to be inconveniently careful about your feelings, and
to put themselves out in various ways in order to avoid
hurting you.   Now, that sort of thing is out of all
reason.   None of us relish walking about "on eggs."
You really have no right to make such demands upon

common good nature. You should therefore take your own case in hand for the sake of relieving other people of unnecessary trouble. I know several timid souls for whom one must always do a great deal of social fussing; they must be introduced, must be looked up and dragged out of holes into which they have crawled, must, in a word, be nursed and coddled until one might almost wish they would form a society of diffidence and herd all together. If you are of this tender, sensitive class, then, you ought to brace to a little effort looking toward a measure of unselfishness on your own part.

Nevertheless, the remedy does not involve thought in the nature of worry, but rather the determination to take a stand among people as able to care for self in all social relations, thinking always of entire ability to do so, of ability now in exercise, and of the idea as wholly free from all thought of worry or personal distress. In other words, you are urged to strip the courage-mood of every atom of worry or doubt by maintaining constantly the ideal in mind of yourself perfectly self-possessed among all classes of people and under any conceivable circumstance!

TENTH REMEDY: *Dismission of the Shrinking Disposition.* This remedy is very similar to the foregoing, but is given because it may suggest a somewhat different phase of the work. You are urged to dismiss from all thought the notion of your shrinking disposition, by putting it instantly away whenever it arises in consciousness and immediately thinking of some agreeable subject suggestive of courage. You will find it helpful in this effort to *imagine yourself as carrying on a lively conversation with some person in whose presence you are usually timid and as being consciously on a level with such person and entirely at ease.* This regime is of great value, and should be persistently practised for a period long enough to make such imaginary states of the self habituated and usual.

ELEVENTH REMEDY: *Forgetting Self.* The secret of timidity, diffidence, bashfulness, shrinking, and the like, lies in the auto-suggestion of perpetual and pronounced self-consciousness. You are abnormally self-conscious in the presence of others, and certain physical effects follow which in turn react upon the mind: the lips tremble, the hands are in the way, the breath is unnatural, the voice is low, and so on. I might, therefore, advise suppression of these physical signs, for the moment one becomes conscious of them timidity increases. *Fear feeds on bodily expression.* It is, indeed, helpful to force down, so to speak, all such manifestations by a resolute bracing of the self against them — that is, in some cases. But in view of the fact that such an effort may in other cases only accentuate the trouble, I suggest a better method, at least an additional one, which consists in acquiring the art of self-forgetfulness, since, when one is unconscious of self, timidity and its distress must necessarily vanish.

In order to this diminution of awareness of self, you should practise trying to place your thoughts on those with whom you are timid, when in their presence, as being homely, awkward, conceited, blustering, ignorant, selfish, and the like; or, as being handsome, agreeable, well-informed, friendly, etc.,— but never as being superior,— so that you cease to think of yourself and have only such thoughts about others as will tend to eliminate occasion for timidity when with them. During the continuation of this regime, which may consume months, you are urged to engage in conversation with the people with whom you are nervous, always seeking to bring the matter around to some field in which you are especially at home. In so doing, you will obtain a double result: you will interest your hearer because you know your subject and can give him information unfamiliar to him, and you will become interested in the conversation yourself, and thus in the warmth of a two-fold interest your self-consciousness will tend to wear away. If conversation, now, should chance to be out of the question, you can at least concentrate your powers on the task of pleasing the other person, and thus, again, succeed in forgetting self. The main principle suggested in this remedy is the law that timidity is lost in self-forgetfulness, and any method which involves that principle, whether those above given or such as you may yourself devise, will prove helpful.

TWELFTH REMEDY: *Maintaining the Attitude of External Interest.* One characteristic of the timid person is the self-centre. Such an one does not mean, perhaps, to be selfish, yet himself is nevertheless and naturally the centre of feeling and thought. If this is your trouble, you need to "get out of yourself," to shift the main point of interest. You are urged, then, to become interested, not necessarily in others as a matter of theory or concession, but in what others are saying and doing, both in your thought and in your conduct or contact with them. It will assist you in this effort to maintain in the presence of others the attitude of external interest. By so much will you cease thinking of yourself, of your gestures, of your manners, of what others may be thinking or saying about you. In connection with this, it will be well to cultivate indifference as to whether or not you attract or please people in general, or as to any sort of opinion you may or may not inspire. Such indifference, of course, is not an ideal for the common life, but it is a necessity in the case of the timid person because it braces him against his fault and helps him to overcome it. If you will begin the work by assuming the external signs of interest in thoughts and doings not your own, you will find something of real interest springing up, and, in the meantime the self-consciousness of timidity will by so much decrease in your life.

There are, to be sure, certain constitutional phases of shyness, diffidence and awkwardness which appear to be exceedingly stubborn in refusing to yield to self-discipline. Some of our greatest souls are thus handicapped through life. Nathaniel Hawthorne was never able to overcome shyness and consciousness of his own manners. But Hawthorne was more or less recluse, and who shall say that his efforts for mastery in this matter were really intelligent and persistent. It is exactly in point that Archbishop Whateley, who tried imitation of others, and failed, finally discovered for himself the secret of freedom from embarrassment, as will be seen in the following remarks:

"Why should I endure this torment all my life to no purpose? I would bear it still if there were any success to be hoped for; but since there is none, I will die quietly without taking any more doses. I have tried my very utmost, and find that I must be as awkward as a bear all my life, in spite of it. I will endeavor to think as little about it as a bear, and make up my mind to endure what can't be cured." Then his shyness disappeared, because he thought no more about the matter than a bear would have thought. Afterwards he wrote: "I succeeded beyond my expectations; for I not only got rid of the personal suffering of shyness, but also of most of those faults of manner which consciousness produces, . . . and therefore giving expression to that good will towards men which I really felt; and these, I believe, are the main points."

THIRTEENTH REMEDY: *Meeting People Half-Way.* I organized a men's club "for the sake of the other man." Here gathered scholars and "carriage men," successful business men and odd-job men, with every other sort. Immediately segregation began. The self-possessed people fell into groups here and there, and the timid kind unerringly got together and hunted up the retired corners. Not in ten centuries will you acquire confidence by herding with timid folk. There is but one thing for the timid to do: elbow their way up to the other variety of human nature and get used to the feeling of being there. This method may seem very "forward," but forwardness is always a small vice at the worst, and in the timid person it will prove a pronounced virtue. As a matter of fact, the timid man's suggestion about "forwardness" is merely his excuse for remaining timid. So fine a degree of modesty amounts to nothing in your case. If you have that virtue "down fine," you have the vice of diffidence "up large," and life will bear a better balance. You are, therefore, urged to seek opportunities for meeting people of all sorts, as often as possible, refusing to yield to your shrinking impulses. And when the opportunity is yours, you are urged to "go half-way" or more in the meeting, for the sake of getting used to the idea and the act of making the advance, which means, a contribution toward your cure. Those whom you will meet will always be glad to receive your advance if they are worth while, and you may, by the very determination of making the advance, come finally to a beautiful indifference in regard to those who are not worth while. Indeed, you will see that the person who does not meet you in a friendly way is precisely of the other class — not at all worth anybody's while. Let no man suffer fools to upset his peace of mind.

FOURTEENTH REMEDY: *Curing Fear of Criticism.* Timidity, diffidence, awkwardness, usually feed upon fears of possible unkind opinions beld by those one meets. Although you may not have analyzed the trouble, in your unconscious self you are afraid that others may or do think illy of you. But this means, in other words, that you are already thinking ill of other people. You meet men and women, and immediately entertain the poor opinion of them that they are thinking poorly of yourself. You can lay aside this habit. You can cultivate the habit of thinking well of others, and, hence, of assuming that they think well of you. You need not imagine that they admire you; it is enough that you cease judging them in advance as unkind critics of their fellows. You can think of them as honest, sincere, kindly disposed. This will infallibly help you. The moment one begins to entertain agreeable thoughts concerning his fellows, that moment one begins in some degree to be interested in them, and by so much to forget one's self. And then timidity and embarrassment disappear.

FIFTEENTH REMEDY: *Recalling Mistaken Fears.* One said to me: "When I first met you, I was afraid of you. It 's different now." But I had not changed. His former fear I laughed at. He saw at last how groundless his timidity had been — for I was merely an ordinary human being, "pegging away" at my life's work. Doubtless there are those with whom you also

are now at ease but whom you once feared. You see
that your timidity was a mistake and utterly useless.
It is precisely so in every other case. You are therefore urged to review your history and to profit by the
errors of the past.

SIXTEENTH REMEDY: *Scotching Suspicion.* The
timid person is almost invariably suspicious, though
frequently unaware of the fact, imagining all sorts of
criticism and ridicule on the part of others, and thus
creating occasion for his diffidence. This condition of
mind reacts, of course, upon himself. The suspicious
soul telepathically suggests the superior feeling to
those with whom he comes in contact, and so arouses
what he fears, or induces effort to be rid of that feeling,
and thus causes in them a doubly disagreeable state,
superiority and the revulsion against it, which state is
naturally connected with its cause. For your own
sake, then, you are urged to thrust aside all suspicious
feelings as indicating a mere characteristic or habit
because they are unworthy of you and will surely react
in an evil way against you.

SEVENTEENTH REMEDY: *Ignoring Boors.* The
above suggestions have in mind, of course, the average
quality of human nature. There are those, however,
who are not amenable to the laws of courtesy, of whom
one can scarcely think well and in whose affairs only
saints can become interested. Against the coarse,
open brutality of such people no regime is practicable,
so far as timidity is concerned, save the cultivation of
total indifference toward them. Timid souls would
best avoid this class. If you must have dealings
with them, indifference seems to be your own only
recourse. It will assist you in securing that attitude
if you will remember and always assume that you are

really their superiors and therefore have no occasion for being nervous in their presence. You need to develop a mood which will make you at ease with such people, and this you can do by asserting your will-power against your tendency to timidity and in favor of your superiority above them. A suggestive sentence would insist in this way: "I will not fear you, for I am certainly your superior and have not the least occasion for timidity."

EIGHTEENTH REMEDY: *Cultivating Egotism.* One of the main factors in the cure of timidity consists in a comfortable feeling about one's self. You observe that the genuine egotist is never shy if he is of the assertive variety. He is not a coward; never awkward or nervous; does not know how to be gloomy or depressed; is incapable of laziness; will not permit himself to be a beggar. He is courageous, easy in manner, of good nerve-tone, cheerful, hopeful, inspiring, industrious, pays as he goes. He gets on. He brings things around. He makes the world lively. He carries sunshine with him. He is alert, curious, quick, inventive, a creator of values. He is an incurable species of humanity, for he needs no cure. His egotism is an asset. The world wants him, not cured, but raw, exactly as he is. We do not like him, but we all know his worth. He thinks well of himself, for the reason that he really is something to think well of. His mood, his attitude toward himself and the whole earth as his own, are preëminently worth while. Every timid person who despises him might imitate his egotism with great advantage to himself. The egotist is the scared man's very best example. It is not worth while to underestimate the self. Overestimation of self, if accompanied by great and well-directed will-power and ambition, is an inexhaustible source of energy and inspiration.

You are urged, therefore, to think well of yourself. You are in the habit of thinking ill of yourself, at least in some respect related to your timidity.   How can you expect others to think well of you when you depreciate your own value?   You must improve your self-estimate by persistently suggesting to your deeper mind various good and admirable qualities which you possess, by enumerating frequently your pleasing traits and abilties, and by seeking to develop them and to cultivate others as they are brought to your attention.   In the meantime, you should conduct yourself exactly like a genuine egotist, ignoring all fear of criticism in others, and browbeating your way through all opposition, whether created by outside agencies or by your own inner experience.   In time your affected egotism will come to a reasonable balance with your natural modesty, the latter growing less and the manner of egotism imparting to your inner self a better actual self-estimate. A "new birth" will take place: you will discover the courage-soul in the room of the old timidity.

NINETEENTH REMEDY: *In Touch with the White Life.*   Above all, one who is determined to cure in himself these varieties of fear must keep himself in touch with the Universal Goodness.   I do not refer to religious ceremonies or theological methods. This touch of harmony is as old as the race; it is harmony, with consciousness, of feeling, of thought, of will, of conduct, with the well-wishing infinite System in which we live. It is a sense of oneness with all that is good, and true, and beautiful. It is the inner possession of the White Life. That is peace, self-poise, and it means courage.

How may the touch of the White Life be secured? As frequently as may be convenient, you should go apart by yourself where quietness reigns. If this is at any time impracticable, you can shut the world away from thought, and shut yourself into yourself. Now think of your soul as the center of all existence, and proceed to imagine innumerable light-rays pouring from every point of space in toward yourself,— falling quietly and incessantly upon your innermost self's centre. Think of these light-rays not as unmeaning things coming toward you, but as forces raining into you — light, life, power, beauty, goodness, courage. When this feeling of receptivity is secured, think of yourself as living the *white life*, and resolve that in all things a *white life* you surely will become. Then send out in thought upon the countless rays of light imagined intense and honest well-wishing to every existence, animal, human, unseen — all save evil, of which think not at all. Make this communion with the White Life a daily regime. You will as certainly come to a larger life as the dawn will follow the night, and in that larger life, if you have endeavored to observe the remedies given in this chapter, will infallibly emerge a courage for people and events which will become to you as the breath of morning and the inspiration of a new discovery.

FEAR NOT THY FELLOWS.

Fear not thy fellows:
For some are *slaves* — be free, and assist;
And some are *ignorant* — be wise, and teach
And some are *enemies* —
Selfish and blind, they seek to do thee hurt
For what they misconceive as gain —
Be valiant, and make their good thine own;
And some are *false* — be model of a golden honesty;
And some are *lovers* — love better, and all worship sanctify
And, if Grief catch thee with another's hand,
Leap to thy centre-consciousness serene,
"I am! I am Power!"
Nathless in the impenetrable Holy
Of unimpeachable motive.
                                        — THE AUTHOR.

CHAPTER IX.

Some People We Fear.

"The man who, outside of pure mathematics, pronounces the word impossible, lacks prudence."— *Arago.*

ONE Universe there is, essentially the same in all its parts — of the essence of Mind.

To the Universe observed objectively we give the name, matter.

To the Universe observed subjectively we give the name, mind-self.

If the objective Universe is essentially Mind, it knows itself as mind only.

If the human self expresses in body, it knows itself as psycho-physical.

Matter to itself, then, is expressed Mind.

The self-mind is existing and expressing mind.

To the human self the Mind-Universe is objectively expressed as matter, and subjectively in the psychic factor.

All expression, in either case, is conducted by signs — marks, traits, or the like, which are susceptible of interpretation by knowing mind. Both the Universal Mind and the human mind-self can only know either mind and the self through the signs of mind-activities. The discovery and interpretation of such signs bulks so large in the mental life that it has only one other rival, the using of such interpretation in the interest of the completest personal being.

The Universe a System of Signs.

The world we live in, including all other humans besides your self, constitutes, as expressed in external form, a vast and complex system of individual and more or less definitive signs, since that world is a vast and complex expression of mental reality. Nature is like a huge manuscript written by an Unseen Hand, some of the letters of which move about from place to place, while others appear to remain in a stationary position. As the characters on a written page are signs which we have learned to understand, so the world of things consists of signs which suggest or induce in us certain mental activities by way of interpretation. In becoming acquainted with Nature, your mind, your knowing self, does not go out to objects external, nor do the latter pass into the self. Disregarding the body, it is to be understood that nothing goes out of the self or into the self in the act of knowing the external world. The world of objects exists and remains outside the knowing self, exists in the objects as signs which induce or suggest innumerable thoughts and feelings in the observer. What we know of these signs is simply our interpretation of them: it is what we conclude they are and mean.

The successful human life, then, involves, for example, three questions: What are the facts about us — the signs or realities as they actually are? What attitude toward such signs or objects or facts and their sure meanings is best for individual welfare? How shall we successfully apply that attitude?

Personal unfoldment consists in trying to answer these questions in such a practical way as to "make good" for the most truly successful life.

Let us now ask what these object-signs are in the world of Nature.

NATURE AND HUMANITY ARE MOVEMENT-SIGNS.

Our first study concerns movement, one of the things hardest to be explained in the whole Universe. The world seems to consist, as science informs us from its necessary point of view, of matter and force. But the word ''matter'' is merely a sign, written, printed, thought, spoken, for a certain other sign, the external ''matter itself''— which also is to the human mind none other than just a sign of some reality objectively observed. The first sign is a word; the word-sign stands for the something-sign. We understand the word-sign; we form some notions about the something-sign; but the essence of the latter sign no one knows, or ever will know, since the sign is of mind-reality, and mind to itself is essentially unknowable save as a system of activities. Nevertheless, we all agree that the something actually exists, for otherwise we should not have the word-sign and the thought-sign at all.

The word "force" is also a sign, and it stands for—simply an idea. Force can no more be explained than can motion. Force in itself is always an inference from observed activity, but no one has discovered the essence of what is called force. Matter and force are inferences, but movement is beyond doubt, whatever its origin.

The thinkers of the ages, discovering perfectly evident motion everywhere, began thousands of years ago to surmise that things which are apparently inert were nevertheless incessantly active. The birth of chemistry confirmed these surmises, and led to the

modern conclusion, which is a scientific re-statement
of old Greek guessing, that all things involve absolutely
ceaseless movement within themselves. When we
run this conclusion down, it is seen that it is only
true for science, since in a Universe which is essentially
all mind there can really be neither space nor motion,
but only conditions and changes in the Universal
Mind's Thoughts. For practical purposes, however,
the conclusion must be accepted. On examination,
the conclusion assumes two forms: the metaphysical,
that all things are in a state of flux, are forever becoming and forever ceasing; and the physical or
chemical, that all things are what they are because
of molecular activity. Thus the world of material
Nature and physical man is simply a huge system of
movement.

MATTER AND ETHER.

Formerly we were told that matter is composed
of molecules, which in turn consisted of atoms, the
smallest divisible particles of matter, and that the
molecules were active or moved in grosser matter,
or among themselves, while the atoms performed
similarly within the molecules. To-day such molecules and atoms are regarded as very "lumpish" affairs,
for we now believe that the atom itself is an assemblage
of "corpuscles." Yet here also, incessant activity
prevails, for the final constituents are forever engaged
in movement of inconceivable rapidity, at the rate
of from 10,000 miles to 90,000 miles a second.

When we ask science what the corpuscles are,
one of the latest answers refers us to electricity. "Any
mass of matter is x-molecules, a molecule is y-atom,
an atom is z-corpuscles surrounded by positive electric-

ity, and a corpuscle consists of a unit of negative electricity." Matter, then, consists of a certain definite number of established or more or less permanent modes of motion, and the innumerable objects of Nature, so far as concerns their material, are thus seen to be simply varieties or individual specimens of etheric movement.

Nothing exists save as it acts, and it is action that constitutes things themselves. Nature, including man, is a vast complex of movements which, as observed by us, become movement-signs. These movement-signs we investigate and interpret, and with the interpretation, corresponding in a way, and thus varying, with everything that exists, we build our thought and the whole philosophy of life.

If, now, any material object is simply a kind of established motion of the ether within the ether, the human body is precisely the same. And whatever may be said as to the nature of life, it is also exactly this, so it would seem: a mode of motion within material molecules (since we know it only in connection with matter), and motion of the ether within the ether (since molecules themselves are such modes of motion). Whatever, again, may be said as to the nature of conscious thought, since it takes place within the material brain, it is, as well, precisely a mode of motion involving ether within ether.

The law of inertia forbids that we refer the origin of that motion to the ether itself, for such reference would require that we conceive some original ether without motion, which is inconceivable under the law that a medium not in motion cannot begin motion without the agency of some external force; the original motionless ether can stir "neither hand nor foot"

until moved upon by reality apart from itself. Even
if life be indeed a mode of motion, the specific character
of that motion may differ from other forms of motion,
say, gravitation, or heat. We may not affirm that
life, a movement within ether, is identical with molecular action, a movement within the ether, simply because
we do not know. But we may say, that life, whatever
the character of it, emerges in motion of the ether within itself. Similarly, the exact kind of etheric movement involved in consciousness and thought would
not necessarily, even if we knew it, resolve itself into
a motion identical with that represented by molecular
action in the brain, for the one movement, though
associated with the other, may stand for a very different reality. Our personality involves innumerable
etheric movements, but it cannot be set down, offhand
as the same in origin and nature with the movements
which constitute physical nature. To say that because
matter is always associated with life, matter is life,
or life is an expression of matter, is equivalent to
saying that because houses are associated with men,
men are houses, or houses are men, or men are expressions of houses. The conclusion may be true, but it is
not demanded by the association, and the reverse
may be true as well.

Your Self and the Ether.

We are justified, therefore, in affirming only:
that the human personality consists of a complex
system of activities or movements which take place
within the material body, so that all such movements
are fundamentally activities of the ether within itself,
it may be occurring laterally, or in undulations, or in
rings, etc., and that of these movements some are

induced by the outside world, some by life acting in
the body-realm, some by the psychic self.

As we may think of a tree as a system of etheric
motions or activities located in one general place,
or of a bird as a similar system capable of transfer
in toto from place to place, so may we think of human
beings as moving systems or centres of activity
occurring in the ether and capable of voluntary transfer therein. Personality is a definite, though never
clearly limited, sphere of such activities, in which
the physical and psychic factors play mutual parts.
Be the psychic factor what it may, it dominates more
or less, and ought to dominate entirely, the physical.
Inasmuch as flesh, bones, nerves and blood are merely
forms of etheric action established as forms, the
general state of activity in the body influences the
surrounding mass of the medium, for *a centre of force
immersed in a medium of which itself is a part, must
disturb that medium by its activities*. Personality, then,
really involves a complex of motions *beyond its con-
stituent ether*, setting up many varieties of movement
in its immediate surrounding neighborhood by way
of transmitted and transformed motion, in straight
lines, vibrations, vortices, and so on. Your personal
sphere of unseen activities is larger than the bodily
outlines, some movements which you originate running
"the diameter of the Universe," most of them, however, being condensed, so to speak, within a comparatively small area, and all springing up throughout
the physical structure incessantly during life.

In the purely physical functions of the body, as,
say, the circulatory system, heart, lungs, stomach,
nerves, etc., the activities involving the ether are
more or less regular, and are conducted without con-

scious effort.   The movements which indicate volition,
thought and feeling, however, while regular in their
larger phases because they are the products of psychic
habits, are nevertheless incessantly varied and to a
degree confused.

The average person, then, represents a system
of very complex ether-movements, some of which are
automatically regular, some of which are volitionally
regular, and very many of which are exceedingly
irregular and constantly modified and changed in
all sorts of ways under the varying conditions of life.

It is at this point that the difficulties pertaining
to personal relations appear.

RIGHT LIVING INVOLVES RIGHT ETHERIC ADJUSTMENTS

If you will imagine a sphere several feet in diameter consisting of complex movements of some perfectly transparent jelly-like medium, and if you will
suppose yourself occupying that sphere and causing
such movements, and then remember that you are
surrounded by thousands of other spheres (personalities)
each a dweller within a similar sphere and constituting the activities and characteristics of that sphere,
you will see that we are all not only causing disturbances in the Universal Medium, but also receiving into
our own sphere movements induced by others.

Recalling, now, the thought that Nature is a
vast system of sign-objects, that is, of movement-
signs, it is evident that, if we are to understand Nature
and her objects, we must learn to discover the sure
meaning of such signs.   Precisely so is it with regard
to human beings.   A human being is to each of us
simply a sign of some existence which we have learned
to interpret as "man," or "woman," or "boy," or

"girl," or "John," or "Mary,"— this or that kind of individual human. This learning how to interpret personal sign is one of the most important things in life, because it is the first step toward that right adjustment of self to others which insures greatest success in practical and ideal living. Thus we come to

A PRELIMINARY PRACTICAL REGIME IN THE PRESENT WORK: *Reading Personal Signs in General.* You are now invited to engage in a study of the people whom you know, trying always to solve this question: *What kind of sign is each man or woman I meet to me?* A sign, for example, of dullness, brightness; slowness, quickness ; irritability, calmness; close, free-handed; morose, cheerful; tricky, honest; low, honorable; etc., etc. If you will proceed in this way, deciding always why you come to your conclusions, you will ere long develop a clean-cut understanding of the people you meet, so far as their external signs indicate; you will, that is, be able to interpret their personality-signs, and thus learn how the most effectively to adjust yourself to them in practical affairs. For detail methods of adjustment you are referred to the author's work, *"Power For Success,"* which fully discusses this important subject.

The question, now presented a second time, What is the relation which the individual must come into with other people for his own greatest welfare? involves just this matter of interpretation of personality-signs which we have indicated. The truth is that we do not reach our highest attainments because we do not adequately know the signs of men and women with whom we deal. But the completest relation involves not only correct interpretation, but also right adjustment to the persons whose signs we interpret. If we interpret them incorrectly, our adjustments will be false or misleading. If we interpret them correctly, we may, nevertheless, fail in the best adjustments. It comes out, then, that life is no matter of mere happy-go-lucky, hit-or-miss contact with people, but really a wonderful science requiring the very best in us properly to master. And, since no one is great enough to master the innumerable details of this science, we are left to acquire and practise the great trunk-line principles which human experience has proved to be the most surely calculated to make for development and success. These fundamental principle are the moral laws and the dictates of what we call common sense. And common sense has worked out this *universal law:* that *if you desire to get on with people, you must find out what their personality means* — must interpret their self-signs — and so adjust yourself to them as to secure some kind of harmony with them or to repel or control any of the etheric movements which may proceed from their personal spheres and enter or strive to enter your own.

These two phases of every human being's life-work, *interpretation* of personality-signs and *adjustment* to personal etheric spheres, either by harmony or control or repulsion, constitute the art of arts which is open to and possible by all who may read these pages.

Fear Means Surrender to Interpretation of Personality-Signs.

It is because you interpret the personality-signs erroneously, or, whether you interpret them incorrectly or correctly, yield to the interpretation, that fear or timidity and nervousness seize upon you in social or business contact. If you would say, in regard to

such signs: "These signs may be intended to awaken
fear, or they may be merely of a character suggestive
of fear to the common run of people, but I refuse to
so interpret them, and they do not mean fear to me;
now, how shall I adjust myself to them in such a way
as either to repel or control the etheric movements
which they indicate as seeking to enter my personal
sphere?"—if you would say thus, you would find yourself in time altogether free from the fears or nervousness which the signs usually induce. In other words,
you have it in your power, first, to learn what personality-signs are; secondly, to repel them if they signify
evil of any sort to yourself; and thirdly, to control
and use them for your own good, if not of a hostile
nature. This brings us to the practical work of the
present chapter.

ADJUSTMENT TO FEAR-SUGGESTING PERSONALITY-SIGNS.

You are therefore invited to practise the following
as long-continued regimes in your daily life.

The work now involved I indicate in two sections:
The Golden Regimes of the Masterful Self, and, *The
Iron Regimes of the Self Striving for Mastery*. Into
the second work must always be carried the first,
courageously and confidently.

I. THE GOLDEN REGIMES OF THE MASTERFUL SELF.

You are urged to practise for long the following
regimes:

FIRST — THE GOLDEN REGIME OF INNER ETHERIC
CONTROL. This regime consists in the constant reiteration, until it becomes the habituated idea of the self,
of the affirmation: "*I am now under perfect self-control,*

*quiet, powerful, fearless; my own etheric activities being
regular and harmonious, and all incoming movements
being reduced to order and subject to my will.*" This
sentence, or the substance of it, really and confidently
pronounced by the self, will quiet any burst of anger,
quell any impulse of fear-feeling, establish your inner
personality against any evil influence, and in time
bring you to splendid mastery of your entire self —
if only you will persist in the regime — and *act* accordingly.

SECOND — THE GOLDEN REGIME OF THE IMPERIAL
WALL. You have it in your power to build around
your personal ether-sphere a wall which no influence
can penetrate while you are on guard (as you may
habitually in the subconscious self become), without
your consent. You are invited to try the method following, asserting daily from time to time: "*I am not
only master of my personal sphere of the etheric activities,
but the subjective self of me is learning how to obey my
orders to wall out, by imperial degree, all things contrary
to my best interest — drawing a circle beyond the outer cir-
cumference of that sphere more potent and impenetrable for
protection than the mystic ring of Rome, so that I, within the confines of my own kingdom, am secure from all
assaults suggesting a fear or threatening evil.* The
king may not be disturbed in his castle, and I am
the king." This regime will ultimately give you
remarkable power in repelling the psychic assaults
of life, both from human beings and from invisible
hostile forces. Remember, and lay hold, and conquer!

THIRD —THE GOLDEN REGIME OF FRIENDLY
INVITATION. You are now urged to make the following a lifelong habit. In this regime you affirm for
many months: "*Master of my own personal field*

*of etheric activities, and surrounded by the Imperial
Wall of Exclusion against all seen and unseen hostilities,
I, nevertheless, preserve the utmost friendliness toward
all existences that are in harmony with human welfare,
and I send out to all the world the cry of Peace and Welfare,
and I open the Imperial Gates to every good and helpful
influence, my Citadel being even now a centre toward
which the Universal Forces and human helpfulness
flow steadily and unceasingly.* With all right lives
I harmonize! To all honest souls I go out in the spirit
of friendliness. All etheric movements meaning human
happiness I receive and bring into relation with my
own. Peace to the world, and co-operation!"

The purpose of these regimes is evident. If you
will observe them, you will infallibly find yourself
coming more and more to golden mastery of the self in
all your outlook on human life. In the meantime,
the Iron Regimes, which are practical in a detail sense,
will reinforce the Golden Regime and prove immensely
valuable in the growth of courage.

II. The Iron Regimes of the Self Striving for
Mastery.

In the preceding work there is a genuine striving of
the self for poise and control, of course, but the spirit
sought is more easily and more quickly secured,
perhaps, than are the practical details of the labor
now to be entered upon, and the idea of effort is therefore here more particularly emphasized. We have,
now, the following:

First Iron Regime: *Of Correct Interpretation.*
Remembering our theory of signs, we may formulate
a general sign-outline of the people we meet, as
follows:

The sign of the *sarcastic.*
The sign of the *ridiculer.*
The sign of the *egotist.*
The sign of the *brusque.*
The sign of the *crafty.*
The sign of the coldly *indifferent.*
The sign of the *rowdy.*
The sign of the consciously *superior.*
The sign of the *malevolent.*

This outline does not, of course, exhaust human nature, and is presented in no pessimistic mood of mind. A much longer indication of attractive signs might be worked out, since man, the world over, is more worthy than ignoble. The outline has its purpose in our study of fear and the growth of courage. We have here a fair list of the signs of people whom you, perhaps, fear, and the showing is made in order to suggest the remedies.

Fundamentally considered, the physical and the psychic life of all human beings correspond, field for field; there being one general physical life and one general psychic life covering the whole humanity. The chemistry of bodies is universally one, and one is the essence of the human self. In the common field of physical substance there are individual differences, of course, as in the blood, for example, wherein may lurk an excess of some one of the poisons contained in the Great Sympathetic System, which excess (or lack) may kill or induce insanity, or as in other functional structures, which may give the body some characteristic tendency. So, also, in the common psychic ground, variations appear which individualize the person. In either case the differences are due, it would seem, to departures from the general etheric

movements common to the whole of human nature.
Regarding the general movements as signs to which
we give current interpretations —"man," "woman,"
"health," "power," "attractiveness," etc., we may
say that certain etheric activities in the personal
field are interpreted as *kind* of man, woman, individual,
spirit, and so on. The *observed* signs are very evident
facts, but their *origin* lies in subtle, invisible etheric
activities in the physical (and by personal inclusion,
the psychic) fields, and if we could pass beyond the
cruder facts,— the facial expressions, the voice and
word, the external conduct,— we should still be dealing
with movement-signs — those of the ether within
itself.

If you observe smoke-rings, you know that here
is rotational movement; if the smoke streams away,
you know that here is an underlying transitional
movement; if the smoke volumes and billows, you
know that here is a chaos of movements. So the varying ether-movements reveal first in the crude or evident facts of life, indicating sarcastic, or cold, or brutal
dispositions, and the like. Your conclusions about
people are your interpretations of the signs that they
habitually carry on the outside. Interpretation,
then, is one of the tasks of life. It is error, however,
to rest content with the merely evident signs, but
we should seek to know the slighter and more difficult marks, since these originate in subtle etheric
activities and have to do with deeper realities of the
personal self. Such realities may, indeed, when
discovered, modify very greatly the interpretations
which are based on observation of the cruder personal
evidences. Thus, the sign of sarcasm may be frontal
to a further sign of actual kindness, that of coldness

may overlay simple dignity, or defensive reserve, or timidity, and so on.

Always, then, the handling of fear must involve correct interpretation of person-signs *taken together*, so far as these may be discovered. Securing such correct interpretation requires patience and intent observation and the controlling of conclusions until the latter seem inevitable. That sentence, indeed, outlines the essentials of all possible regimes for fears of the kind now before us. Fear is always in a hurry. I do not mean merely that its tendency is panic. I mean that the mind of fear is spasmodic, partial in its observation, hasty in its judgments. It welcomes signs that feed and stimulate its own nature; it moves by jerks and rushes; it grudges controlled deliberation. It wants the conclusions —"Cause for fear! Get away!" It is unable, of its own motion, to secure the interpretation —"No cause! Hold on! Fear-Sign modified! Now for the real facts!" Hence, the sarcastic person is always to be feared; the ridiculer is an occasion for agony; the egotist is a pest; the brusque is a bear; the crafty is like a snake; the cold is a block of ice; the superior is a judgment on "white trash;" and the malevolent has murder in his eye; — all when the very *reverse* may be true, if only the *inner* signs could be discovered. As a matter of fact, some sarcastic people carry the proverbial big heart of the ox. There are people who ridicule only those whom they love; it is mere play of affection. My friend, the gem expert, always has his sport at my expense when others are present, but his loyalty is unimpeachable. Similarly in the various cases mentioned above: the inner sign reverses hasty interpretation of the more evident. Even the malevolent

man may prove a coward. If there be a "boss"
devil, he exists because he fears the whole vast Universe. Every soul that entertains fear, banquets at
hell's table. Remember, and hold fast, and conquer!

We see, then, that the people we fear may have
been misunderstood. Along with every cure for this
sort of trouble, therefore, must go—

SECOND IRON REGIME: *Of Control for Interpretation.* This means the control of all fear-impulses
until the exact truth is discovered. If you fear the
varieties of people you meet as here outlined, your
remedy consists in affirming: *"I fear you not until
I know there is actual cause for fear."* You so affirm
and you thus suppress the impulse to yield to fear,
and so hold yourself courageously. Our life is a
satisfaction of impulses. The impulses spring from
very deep sources, at times; in body-tissue, perhaps;
even in the elemental cells. If an impulse of fear
arises, it must be substituted by an impulse of courage-
thought. You can train the tissue and cell and self
to satisfy in the fear-impulse by forever yielding to
the demand. You can train these factors to satisfy in
the opposite action by commanding the subconscious
self accordingly and thus by creating a tendency in
tissue and cell toward courage. The fear-impulse
habit *seems* preferable so far as satisfaction is concerned
because this satisfies not only the instinct of self-
preservation, but as well the feeling of self really
preserved. But the seeming is false. The outcome
of fear is the lessening of self; the reward of courage
is an increase of self. The satisfaction of self increased
is the supremest in all existence.

Thus, you should affirm as above, persistently
and confidently. Of course you do not perfectly

succeed at the first, for you are establishing a new mental habit, and one which "goes against the grain," and such a goal requires time and effort. But if you resolutely continue in the regime, you will infallibly conquer the rush-tendency of the fear involved.

In time you may still hold to your original interpretation of the external personal sign; you may still say, "Here is a sure sign for fear," but a strange thing will now appear: you will find that the *fear*-factor has become merely a *reason*-factor in the field of self-interest and self-preservation. The reason-factor displaces the fear-feeling. You will take care of yourself, but distressing emotions will have disappeared. The fearful person who can develop self-control for correct interpretation of fear-signs, will infallibly find simple reason-signs in their place. Since this book is a fear-killer, not a mystical body-guard against danger or hurt, our goal will in such case be fully realized. Whatever reason may say about the sarcastic person, or any other disturbing sort, fear as a feeling is now dead. The idea of fear has lost its power. Reason, like the white corpuscles of the blood, has devoured its enemy, fear.

REGIME CONTINUED. *Of Interpretation for Control.* It is useless to defer a judgment unless you seek a better one. The purpose of the preceding regime looked to the habit of suppressing impulse until justified. *Deferring fear long enough means starving it.* In the meantime, however, a correct interpretation must be sought by re-reading evident signs, by unearthing subtler signs which may modify the former, and by relating such subtler to the cruder signs observed. In other words, you are urged not to conclude that you ought to fear,— the sarcastic person, the cold, the brusque, and so on,-- but patiently to study your man and discover whether or no some deeper sign in his make-up may not appear which in itself shall modify your interpretation of him, and thus show that you have no occasion for fear at all. Here is a long regime, to be sure, yet one of the greatest value, since it is really practice in self-control and the elimination of the fear-impulse. If your final interpretation rids you of cause for fear, the result will amply repay your labor.

Nevertheless, this victory is only partial, and it is rather cheap at that. If you fear not one person or another merely because you have discovered no cause for fear — for example, that the supposedly crafty is honest according to his standard, the brusque really kind hearted, the malevolent a coward, and so on, you have not injured fear at all, but have simply left it ready for you on the very next occasion. The battle is yet on. If, then, you find that your original interpretation of the person dealt with was correct, that it still holds, unmodified by any fear-dispelling elements in his character, it remains to go on interpreting the facts correctly, exactly as they are. But when you do this, clearly and coolly, you actually begin to displace the fear-thought and fear-impulse by deliberate reason. You are trying to understand the situation, which is a matter that fear-feeling never does and never wants to do. Now, this is precisely our goal. You find out why you fear a person — meanwhile repressing the fear-thought and the fear-impulse and controlling self *for* a correct interpretation, and you thus discover that you have *bona fide* occasion for adjusting yourself to that person, for handling that person, one way or another, in your own rational self-interest; but no cause whatever for indulging the fear-feeling, because you now know him, and know exactly what to do with reference to his particular case. *If we know what a person is, how to handle him, then how can there be in him any cause for feeling afraid of him?* We have thus gotten rid of the fear-feeling, and have left — merely facts for reason to deal with. The person may still be dangerous, still design evil to us, but the case is now one for the steady address of reason, and all occasion for agitation or distress of any sort has vanished.

We come, then, to specific treatment of the fears indicated in the outline. The regimes that follow, like the preceding, it should be remembered, are to be applied as the case requires, now to a particular variety of people, now to several varieties, now to all varieties here listed or to your own thought suggested.

THIRD IRON REGIME: *Of Confession and Brotherhood for Raw Human Nature.* The most of us are still in the raw state of human nature. The "clay" of personality is "good stuff," but it is often angular, unpolished, irritating. In pain it becomes heated, and it cracks. By attrition it is rounded and smoothed, but it is also sometimes broken. It is — just as it is — packed into communities, societies, continents, centuries. And thus characteristics become jagged points, rough edges, afflictive surfaces.

Now, every piece of the human "clay" is tempted to *suppose* itself *whole, sound and right.* Each soul feels: "The difficulty lies in that man or that woman. These people are wrong, and they hurt me." Meanwhile, the raw nature of the self is apt to be ignored or unrecongized, and intolerable demands are wont to

be made upon other people to endure us and to afford
us comfort, profit and pleasure. And fearful people
are the most intolerable in this respect. For the things
noted are true in every human being. We are all more
or less undeveloped; we believe ourselves to be in
the right; we ask freedom for personal expression;
we desire that others shall be careful in relation to
ourselves — and we forget our own unfinished and
unreasonable state. We fear, and we wish a cure
for fear, yet we very slightly emphasize the fact that
we are as others are, and that these others may fear
also and have the same desire for freedom therefrom.
Ourselves are human; other people are — just occasions for fear, scarcely human, excessively disagreeable. Fear is the most selfish thing in the world.

You see, then, that we must return our minds to
fundamental facts. We also are in the raw. Other
people are really human.

You will find it wholesome and vastly helpful to
force yourself steadily to realize other people *in* their
human nature: more or less imperfect, more or less
ideal, always pursuing self-interest, in greater or less
bondage to one thing or another, disturbed by foolish
fears, trying to live, trying to adjust to life, trying
to succeed. You may often banish all sorts of uncomfortable thoughts, feelings and impulses by saying,
and repeating, and realizing: *"Why, that is just a man
—just a woman — a human being, the common nature
bulking large in him or her as also in me. That's my
brother — my sister. He and she would not hurt if
they knew me, since I wish them well, and I will see
to it that they do know me — as I am, wishing them
well."* You are commended to this attitude. To
brother the world is to build the king's courage.

The facts, however, that people are sarcastic, egotistic, supercilious, and the like, cannot be banished by mere theory, You who insist upon this truism are, therefore, invited to enter on a further regime given below.

FOURTH IRON REGIME: *Of Association with Sarcastic People.* When we become familiar with people, they seem somehow to have changed. At the first meeting, the very "newness," and some particular feature or characteristic, seize and hold our attention, and it is as if these things constituted the whole of the persons themselves. Later, however, other features and traits come into conscious view, with the result that the general appearance is by this fact more or less modified. So in our present study. The sarcastic person, for example, is never quite the same to you after acquaintance that he was at your first meeting with him. You often find that first impressions have not been exactly correct. It is for this reason that you are urged to acquire familiar first-hand knowledge of the sarcastic person's inner-self. In any event fear should never be based on mere hearsay. You may finally discover that this person's characteristic is entirely harmless after all — just a trait, a foible, not in the least an occasion for disturbance. In the meantime, it is suggested that you be master of the self and hold to the front the mood of confident courage. Do not suffer depression because you do not forthwith succeed in your efforts, but resolutely continue the regimes here set forth. Above all, do not avoid the cause of your fear. Rather associate with the sarcastic person, find him out, get used to him. During this effort, cultivate the smile of indifference and the feeling of being out of

reach of his shafts of wit and acid. The discovery by
this person that his sarcasm does not disturb you,
will destroy the zest of his indulgence, and the outcome
will be its discontinuance so far as you are concerned;
or, at any event, you will consciously escape his power.
If you lose the impulse of fear and the cringe of hurt
because your courage has lifted you into another
world, the goal is then attained. You now know
this person, are accustomed to his ways, and know
how to handle him, to adjust yourself in relation to
his habit, and so have gained the victory of freedom
from fear.

And remember, that the moods contrary to fear are
omnipotent in respect to its feeling and disturbance
by just so much as you secure and *control them from
the radiant centre of peace and good will.* To that
centre comes every soul possessed of the loftiest
courage. This is not a "preachment" on idealism or
being good; it is merely the very best sort of common
sense. Kirschoff, by means of the spectrum, discovered gold in the sun — the essence of gold. But
no man has ever discovered in that centre of fire
and light traces of sewerage or signs of a prize-fight,
because our sun is a consuming furnace. The true
radiant centre in any human soul always destroys
both hates and fears.

FOURTH IRON REGIME CONTINUED: *For People
Who Ridicule.* A further occasion for the present
regime is found in the fear of ridicule. Now, the
weight of ridicule depends upon its source. If it
proceeds from people who are beneath you, in your
knowledge of them, only the slightest effort, if any,
is required to ignore it. One may be laughed at by
inferior folk without a feeling of distress. Children

who shouted of old: "Go up, thou bald head!" did not deserve being devoured by bears — and no honor to the prophet or his primitive God that the history records the event as having taken place. The children knew no better — and the prophet *was* bald. Here is a symbol, then, of a class who indulge in ridicule. You need not fear fear thus caused, because such fear is itself ridiculous. The trouble with your distress on account of ridicule, however, is not so easily disposed of, since its secret is the fact that the occasion may actually obtain in yourself. There may be reason for such ridicule. This suggests the following regime:

FIFTH IRON REGIME: *Of Self-Reform.* If it is only when ridicule arises within your own ranks of life, or from superior ranks, that fear seems to be justified, then it is suggested that you do all in your power to remove any possible occasion therefor. Let us understand, however, that the fear-feeling (and it is this only that hurts) is never justified by any kind of fact or condition in life. The thing which may be justified is reason, based on facts, and acting calmly in wholesome self-interest. Such reason always wants to know what the facts are. If the facts are that the fearing person is open to ridicule — or the irresistible smile — and exposes himself thereto, those facts are either beyond his control or they are subject to removal. In the latter case the burden of effort should go, not to his struggle against fear, but to some change in the facts. When the cause of ridicule is removed, the problem of freedom from its fear is solved. The invitation, then, suggests the elimination of all occasion for ridicule in the person suffering from the distress of it. This may turn out to be a very difficult

task, of course, but the encouragement is certain
that the transfer of attention from ridicule and its
pain to self-improvement and the thought of victory
with the consequent dawning of courage will dispel
fear and begin to introduce the sense of respect —
self-respect at least, attracting the respect of
others.

SIXTH IRON REGIME: *Of Self-Valuation.* Since
the cause is not always removable, this regime seeks
to counteract the fact. Once lived a lovely woman
who was a dwarf. After every appearance on the
street, she sobbed herself ill. Children had ridiculed
her deformity. This woman should have remembered,
with pride: "No one who knows me ridicules my
misfortune. I am myself — power — beyond the hurt
of infants either of years or of mental growth." Moreover, she should have cultivated acquaintance with
these children, and their love and regard. Such an
attitude must have greatly smoothed her way. The
suggestions apply in all similar cases. Whatever be
the occasion of ridicule, if you cannot remove it,
cultivate something of the stoic's indifference through
loyal appreciation of the nobler self with which you
are surely endowed. There is a mood of self-valuation
that lifts us above the smile or the jeer or any affront.
Insist on thinking well of your own personality.
Remember, and hold fast, and conquer!

If you chance, in some innocent way that is not a
misfortune, to be ridiculous (which is at one time or
another the fate of most of us), and those who cannot
suppress the sense of humor are worthy your respect,
it is suggested that you admit the facts — as, say,
in dress, manner, occupation, particular act, or what-
not — and then join in the laugh. Nothing disarms

the laugh of ridicule like the laugh of good nature. Acquire the divine gift of laughter! Remember, and hold fast, and conquer.

SEVENTH IRON REGIME: *Of Self-Valuation Continued against the Egotist.* A third variety of people whom you fear is the egotist and the really superior person. If the word, "fear," seems here too strong, it is nevertheless true that you are uncomfortable with the people indicated. They inspire within you a feeling of inferiority, and in their presence you are in some manner overcome, more or less, so that always you "put your worst foot forward" when under their observation. Such is a general statement of the case. You are asked, then, to scrutinize the following statements in regard to their possible relation to yourself:

Statement One (As to all the fears here mentioned). It is the consciousness that you are under observation which induces your embarrassment. So long as you know that people are unaware, and will not become aware, of your presence, you experience no emotional fear of them. Now, it is very likely that they do not observe you as inferior in any way, and perhaps do not particularly observe the characteristics which you imagine would suffer in comparison with their own. In other words, the substance of the details of their supposed observation may be purely imaginary on your part. You have *created* an observation or a thought for these people of which they are entirely unconscious. This may, at least, be the case.

You are therefore invited to practise total indifference to the supposed (or, possibly real) critical observations and opinions of all so-called superior people — especially of all egotists; — that is, to cease *imagining* such critical observation as a fact. The method consists in assuming that the person in mind does not critically observe you, and that he is of a friendly disposition toward you. The regime totally *disregards the facts* in any case; no matter even if you know the observation takes place and is critical; you are to assume — think, assert —that there *is no such observation* and that the person is most friendly toward you in all his thoughts. You are distressed by supposed criticism; the remedy will be found in the persistent possession of the idea that there is no criticism at all. You crowd out your fear by saturating mind with a thought which does not lead to fear, but rather suggests self-satisfaction and courage.

Statement Two. The truth is, oftentimes, that those whom you hold to be egotists or consciously superior people, *entertain precisely the same opinion of yourself.* As those whom you may fear may fear you, — in which case either occasion for fear is outlawed or negatived,— so, many who embarrass you by their imagined superiority regard you as talented, worth fearing, perhaps, or an egotist. This regime, therefore, urges you to cultivate a high opinion of yourself — in the interest of the conquest of fear. The apparent vice in such a suggestion disappears in its purpose, the building up of a foundation for courage. Moreover, if this particular fear is your trouble, an increase of self-valuation is your special need. Excessive egotism may be a disease, but there is no doubt whatever that the fear-feeling because of other people's superiority is a disease, and a very subtle one, as well. Personality in health always thinks cordially of itself, for the thought is one phase of the instinct of self-preservation. And ,whatever may

be your opinion of the egotist, he may truly represent a
great value in life.   When egotism signifies the thought,
"I am power!   I know what I can do!" it is then a
virtue because it is an asset, a stimulant, a cordial
to courage.   The thing this world needs most is large
and prevailing courage.

Statement Three (for all chapters).   I say there
is no value in self-depreciation, abnegation, humility,
and that these qualities are often vices and enemies
to human welfare.   Reason demands that a soul assert
itself as a sovereign traveler toward a glorious destiny.
Assertion, not humility, is the virtue of developing
life.   He who, in the equity of universal brotherhood
and the *white life,* assumes: "I am I — sovereign
among human lords," and asserts himself for all
rightful sovereignty, by so much aids the nature of
things toward the "one far-off, divine event" of
perfected worlds.

I distinctly deny that the lordliest of earth's
inhabitants was meek and lowly except in the sense
of being in harmony with the Infinite, and I affirm
that He was the most self-assertive and imperial
exponent of balance — in miraculous equilibrium the
most self-assertive and imperial soul — the world
has ever known.   To imitate this king is — to "call
no man master."

Those who embarrass you because of their superiority are very likely calling you "superior."   I have
been unreasonably lauded by people whose presence
demanded the application of my own regimes.   It is
probable that a similar disclosure might be made in
the case of every human being.

The affirmation of your own power and value,
couched in words, thought with emphasis, continued

into settled habit, is, therefore, the injunction for this form of fear.

Statement Four (for this regime only). The "worst foot" is almost always a fiction, or becomes fact by blunder-inspiring imagination. You are urged to persist in the effort to banish the thought of this "worst foot." It is also suggested that you refuse to call up or dwell upon any supposed instance of mistake or of awkwardness in your past experience. Feed on the happy memories! Erase from memory every fact, incident, experience which you believe has showed your weakness! Live alway on your own signs of power! Remember, and hold fast, and conquer!

You are also urged to rid yourself of the habit of thinking, "I shall not be myself in this person's presence." The positive method therefor is now the affirmation — in thought-words — emphatically spoken (mentally), repeated again and again and again, *"I am myself! I am power! I also am worth while! I am free! I am courage!"* In order that you may cultivate a good solid sense of your own abilities and value, you are urged to think these things, assert them as true, realize in mind-feeling precisely these and no contrary. Remember, and hold fast, and conquer.

Statement Five (for all chapters). The vast majority of people think too little of themselves. *False religious teaching has made us feel that it is evil to think well of the self.* It is, on the contrary, evil to estimate self as a "worm of the dust," or any such thing. It is because I so believe, and to cure all fears, that I have written the suggestion above italicized.

Statement Six (for this regime only). In all common thinking it is assumed that a "better nature" advises against self-assertion. But by what criterion, I ask, are we to discover this "better nature?" A better nature than is sometimes in evidence we certainly all possess, yet I am unable to see that those advices of the so-called "better nature" which persistently go "against the grain" and demand disagreeable self-effacement are necessarily right — as a matter of exact fact. We may think, with the philosopher, about the "Changeless and True Consciousness" and the "Fickle or False Consciousness," and hold that whatever the "Changeless" or "True" affirms must be right and should be obeyed. The clear fact, however, is that we are one unitary consciousness, educated in one way or another, and morally educated in the West of the world to believe that the "better nature" ought to advise all sorts of things contrary to a so-called "evil" nature, and that when it does so advise, it is for our good. But the moral education of the world's Eastern consciousness does not always agree with the details of the Western education. It is a question of education. And in the West it has turned out that the "better nature" has advised things that have subsequently been held wrong. The conclusion is that the "Changeless Consciousness," or the so-called "True Self," has shown itself mistaken and has no infallibility; is precisely as ignorant as the man whom it tortures — for the simple reason that it *is* the man. You see, therefore, that no one's mere inner feeling about a supposed virtue is to be accepted as law. The "better self" may be mistaken. *Our true teachers are reason, experiment, experience.* Always the question of virtue is this: Does the idea, belief, act, work well among all people and in the long run? If so, the thing is right. There is a kingdom of law

— the Universe of Law — which infallibly works well in the long run. This law is *right* because it *works well*, and it *works well* because it is *right*. The Universe must be self-preservative for highest unfoldment. The long-run working of things cannot be destructive. The working well means some kind of esential preservation for development of possibilities. Only trial can find out what works well and is therefore right. No one's mere feeling can decide a right or a wrong, since no feeling can determine whether or no a thing will work well, universally and forever. Only experiment and experience, interpreted by reason, can so determine.

I do not mean, however, that you are not to go by your feeling of right and wrong, for the feeling is a product of past human experiment, experience, and reason. I mean that you are not to suppose that because a thing seems right or wrong for you, it is therefore right or wrong for all and through all time. This distinction invites liberty of thought, and it surely would have saved the world much close contiguity to hell and many people great suffering, on the one hand, and intimate relationships with devils, on the other hand.

Statement Seven (for all chapters). It has never been demonstrated that fear and self-abnegation have worked well for man. These things in themselves have always worked evilly. And forever, on the contrary, when man has sought self-interest *consistently with other-interest,* asserted all his well-working powers and put fear and self-belittling totally out of his life has he unfolded and come to success. Hence the advices of this regime.

If your consciousness of other people's superiority

induces embarrassment, your remedy, in addition to
the suggestions of preceding regimes consists in
meeting such other person's atmosphere with a positive outgo of self-assertion and courage from your own.
This brings us to a further discussion.

EIGHTH IRON REGIME: *Of Offsetting Assumption.*
Having entered the work of self-valuation, you are
now urged to repel the influence of those who evidently
feel their superiority and embarrass you by throwing
out from yourself a counteracting influence. The
will, in this regime, acts from the vantage-ground
of your habituated self-valuation. The latter is the
leverage of the will. It is always to be remembered
that the will can never achieve anything without
some solid ground for its action. If you belittle
yourself, you cannot will aggressive antagonism to
superiority, simply because you have already surrendered. So long as you admit superiority, you cannot
overcome fear of criticism. Affirming the superiority
or the worth of self, you have ground on which to repel
or will repulsion of embarrassing influences. On this
affirmation-assumption, you should in thought go
out by will to meet the superior person's atmosphere
with a positive assertion of antagonism; that is, by
thought and force of will, surround your person with
a vibrant antagonism (feeling) to his overweening
self-sufficiency. The fact that you are doing so should
not be evident to that person, of course. The regime
consists in quietly resisting (affirming that you resist
— assuming a mental attitude that thinks resistance
to) his aggressive, self-assertive personality. Whatever you believe this person to be in his attitude toward
yourself, that you are to be in thought and feeling
toward him. In the meantime it is suggested that

you hold steadily in mind the absurdity of this person's egotism, proceeding all along to study his characteristics as a source of amusement to yourself. How can you suffer embarrassment with one whose assumptions are ridiculous? The methods thus indcated will, meantime, beget familiarity with the person in hand, and you will become in time so accustomed to the thing you have feared that fear will vanish for lack of fresh inspiration. Fear always dies with its old impulses, and if you can exhaust these impulses, your task is accomplished. The study for such inspirations thus brings us to a further regime.

NINTH IRON REGIME: *Of Character-Analysis.* There are certain types of mind which can only find expression in vociferous talking. With such people you are, perhaps, ill at ease and not in full command of yourself. Always in their presence your ideas seem weak and your language inadequate. They overwhelm you. It is likely that you really fear them.

Now, the loud talker commonly believes himself right, at all times, on all subjects. His emphasis of voice and words is due to this supposition: the power of self-conviction is in him so great that it compels immense vocal and linguistic activity. Some psychologists would say that his vocal and linguistic activity induces the habit of opinionativeness, as they affirm that a man fears because he runs rather than runs because he fears. It is probable that the people before us are loud talkers because they believe in their own opinions in a rowdyish way. Some minds are deficient in equity — everything is, with them, just hard law and fact. Such minds do not think of other minds as possibly being correct in their action. Others are so constituted that what they see exhausts all vision: there is no world besides their own. In both cases violent expression is indispensable to the mind's life. They must think with triphammer blows or air-blast rushes and talk like a steam siren.

This analysis suggests the remedy for fear of such persons. *They are not worth the fear.* If you are thus troubled, you are urged to remember that you are surrendering peace of mind to another person's constitutional weakness or mental defect. A studied recognition of the loud talker's psychic deformity will breed in yourself a feeling of indifference to his voice and opinions which will effectively destroy all fear in his presence. Such a course may also beget a sort of tolerance born of pity for his unconscious mental exposure.

Among such opinionated people is found that happy class whose interpretations of law and fact always run their way. I have discovered, however, that these are sometimes the quietest and least obtrusive of personalities. As an illustration, here is a man who never intrudes his presence or his opinion upon others, and yet no case in which his interests are concerned could be conceived wherein all the law and all the facts would not naturally, rationally and inevitably make his way. Thus would any intelligent person, court or jury — even the Almighty — surely hold. This man is as mild as a lady, but his way of seeing things is a mental law for all mankind — and he cannot help the fact that it is so. The son of our illustrating friend is exactly like the father in this respect, except that the son's opinionativeness breeds the loud voice and the confident word. I once asked the son if he ever made any concessions on any subjects. His ears heard the question, but the rush of his mind induced mental deafness, and the matter in hand was bombarded with stock-phrases. The man could not help himself. Since such was the case, he seemed no occasion for fear. You can calmly endure the loud talker if you know him and understand how helpless he is before his own psychic impulses. Whether loud or mild, his interpretation of all things by his own light and interest is likewise merely a deformity, to be classed with nearsightedness or defective hearing.

Having read the psychic signs of your man, now, you see that embarrassment or any sort of nervousness on your own part must result simply from your own weakness. If you persistently consort with these people, come to see through them, and then resolve to be rid of your fears concerning them, their influence upon you must necessarily cease.

This regime has referred to two classes only, but it is more or less applicable to all the varieties of people mentioned in the present chapter, with the possible exception of the malevolent.

Somewhat allied to the classes above discussed is the kind of people who are called brusque or bearish. The brusque person hurts the feelings of others either because he is naturally harsh or because he likes to do and say the unexpected thing. Mental pain resembles the sense of humor in respect to the thing not expected: the shock emphasizes the feeling. You cannot foresee the brusque person. It is not his word alone, nor his act alone, that you fear: it is the rasping cross-cut of the unexpected thing. This man knows things, when you think he does not know them, and he never says or does as you would like. He is usually "contrary-minded," and he enjoys the fact. Brusqueness is always due to the possession of a certain amount of wisdom, keen opinions, and an indulged fondness for startling others by the unusual expression of uncommon notions contrary to the general run. Sometimes it covers the kindest disposition of heart, sometimes it backgrounds in a tragic past, sometimes it is the guise of an ugly soul. You fear the brusque person because he gives you distress. This distress is itself a fear. You fear a fear, you see, and that fear you indulge for a poor human specimen whose centre of etheric action is either

Altogether kindly toward you,

A guard for the buried past,

A weakness of contrariety,

A childish fondness for surprise,

Or an unworthy love of pain in others.

You are invited again to read the above interpretations, as you pass into the following regime:

TENTH IRON REGIME: *Of Counter Analysis of Brusque People.* The re-reading suggested gives us certain curious results in which you will discover again as always heretofore the foolishness of fear in its emotional aspects.

To fear the *kindly* heart is, of course, unnecessary. You are invited always to search for the kindly heart in this world. If you assume the corresponding mental attitude, the etheric movements of your personal atmosphere will influence the atmosphere of even the brusque person to disclose his real nature. If he turns out to be ugly, you are so far on your way in the matter of handling him. If he turns out to be kindly, there's an end. The talismanic sentence here may be: "*I give you good will for good will.*"

To fear a man's self-covering which he throws around himself because of his past, is weakness. You

are invited to ignore the fact that he has any past —
it is his own — and to assume the iron mask against his
present. Our talismanic sentence now is: *"This mere
covering of yours is harmless. Wear it, if you will.
It cannot contact with my soul."*

To fear the mere word or manner of an *ugly* person
is to surrender before you are really hurt. You are
invited to assume the attitude of alertness, without
its external signs, and, meanwhile, inwardly to smile
at his manner and word. The concealed attitude of
alertness discerns the other person's actual intentions:
the latter give you information because you are psychically receptive and awaken within you certain pro-
tective impulses. As a general rule, these impulses
should be obeyed, since they proceed from the alert
subconscious. You are thus acting, not from fear,
but in accordance with the highest reason obtainable.
The talismanic sentence may be as follows: *"I am
alertly listening that I may catch your real intentions
and hear my subconscious warnings and commands with
regard to the same. Your external signs are harmless."*

To be suppressed by or to fear another person's
mere contrariety of speech and action, is to yield to the
unexpected when it ought to be anticipated. If you
know a man will surely say or do some unusual thing,
the remedy consists in bringing to the fore and utilizing
that knowledge. The talismanic sentence is: *"I expect
you to speak and act contrary to all precedent and reason,
for such is your weakness, and I am therefore on guard
against the desired effect of shock and disturbance which
you seek to produce."*

To fear one who takes unworthy pleasure in another's pain, is to place yourself below that person's
level. It is your privilege mentally to rise above him,

and, while guarding in all ways against actual hurt, to shake off all feeling of fear by sheer imperiousness of willed courage. Hence the talismanic sentence: "*Your unworthiness condemns you, and my courage not only defeats you but compels your respect.*"

The brevity of these suggestions may tend to obscure their value, for they are easily read and easily forgotten. You are therefore urged to apply the regimes in actual and prolonged work. It is error to expect that inveterate tendencies can be overcome by the mere reading of a book. The law that reaction exactly equals action holds universally good. The effort to reform a tendency must equal the action which has developed it. The reform may proceed more swiftly, however, if only that sovereign creative power, the will, be brought resolutely to bear on the effort. This fact insures your success. But you are invited to remember that the most strenuous and exacting and wearying thing in the world is prolonged vigorous action of the will set to one achievement. It is for this reason that people fail. The book you are reading instructs in a fine work, practically and correctly, but the book cannot furnish the action. All rests with the student — who must be a *reader* and a *doer*. One who owns the power-books has revealed in correspondence this common trait: "The mind that is avid for more and more instruction, none of which it is (seemingly) willing to act upon and make good." It may therefore be urged that you actually and persistently test the regimes here set forth. If you will do this, the result is inevitable. Courage will arise from the grave of fear. Remember, and hold fast, and conquer!

In addition to the above regimes, you are now requested to observe the following:

ELEVENTH IRON REGIME: *Of Like for Like.* Mere retaliation is always weakness, and is therefore not advised by this regime. The method is purely one of self-defense, and should always be so accepted. You are seeking freedom from fears, so that apparent retaliation will be justified provided no reaction of irritation go with it. Maintaining perfect calmness, you are now requested to meet brusqueness with brusqueness, contrariety with contrariety, surprise with surprise. In attempting this work, you must remember that you are trying, not to cure the other person's faults, but to conquer your own fears because of his faults. Should the method develop controversy, it must be abandoned for the time being, for its continuance would then lead astray. The point is, that you are to maintain inner calm while quietly employing the other man's weakness. The idea is, not a deadly duel on your part, but a fencing with a choice of weapons left to the opposing party. Whatever weapon he may choose, be you the better of the two. This regime, be it understood, of course, is to be resorted to only as a final effort in the interest of courage, and always must the fact be kept in mind that it requires the very highest skill, since you must, simply *must*, maintain perfect inner poise of mind and nerve. The questions are —"Can you be brusque and self-controlled? Contrary merely for the sake of peace and quiet? Contrary in the interest of ultimate harmony?" The answers are affirmative, but you are urged to remember with Epictetus that a gourd does not grow in one night. The regime assumes that you are determined to prove equal to its demands. This being so, you will find developing within you a feeling of indifference for all those elements in the brusque person's character which heretofore have inspired your fears, and such indifference will undermine and destroy the fears themselves. In the meantime, the brusque person, discovering that he is unable to move you, will weary of his attitudes. He cannot forever beat the wind — which he neither retards nor deflects.

Moreover, since brusqueness is a weakness, and since weakness is gregarious, the brusque person shows a failing in his fondness for the respect of others —of some one or more human beings. Now, respect lies not very far removed from fear. Sufficiently dilute your fear of a man with negative feeling, and it becomes respect only. Or, sufficiently inject positive feeling into mere personal respect, and you have a case of fear. You respect a neighbor. Infuse a certain feeling into the respect: you now stand in awe of him. Increase the awe to a given degree: you are overwhelmed with fear. It is said that "the fear of the Lord is the beginning of wisdom." This means that wisdom begins in acknowledging a Being who can never be exhaustively known. You cannot merely *respect* the Infinite: the feeling you entertain for the Infinite has *too much feeling* to be other than just fear-thought or awe. Always shall you (justly) fear-thought — in reason acknowledge that Infinite, for, as you unfold yourself to increasing apprehension of Him, it is He (the Infinite) that you unfold, and that Infinite — and yourself, petal of the Unspeakable Flower of Reality — is forever subjectively More both to Himself (that Infinite) and to you — the petal on the Flower. Always shall you fear-thought your finite and that Infinite Self, since you can never exhaustively know either the one of the other. The Infinite Subjective — your "Great Within"— cannot exhaustively know Self, for the Self infinitely underhides the knower. So, the More, the limitlessly unexplored of *you*, shall always underhide your self-knowing. One ideal of life is self-respect, and it needs but to know self but a little more deeply to stand in awe of its immensities, and in that awe the human being finds the first shadowy substance of that true wisdom which is "the fear of the Lord."

These reflections bring us to the conclusion that fear for any *human being* is indefensible, since each one is ideally a phase-person of the Infinite Unsearchable, the "I Am That I Am," so that you are yourself even such an one, royally dowered, and need fear none who is also just a phase of the Universal Life. And if some people are practically mal-developed or partially developed phases of that Infinite, their traits which you fear are mere weaknesses, and, therefore, no occasion for fear at all.

The brusque person desires respect from others. His methods of seeking what he desires are merely false. Were the methods normal, you would not fear him. Being false, they are open to criticism; and because open to criticism, are unworthy your fears. False though they are, however, you are at liberty to utilize the end he seeks — your respect — the *idea* of respect — for your own freedom from his thralldom. You are, hence, invited to meet his manners and words with studied respect for his opinions, ways and character. You thus not only communicate to him agreeable modifying ether-movements; you also develop within yourself a feeling of genuine courage.

TWELFTH IRON REGIME: *Of Respect-Winning Efforts.* The desire for respect usually carries with it a good valuation of the self-respecting attitude. The brusque person — indeed, any of us — respects respect. In this feeling we disclose the qualities which we desire.

The thief respects in another the traits and skill he covets most. The ideal man of honor values those characteristics which he seeks to embody. Evidently, then, the winning of respect must be preceded by the discovery of the things other people profoundly desire by way of qualities, traits, manners, characteristics, and the like. If only you know the secret ideals of men,— money, power, learning, etc.,— you possess the key to their regard. Recalling, now, our previous study of human signs, both visible and hidden, it is certain that if you can win the respect of the person whom you fear, so that this respect becomes mutually known, you will infallibly have banished all occasion and impulse of fear in his presence. For this reason you are invited to study your man, to get at the qualities he craves most in himself, and then to embody them in yourself — to imitate them while cultivating them, if they are to you respectable, and to imitate them, whether or no, so far as concerns a cure of your fear. You need not cultivate unworthy qualities, of course, in the pursuit of this regime. Becoming a thief does not win a thief's respect, although becoming a skilful one may do so. People admire excellence in what themselves are, but they really respect excellence in qualities which they feel they ought to desire. Desire never grows on the one level alone. Always are there deeps under deeps in the world of desire. Somewhere in any man are the deepest desires of his life, and these deeper desires run toward the highest idealism — so far as the man can make out his ideals. If, then, you imitate the brusque person's brusqueness (except as in a former regime), you fail to win his respect in the true sense. You must find the qualities which he craves in his better soul. Hence, you are urged to imitate and cultivate these until they are you own, and so urged with the assurance that you will thus infallibly win his respect. Meanwhile, you have banished fear and called courage to the fore.

THIRTEENTH IRON REGIME: *Of Quiet Self-Mastery* (for all chapters). If, in the presence of any person whom you fear, you will retire into an imaginary stronghold, moated on all sides and with drawbridge up, you will be enabled to repel all assaults, whether of visible word or act, or of unseen etheric movements. You here never let yourself go. You here always refuse admission to any disturbance. Safe within, and viewing this person through barred plate glass, as it were, you say: "*Since I am here, in perfect command, none of your words, opinions or acts, have power to reach me. I am immune to all your attacks.*"

FOURTEENTH IRON REGIME: *Of Simple Dignity.* The quality of dignity is seldom a birthright, is capable of being overdone, and may, in admirable form, be acquired by long-continued, intelligent effort. By the majority of people this high value is seldom attempted because of a vivid conception of its spurious imitation. Dignity in one person you admire; it is seen to be genuine. Dignity in another person you condemn because you know it is false. The present regime, then, urges the cultivation of a dignity that befits your personality, your life-level, your occupation, and any particular occasion. What such a dignity is you must discover by looking within for the ideal which seems to be right to *you*, as made certain by the reception of it which other people may accord. When you feel that you are right about a thing, criticism simply refers the feeling to a deeper phase of the self, and in the long run the deepest self, called upon for decision in the matter

by such criticism, will give you the last word; that is
for *you* the right conclusion. You are urged to seek a
true conception of dignity fitting for yourself, and then
to adopt such dignity, standing, meanwhile, within
your citadel or stronghold, and, thus panoplied, to
ignore the intention lurking behind sarcasm, ridicule,
or brusqueness. You will find assistance in the thought
and words now given: *"I value myself too highly to
retort, or to cringe, or to fear. 'None of these things
move me.'"*

FIFTEENTH IRON REGIME: *Of Using People for
Practice.* By so much as one learns how to use another
person for any purpose, by so much does one lessen the
possibility of fear for that person. You thus turn the
one you fear into an instrument of practice for overcoming the fear. If you will apply the regimes of this
chapter, seeking to know sarcastic, egotistic, superior
and brusque people, you will infallibly find yourself
rising above them, or becoming immune to them because of the very familiarity induced by the practice,
no less than because of the practice itself. For example:
you fear some overbearing person, but you set him up
as a target for these regimes; you make him a stone on
which you sharpen any method; you compel him to
serve you as a test of the regimes outlined. Always
during the process, you mentally inform him: *"Why,
you are an implement on which I am practising and by
means of which I develop a perfect courage."* Observing
these instructions, the death of your fear is guaranteed.

SIXTEENTH IRON REGIME: *Of the White Life.*
When you are consciously right — right in yourself,
in your position, in your attitude and speech — you
have but to remember your fortress and the iron mask
of dignity to render fear a foreign reality. Conscious-

ness of being "out of true" somewhere must of course breed cowardice. A sense of right needs but the command of will to summon invincible courage. The sarcastic person, the boorish, the one who ridicules, the brusque, the superior, even the malevolent, cannot inspire fear in the soul that knows itself to be right. So, the deformed Roman philosopher told all Rome and Cæsar, under the guise of a dialogue, that no thing or man could do evil to him, the noble soul, whose bodily mask was like to a broken back. "*Now can no evil happen to me; for me there is no robber, no earthquake; all things are full of peace, full of calm; for me no way, no city, no assembly, no neighbor, no associate hath any hurt.*" For you, as the Hindoo sages well say, are not there eyes, hands, body, flesh, blood, nerves? You are *you* — infinite in your "great within," deathless in that infinitude, impregnable in your harmony with right.

The Universe is a vast complex of etheric movements,— vortices, rings, undulations, translations,— every type of which is established and in that sense permanent, no individual movement of which can be destroyed except by conflict and in the interest of the whole. Imagine one ring always preserving harmonious relations with all other movements — the adjustment intended by the nature of things. This ring possesses, therefore, the power to repel where it cannot adjust, and can by no possibility be destroyed so long as such harmony continues. The ring is your psychic self when consciously right. The Universal System guarantees you while in the right. And here is your sovereign remedy for fear and your breeder of courage-consciousness, invincible right living and being.

Observe, however! Right, as a known possession, may not always obviate the feeling of fear, because men and women do not know how to use the sense of right. The use of a consciousness of being right is outlined in this book. You are urged not to be content with a knowledge that you are in harmony with the nature of things, as is done in countless cases, but to apply that knowledge, as, by this talismanic sentence: "*I — myself — am courage, to the full limit of being now consciously right in my intentions and my actions and my existence.*"

And observe, again! No method may slay fear at a stroke. You have the wind and tide of fifty thousand years of evolution to contend with, it may be, and you are therefore invited to maintain patience and persistence in your efforts to be rid of fear. Moreover, you have *with you* the ultimate intention of that fifty thousand years, so that the fears which have come to you out of the long past may surely be slain by the struggles of your life, and the courage, which that intention of evolution has had always in view since "star-mist and fire-dust" became tenuously real, may be developed to all your need by the persistence of just this little thing — your will. Remember, and hold fast, and conquer!

The will, set to a good purpose, is the Universe on the march.

SEVENTEENTH IRON REGIME: *Of Feeling Debarred from Reason Against Crafty People.* Fear in regard to crafty people (and in all the cases cited in this chapter) is an emotion imposed upon reason. This feeling is absent where the person is not supposed to be, say, for example, crafty. Recognition of the signs of such a character calls upon reason to be on guard, and this demand is a phase of active self-interest; but exactly at this point the psychic addition occurs and the fear-feeling arises. To permit that addition is to overthrow reason rather than respect its dictates. The feeling is unnecessary, for reason will attend to all the facts without the feeling, and the unnecessary addition can accomplish no single thing except to injure the one who indulges it. You are therefore urged to discriminate between your recognition of the signs of craftiness (or any other unworthy quality in those whom you meet) and your instinctive impulse to conserve your own self-interest, on the one hand, and all feelings of uneasiness, foreboding or fear, on the other hand. And you are also urged, while properly alert in the recognition of the signs of craftiness (or other quality), to resolutely eliminate every feature of disturbing elements, that is, of fear-feelings and fear-thoughts. To accomplish this, you banish such feelings, you rise above them, you substitute the thought and mood of courage — try to feel courage. The talismanic sentence is this: *"Alert toward all your machinations, I indulge no emotion whatever concerning your intentions. I am courage in the face of such intentions."* The goal, here observe, is not prevention of craftiness in other people, but is destruction of fear-feeling induced by craftiness. Not all the books in print might accomplish the former goal; the second may be achieved by one power — your will.

It is now asserted that *whoever fears — in the feeling-sense of this book — anything in earth or heaven or "hell," fears solely because he wants to fear.*

It is possible to live the span of one human life without one fear. There are those who actually so live. They stand for a true self-interest, of course, and they try to protect their own, but they do not know the feeling of fear.

It is now further asserted that any mere quality, such as fearlessness, which any human possesses natu-

rally, any other human being may acquire by intelligent
and persistent effort — referring, however, to reasonably normal classes.

EIGHTEENTH IRON REGIME: *Of Self-Interest
Reason Against Malevolent People.* Actual malevolence
is not often observed. In the great majority of instances
injury to others is due to a malevolent impulse which
is momentary or really foreign to the person in which
the trait appears. Here is a case of average human
nature gone wrong, not of wrong human nature developed. There is a difference. Let us say that
Milton's Satan is the negative of demoralized holiness.
Goethe's Mephistopheles is the positive of developed
evil. The ancient Greeks never conceived of either
character.

Rome could give us in her last days an "incarnation" of Satan, as seen in Nero, who was affirmatively bad—in his later life: an evolution of the death-
throe of Rome. Alexander the Great or Napoleon was
the negatively deteriorated struggle of life's expression
of power. The real "bad man" is seldom discovered—
and he is always insane. The right-man twisted is
everywhere in evidence. In the one case we have concentrated etheric anarchy against whatever is *because*
it is. In the other case we have merely etheric confusion.

It is a fact that you can so cultivate the farsighted
self-interest reason, acting always in the mood of right
and courage, that you can pass through any experience
with malevolent people, either of the kind who are
developed evil, or of the kind who are the degenerate
of the human average, maintaining all senses alert for
the long-run best thing under the circumstances, and
with absolutely no feeling of irritation or of fear what-

ever. To achieve such a desirable goal, you are urged to follow all the regimes of this book, so far as applicable to your case, until self-poised self-control, acting on the farsight of your best interest, together with a combining sense of courage and power, have become habituated with you and identified with the deepest things in your nature. These desirable results you may surely bring about, if only you will persevere in your efforts. Remember, and hold fast, and conquer!

LIFE'S RELATIONS.

The relations of life are not tyrannical
In the Plan of the Nature of Things.

Why, now:
If I clasp your hand, must I let it bind me?
If I catch your step, must I lock-step with you always?
If we vibrate brain-purpose together,
Must I or you bow knee to you or me?
If we meet in the pure flame of love,
Must time find us, not twain, but just one sole?

I hold to my Self.
Out of the star-depths Self came;
Into the star-depths Self goes.
I must keep mine individual Name.
I say! Let us two (or more) walk together
On the long, long way of life —
Or the skies be fair, or in every kind of weather—
But, pray you, have done with ownership!

For I am I,
Unquenchable, indestructible, unbindable;
And I give you — mayhap the half of me,
But no more, on pain of the loss of my Self.
What will you? A *live* soul,
Or a *part* of your *dead* Self?
(For he who insists on the whole of another
(Dies in himself and the other entombs
(In a death-smelling sepulchre).
Nay, soul! I stand in awe of your selfhood —
Reciprocate! . . So . . now I see harmony
And power for each!

I will pair with you, my friend;
I will surrender and adore, my beloved;
But, be thou THYSELF, as I am SELF.
So shall either for other sing,
With all the uncounted,
"*I am! And I am! And I am Power!*"

— THE AUTHOR

CHAPTER X.

SOME OF LIFE'S RELATIONS.

"Have the honor due
In living out thy nature."—*Robert Browning.*

EXPERIENCE marks man the superior animal. It is only through experience that we can know. Even the instincts are mere impulses of human nature, and we can know what they are and how they work, not before they have occurred, but thereafter. So, also, innate intuitions of truth obtain as impulsive activities of the self in mind, and that the intuitions are truths can be determined alone by experience. Knowledge is an established reaction to the real contents of experience, but experience only can give these contents. Consciousness is a first form of experience, but neither the consciousness as such nor the self as a self comes to recognition prior to the experience of consciousness and of self.

KNOWING IS AN OUTCOME OF EXPERIENCE.

You can know nothing save as you have experienced a definite something, and when you have done this, you must know what you know or have known. The worm is acted upon by outside influences, for example. The worm re-acts—acts in response to the influence. It may be that the worm will thereafter pre-act in order to prevent such action upon it by outside forces. Indeed, under given conditions, the worm will always do so. If the conditions vary, the worm-action will vary.   The worm's nature simply expresses itself in impulses — re-actions induced in every instance by the outside force, but caused by the nature which is itself.   It is error, however, to say that because the worm acts differently under differing conditions — to prevent action upon it by fire, say, a second time — that the worm *knows.*   *Something,* indeed, *does* know: Nature knows; the Universal Mind knows *for* the worm, but the worm does not know *in* the Universal Mind. The thinker knows his thoughts, and the thoughts act according to the thinker's nature; but the thoughts do not know themselves or their actions in the thinker. So, the worm does not know.

Higher in the scale of life, the being there acted upon seems to individually represent Nature in knowing that it is acted upon.   In the former case we say, "Instinct is at work."   In the latter case we detect the beginnings of intelligence.   The dog has the primitive elements of experience, and knows in a measure corresponding thereto.

Finally, when man is acted upon by outside influences, he knows *what* is going on: that something is going on, and that the going-on relates to himself. Moreover, he can mentally affirm the thing just written. He knows that he knows.   And he can also affirm this last statement.   He knows that he knows that he knows.   It is this reiteration of this knowing that makes man capable of experience in its fullest scope.

Experience Analyzed.

Let us throw these thoughts into staccato:
In experience you are affected *by* something.
You know that you *are* so affected.

You know that what affects you is a *something other* than yourself as affected.

By so much you know *that affecting something.*

But you are able to *remember* all this, and to *act accordingly* in the future.

Experience, then, consists in being affected by something, knowing the fact, and being able to use the knowledge with reference to self and conditions.

Now, you cannot have an experience unless something comes into relation with yourself. Such relation secures the knowing. That is the only way in which anything can be known. You can *know* nothing outside your experience.

Take, for example, a word in the dictionary. It is a strange word, and you are ignorant of its meaning. Its definition consists totally of words that are equally unknown to you, and your ignorance remains as in the first case. If, however, one of the defining words is understood by you, that word becomes a clue, and you may turn, now, to its definition, and find there other familiar words, until, by a round-about way, you find out what another word in the definition of your first word means. You have started in on a voyage of discovery. When you have finished this work, you understand every word in the definition of that first troublesome word, and, therefore, the meaning of that word itself. But you will know that word only as you come to know every identical word employed in its definition — provided all its defining words are themselves necessary and correctly defined.

But your first clue-word — and every other word studied in the voyage of discovery — represents some experience in your past. You have to experience words — at least their individually major part — in order to know them. And you have to know experience in order to know that you know. When you thus doubly and triply know — you understand.

What is Courage?

If, then, you desire courage, you must know what it is. But you can never know courage prior to having experience in courage. You see that in the intelligent study of words you must find something of your past in them, — in their meanings, — and in order to understand them at any time you must put yourself into them. In order to know courage, you must have had in experience some of the elements of the quality, and in order now to know what courage is you must think those elements into the word, "courage."

In the dictionaries the definition of the word, "courage," amounts to this: "Courage is courage," since the qualities which are given to state what courage is are all equivalent to courage. The word comes from the Latin, *cor*, meaning, "heart." We say, "Be of good heart," meaning, "Be of good courage." The word, "concord," also comes from *cor*, as though to express the idea of a function working in co-operation with all other functions. The outcome is well-being, as well-being is the outcome of such working. Courage, then, is a working of the entire system in the sense of welfare promising to continue. In a state of courage, there is a consciousness of power-poise equal to apparent danger, and this sense of power-poise sometimes throws the self into danger with rush and enthusiasm. *Courage is a sense of ability to maintain personal power-poise against threats of injury.*

PHASES OF REALITY.

This personal power-poise comes as an **experience**, whatever may be said of the quality itself. At once we are carried into a wide field of interesting thought, as follows. Every individual object of existence, every truth, every law, every physical and psychic state, is many-sided. This is not only because existence is never a barren unit,— a " thing in itself,"— but because all things that continue — and so, exist — must change. Things, states, acts, therefore, are never the same for any two or more continuous moments. At any instance they have phases, for change is a process, and a process involves parts and successions of states. At each succeeding instant the phases change, for the reason suggested. Whether or no the phases and changes are actual because objective in themselves,— really in the things, acts, states,— or actual because subjective in the human mind, nobody knows. You can only know in yourself; you cannot go outside of yourself in order to know. It is certain that when you know a thing, you have built it by mental experience, and that when you know a thing more completely, you have simply added to that building by experience.

Most people are apt to assume that they know an object, truth, fact, law, act, state, when they have learned *something* about the matter — have had phases of a total possible experience in relation to it. We now see that this is error. The unknown phases of any object, etc., may, indeed, uncover more or less to the mind, or old phases may be newly presented, or the thing to which any phase belongs may change. The field of knowing is thus seen to be infinite. You will find it interesting to select any object or truth which you imagine you know exhaustively. Nothing can be so known. To the Infinite the final inexhaustively unknowable must be the Infinite Self.

COURAGE ALWAYS PARTIAL.

Courage, then, can be known by any one person only in part — so far as his experiences go in the matter. There are phases of courage which you do not know, and which you never will know. An example might be —facing an Arctic winter solitude with a madman for a companion. There are phases which no human being has ever known. Here the example might be — facing in spirit the sudden wreck of the starry heavens. One phase of courage is unknown even to the Deity — that required in facing His own death — because He is the Infinite.

The study of this book, it is now observed, must indeed be partial only. It must be partial as concerns the entire volume, and it will be partial in the study involved in any page. *You will understand up to your own level. You will profit according to your will.* On your level, your experience will determine what you shall realize. Some of these chapters, some of these phases of fear and courage, you will not understand at all, because your experience has fallen short in some particular aspect of the discussion. At every page this has been demonstrated by some one among the book's thousands of readers. The fact, however, is not due to any lack of intelligence on the part of its readers, but is due to the limits of personal experience imposed by the nature of things.

Intelligence is the "chooser between." Always you have to choose between experiences, in order to understanding and mental development.

APPLICATION TO LIFE'S RELATIONS.

Now, the discussion of the present chapter affords illustration of the foregoing suggestions. Human life is a tangle of relations, and in these relations we come to knowledge through experience. Nevertheless, it is evident that multitudes of people have no experience in many relations which are entirely common. Moreover, no one experiences the whole of any given relation. And again, thousands in the full experience (broadly speaking) of certain relations, remain during life largely ignorant of the meaning of very common words involved in such relations.

You are familiar, for example, with *crowds*, but you do not know what it means to face a crowd when it is in a certain mood, say, of anger or of ridicule. When you think of a mad mob calling for your death, you begin to experience a feeling of fear — at least, the idea of fear, because you have had the feeling or idea of fear in other experiences, and this fact gives you power to imagine fear of a mad crowd. You cannot, on the other hand, *realize* courage before a mad mob unless you are really courageous, and the *actual courage-fact* you cannot know unless you have *stood at bay* before such a crowd.

The relation of true *marriage* affords a further example. All know, in a way, the meaning of the words, "husband" or "wife," just as all know in a way the meaning of "love." But it is experience that really defines these words, and unless one is actually married or really loves, one cannot know the words, "wife," or "husband," or "love." Millions of people live in the relation indicated, and one out of a thousand knows the majesty and power and glory of physico-psychic passion. Few, indeed, know what it means highly to mate with a human being. The ideal ends in tradition, fiction, poetry, painting, music, but that world which we call the real knows the state and the relation about as much as an ape knows Mozart, Beethoven's Ninth Symphony, or a kitten knows a Stradivarius. And it is not in a spirit of pessimism that these words are written. They are merely and strictly in the line of the present study.

A further illustration is seen in the idea and the fact of *individuality.* We know only as we experience. Few people experience any the least individuality, and few, therefore, know this splendid reality. That is to say: while all are individuals, the vast majority of men and women fail to be, freely and utterly themselves — even their better selves. The land of the free and the home of the brave is very largely the land of the bound and the home of some variety of fear. These things are not said in the mood of criticism, be it again observed. They simply confront us in the study now opening.

It is life's relations that develop the facts before us. Were a man alone on a desert island in the Pacific ocean, he might well be free and brave — in a way. To individualize himself to the limit of ability and opportunity would even then be difficult, for a man so placed would have to confront himself — and Nature — and the stars and the sea — and the world's traditions and education and a devilish misconception of religion. These things would confront this man in his thought, and if he would really individualize, he would have the task on his hands of conquering every item above mentioned. We prefer the city to the desert. In the latter the demand is incessant and insistent; in the city it is confused and put down, and we are relieved of the awful pressure of life.

Nature and civilization have always conspired to oppose individuality.

Religion, as man has made it, distorted by creed, bound by ceremony, overloaded with institutions, envenomed by selfishness, and made absolutely horrible oftentime by cruelty,—has fought in blood and fire to prevent and destroy individuality. These oppositions vary mightly.

The explanation of *Nature's* apparent hostility toward a true human individualization is the fact that by her oppositions she has sought to discipline and browbeat and inspire man into splendid assertion of himself. We may say that Nature has no real intentions, yet the outcome is the same — individualization. Or, we may hold that Nature is a complex Thought of the Infinite, and then the evident purpose of life's roughness is precisely that — individualization. The more the individual becomes himself, — independent and real and assertive, — the more Nature loves and assists him.

Civilization is apparently opposed to the individual in its real intentions, but the outcome of the actual working of things is more and more the man become himself. Anciently, man understood that he was always dealing with person in his civilizations, yet he never got hold of the true meaning of personality as a real and a sacred thing. The idea is not to be found in Greek literature. Only after man had philosophized and built empires and ruined his own systems and at last begun to dream of freedom, did he really personalize himself. When he did so, he caught his first glimpse of high-browed individuality. Just as much as civilization has dropped absolute monarchs and kings, has it discovered that the one only thing worth evolution and starry systems is the individual come freely and utterly to his own kingdoms. The modern king is simply a symbol for modern government. The absolute monarch died long ago.

There is very little individuality in the completest sense because public opinion and convention and fear are so universally and unrecognizedly the rulers of life; but more truly because so few people have any experience in the individualization of the soul. The meaning of the word, "individuality," in the sense of experience, is almost unknown. For you can only know through experience, and only can know what experience has given you. If you would realize this splendid thing, individuality, you must begin by striving for experience beyond your past, since you can only know as you experience, and if your experience has been ordinary, your limited knowledge (realization) also limits your ideals, and the poor ideals hold you to the past commonplace and enslaved reality.

The courage of individuality is the sublimest possible type of courage known or conceivable. When you come into full individualization, your courage will be of full stature, like that of Peruguino's Michael the Archangel of War — who is the Minister of Peace. By so much as you strive after full freedom of self, by so much do you breed courage in the soul. This is the finest comment on your nature — that if you really become yourself, you will be courageous. And by so much as you strive after full-orbed courage, by so must your soul comes free. In freedom the self experiences entire individualization. Remember, and hold fast, and conquer!

COURAGE AND INDIVIDUALITY.

The courage of individuality, realized in experience, is master of all life's relations. The individualizing self can entertain the fear-feeling in presence of no crowd or mob. Asserting its own throne and kingdom in the law of interest-balance, it neither yields its existence nor calls for the surrender of other individualities. It never breeds fear in any human with whom it stands in relation, nor does it abate its courage in the maintaining of its own identity. This is the ideal. Here is the goal of our seemingly aimless digression: the courage of individuality realized in spite of opposition, by reason of opposition, in every relation of life. That ideal goal may thus be stated:

The royalty of the human
Resides in the powers possessed
By any,—
And the human kingship issues
From the development of those powers;
But the reality of sovereignty
Is the courage of self,
Asserted before all odds
For the right and the power to be,
In every condition and relation,
ONE SOLE HUMAN,
Always and increasingly free,
ITSELF — *and that alone—*
AT ITS BEST — *and nothing else or less:*
The assertively evolving individual.

The forces which obscure and prevent this goal are seen, in part, in the various relations of life. Some of these relations concern a number of people grouped together, while other relations concern one or two individuals only.

The significant thing, now, is this: the man in relation with the crowd is merely an individual (in the common sense of the word), as are those who confront him merely individuals, and whether one confront many or one, nothing is there save individuality, in its common form, so that the only salvation of any situation in life's relations is individualization at the human best.

We now proceed to ask: What is to be understood by the "human individual"? And what are his privileges, rights and duties?

WHAT IS THE INDIVIDUAL?

One highway of answer is as follows:

The world in which we live exists as (a) object — a system of objects; (b) as action — a complex of activities. Things are, because of action.

The world and every object and action are *expressions of ideas*. Classification is based on this fact. Thus, the Universe is analyzed as Material and Nonmaterial, Inorganic and Organic or Living, Animal and Mineral, Physical Life and Psychic Life, Beast and Human, Male and Female, and so on. In the ascending process of analysis we always find some phase of reality appearing in the next higher order of being which is absent in all lower orders. Evolution is a process of differentiation by specialization climaxing finally in the highest possibility (so far as we know) of every kind of object.

In man, the highest possibility, psycho-mentality, climaxes in *moral relations*.

The broadest human idea, *moral psycho-mentality*, presents *infinite variations*. Each man and woman expresses the idea — a human, which carries with it body-idea, mind-idea, self-idea, the idea of moral completeness in the self.

The *body-idea* varies for the reason that it is a complex idea, and what any particular body ought to be is determined by the arrangement of the *component ideas* involved in parts and functions, together with some *predominant idea* which modifies all these associate ideas.

The *mind-idea* varies, for, while all minds are of one general nature, the mind in each instance is a compound of certain ways the self has of being and doing, and the *arrangement* of the mental factors varies and is modified by some *particular factor*.

The *self* varies because every self is an *unique combination* of personalities and within each exists some *one specific idea* which differentiates the possessor or manifester from every other human being living or dead or yet to exist.

The body, the mind, the self, is each a compound of ideas, and in each case the *arrangement* of the component factors is *itself an idea*. But this last idea is determined by a final all-modifying and climaxing idea as well, determining individuality.

Individuality is the practical and growing realization of the highest idea-thought — plan — purpose — possibility of which the unitary person is capable.

Precisely what this sovereign idea is, none of us can affirm, either for ourselves or for others. Nevertheless, it is the supreme privilege of each to realize in actual life this ideal goal — the idea of the complete self — sufficiently, at least, to make the individual a vast improvement on anything yet known. This privilege is so universal, so august, and so important that itself suggests the supremest obligation con-

ceivable. *We are here to make the most of the self.*
To make the most of the self is to assist the Universe
in its struggle toward perfection. A perfected Universe is nothing more than all its individual intelligences brought to a state of perfection.

*The highest law of life is self-assertion and altruism
so universally balanced that with all men the law may be
justified.*

Reverting, now, to the proposition that the world
exists as object and action, let us observe certain conclusions:

INDIVIDUALITY AND EXPERIENCE.

Experience is a knowing. We know as follows:
Every human self knows *the self* only in action. The
self is known, therefore, as actor. Beyond this we
cannot know self. The self acts — is an actor. That
is the essence of personal life — to act. No other
essence is "knowable."

The actor is Will. Reversed, the statement is:
the self exists only as it acts; the self, then, is the Will.
The Will is the self — primarily.

Body expresses Will. Body is established manifestation of the Will-Self.

The body is not the self — the Will. So far as the
self is concerned, the body must take its place among
other external objects. It is therefore *known as any
object is known.*

Nevertheless, so intimate is the body to the self
that the self could be at home, could live, indeed, in
no other body, and no other body could long hold
together with any foreign self in control.

We know *external objects* indirectly, through the
senses. The world about us exists for us only as idea

— innumerable ideas. Body, as part of the world, exists for its self only as complex idea. In all cases the mental idea compels belief in corresponding reality. World and body are real, but we know them only through mental reaction — action in response to action not of the psychic self.

It appears, then, that our knowing relates to (a) the self and (b) a world that is not self.

The world we know also indirectly through the senses. But the self we know — (it is insisted by many, directly through consciousness, but I here say) — indirectly through its activities. There is no self-consciousness independent of some act of psychic self. Self-consciousness is self-action accompanied by some running mate of other-action. Consciousness may obtain in any intelligence, but self-consciousness can only arise after reaction-cognition of a not-self as such.

If we know self only as it acts, and if each act of the self expresses Will, and if things exist only as they act, the Universe, like the body, is an expression of Will.

The Universal Will seems to be striving toward final expression of the highest idea of which physico-psychic existence is capable. The individual Will knows itself, but *exists* for the realization of its highest possible idea. The pure, unwarped Will *is that idea*, and that idea in purity is the Will. The Universal Will knows itself and exists for the realization of its supremest Idea. The Idea which is God is Will, and the Universal Will is the Idea which is God. Since the realization of the highest idea of which an existence is capable cannot be an *absolute* thing, but must ever be a *relative* thing — relative to developing experience —

God grows. A standstill God is utterly impossible.
Perfection does not consist in realizing the whole of
possibility *now*, but in the realization now of all now-
possibility. In other words, perfection is not a matter
of quantity, but is a matter solely of quality. The
quality of perfection in an intelligent being is the now-
possession of all now-possibilities which minister to
completeness. The Infinite Will, so far as this Universe
is concerned, can only be realized as each individual
Will comes to know itself and to realize from now-to-
now its highest endowments.

The goal of all worlds is individuality attained
through experience with the external Universe and
realized in consciousness of self as completed individual
for any now-period of existence. We are here to grow
a soul individualized by the complete realization of all
its powers at any now-period, recognized as of the self,
and especially of the climacteric idea which gives the
individual its possible history — that which distin-
guishes the person from all other individuals.

This brings us to

The Great Affirmation.

You are now invited to dwell upon these thoughts
until something of the sublimity of the following
sentence inspires your inmost soul — the sentence
fell from the pen of one of the world's deepest
thinkers:

"*The proposition, I am, is an infinite proposition
because it is one which has no real predicate, but which,
for that very reason, may have an infinity of possible
predicates.*"

This statement may be illustrated as follows:
I am — that is, I = I.

I am body: forever some kind of body. I, body, perfectingly am — *eternally*.

I am mind: forever some development of mind, never exhaustively unfolded. I, mind, unfoldingly am — *eternally*.

I am self: forever a complex, making toward realization of my individual climaxing idea, but never manifesting this as a finality because it is a limitless thought. I, individuality, am — *eternally*.

Catching something of the inspiration of this notion of sovereign individuality forever realizing and never exhausting, you are urged now to resolve:

"*From this high day onward I resolve to be all my self at its known best: freely, solely, wholly, independent of all fear, coercion, opinion, belief or law not based in reason and motived in human weal.*"

The possibility of this resolution is more or less questioned by all the common relations of life. Always the question (and the usual assault on the theory) beget fears; and always, nevertheless, the fears constitute a demand for courage. Hence, our methods of dealing with them take on supplementary aspects. If you wish to achieve individuality, you must cultivate courage. But, again, if you wish to achieve courage, I know no finer method therefor than the steadfast assertion and development of individual selfhood. Having, then, the culture of courage as your goal, we shall also make for the companion goal in the regimes that follow. Both goals are sought in the methods, and the methods or regimes work themselves out through those relations in life which threaten, yet may really assist, the full individualization of the self. And so we come to our regimes.

REGIMES: INDIVIDUALITY-COURAGE THROUGH LIFE'S
RELATIONS.

I. FIRST RELATION CONSIDERED: *Fear of Husband or of Wife.* It should be observed that you are
not here instructed in the matter of getting on with an
uncomfortable person; that is an endless subject. Our
discussion solely concerns courage cultivated for the
sake of happiness and self-realization where some form
of fear obtains in either woman or man for the other.

FIRST REGIME: *Dispelling Fear in the Fearful.*
This work should begin with the person who inspires
fear. It is damnable selfishness and selfish damnation
(these words are deliberate and meaningful) to permit
fear in any human being, if the feeling can possibly be
dispelled. You are, therefore, invited to know whether
or not your life-mate fears you, and, if such transpire
to be the case, to make the dissipation of that fear the
chief business of your life. For methods you must look
to your better self, resolved persistently to work for the
achievement of the end. If you will patiently strive
to convince the other person that fear for you is unnecessary, that it really hurts *you*, and that you wish
the feeling to be removed forever, you will assuredly
accomplish the liberation, by so much, of a handicap
to individual happiness and growth.

SECOND REGIME: *The Cessation of Domination.*
Life in such intimate relations tends to develop, unconsciously in one party, unrecognized, it may be, in the
other, habits of interference, dictation, domineering,
disclosed in matters of dress, preferences, antipathies,
reading, thought, use of property and money, friendships, art-tastes, politics, religion, and so on. There
is no justification here. If you say, " Why, this person

has not sufficient judgment for these decisions," remember that life is for growth, that no one can grow
without freedom, that no freedom can be exercised
without making mistakes, and that mistakes are the
necessary cost of that freedom which is indispensable
to development.   You do not own a human soul merely
because you marry that person.   Marriage, like sex,
is a convention and a convenience in universal life's
long history, evolved for the sake of life only.   You do
not exist to be a married person.   You do not exist to
be a male or a female.   You are a male or a female,
and you are married, in order that life — your own and
that of others — may realize individuality.   This relation of marriage is a means, not an end.   The personalities involved can never rightly surrender selfhood to
the relation or to the other contracting party.   The
contract calls for coöperation of body, not surrender,
and mutual coöperation alone.   Otherwise, here is
anarchy.   The contract calls for coöperation of the
mental life, but such coöperation cannot possibly be
surrender or capture.   Also is there here a demand
that soul-life shall be free to grow alongside soul-life,—
soul by soul,— and when the idea " alongside"—*soul by
soul* — is realized, each soul is boundlessly free to
realize itself.

Now, here are some interesting truths which we
may present under the heading, *To Every Soul a World.*
The individual idea constitutes a nucleus,— as, physically in the cells of the body,— and this idea-nucleus
builds for the person his or her world, according to
which, and in which, the soul must grow.   That idea,
if free and developing, determines, as I have previously
said, every other idea in the personality.   Doing so, it
expresses itself in ten thousand ways.   The endeavor

to express the nucleus-idea creates a personal world in which the soul would live — the world of physical action, of dress, of taste, of thought, of amusement, of social or business activity, of religion and dreams and ideals.   This statement is true in each case.   You see, then, that you thus create your own life-world.   Whether or no the ideal of the self be attempted, there is a world for every one of us, and in the sense that the ideal is for all, for each of us there is a life-world which may represent the self at its growing best.   So, in marriage, the man has his world: shall not the woman have hers?   Or, must the woman overspread the man's?   What is the vast importance of a necktie or a millinery hat?   From kind of necktie to kind of religion, such matters are always mere incidentals, since the main thing is forever — just individuality realized.   The clothing and the faith are simply passing phase-expressions of the self individualizing;   are, thus, parts of the person's individual world.   That world belongs to its creator, the man or the woman, and its complete integrity is an inalienable right which no other may justly question, determine or meddle with.   That world may be wrong — according to your judgment, but *your* judgment is for *your* world, and none other.   In later experience the person to whom that world belongs may see that it has been wrong (the necktie an atrocity, the religion more or less mistaken, and so on), but it is the inalienable right of the soul to make its own final discoveries in all these matters, assisted, it may be, by the opinions of others, yet never coerced; to make its final discoveries and profit thereby.   The invitation, then, which our study indicates is that you cultivate a most sacred regard for the other person's individual world and life, refraining from all coercing interference therewith. By so much you will assist that person to freedom and courage.

THIRD REGIME: *Sharing Worlds.* It is oftentimes just the unknown that inspires fear. You do not, perhaps, really know the inner world of the person with whom you are so familiarly associated. That world is, let us say — business, art, society, religion. The other person's reticence walls you out, and you are in awe of him because you are unfamiliar with his realm. Since you cannot break your way into that world, then, the remedy for your fear rests with its occupant. The urgent thing is that he shall open the doors to you so that you may share that world with him. No person may rightly bar out husband or wife from the inner kingdom of psychic individuality, so far as general partnership therein is concerned. Some subtle things are, of course, never disclosed to any human being, and no honorable person fails to respect such sacred factors. Nevertheless, you are obligated by the association of marriage to take the wife or the husband into your confidence in all matters which concern the welfare of the two lives. You are, therefore, urged to diminish reticence and to disclose to the life-mate the greater phases of the inner personal life. By so much, again, you assist that person to freedom and courage.

And there is a reason for this advice, other than the cure of another's fears. We now approach the inner phases of the married life, in order to bring out our thought. The sex-life is universal in all the worlds of plants and animals. The significance of this fact is three-fold:

Sex exists, first, for the perpetuation of life.

But life perpetuates for the evolution of higher forms.

Each individual is a variation from ancestral individuals.

Sex operates, therefore, in a way to combine variations, and thus to secure higher (and varying) individuals.

But the combination of two individual factors prevents either from a fixed perpetuation by restraining its purely individual tendencies. Sex operates to combine variations, but also to restrain tendencies of certain fixed types.

In sex combination, then, the ideal is reached only through the coöperation of the individual worlds — the worlds which build around the nucleus-idea of the soul life.

The person with whom you are associated for life needs your inner world for variational development — assuming that your personality is wholesome and worthy. For the same reason — on the same assumption — you need that other person's world for the best in your life — and other lives to come. By reticence and self-inclosure either person commits a double robbery: the robbing of self of ideas, tastes, influences, experiences which would tend to variation and improvement in the world of self, and a similar robbing to the hurt of the other life-mate. Both parties must remain the poorer for such mistaken method of life in marriage.

FOURTH REGIME: *Assertion of Selfhood.* If fear is your difficulty in this relation, you are urged from henceforth to be yourself, to insist, practically, yet without ostentation, upon your own individuality. Such insistence means two things, which are of the greatest importance:

Individual assertion means, for one thing, the *utmost valuation of your own experience.* It is a charac-

teristic tendency of the timid or fearful person to undervalue personal experience, and hence, his opinions and
judgments, and so on.

But one's own experience is one's own knowing
and developing relation to the Universe. You come to
know and to unfold through your own experience only.
Any other person's experience may be valuable as a
consideration, of course, but even then the real value
of it will issue alone from the fact that the consideration
in some way goes into your own experience. Only
through your experience can another experience help
you. We always are driven back, then, to experience
purely personal to ourselves. It is this experience,
and this alone, by which you are to know the Universe
and thus unfold your individual selfhood.

Now, your experience is, and has been, just itself.
This "just itself" constitutes its supreme value, no
matter what it is or has been. It is, therefore, always
a mistake to belittle one's own personal experience,
since that is the only experience out of which you can
make anything for life's improvement. One who had
had all sorts of "occult" experiences was heard to speak
contemptuously of certain phases through which he had
passed. His hearer remarked:

"You should not entertain contempt for the
egg-shells out of which you have been hatched. You
have gotten past them now, of course, but you have
become what you are through all that past experience."

Here, then, is the suggestion. You have not been
decreed to the experience which your life has developed,
but you have really had just that experience and no
other, and this it is that has made you what you are.
Above all, you are invited to stand for that experience,

to properly value it, not to discount it, to utilize it for the utmost freedom, courage and development.

It is a fundamental thing that if you will insist on your own individuality and experience, courage will infallibly begin to grow in your soul and displace fear and all its fell brood.

Difficulties Confronting Individuality. Now, the determination to be one's self (at the best, it is always assumed in these discussions — and you alone can rightly decide what is your best self)— this determination involves a number of difficulties, to which we now turn our attention.

1. No one's selfhood may be asserted at the expense of any other selfhood. Always, when this is attempted, the self so assertive robs itself of its true best.

Nevertheless, it is error to confuse true selfhood with personal happiness. Self-assertion may diminish happiness either in the one or the other in the marriage relation. This presents the difficulty.

It may be that you are surrendering something of individuality for the sake of another's happiness. This can be none other than error. Such surrender simply perpetuates a wrong. You may say: "If I insist upon being myself, free, active and courageous, this person's happiness will inevitably suffer." A great heresy lurks here. No one has right to happiness at the expense of my selfhood: the Universe is not so constructed. Anyone's selfhood is the sacredest thing in existence, and demand for it is the supremest of duties. One who derives pleasure (not happiness) from the sacrifice of another's happiness (not pleasure) is guilty of gross selfishness, and by so much injures his own personality. One who permits such pleasure (at the expense of happiness) is *particeps criminis* in the ruining of a human soul.

You are, therefore, urged to have the courage of individuality, even at the expense of another's pleasure or selfishness. You can adjust to the individuality of your mate without surrendering your own. This will assist each person in building the ideal life, while surrender will only increase your timidity and fear and permanently injure the both of you. Self-insistence, seeking right adjustment, must infallibly unfold the spirit of courage, and that more and more.

It is a mistake to value happiness (superior to pleasure) as a supreme end in life. The goal of existence is individual development, and this guarantees the highest type of happiness, but all so-called forms of happiness which depend on the sacrifice of that goal (individuality) are false, exactly because they so depend.

2. Oftentimes, in the relation here discussed, one is tempted to sacrifice individuality, not only because of some other person's misconceived happiness, but in the interest of one's own peace in life. Such an one, to describe the fact plainly, prefers a valueless peace to a complete personality. It is a case of psychic abuse of self.

Setting aside all lesser and all false considerations, now, you are urged to stand resolutely and persistently and heroically for that individuality which Nature intended in your birth. You are invited, to this end, to make the following declarations of independence your own for life, whatever may betide as the outcome:

"*I am!*"

"*I am inalienably myself!*"

"*I realize in daily life the supreme idea of mine own individuality!*"

" *I live my own life, freely, fully, courageously!* "

" *I build the inner world of my best selfhood —
and I alone!* "

" *I create the personal experience that is mine —
and I alone!* "

" *I value my personal experience immeasurably.
I is my highway of unfoldment and life!* "

" *I adjust to any person, but I sacrifice no whit
of my personality!* "

" *I wish happiness to all, but I shall be my true
self, at balance with every other true individual, dominated by no false claims of others!* "

" *I seek the happiness of the self at its best, and
none other, and for this goal I pay any price!* "

" *I stand for individual freedom and the courage
of the free soul!* "

" *I am inalienably myself!* "

" *I am!* "

FIFTH REGIME: *Assertion of Courage.* It has
already been suggested that you can only know courage
through its experience. Also, experience has been
divided as outer and inner meaning, experience in
relation to things external and experience in relation
to the inner life. At bottom all experience is internal
— within the self. You experience, in either phase,
through activities of the self. If you had never had
an inner experience effectively denoted by a world of
Nature, you could not begin with experience of an external life, since the objective world is only what you make
it by your perception and thought. You are compelled, in dealing with any new experience, to begin
with your inner world of thought and feeling. If it be
said that we first discover the outside world, and that
we discover the inner world only by reflection, the

answer is that the discovery of the outside world is also an inner process. The only Universe you know you create within.

Herein lies the secret of the *power of auto-suggestion*. In auto-suggestion you assert and assume to be a fact that which has not really become a fact. Yet, by the assertion and assumption you begin to *make it a fact* in your inner life and for yourself. When you assert a thing, you form an idea of it — begin to *experience* it as thought. When you begin to assume the thing as *real within*, you begin to experience it as *feeling*. If you really assert and assume, you not only affirm that it is, but as well that it surely will be — only more so. In other words, in regard to this thing, you decide, affirm, resolve. By so much as you go on with the assertion and assumption, you disclose *persistence*. You see, then, that you now *experience this thing as Will.*

Thus, the inner experience has evolved thought, feeling, Will. You have really experienced the thing with the *whole* of yourself. You have put yourself into that thing. You have incorporated that thing in yourself. By so much you have *become that thing*.

You will find, moreover, a strange occurrence taking place at this point: The *meaning* of the thing will grow on you, and the thing itself will unfold within you. New meanings will emerge. New developments will occur. The process is infallible.

You are, therefore, invited to assert daily for months:

"I am courage; perfect, unflinching courage."

But you are also invited for long to affirm:

"I assume — feel — realize — within — courage; perfect assertive courage."

And you are invited to persist in the assertion and assumption until they become one fact: perfect, unflinching courage.

Always, thus, you will develop new meanings in courage, make these real elements in experience, and bring thought, feeling and Will to bear on the realization of the goal — that is, the entire self as courageous.

This process will bring to you a larger and a richer life. If such a course shall finally mean the severance of the relation of marriage — better separation than the stunted life. That outcome need be rare only, since the human animal is almost infinitely flexible, and, for the majority of people, means good and not ill. But if it chance to mean ill, and demands your last sacred right, selfhood, the final "farewell" seems the only alternative.

II. SECOND RELATION CONSIDERED: *The Home Life — The Child.* The above considerations apply equally to other relations of the intimate life: such as, brother and sister, employer and employee, and so on. Always the solution of fear-troubles induced by close relations involves remedies sought through adjustment and assertion of complete individualism.

One phase of the relation of the home life is not to be sought through the preceding regimes, except in a very general way. The relation of parent and child calls up the elements of such regimes, indeed, yet demands special application up to a certain varying age, from which age the main principle, conceded and asserted individuality, becomes the one admirable guide to the culture of courage. This leads to

A Fundamental Principle in Child Government. Life is an art, and a child's learning of this art must go on under direction until it discovers the fact and the value of personal experience and discovers how to utilize experience in the conduct of its own affairs. The direction which is meanwhile demanded, and the discovery of experience and its utilization by the child, however, are precisely the factors which require care and intelligence on the part of parents. Thus we come to our regimes.

FIRST REGIME: *Concession of the Right to Make Mistakes.* The goal here suggested, *individuality through personal experience,* indicates that the tendency to make mistakes is an inalienable *right* —in so far as these may minister to personal success in the end. Experience without mistakes is an impossibility. This fact must be conceded. Experience profiting by mistakes is the great teacher. This fact asserts the right of every individual to commit some errors in his life, so long as the motive of right conduct prevails. It is here that the right of self-government appears. Before the human self can know what experience is, and what it is for, some one must put his own knowledge and experience in responsible relation to that self. Government must begin with oversight, but go on to the independence of the governed. The right of government by oversight obtains in the interest of the coming independence. The right of parental authority is not based in the parenthood; it is based in the fact that here is a young life which does not as yet know enough to govern itself. For this reason, there is only one goal for the government of parent over child, the development in the child of ability to take authority-government over to self-government. All along, in the young life, since this alone is the goal, it must be conceded that the child has an inalienable right to that degree of self-assertion which involves mistakes. The goal of self-government can never be realized without experience, and without a measure of blunder and folly experience can never occur in the human career.

You are urged, therefore, to concede to the child three things:

(a)   The right to its own personal experience;

(b)   The right to make mistakes in the course of that experience;

(c)   The right to that degree of *courage* which issues from a consciousness of a growing independence and the expectation of a future self-government.

When you succeed in placing the child on the throne of its own judgment-will, you initiate its surely coming final career.

If, in the meantime, you induce the child to depend on itself, to endure the consequences of its mistakes, to understand and profit by its own experience and to be sanely courageous, you initiate, or assist in initiating, its surely-coming final career for success of some infallibly valuable kind.

SECOND REGIME: *Cultivation of the Child's Courage.* The preceding regimes will "make good" for this present regime.   If you throw the child upon its own resources, and teach it to heroize amid the consequences of its own mistakes, you assist in unfolding its courage.   You are urged, however, to go beyond this in the following respects:

1.   Fear breeds fear, and courage inspires courage. If *you* reveal *your* fears, the child will imitate you.   If you *mimic* courage, the child will take your leading. You are thus invited to smother your fears in the child's presence and to assume courage and self-control before it for the sake of a brave young life.

2.   Courage thrives on *encouragement*.   Thus you

are urged always to inspire the feeling and will of courage in the child's soul.

3. Courage expands in the light of *reason*. The fears of human life that have no basis in fact whatever are legion. Here are some fearless statements which all men ought to confront:

There are *Nature-Fears:* savage and child quake in presence of the great Mother.

Here are the *Dark-Fears:* man-child and years-child are always fearful when light fades.

Here are *Death-Fears* and *Grave-Fears* and *Ghost-Fears:* undeveloped mind forever trembles in presence of the Mystery.

Here are *Religion-Fears:* the majority of men and women are by these incessantly haunted.

This book denies the *validity* of all these fears *in toto.* There is nothing whatever to fear in Nature, darkness, death, grave, other-world, religion, in all this Universe: neither Creator nor created. There are dangers everywhere, and this fact calls for reason and self-preservation, but at the same time it admits the statement as correct: *there is nothing in or under the heavens to be afraid of.*

It is heresy and a fallacy that danger justifies fear. Danger justifies only the exercise of reason and the action of the instinct of self-preservation: these only. There is nothing in danger to be afraid of. Danger is to be avoided, met, turned aside, overcome, destroyed (and it may be) without a particle of fear as a feeling, disturbance or panic.

Only one thing might seemingly justify fear — thyself gone wrong; yet even here the call is for the righted and the fearless self resolved on better things through harmony with reason.

First Invitation. I urge you, with these clearing
statements, to deny and sweep away totally and forever every known and imaginable thing —or so-called
reality — as a justification of fear; to be done with
every notion involving fear-feeling regarding Nature,
Stygian Darkness of Empty Space, Death, Grave,
Other-World, Religion or Deity.

Religion, Child of the Infinite, sweet Guide to
reasonableness and wholeness, beautiful Simplicity of
fearless selfhood — Religion has been massaged, and
clothed, and rouged, and starved, and made odorous
of the grave and pallid with death's bloodlessness, until
now she is oftentimes more *prostitute* than Heavenly
Vision, more *tyrant* than Friend, more *devilish* than
Divine, more *feared* than loved — hateful obsession of
souls warped and twisted by innumerable fears.   And
if this seems hysterical writing, remember the long
hysteria of carnage, death, torture and awful fear which
has haunted the world by reason of religion misunderstood and misapplied in a vain attempt to take the
world by brutal force.

Second Invitation. You are invited, therefore, to
destroy all these fears within yourself, and thus to
banish from the child's life the very suggestion of fear,
so prevalent in the common home atmosphere.   If in
this effort you call to your aid your will and your
reason, the child will imitate you and in time will acquire the habit of courage-reasonableness.   The imitation will appear in its objective life because it has appeared in your objective life.   In addition to such outcome, which must be evident, a further result will
obtain: the psychic and etheric activities of your
inner life will, in some way — telepathically, perhaps —
communicate to the child's inner world.   Unconsciously

to you and to him will pass into his deeper mental sphere the incessant suggestion of a reasoning way of looking at things and of the consequent attitude and habit of courage. Your deeper life surely influences those with whom you are intimately associated, and in various "occult" (through natural) ways. You influence others by impressing your inner personality upon all objects of common use, no less than by direct contact.

> The rose that greets an angel's face,
> Tossed to the street, exhales a grace
> Beyond its perfume, as it lies
> Upon a waif's pale cheek, and tries
> Life sordid to idealize.

> The flower from an evil breast
> Has quaffed the soul its hues expressed,
> And she who wears it now must bear
> The life it breeds a-lying there —
> A glittering symbol of despair.

And the truth here indicated is a conclusion from scientific study. It is not as yet "true science," since it eludes the ordinary pickaxe methods of so-called true science. Nevertheless, many facts now conceded in the realm of matter-force or force-matter suggest very strongly that subtle ether-movements are incessantly passing in to and out from every material object, that the human person, be he all matter or all spirit, does originate such movements, that such movements pass from person to object and from object to person, and so, that we are always influenced in "occult" but natural ways by things which have long been associated with human beings, and by the "personal atmosphere" of the people about us.

If such conveyance of influence between persons and things be real. it is surely as real between persons and persons

Always the home-life has its complex personal
atmosphere. In this atmosphere, amid such influences
of things, the child lives. Above all is it constantly
assailed by the unseen forces of the personal life around
it. What that life is, the child is likely to be, more or
less. If the home ether-life, to express it so, is full of
fear, even though unrevealed by word or action, fear
will enter the child's soul. If the home life is vitalized
by reason, freedom and courage, the child's soul will
be subject to the influence of such factors. It will grow
into fearless intimacy with Nature, for example. A boy
just able to toddle about, whose father is a naturalist,
forms a child's acquaintance with a college professor,
and greets him, both chubby hands full of live insects,
with a shout of glee, "Buggums, Bates! Buggums!"
In the same brave atmosphere of reason, the child
should know no real fear of darkness. Here also, religion should mean sweetness and light rather than
rubbishy ceremony, intolerant theology and hell and
deific wrath. And here the All-Good should come,
by inevitable and natural communications, to be the
Eternal Thought Beautiful.

Third Invitation. You are invited to break away
from all bondage and to enter the free world of courage
for the sake of courage. If, meanwhile, you try to
develop the larger life and the true courage in the child,
you will find the satisfaction of the constant response
to your example and teachings.

Fourth Invitation. And you are urged to appreciate
the fact that the child's life and thought-world are real.
The fact that the child's life is imaginative by no means
lessens the reality of its world. The realm of imagination is after all merely the realm of things in thought.
But this is true of the world of external Nature: it is

also, to each of us, only a thought-world — however actual as an external reality it may be — and is. There is absolutely no hard-and-fast criterion of difference between the world of imagination and the world of reality — except that the inference of the latter seems inevitable. The so-called real and the so-called imagined is in each instance, thought, and no more for us. Experience alone can discriminate things of pure imagination from things actually existent aside from imagination. The child's world is all its own, and it is as real to him as the adult's world is to the adult. The child's fears are begotten of this seemingly real empire of dreadful things — which he imagines because he has been taught to imagine it. It is your privilege to assist him in building a thought-world which shall be free from such evil suggestions.

III. THIRD RELATION CONSIDERED: *Sex in the Social Life.* Individual fear for the opposite sex is common. Such fear may obtain as bashfulness, embarrassment, timidity, or fear in the usual sense, or even as antipathy. All these phases may be regarded either as the outcome of unfamiliarity or as the product of traditional teaching. In the one case, sex timidity would disappear with familiar association (sex-timidity should not be confused here with fear of certain individual traits appearing in either man or woman), or with association inspiring regard. In the other case, timidity needs but a just understanding of sex as a condition to reveal the utter uselessness of the feeling. These propositions lead to the practical regimes demanded for development of courage.

FIRST REGIME: *Fear Dispelled Through Social Life.* Every rightminded person naturally idealizes the opposite sex. The tendency to do this is one of the

most valuable of psychic activities. There is in the
human soul a universal initiative in this direction. The
initiative, in other words, is a broadly working tendency,
as the bent toward individuality is a broadly working
instinct. The value of the tendency to idealize the
opposite sex is evident when the general initiative
gives rise to the special initiative of sex-love for some
particular person. The special idealization re-creates
a loved person and builds around that beloved object
an altogether unique world. The one whom we love
is always more the ideal then the real. The lover's
truest mistress is the creation of his passion. The hero
of a woman's soul is only suggested by the actual man.
This fact comes very close to a law which obtains in
religion, as, indeed, the sex-life lies so closely thereto
that it ought always to be taken as a sacred experience.
The Buddha, the Christ,— each is forever a gift to the
worshipping world of that world's own idealizing imagination. Nor does this fact destroy the value of
religion; it really enhances and validifies religion. In
the sex-life, also, no statement of the kinds made above
can destroy the idealization of passion. That initiative
of imagination which leads to sex-union, is the guarantee
of the sex-life, and the philosopher who knows the truth
goes as blindly into love as the veriest boor. In its
general form the tendency makes the sex-life possible.
In its special initiative it makes the sex function actual.

When, however, the idealizing tendency operates to
excess, it begets that common condition, sex-timidity,
or sex-fear. The boy fears the girl and the girl fears
the boy — at the proper age. In either case here there
may not be the slightest consciousness of idealization,
but the tendency indicated lies back of timidity or fear
(other than antipathy) in so far as it is due to sex rather

than to individual traits. The problem, therefore, is this: how to remove the inspiration to fear, yet leave intact the vital idealizing tendency. The problem suggests the present regime. The right social life removes the mystery of the unfamiliar sufficiently to banish fear, but does not touch the general initiative of idealization. Observe, at this point: it is said that the right social intimacy tends to accomplish these two things. Whether or no such be the outcome in regard to the idealizing tendency (or ought to be the outcome), the death of fear certainly does follow right social acquaintance.

If, then, you are timid with people of the opposite sex, your remedy consists in associating, incessantly and in the most friendly way, with individual women or men. You should never yield to the temptation of flight, but should resolutely hold yourself to social contact, however emphatically you may feel at any particular time that this is exactly what you do not desire. Nevertheless, social contact should be social indeed. It is sex-fear which you are seeking to rid yourself of, not fear of individual members of a sex. If you lose your timidity in the presence of some women or some men, your trouble may still linger on. In such case you have merely conquered individual occasions of fear. You are urged to go beyond such accomplishment, and to conquer sex-fear by means of familiar social contact with men or women in numbers, meeting them individually, in groups, in crowds, and to persist in such social contact until the fear for any man or any woman because of sex shall have vanished from your life. With this persistent effort may go, as psychic encouragement, the assertion and assumption of all these pages.

"I am what I am! I have no cause for fearing you.

I am, with you, unobtrusive yet perfect courage." The outcome of this regime is infallible within its intended scope.

The scope of our present work, however, is not designed to cover pure psychic antipathies. Antipathy founded in sex-reality is rare, since the great Nature of Things works precisely to the contrary in the interest of universal evolution. Individual cases of antipathy, therefore, are not common, and when they occur, are abnormal. This fact does not render sex-antipathy the less unpleasant. The experience ought to be unpleasant to the person who has it, and certainly is to those with whom the person comes in contact. If you are conscious of aversion for others merely because they are not of your sex, you are doubly abnormal in case you do not desire a cure of the antipathy, and are emphatically commended to the work here suggested.

Assuming that a remedy for the evil is desired, you should seek to discover all the *fine traits* and qualities, all the *admirable activities* of the opposite sex — doing this with perfect fairness — and, to this general end, all similar factors in individual men and women within the field of your observation. In the meantime, of course, you are urged to ignore, utterly, every other contrary evidence.

The existence of *evil traits* in human nature is to be conceded as of no importance whatever, for their consideration here is absolutely without value. What good can be accomplished by discovering or dwelling upon the faults of other people? The facts "go without saying;" let them alone.

The existence of noble qualities in human nature is also a fact, but of the *greatest possible value*. The search for such qualities and the constant dwelling thereupon always prove beneficial, both to self and to others.

It is not only an evidence of highmindedness, but is also a motive of high uplift in mind to seek, discover, acknowledge and dwell upon all virtues and exellences in the opposite sex.

Should such a regime fail in your own particular case, the only remaining possibility is the birth of a noble passion in your soul for some individual man or woman. When real love for a woman or a man unfolds in the heart of man or woman, sex-antipathy dies perforce. So concluded Oliver Wendell Holmes in *"A Mortal Antipathy."* Thus, to cite another instance, a marvelously beautiful queen had been dominated for years by actual aversion for all individual men, and had endured with the utmost pain the very touch of the king's hand, her soul being as ice at the thought of love; but when the sovereign had asserted his kingship and had proved himself so truly a monarch that he inspired an impossible passion in a daughter of the people, the queen's heart yielded and she discovered within her soul a great love for the man — too late. And then the queen became the superior — a woman in love.

SECOND REGIME: *True Knowledge of Sex.* It is an evidence of the preëminence of Nature that the physician, the surgeon, the scientist, may know human nature to the last knowable atom, yet retain the idealizing tendency here suggested. A truer knowledge of sex would certainly dispel many false views of men and women for women and men. Especially is the notion of the superiority of one sex over the other entirely groundless.

There is no fundamental *entity* which we are to call sex. Sex is not, so far as we can perceive, a psychic

reality in itself.   The ascription to Nature of male and
female essences is purely imaginary.   Similarly, the
notion of two coöperative principles in Being, or in
Deity — the notion of the Divine Fatherhood and the
Divine Motherhood — has merely a fanciful value.

Many scientific works appear to assume that sex
is universal in the sense of being fundamental, and in
some instances writers in the science field go so far as
to speak of the "male" cell and the "female" cell. Such
cells may indeed issue from male or female bodies, but
there is no real sex in either instance.   Either "male"
or "female" cell will reproduce female or male forms
of life, indifferently, up to a certain larval stage of
physical life.   The one form of cell has been seen to
enter the other form, and, before the two had completely
united, before the inner nucleus of the one had merged
with the nucleus of the other, the whole has been
divided (in experiment), so that the two nuclei occupied
the one portion of the division, the other portion being
without nucleus,— and each portion has produced a
temporary living form.

The union of the male and female cell is conjugation, and the function of conjugation is restoration, so
to speak, of energy.   The cell, without conjugation, is
capable of a larval form of life, but its energy is not
sufficient for the further development of that life.   Conjugation affords a condition in which is supplied the
greater energy demanded for the fully developed type
of life.

The factor, sex, is functional, not essential — not
of the essence of things in itself.

The fundamental function of sex is conservation
of energy.   In mathematical physics, the parallelogram
of forces illustrates this truth.   Two forces meeting

at right angles, proceed combined on a line of forty-five degrees. Sex corresponds to the forces: the resultant action is not a fundamental; it is merely an outcome of the meeting. The sex-correspondence is not the two lines of force, however, but is merely the fact of the to-be coöperation for the resultant. Or, to illustrate in another way: a thought has its own mental energy, and it may fail to realize its own possibility until it is re-energized by contact with another thought. The function of contact is not of the essence of thought; this is incidental to the upholding of the thinking activity.

Sex is functional to the physical life we know; but it is not of the essential nature of the psychic life, *so far* as we know.

There can be no superiority based solely in or dependent on sex. If two factors are indispensable to the production of a third — not in its initiation, but only in its completion — the conclusions are:

Neither is essential to the nature of that third;

Both are essential to the completion of that third;

Neither can be superior to the other, so far as its own existence or nature is concerned — at least, evidence of such superiority must be looked for elsewhere.

The superiority of man regarded as a class over woman regarded as a class is not demonstrated by history, since the question of superiority must involve those elements in which women surely are superior — thus far in the world's life. (The apparent contradiction here is balanced by the ensuing paragraphs.)

The superiority of woman as a class over man as a class is equally not demonstrated by history, since as truly the question of superiority must involve those

elements in which man surely is superior — thus far in
the world's life.

Human superiority is wholly *individual,* never a
determination of sex.   If an individual man proves to
be superior to some individual women, this is a case of
individual (not sex) endowment — a fathomless mystery — and of personal effort — a very plain affair.

If an individual woman proves to be superior to
some individual men, this case is explained precisely
in terms of the former statement.

We are compelled to deny the actual superiority
of men in any large and fair field. And we see no
reason for holding that woman is in any actual sense
superior to man.   Whatever degree of inferiority or
superiority appears anywhere in members of either sex
is due to the *social history* of the two sexes.

If, therefore, you are hampered by fear of woman
because she is woman, you should remember that she
is simply a human being, primarily, and a woman,
secondarily, because of her marvelous part in the drama
of life.   And the same proposition applies if you are
fearful of man because he is man.   If you are right-
minded the rude truth about the other sex — that the
individual woman or man is just human, body and self
— will assist you in meeting the other sex without fear.
Moreover, the fact that woman instinctively tries to
surround herself with mystery and beauty will clothe
that rude fact with ideals essential to her place in life.

In London's "*Martin Eden,*" the woman whom
Eden loved stained her lips eating cherries. So, she
was human, after all.   "She was pure, it was true, as
he had never dreamed of purity; but cherries stained
her lips. She was subject to the laws of the universe
just as inexorably as he was.   She had to eat to live,

and when she got her feet wet she caught cold. But that was not the point. If she could feel hunger and thirst, and heat and cold, then she could feel love — and love for a man. And why could he not be the man. 'It 's up to me to make good,' he would murmur fervently. 'I will be the man. I will make myself the man. I will make good.' "

Our regime consists in the two suggestions: Remember the fact that every woman is simply a human being, fundamentally like your psychic self. And, remember, too, that her ways, adornments, mysteries, are just the instinctive efforts of her psychic self to play its part in life's huge history.

Reversing the matter for the opposite sex: Remember that a man is merely a human being, and that his aggressive ways are but expressions of a psychic self whose first law is to die for the object of its love.

These suggestions are based on sex considerations only. If the individual man or woman proves fearful by reason of traits peculiar to individuality as manifested, the present regime must give way to other methods as herein outlined.

IV. FOURTH RELATION CONSIDERED: *Employer and Employee.* In *"Power For Success"* the relation of employer and employed is discussed with reference to getting on in life. That object of effort is not now before us. Our sole concern is the destruction of fear and the development of courage in either master or servant. (These words are here used because of the wide scope of their meaning). The relation, then, suggests:

The Employer's Responsibility. Respect for rightful authority is always legitimate, and respect for the man who deserves it is admirable. The feelings of respect, deference, veneration, have nothing necessarily to do with fear, however. Neither the feelings nor their corresponding attitudes involve distress, nor do they tend to initiate flight. These are the characteristics of fear in all its forms: a sense of danger, a nervous disturbance, an impulse to get away from or to overcome the inspiring cause — some instinctive action which means self-preservation. The action, flight, even in assault by the fearful, is negative (though positive in its manifestation), really signifying an effort to put the cause of fear away from the self. If, then, the employer, or anyone in authority over others, arouses such psychic activities, let him remember that he has induced fear in a human soul.

Such inspiration of fear is not always conscious in the employer himself; nevertheless, the contrary is often true. And the man who becomes timid, bashful, fearful, in the presence of his employer is not always really conscious of the fact; but the contrary is very frequently the case. Responsibility comes up in both instances. Nevertheless, the greater fault lies with the *employee*, since the fear is his and the cure must be sought in himself. No man need in any degree be fearful of an employer if he wills, desperately and persistently, to be self-possessed and courageous. Provided, the employer be a human rather than a beast.

The employer who consciously inspires fear in his people is a demon if he enjoys that fear, and unfit for his position if he is indifferent. So, also, of any person who controls labor. The conquest of fear, then, raises responsibility for the employer. With him should our regimes begin.

FIRST REGIME FOR FEAR IN THE LABOR-WORLD: *The Employer's Responsibility.* If you are an employer, it is suggested that you begin the effort to lift yourself above the level of mere business.

I do not undervalue the business world. That world is of the very greatest importance, since, as things are at present, it supports all other worlds of human activity. Nevertheless, to be a *mere business man* is to be a very poor thing; as poor a thing as to be a mere artist, musician, poet, lawyer, physician, minister. No vocation can be as great a thing as is this thing: that of being a whole human. Your supreme vocation is the making the most of yourself and your life. What men call their *vocations* should be their *avocations* simply — the chief business being the unfoldment of individuality to its best estate.

If you say, or think, "rubbish," the rubbish is in your own head.

Business goes on for the accumulation of money. The cause of its great bulk is not the support of others and the fostering of culture; the bulk is purposed in money-making. Everywhere *mere* money-making absorbs the business world.

Money-making is certainly legitimate and praiseworthy as an avocation. As a vocation, it is degradation.

The mere business-man money-maker sacrifices the cream of life for the golden pitcher. The pitcher is needful,— gold or pewter,— but of what value is it if you have nothing within? This man swamps himself in effort which cannot possibly build the greater self so long as that effort is the main thing. And so, we come to one of *two bottom facts* in the realm of employment — that

The business man often puts his mere business above humanity; and that

The employee does not care for his work as work: he cares for it as only money-getting.

Both facts constitutes selfishness — which is the sole hell of a struggling universe.

When the employer is conscious that he inspires fear of any sort in any employee, the fact calls for effort on his part to dispel that fear. You must face the responsibility of the relation. And all responsibilities have this rather uncanny character: *they are neither settled nor disposed of by denial or neglect.* They are always there — just where they were born. The only way in which to get rid of a responsibility is to take it up and do the thing required. If you would get past a duty, you must eat it, absorb its essence into character. This is the whole of life — digesting and assimilating responsibility. Duty has been called "hardtack," but if you take the right view of life you will find the hardtack turned into truth, love, service, self-development: it will appear in brains and heart and manhood and womanhood. I do not preach in these words; I simply speak common sense. The principle runs clean up to the top of things. There is only one true God: That Which Lives By Doing Right Always.

You are invited as an employer, then, to resolve upon the removal, so far as your ability permits, of all occasion for fear of you in any man, woman or child whose labor you employ. If you cannot rule except through fear, that fact calls on you to surrender the position you hold: you are too weak for the place. The resolution indicated involves several important details.

First Detail for the Employer. To the end suggested, you are invited to regard your people from henceforth as altogether human, entitled to the best life that they can win, with their endowments, under the circumstances, and with your reasonable assistance.

Second Detail for the Employer. You are invited to put your business, in every single transaction, up on the level of an uncorrupted conception of right. A politician said of a great soul who had come to high office, and who yet repudiated all evil schemes: "Why, he simply does right the whole damn time." This second regime is fitted to awaken a similar surprise — perhaps in yourself — but it is the only way. The satisfaction that comes to a rotten life is not worth the candle.

Your business would go to pieces on that plan? On any other plan *you* will go to pieces. Let us see:

You desire that your wife and daughter shall be virtuous "the whole damn time." Doubtless they are. Yet some women are not. Among these there are some who declare the ideal life impossible. They cannot live as they want to live and be rigidly right every single time. Here we have the prostitutes among women: known or unknown, housed or homed, kept or married.

And the business man who is dishonorable, less than honest, slack in exact right dealings with public or employees, puts himself on the level with women who are housed, not homed, kept, not married. Differences of opinion on this subject are valueless. The thing is precisely as written. Should these statements and the present detail be repudiated by some chance reader with the remark, "This would destroy business," the reply is, "So much the worse for business"— and the man. Unyielding virtue destroys the social evil. But there are thouands of employers — business men — who contradict the objection. The business world would be infinitely better were the contradiction universally carried out.

The philosophy which has come to be called Pragmatism holds that any claim, proposition, law, truth, can only prove itself right by its practical working-out in human affairs. There is no other test.

But the application of the test is critical. It is hastily concluded that a man's life or methods have been right or justifiable because they work out for some elements of "good." The formal statement needs analysis and illustration, therefore. The world of employment validates the statement, in claim, but really shows that the usual illustrations should be reversed. Let us see.

Example One: A man accumulates a tremendous fortune and builds public libraries over all the world — with his name somewhere on the building walls. This is a good. A *vaster good* might be — an unmonopolized market, many independent enterprises, labor better paid and pensioned. The pragmatic philosophy here is somewhat clarified. Example Two: A man accumulates satanic wealth and founds colleges and universities. This is a good outcome. Perhaps it would prove *better* in the end for schools of learning if they could practically represent their own scorn for the mere money-getter and look to sound business and the people for their support. A substitute for the "good" in this case would be, again, an unmonopolized market, independent enterprises, better paid and pensioned labor. Thus further with the pragmatic philosophy as usually applied in such cases.

Many men define "good" as the thing they want.

The world does not exist *because* of business, whether honest or dishonest, but in *spite* of *dishonest* business and *because* always there are business men who try to do right "the whole damn time."

Third Detail For the Employer. Any man's relation toward labor demands equity. Equity is no more than justice. Equity in the English Common Law, however, sprang from two facts: interpretation of law was always a matter of opinion; the opinion tended to crystalize into rigid forms. Only as interpretation could find a door opening toward improvement — toward a higher ideal of justice — could real justice be done without violation of established precedent. Equity and Equity Jurisprudence were the outcomes of an effort to find that door.

No matter what a man's notion or acceptance of truth may be, if his attitude is not free and open to new conceptions, his "truth" may become error and his love of truth mere jealousy for a dogma.

Here arise the falsities of science and religion. The scientific attitude sometimes petrifies and becomes totally unscientific, so that love of truth is lost in the bigoted worship of a fetish. The phenomena of spiritualism, to cite an instance, were scouted, scorned and wilfully ignored by great scientific minds for many years until the age of the psychic factor inspired courage in a few investigators. Religion, again, has always been cursed by the theological bony system strapped on the outside, and theology, absolutely man-made, with no more God in it than in art, literature, science, or a henhouse, although with just as much,— *now and then,*— has been first a vital necessity of inquiring thought, then inevitably a marbleized mummy: Pharaoh trying to rule the world of later history — and so in every age. Always opinion issues from interpretation, and always interpretation hardens into fixed forms. If that which acts behind interpretation is to live, there must be the open door of re-adjustment. Nothing is true merely because it has been true. Truth now is because it is now-truth — and none otherwise.

The question of justice from employer to employee, to return to our regime, must always be idealized by the attitude of equity. When not so idealized, justice becomes rigid, an iron hoop all round the heart of business, and inevitably, thus, becomes injustice. Equity is not some sentimental ideal. Equity is justice striving to realize itself in new situations.

When you subject yourself to a fixed system of rules for the regulation of your conduct, you eschew the one fine thing in that system — the desire to do a little better. The ten commandments had to be completed by two other laws — and centuries of improving interpretation of those two additions. When you say, "The highest right thing I can make out— 'the whole damn time—'" you have all the rules *plus* this one saving thing, *the desire to do a little better.* Then your "Common Law" unfolds its flower, "Equity."

The detail, you see, calls for equity in your dealings with labor. This equity does not put itself on the usual financial basis: As big a fortune as possible whatever becomes of labor. Equity is demanded because that statement (Equity does not put itself on the usual financial basis) represents common notions of justice. No man starts in business for the sake of being unjust. The man wants to do justice by all. Methods which mean "success" come gradually to define what justice is, then opinions about justice petrify, and then the real justice — that of equity, that of new and human conditions — disappears.

The Equity-Detail thus suggested involves: (1) A reasonable *return* on the capital : money, time, effort and brains. But the valuation of brains does not base on a crook's notion of skill in robbery, since this would "in equity" give the Universe to one or two men in history. Such a true reasonable return may represent a fortune of millions, it is right to say, but it can never carry with it a gigantic monopoly, corrupt legislation, dishonesty of any sort, nor scanty wages, long hours, and the death of human sympathy as its legitimate price.

(2) Conditions of labor conducive to the best of body and mind, so far as possible, and consistently with reasonable equity-success.

(3) Shouldering responsibility usually shirked under the fellow-employee law.

(4) Hours of labor free from the coercion of labor societies and selfish business: long enough for capital's rights, short enough for labor's welfare. Equity! Equity!

(5) Wages of labor based on the ideal of coöperation. This may not involve the actual coöperative plan, since employees seldom reveal sufficient wisdom for that plan. It involves a fair (Equity!) distribution of the final net products of the coöperation of employer and employee.

(6) Interest in every employee outside the business plant.

(7) Advancement in position and reward conditioned on worth.

(8) An attitude toward every man, woman and child which shall, thus based on downright good-will, encourage all true courage and independence, yet demand personal respect and perfect adjustment to authority.

These details will infallibly work wonders toward the development of courage in all the world of labor.

If they should be labeled, "sentimental," "ideal," "impossible," "rubbish," very well. The author is not striving to coerce his readers, who rightfully have their own opinions; he is endeavoring with friendly motive strictly to adhere to his task, the inspiration of courage and the slaying of devilish fear.

SECOND REGIME FOR FEAR IN THE LABOR WORLD: *The Employee's Responsibility.* In the work of driving fear out of the world of business, the employee's responsibility is exactly equal to that of the employer. Hence we come to —

Labor's Responsibility for Courage. The mere business money-getter is evidently selfish. Unite this fact with labor's indifference to its work *as work*, and you have the twin supports of fear in both employer and employed. If the former is called upon to do what he can, as in the preceding regimes, to eliminate fear in his people, the latter should avoid occasion in the employer of fear for the employed. A master's fear of his servants is not even natural. The fact that he is in business indicates his initiative and courage. In him, then, fear is inspired by something which his people are or which they do.

No wage-earner or salary-earner should fear any man on earth. No employer should fear any wage-earner or salary-earner, since he also is a man, and as well an employee.

But the business man is constantly aware of the occasion for fear in his relation with business. This occasion for fear is two-fold.

First Occasion for Fear on Part of Employer: The employee is not always practical and sane in his attitude toward the employer. He also both wants and withholds things unjustly. His notion of justice also often lacks the sense of equity. He sees his own case: there 's an end! He does n't know as much in regard to the relation as he should seek to know. He does not try to know. Associations and unions back of him (or which he backs) represent these statements because such associations and unions are his own building. Organization is essential to his welfare, but he can and he will organize only himself. He organizes all his faults and follies and ignorance, so far as his relations with business are concerned. Conceding that he and his unions have their splendid points, yet squaring to facts, you see that labor is about as often wrong as right, about as insane as capital. Business courage may be willing to face equity, but employers, for the most part, fear the inequity of organized labor, insistent often on what cannot be granted, fully as much as they fear the unexpected in trade. If the employee, then, wishes to remove fear from his own soul, he must establish such relations with the employer as will remove the cause of fear from his own ranks. And so, our invitations:

First Invitation. You are urged, therefore, to take your stand as an individual for equity in your working life. No man can develop courage while conscious that he is wrong, or even that he *may* be wrong as a matter of practical fact. This invitation signifies independence of organized tyranny, whether that of wealth or that of labor. If you fear the business world, you have equal cause for fearing the tyranny of your own ranks. So far as courage goes,— which is the motive of these pages,— it is imperative that you permit no society to dictate to you the number of hours you shall work, nor wages, nor conditions of labor. You are urged to be and to remain a free man, working when you will, where you will, for whom you will, at what wages and for the number of hours you will, and under conditions as you will, with fears for no demagogue or organization whatsoever. The cost may be heavy, since you have to do with human passions, but this book holds that the goal is worth the cost.

He who suffers labor organizations to supplant his human sovereignty proclaims the coward. He who essays to control the sovereign individual in the world of wage and salary by organized capital or organized labor proclaims the tyrant. Tyranny has no real courage.

Second Invitation. You are thus invited to stand in your labor world, organized or otherwise, for sanity, fairness, full justice, which is full equity.

Second Occasion for Fear on the Part of Employer: The second phase of the occasion for the employer's fear of the employee is the fact that labor does not care for its work as work. The prevailing goal of labor is the pay.

This goal has a fair look. For what *does* a man toil if not for wage or salary? But this, again, is mere money-getting. And it is in the majority of cases *small* money-getting. Seemingly justifiable might be the striving for a mere fortune. When the striving is for a mere little sum, manhood sinks in degradation. By so much as labor becomes merely an effort for money, the thing assumes this equational form: *As little labor as possible for as much money as possible = dishonesty.*

The employer whose rule is, *As much as I can get for as little as I must pay,* is guilty of that dishonest type of business which dishonors finance. This proposition will carry the laboring man as truly as the business man. One personality is as low as the other.

The Difference Between Labor and Work. The wage-earner and the salary-earner fall into confusion in the use of the words, *"labor"* and *"work."* It is everywhere assumed that an employee is paid for his labor or for his work *as one and the same* thing. Hence the notion of little labor, much pay.

No business man in the world pays his employee for his labor. Labor and work *ought* to identify; but they do not, as a general thing. Labor is muscular or mental effort; it is the expenditure of force. The phrase, "the labor of a machine" is never used, because machinery is valued for its *work*, and it does not *labor* at all. In the machine energy is engaged in doing work. We measure energy solely by its work. That is to say, energy is gauged by what it does, machinery is valued for what it accomplishes. Labor being mere effort, *nobody pays a cent for it.* Work being the doing of something, is *entitled* to wage, salary, fortune.

You are not paid for eight hours of labor. As well might a business man hire you to swing dumb bells. You are paid for the *things you accomplish.*

This is the true discrimination between labor and work. Nevertheless, employees manage their effort in a way to contradict the proposition. In many instances they are *actually* paid for mere labor rather than for the real value, work, because their aim is, "As little done as possible for the effort I make." Thus they are tempted to think of their employment as so much *time* put in at so much *per unit* of time. In order to meet this fact, the employer plans to get as much out of his people as he can at as small expense as the situation will permit.

I hired a carpenter in the construction of a small building. I worked with him day after day. I did

not want to kill the man.   He did want to get in as
many "hours" as possible!   He put in a bill for "work,"
I paid him for a lot of needless muscle effort.

The element of time is purely incidental in the
business world.   Employers do not pay wages in order
that employees may get through eight hours of time.
Wages and salaries are based on the idea of values
secured during the day, month, year.   To meet this
rightful claim by time-killing is robbery.

The cause of the confusion indicated is the fact
that labor does not care for its work as work.

Work, properly viewed, involves four things   (a)
Enjoyment of a finished product, as the artist's enjoyment of his picture, marble, music;

(b) Pride in the finished product, as the handi-
craftsman's pride in the result of his skill;

(c) Pride in the skill involved, as the journey-
man's pride in the technique of his craft;

(d) The honest purpose to give value for value
— which means, to do one's very best.

No employee who seeks to practicalize these factors
and stands for equity in his own relations and those of
his organization toward his employer, will inspire or
prove an occasion for fear in the business man.

The invitation, therefore, looks to employer and
employee alike:

(1) To the employer: to demonstrate his own
equity and to refuse manifest injustice, with this resolve: *Fiat justitia ruat coelum* — "Let justice be done,
though the heaven falls."

One class of people especially needs an infusion of
back-bone in this matter: employers of household help.
Women are afraid of such help, from cook to lady's
maid.   Two things will instantly remove this fear: A

fully human treatment of help; ability and willingness to get on without such help. The consciousness of being right, and so of being independent — this is the nursery of courage.

(2) To the employer, again, to decline to entertain fear for any human in his employ. You are invited to face labor with equity and to hold fast the courage-attitude against all inequitable demands from the labor world. Many a business man has won out on precisely that ground.

(3) But the invitation also looks toward the employee. The latter must love his work. Hence—

Third Invitation. You are invited to get rid totally of the notion that you are paid for your time. Practically that is what labor is paid for, but this is not because business has *agreed* to the plan, and it is wholly dishonest.

Fourth Invitation. You are invited to hold steadily in mind that you *ought* to be paid *only* for valuable things accomplished in the shortest possible time, reasonably speaking. The muscle-action of slavery is justly measured by mere time — since all value goes to the master, and the slaves' energy must be renewed. You are a workman on the level of equality involved by freedom, and this fact demands brains and the use of them and the equity which ought to go with brains. Hence, you are invited to substitute the idea, work, for the notion, time-labor, both in your thought of your occupation and in the activities involved. Only thus can the human machine become a man. The best way in which to get out of the machine-life is to cease being a mere machine-man.

Fifth Invitation. You are invited to seek *enjoyment* of the finished product of your effort. There is

nothing a man does in which he may not put some skill,
and there is nothing requiring skill that he may not
enjoy. If your best goes into your work, enjoyment
is surely there.

Sixth Invitation. You are invited to cultivate
pride in the finished product of your effort. You cannot enjoy that product unless it merits your pride, and
you cannot take pride in it without enjoyment as well.

Seventh Invitation. You are invited to take pride
in the *skill* employed in the very best thing you can do.
Such pride is the wine that stimulates human evolution.
Nothing is more conducive to the magnetism of art and
craftsmanship than pride in bare technique of skill.   It
begets a fine personal feeling which infallibly lifts the
person to a higher level and establishes superior etheric
activities that must in the very nature of the case mag-
netically influence all persons susceptible to the higher
values of life.

Eighth Invitation. And you are invited to enter
the ranks of the sovereign few in this world whose law
is : the best of myself in every undertaking of body
and mind.

These invitations bear directly on the culture of
courage. He whose service is thus determined has
built for himself a foundation rock of courageous independence. This man may say three things against all
odds:

My will is — an honest day's work for an honest
man's pay.

My pride is — an able man's skill in an honest
man's task.

My courage is — a free man's claim for an honest
and skilled man's work.

Ii, now, the usual selfish indifference and brutal

selfishness of capital confronts you, you are invited persistently to resort to the powers of your own psychic self for the culture, through sheer assumption and will, of the courage that may be demanded by the very condition in which your difficulty lies. The time for courage is when things go badly. And kindly observe that the theme of this book is courage, and, *directly*, nothing else. It seeks, not to solve problems, but only to instruct for courage. Were conditions not adverse, courage were not called for. It is because things are as they are that you need to specialize on the unfoldment of courageous independence. This, then, be your talismanic sentence: *"I offer the world, not time nor toil, but work — the best thing I can do to-day, and better to-morrow; and I will be no man's machine, and I will fear no employer, and I am power amid all conditions whether of muck or of gold. Man lives here but once. Therefore, here I live high the life of an honest soul."*

THE RAW MATERIAL.

All about me I behold
The raw material of man:
Rough, angular, uncouth and jagged,—
Tossed and whirled, bruised and broken
Like iron shapes in the foundry's smoothing cylinders.
The heat of the strenuous moil is terrible;
The dust strangles;
The sudden and fierce contact is war!

I, too, am a part of the culturing process
Which makes of the raw some statues of the gods.
Therefore, I will set myself in opposition to all hurt,
And I will suffer the grind with a smile,
And I will take on equality with the best,
And I will assert my soul, and fare on
Resolute to win the wealth that's mine,
Win of the place that awaits me,
Win of the deep, wide richness of soul I inherit,
Win of the White Life's nicety and power.

Some day, afar up, I shall stand
Looking back on the cylinder-life,
On the plane of the raw and the painful,
On the planet of war and defeat and poor death,
Elate, having climbed to mine own —
No shapeless Thing,
But a human that's worth the cost.

— THE AUTHOR.

CHAPTER XI.

THE FEARFUL CROWD.

"Neither God nor devil, but a man."—"The Man Who Would Be King."

CURIOUS is this feature in fear-hallucination that one may be apprehensive before a crowd while consciously indifferent toward any of its individuals. An hallucination may be sufficiently defined as an impression not founded in fact. The apparent foundation for this fear is the notion of fear-worthy danger to self threatening injury or loss of reputation. This is an old error — that danger is something to be afraid of. The recognition of danger should not be identified with the emotion of fear or with a feeling of nervous apprehension. Always danger may exist without inducing fear. In regard to the crowd, the word hallucination is doubly applicable, therefore, because the crowd-fearing person assumes that danger justifies his fear, and because he manufactures a mysterious something in the crowd which none of its individuals supplies. If he is not afraid of any individual in the crowd, fear before the crowd is his own creation. If, however, the crowd portends an injury which no individual could portend, it is error to suppose that one may justifiably be fearful in its presence. No matter where you find fear, nor from what point of view you approach it, clean thinking always destroys its justification.

Fear because of numbers exhibits in three phases: Fear of the Crowd Hostile, Fear of the Crowd Human

merely, Fear of the Crowd Critical — the mob, the
mass, the audience, the public. We take up these
varieties in their order.

The crowd critical furnishes audience and builds
public opinion. The human mass exerts a physical
and a psychical influence toward which some organizations always, and most organizations now and then,
are antipathetic. The hostile crowd is comparable to
a wild animal.

But always man should stand before that crowd
serene, self-poised, alert, unafraid. You are invited to
make that statement a sure conviction in your soul.

I. FEAR OF THE CROWD HOSTILE.

Fear of a crowd may assume one or other of two
forms: *physical nervous excitement* reacting in mind,
or *psychic apprehension* reacting in body. In the
first form excitement threatens to beget fear in the
self psychic: the nervous activity may affect the subconscious mind and start a panic. In the second
form excitement threatens to overthrow physical control and to disclose fear tending toward panic.

One aim, then, must be to get *control* of the *nerve-
centres* by an instant and powerful effort of will and
through the discipline of constant practice, both in
thought and before the crowd itself. *A second aim*
must be to get *control of the body* — hands, feet, muscles
of lips, eyes, nose,— secured, again, by will and thought.
In the presence of danger, psychic fear-action tends
to express physically, and physical fear-action tends
to react psychically — in either case increasing the
fear-feeling. You, therefore, wish to master the physical and psychic signs of fear *before* these master·you,
or, in order that they *may not* master you.

Now, voluntary will-action is always preceded by idea in the conscious self. The governing idea in the subconscious self is self-preservation — protection of the individual. This idea takes care of automatic and reflex will-actions, as, eye-winking, dodging, assumption of defensive attitudes, and the like. All these, together with physiological processes, even the wars of the phagocytes in the blood against hostile organisms and substances, are efforts of subconscious will, for the will is the man, the man is will.

When you will to do a thing, this is because an idea has arisen in mind which suggests the action involved. You do not think thoughts; thoughts think themselves. You can will to engage in the activity of thinking further about some given thing that has occurred to you, but you cannot will to think any given thought, for when you seem to do so, the thought is already before you. You can will to stop thinking about a given thing, but the will-act here is preceded by the idea of inhibiting a given thought or line of thinking. You see, then, that you are able to inhibit thoughts.

You do not, furthermore, create thoughts; thoughts emerge in mind. You cannot destroy thoughts; you can simply stop thinking along a given line of thought. Here also idea precedes will-action.

When a given idea becomes strong enough — to do a thing, to think about a thing already in mind, or to stop thinking about such a thing or along a given line, you act, and when you so act you simply let the idea have its way in suggestion of action. Then the expression of the idea — in further thinking or in cessation of a given line of thought, or in the doing of some act — takes care of itself. You do not have to

carry out that expression; the expression carries out
itself. If, for example, you yield to the idea of moving
your arm, the arm-movement follows; you do not
trouble yourself with the process. The will does not
move the arm, the will lets the idea move the arm.
Thus with all your mental and physical actions. *The
will is idea become dynamic* (or ruling). The will is the
man because the man is thought — a complex of thought
— constantly going over from a mere ideally static
condition to a practically dynamic state. We note —

Elements of Physical Fear. The nervous excitement of the first phase of fear above mentioned is due
to a psychic state which is primarily nothing but a
complex of ideas, as follows:

    (*a*)   The Idea of *Danger*;
    (*b*)   The Idea of *Injury;*
    (*c*)   The Idea of *Weakness*;
    (*d*)   The Idea of *Flight*.

The idea of weakness and the idea of injury (or
suffering), combining together, constitute a feeling.

The physical distress and activity caused by
fear are all results of such idea-complex working without restraint and upsetting poise through nervous disturbance. The idea of danger becomes a complex
thought-action among nerves, emotions in the mind,
quivering of the lips, distention of the nostrils, dilation
of the eyes, quickening of the heart action, backsetting
of the blood, retreat of the mouth secretions, hasting
or retarding of the breath, weakening of the muscles.
The bare idea of danger multiplies with wonderful
rapidity into just this complex brood of mere thoughts.
So far as the fear is concerned, there is absolutely
nothing here but unreasoning, unchecked, fecund
thought — and will *i*n the sense above indicated.

The subconscious idea of self-preservation invades the conscious mind, and the subconscious will erupts out of its field into that of self-control, and so stampedes the conscious will. Thus, what appears to be automatic or reflex is really result of pure will considered as the dynamic of thought. What seems to be without will or against will is simply will running riot under the increasing spur of idea left free to breed after its own kind, or is simply rioting thought unchecked by will under the sway of reason.

This idea is primarily self-preservation. If that idea is controlled by the idea of reason-mastery, it serves its purpose fully.

Secondarily, however, that idea breeds many others if it is not controlled, among which is the notion that danger is something to feel afraid of. The moment this idea —"to feel afraid of"— is conceded to be legitimate or is given freedom, that moment all the processes just noted begin to arise.

Always, then, fear has to be met by idea and will — by the idea of will-power and the idea of control. Fear is wrong idea and will gone wrong. It must be met by right idea and will come right.

Idea and will of self-preservation are right in themselves. The right and the wrong here depend on the meaning of self and the meaning of self-preservation. Let us observe:

With the emphasis of meaning on *body*, the *coward* has his invitation. The idea of self-preservation is then body-preservation.

With the emphasis of meaning on the *psychic self* (the inner self), *courage* has its invitation. Self-preservation is then preservation of that which nothing material can hurt.

With the emphasis of meaning on *now*-preservation of any value *less* than the true inner self, the idea of danger coöperates to beget and spread fear.

With the emphasis of meaning on *long-run* preservation of the *true* inner or higher self, the idea of danger suggests self-control and facing and dealing with danger, and begets indifference to all things having power only to injure body or present material conditions. This analysis brings us to certain regimes which are of vital importance.

GENERAL REGIMES FOR FEAR OF CROWD HOSTILE.

FIRST GENERAL REGIME OF CORRECTED IDEAS: *Body or Soul?* Remembering that will acts in all that you do, and that will acts only in conformity with idea, you are invited to substitute for the usual valuation of body the true valuation of the higher, the entire, self. You have always thought of the welfare and painlessness of body as immensely important, and the law or bent to action of self-preservation has tended to action uncontrolled by higher considerations, so that danger has made you fearful. You are therefore invited to displace the emphasis of valuation from body to greater concerns, and, thinking more of the true self as absolutely immune to all evil not self-induced, to cultivate a reasonable feeling of superiority over merely physical danger. The banker will not greatly worry about the outside shell of his vaults so long as no thief can injure his gold. You are the banker, and your body is but the vault (in the sense here intended) wherein are values good enough to justify all the ages of evolution. The Universe begat and developed those values, and it thinks not too highly of matter, muscles, nerve, organ, but really justifies in the self of you which expresses in body-forms of matter. The idea of reasonable indifference to body-hurt will infallibly inspire will to right control of activities that stand for true self-preservation.

A practical method for realizing this regime consists in emphasizing some such thought as the following: *"I, myself, express in body, shall survive body in its present form, and shall always be able to express adequately in some body, whatever the present may do or become. I am no slave to body. I am master of any condition that may come into my physical life."*

SECOND GENERAL REGIME OF CORRECTED IDEAS: *Now-Preservation or Long-Run Preservation?* In a similar way are you invited to give less weight to any given moment in your life and more weight to its long-run values. The surgeon's subject must first in idea set his future over against the present crisis. Seldom do we need to go beyond the idea of some physical or immediate danger as opposing long-run self-preservation. If such idea must become actual, it is then fine training for courage (and the man's *best* courage) to sacrifice present preservation for future. It will, therefore, prove infallibly helpful if you will companion, for long and adhesively, with this idea: *"Body or soul in danger, it is the long-run welfare I seek, and so surely as I stand for the long-run highest and best in me, nothing can essentially harm me, the inner man. Therefore I fear not!"*

THIRD GENERAL REGIME OF CORRECTED IDEA: *The Honor of the King.* It is not in the power of devil or man to injure a soul that is buttressed in honor and sublimely careless of body harm or present non-psychic disaster. The way to courage leads high. If you would attain the courage-confidence that fears no evil, you are urged to live the life of conscious moral harmony and human honor. It is assumed that such is indeed your life, and in that assumption you are urged to reap all the benefits belonging thereto, one of which is absolute fearlessness. It may be that you have forgotten your right, however, and, because of that possibility, you are now invited to assert your own integrity, in your own mind, and to claim that in your conscious honor you have no need of fear because there is really nothing to be afraid of, since no force operating on this earth can affect your real self without your will, and your will is unalterably set to moral harmony and human honor.

But, now, in association with these regimes should go certain others which are based on our analysis of the fear-thought — regimes of a more particular nature. This fear-thought, as we have seen, involves the ideas of danger, injury, weakness, flight. And usually, the idea, "I am afraid," which is an interpretation of physical and mental states.

The culture of courage before the hostile crowd — indeed, under any circumstances — involves the *substitution* of these dispiriting ideas by their exact *opposites*. Such substitution must be complete, so that all merely negative attitudes retreat before attitudes which are positively inspiring. Regimes for this work may be suggested as follows:

SPECIAL REGIMES FOR FEAR OF CROWD HOSTILE.

FIRST SPECIAL REGIME OF SUBSTITUTION OF THOUGHT: *Danger Denied or Minified.* Emphatic ideas "reverberate" throughout body and soul, tending to induce all sorts of action according to their

nature. This action the subconscious self, making
over through heredity from ancestors, has learned to
associate with the corresponding ideas. How much
this statement is true cannot be said, but enough
evidently for the inheritance of instinctive life. But
the great bulk of action going with ideas has to be
learned in a more or less conscious way. Under the idea
of danger, your subconscious self tends to stir up the
whole physical system in the interest of self-preservation. This was the great primitive function of the
subconscious self before higher mental functions began
to unfold in the conscious self. As some sea-plants
are anchored by a cord or cable many feet long, so the
instinct of fear is anchored by heredity running through
centuries back to the man-animal whose whole business
consisted in trying to stay alive.

The idea of danger stimulates physical activities
--hich we have all learned. Here is the "line of least
resistance." To act as suggested by the idea of danger
is the easiest thing to do. Hence the physical functions naturally, as we say, act in their accustomed
fear-inspired way unless they are checked.

Now, it should be remembered that will is *initiative idea*. What seems to be a separate power (will)
is nothing but idea. There is nothing in the universe
but thought-action and thought-"substance." As a
matter of fact, thought-action is the fundamental
"substance" itself. So, if you fiercely try to check
activities while holding fast the idea which has started
them, you contradict will in the sense that you are
only using a statement that the ideas shall not go on
while all the time that stronger idea which has held
the throne for centuries in the subconscious self of
ancestors, and now holds the throne in your own self,

is really saying that they *shall* go on. The remedy for this state of things lies in the reverberating power of an opposite idea.

You are therefore urged to call up always, when facing the hostile crowd, the thought that there is no danger, at least that it is not near so real or so great as may appear (remember that the idea, danger, need not be, and is not, the fear-feeling). A talismanic sentence may now be given for the realization of this work:

"*This danger is imaginary. There's nothing in it!*" *Or:* "*The danger is not nearly so great as these people seem to pretend. They do not even intend danger to me!*"

Kindly observe! The suggestions here offered concern not at all your *escape* from the danger of the crowd or your protection while facing it, nor the success of your display of "nerve," nor the difficulty of carrying out the suggestions. The present theme is courage, not self-defense, substitution of ideas, not overawing the mob, the conquest of fear, not an easy method for working "miracles."

You may get hurt by this crowd; but why add the preliminary hurt of the danger-thought run riot? The "nerve" display may be feeble; but the memory of a good effort will linger long in your mind. The substitution of "no danger" may prove difficult; but the difficulty will give you future confidence if you overcome it. There are no miracles, and nothing is "easy" in this world. Resistance is the price of organization, for organization is harmony-centred resistance, and organization by self-effort is the price of growth. There are many "new thought" books, and they are made "easy" enough, heaven knows; but they also die easily, as we all discover.

Infallibly, if you employ the talismanic sentences given, will the rioting idea of danger be calmed and diminished in power. In that event, you have achieved victory, because you will have then acquired the initial power to check the first impulses of fear-action anywhere within your personality.

SECOND SPECIAL REGIME OF SUBSTITUTION OF THOUGHT: *Strength and Ability Asserted.* It may be thought that danger awakens a mere feeling of weakness, and that one is not responsible for the working of natural physical laws. But this is error. The human personality is agent, therefore intelligence, therefore will. All its activities originate in and make for knowing. Feeling is a result of some form of knowing. In the subconscious self it is the idea which first comes to existence, and feeling is reaction to that idea. Feeling obtains in the conscious self as a report of the idea. The feeling of weakness is created by the idea of weakness in the subconscious self. You could not feel afraid if you had no idea of danger, and you could experience no feeling of weakness if you had the thought of completely adequate power successfully to cope with danger.

You are invited, then, to resolve on vigorously and willfully thinking strength, adequate power, when the hostile crowd confronts you — or in the presence of any sort of danger. Of course this will be difficult, but if you persevere the effort will in time beget the required confidence. The effort consists in switching the mind off from the danger-weakness idea onto the notion of full power A sentence talismanic may well be: *"I am power! I can perfectly cope with this danger! Body and soul are electrically charged with courage-confidence—courage-confidence—courage-confidence."* Thus you will displace in subconsciousness the idea of weakness by the energetic thought of power. By so much, then, the weakness feeling fades before the feeling of adequate power.

THIRD SPECIAL REGIME OF SUBSTITUTION OF THOUGHT: *The Stand-Your-Ground Idea Maintained.* When you remember that feeling reports idea, and that action expresses feeling, you see that flight is merely the idea of weakness (born in the subconscious self, developed in the conscious self) carried out. It is suggestion: "Crowd hostile; I am weakness; run!"

Now, all feeling tends to spread and to multiply. It spreads throughout the system. This spreading forth induces action in the nerves and organs — or constitutes such action. That action suggests anew the original ideas — weakness — flight. When you yield, it is because the idea of flight has been suggested. The flight is action of the whole person. This in turn grows every instant, suggesting *more* action. The result is a panic. If these activities cannot expand with the growth of the fear-idea, there is collapse. There is more activity within the personality than can be taken care of, and the whole personality is swamped.

It is in this sense that we say that *we fear because we run.* We fear because we know — have the idea of danger — a mental action; think weakness — a mental action; feel weakness — a psycho-physical action; turn, flee — a physical action born of the idea of flight.

The remedy, then, must initiate in ideas. First must arise or be compelled the idea — "Danger nothing," or, "Danger slight;" then must be forced the idea —"I am equal to this situation;" and so must be cultivated the idea of *steadfastness* in presence of danger, whether or no. In the latter case a talismanic sentence may be used: *"I am master here, and I stand solid — solid — solid."*

You are therefore invited to combine this regime with the preceding, and to practise the combination for long, until courage-confidence becomes habitually your main thought in regard to danger, whether conceived or present.

The last element in our analysis will then have disappeared, for the ideas substituted cannot possibly comport with fear, — either of thought or of feeling. Your success will be measured by your effort. It is not said that you will succeed easily or after a brief effort. It is insisted, however, that sooner or later you will infallibly banish the fear-feeling from your soul, confronting any hostile crowd, if you persevere in the regime.

II. Fear of the Crowd Human — The Mass.

The idea that lies back of this form of fear may be one of several. Every such idea has a physical cause, only, or a psychic cause, or a psycho-physical cause (sources co-operating). And these causes may obtain in yourself or in others — that is, the predominating factor of the cause may operate in kinds of human nature met with, or in your own personal variety. What you are, this, indeed, determines the matter, but what other people are gives this determination its occasion. *Your* nature asserts itself *because* of *other* natures presented to you.

Whether such causes of fear of the mass be physical or psychic, they differ from the causes arising within yourself. You are — *what* you are; and, if

you fear certain *other kinds* of people, the reason is that
they are *not* what you are. Opposites may be affinities, but only where the one supplies what the other
lacks, and needs or craves. Where one fails in such
respect, there is indifference in the needing or craving
person. Where one is opposite only, and not com-
plementary at all, antagonism is inevitable if there is
contact.

The present thought may be indicated in the
following rather loose analyses (read across page):

You are Physical Person	*Others are* Physical Person:	*Relation :*
Cleanly,	Unclean,	(No complement)
Well,	Diseased,	"
Elegant,	Uncouth,	"
Robust,	Weak,	"
Finely atmosphered,	Contra-atmosphered,	"
Sexually right,	Unholy,	"
Etc., etc., etc.	Etc., etc., etc.	"

Outcomes of contact: Aversion and fear in your relation to such.

Were you some *different* constitution, you see that
the outcomes would not be the same.

This sketch may be supplemented by scores of
other oppositions. It is therefore merely suggestive
of the truth here under consideration. For example:

You are Psychic Person :	*Others are* Psychic Person :	*Relations :*
Educated,	Uneducated,	(No complement)
Wise,	Fools,	"
Courageous,	Cowardly,	"
Fine grained,	Coarse grained,	"
Moral,	Unmoral,	"
Positive,	Negative,	"

You are Psychic Person :	*Others are* Psychic Person:	*Relations :*
Artistic,	Commonplace, (No complement.)	
Inspired,	Stupid.	"
Etc., etc., etc.	Etc., etc., etc.	"

Outcomes: Antipathies and fears in your relation to such.

Always the opposition means the preponderance of qualities without complement of things needed or craved.

You are Psycho-Physical Personality :	*Others are* Psycho-Physical Personality :	*Relations :*
(Various undesirable qualities)	(Various opposite qualities)	(No complement)

Results: As in preceding cases.

When the antipathy of your nature to other opposite non-complementary natures passes a certain limit, — always variable — determined by your sum-total nature and particular circumstances,— the ideas underlying opposition merely become transformed into the ideas underlying the feeling of fear: danger, injury, weakness, flight. Antipathy has now developed into fear.

This is in the case of yourself in contact with other individuals.

Sometimes the antipathy or the fear springs from facts which you yourself recongize. As often, perhaps, causes that you cannot detect underly your attitudes. Thus appear our regimes:

REGIMES FOR FEAR OF CROWD HUMAN.

FIRST REGIME: *Ignoring Antipathies.* In this case, dealing with individuals, you are invited to ignore mere antipathy. You are what you are;

others are what they are. Do not trouble yourself
about the attitudes which they induce on your part, or
exhibit on their own. This book believes that forced
and conscious attempts to overcome natural antipathies are wasted because they must prove futile
in the end. For, they are expressions either of fundamental things in your nature or of mistaken impressions. In the former case, reform is impossible. In
the latter case, it is the impressions that must be
removed or corrected, not the antipathies, which will
take care of themselves, and experience alone will avail
in revealing the mistakes and learning how to correct
the impressions. Such experience needs no forcing;
it will come along in its own time.

But the feeling of fear is another matter, and
should be taken in hand, vigorously and persistently.
Remembering that we are dealing with individual cases,
you are now invited to reason with yourself somewhat as follows:

SECOND REGIME: *Recognition of Individuality.*
"This person for whom I feel aversion has his life,
as I have mine. We are entitled to the two lives.
His qualities need not touch my personality. I am
power! I live my own life. I see to it that this person
shall never penetrate my world nor share my life's
atmosphere. Why should I fear? Why should I feel
that which is merely hateful to my mind but cannot
touch my real life? Though he breathe the same air
and behold the same things as I, we two are apart —
as far as the east is from the west. I do not fear him!"

The purpose here is merely the substitution in
your thought of ideas breeding courage for those that
tend to breed fear — and to hold to that substitution.
So doing, you will infallibly check or cure fear for op-

posites who do not and cannot complement your own nature.

It is a curious thing that some people are disturbed by fear for kinds of personalities in numbers for whom, as individuals, we have seen, they entertain merely antipathetic aversion, or, it may be, even less. That is to say: the emotion of fear arises because of mere *numbers* — the *individuals* arousing antipathy only. Here, again, suggestion is at work. For the individual A, or B, or C, and so on, there is aversion without fear-feeling, perhaps, because the fear-ideas of danger, injury, weakness, flight, do not arise, but the individual A and B and C and so on, *as a crowd*, do suggest the fear-ideas in addition to the thought or feeling of aversion. A man or a woman may face any other man or woman fearlessly, but many men or women suggest, out of the antipathy, an idea of harm. Sometimes the process occurs only in the subconscious self, and then there is a vague sense of uneasiness which may grow into fear. Sometimes the process works up into definite consciousness, and the feeling is no longer vague; it is something more than uneasiness — and is likely to become fear.

THIRD REGIME : *Let Yourself Alone.* Such aversions are not worth an effort toward removal so long as they are undeveloped into the fear-feeling. (The matter is not here a consideration of morals, but relates to courage only.) It is sound sense to take ourselves as we fundamentally and distinctly are. You are invited to set about doing this for the rest of your life. A vast deal of unhappiness and wasted energy springs from this notion that we must revolutionize our characteristic nature, a notion which is fostered by false religion, that somehow man's chief business consists in

becoming something totally other than he is. For
example: sex must suicide, ambition must be strangled,
body must be "etherialized," mind must empty itself,
and so on. And thus, since natural antipathies are
conceived as growths of the depraved natural man,
they are to be rooted out as in themselves necessarily
evil. But this is an impossible ideal born of a misconception. A thing need not be evil merely because
it is natural. All truly natural things are good —
at least free from what we call "evil." A natural
antipathy cannot, in the nature of things, be evil in
a moral sense. Whatever is of nature — fundamental
nature — has a profitable meaning for the whole system
of things. Real evil is unnatural. Hostility in the
form of desire for the injury of another person is evil
because it is unnatural, and it is unnatural because
it is contrary to the good of the whole. You may be
aware of antipathy without hostility. Your fundamental aversions (which can be discovered only by
experience and reflection) are expressions, not merely
and alone of what you are, not merely and alone of
what others are, but also of a *relation* — in the abstract
or in the concrete — of one kind of person to another
kind of person. You are, for this reason, invited to
forego the futile effort to change the basis and essence
of your make-up, and to let yourself go *in* those antipathies which mean no harm to others, but signify
reasonable freedom in and for your own (and their)
selfhood.

It is no more reprehensible to take your *natural
antipathies* as they are, without worry, than it is to
take your *preferences and likes* as they are, without
moral uneasiness. Your antipathies run, neither
necessarily to right things nor necessarily to wrong

things. Antipathies are outcomes merely of personality related to personality (if they are fundamental).
All this is true of likes and preferences, which also run,
neither necessarily to wrong things nor to right things.
Likes and preferences are mere outcomes of personality related to personality. Whether preferences, or
likes, or antipathies, as natural expressions, signify
evil to any one, depends, not on motives, for motive or
intention behind an attitude introduces things entirely
different from natural like or dislike, but depends
upon what *follows* the feeling of antipathy or like. If
you take an *aversion* as a *luxury*, this is a form of
selfishness. If you take your *likes* as luxuries and so
as standards for others, here also selfishness appears.
It is possible to let yourself go as you find yourself,
through experience and on reflection, to be, without
strain to eliminate likes and dislikes, without making
them luxuries or standards for others. You are, therefore, invited to declare for your own selfhood, and for
freedom in all natural antipathies and affinities,—
but taken as no luxuries, kept to yourself,— and to go
no farther in the matter. By so much as you do this,
you of course grant all other persons similar right to
their freedom and their nature. Thus you omit from
your life a very active cause of social criticism and
friction.

But by so much you also put away the feeling of
fear originating in antipathies. For then you do not
care about these antipathies. You feel them: well
and good; let them go. The matter is not important.
So, also, you know that others feel antipathies: let
this go as well. Coming to such negative attitude
toward aversions, you find the inspiration to fear
gone. Indifference toward a thing or person, as a

personal attitude, cannot coexist with fear for the thing, person, attitude.

FOURTH REGIME: *Indifference Toward the Mass Units.* This analysis of any mass or group of people, thus disposed of, should obtain in relation to the group or mass. When you become indifferent toward your own aversions for all a's in the group A, and so on, and toward all antipathies in that group A, your antipathy for that group-*kind* of people loses foundation, dissipates. Take the item in the second analysis on page 324 "coarse-grained." Say this is group A. You think of a-(Smith), or a-(Brown), or a-(Jones), and so on. You take the antipathy for coarse a-(Smith) or any other member in the group, just as it is, and let it go; cease bothering about it; you stop worrying about it, since it is just a fact of your nature. You no longer care about this coarse-grainedness in a-(Smith) in itself, since its presence in Smith is indifferent to you, because it is just his, not yours, of his nature, not of your own. You simply let the thing go at that. You do not care about Smith in his coarse-grainedness, nor about coarse-grainedness in Smith. Then what obtains in Smith's case should obtain in Brown's and Jones' cases. Then the whole group — a-(Smith) — a-(Brown) — a-(Jones) becomes indifferent to you — just a "do n't-care" thing. You soon discover that your fears born of natural antipathies have vanished. For it is absolutely impossible to fear anything so long as you are wholly indifferent toward it — do n't care about it.

There is no form of fear without some form of interest in the thing feared. This study gives you the fear-cure of indifference. If you fear because of antipathies felt toward people, you will continue to fear so long as you nurse interest in those antipathies. When you regard such antipathies with indifference, your fears will vanish.

FEAR INDUCED BY ATMOSPHERIC TOUCH.

The preceding considerations have to do with conscious conditions and activities. The underlying spring of fear is the subconscious life. People for whom you experience natural antipathies trouble you, however, by action on your subconscious self more truly than by action on your conscious self. Very likely your antipathy and fear result from these subconscious, rather than the conscious, activities, affecting you, primarily, in a subconscious way which reports finally in your conscious life. You may say that you ought not to be antipathetic or fearful in regard to groups or masses of people, but you nevertheless experience these feelings, often beginning with simple uneasiness alone. The case seems to you inexplicable and hard to master.

We have here *antagonism of personal atmospheres.* Such antagonism has a psychic cause, but the first expression of that cause occurs in your etheric sphere.

We need not say more about the ether at this point than that it is the hypothetical medium of activities or mass of activities which lies at the base of all matter and founds, pervades, saturates and surrounds every individual object of material existence. You have your physical neighborhood of etheric activities. Call this your etheric sphere or atmosphere. The etheric sphere is what it is because you are what you are. Your psychic self appropriates and molds the ether in definite ways. Your established, regular complex way of being and doing establishes in regular-ity those etheric activities the final manifestation of which is your body: that is, your kind of body, your particular personal body. The body being a final manifestation of these activities, the latter affect a "field" of the ether. In all bodies this is true: The character of etheric activity, psychically induced and established, is reflected in, goes over to, this etheric field immediately surrounding the body. Your body is not a closed thing, like a hollow glass ball. It is a living thing in relation with the ether of which it is a manifest, immersed in which it exists and acts.

Science declares: "While it lives, a living substance by the act of living creates in the environment around its semi-fluid body whirlpool movements *which count for a great deal in the determination of its own form.* Thus, just so long as it survives, the living body carries along with it, not only its own substance, *but also a certain system of movements which it imposes on the medium in the immediate environment of its body.*"

This must also be true of the etheric environment especially, since every material body is saturated with the etheric medium or exists by reason of etheric activities.

Thus, the character of the etheric movements external to a body is also a definite thing. Because the character is definite, the etheric sphere or atmosphere of a body has a limited power of harmonizing with other spheres or personal atmospheres. (See "The Personal Atmosphere.") When etheric activities of one atmosphere do not harmonize with the activities of another atmosphere, when they interfere with, oppose, disturb, those of another atmosphere, one of the persons, perhaps both, is or are psychically affected, and the outcome is vague uneasiness or positive antipathy in one or the other.

You may not, then, consciously feel aversion or fear for any individual in a group of people, while antipathy developing into fear may arise when you confront several people of such a group. Their personal atmospheres, insufficient in any one case to induce antipathy or fear in you, excite these feelings because they combine, and, so combined, assault your personal atmosphere, and through that your psychic self, so powerfully as to disharmonize your regular etheric activities and your subconscious self. Then, it may be, the final outcome appears in your conscious mind. And so we learn —

FIFTH AND SIXTH REGIMES — FOR FEAR INDUCED BY ATMOSPHERIC CONTACT: *Indifference and Resistance.* The remedy is two-fold : the cure by indifference and the cure by self-assertive resistance.

(1). You are invited to recall the suggestions related to the cure by *indifference,* and to make them effective by the simple, yet emphatic and persistent assertion: *"My antipathy for any and all of you, or of you for me, is a matter of entire indifference to me: let it go! I do not care about you. Even though I feel aversion for you, or you for me, the fact is of no importance whatever."* You thus kill fear for a group as you kill fear for an individual.

(2). The cure by *self-assertive resistance* is allied to the preceding. In the one case we have resistance through aroused and maintained indifference. In the other case we have resistance through aroused assertion of self. The former method consists in control of feelings by accepting them as *devitalized* and of *no importance* — destroying their value, "letting them slide" as of no significance or power. The latter method consists in control by thinking and willing *repulsion* of all etheric activities and psychic suggestions of disagreeableness or danger. In this method you are invited to affirm, vigorously and confidently: *"I hold to myself! I throw my will out to the whole field of my personal atmosphere and maintain throughout a positive attitude of resistance to all your etheric activities and psychic influences and suggestions. This attitude meets your group and kind of personality. I repel you. I close you out. I do not care about you, and I do not suffer you to share in my life. In my antipathy and because of it, and beyond my indifference, I do not fear you."*

III. FEAR OF THE CROWD CRITICAL—THE AUDIENCE.

Fear of the crowd critical has to do with *audiences* and *public opinion.*

1. *The Audience.* The fear-feeling which an audience excites involves very keen suffering. And the fact that the fear-suffering is measured by the sensibility of the speaker does not make the suffering less significant. Our pains and our joys are always gauged by what we are. One who experiences all the pain of which his nature is capable will not condemn his failure to rise above it merely because others are capable of experiencing greater pain. Nor may he who feels happiness as keenly as possible to him justly belittle that happiness for the reason that others are susceptible of greater joys. The vase and the sea-valley are alike in this: both are full — and can be no more. You are invited, therefore, to accept your capacity for suffering or for happiness as the case actually is, neither belittling nor exalting.

Nevertheless, it is a law which all should accept, that *the greater a person's capacity for joy, the greater also his capacity for suffering.* Of course the reverse is also true.

Feelings and emotions depend on two things: thought-power and sensibility. All emotions, feelings, passions, have behind them as cause, either in the conscious or the subconscious self, some specific idea. If you are capable of many and great ideas, your capacity for happiness and for suffering corresponds — to a degree. But the extent of the correspondence depends also upon your sensibility. The sensibility of a person is based on his physical and psychic constitution. The correspondence runs two ways: to his nervous organization and to his thought-life. When the thought-life is rather poor, but the nervous organization fine, *physical* suffering is determined by the organization. When the thought-life is large and rich, but the organization comparatively less refined, *physical* suffering is again determined by the organism. When the thought-life is poor and the organism coarse and heavy, capacity for physical suffering is relatively *small*. If the thought-life is large and rich, and the organism fine, capacity for physical joy and suffering is correspondingly *great*. Similar propositions might be set forth in regard to psychic happiness and pain — except in this respect, that a fine psychic factor cannot exist in a *truly* unworthy body. The real body reflects the real soul. *Externals* may apparently, even actually to a degree, contradict this statement, but always in that case the psychic factor has been more or less defeated in its work of expressing character — defeated by oppositions and activities of the environment. With this understanding observed, it is now further held that *the emotions of happiness and suffering depend on sensibility*, but sensibility of a *psychic* rather than a

physical nature. This proposition must be now analyzed.

Feelings and emotions of the purely psychic nature
depend on thought-power and sensibility. A large
and rich thought-life involves a degree of sensibility,
but the sensibility may be comparatively less than
the thought-life would seem to call for. This appears
when we discover the *meaning of sensibility.* In the
physical life sensibility is reaction to external and internal conditions: your *physical sensibility* is great
or keen when you react quickly and intensely to outside things. And this is true when one part of your
organism reacts quickly and strongly to conditions in
any other part. Psychic sensibility is similar : if reaction of the self in its idea-power is swift and intense
in relation to the outer world, — and this really means
action of the mental self, — there is great and lively
sensibility. But sensibility here means *suggestibility.*
In the body all activity "reverberates" throughout the system — affects in some way that whole
system. This is the physical correspondence to
psychic suggestibility. If the external world raises
an idea in the mental self, or if an idea arises in
the mental self without immediate association with the
outer world, the idea suggests other ideas. When feeling goes with the *suggesting* idea, it multiplies by so
much as the *suggested* ideas arise swiftly, are clearly
defined, and are intense and in turn suggestive. A
large and rich thought-life, then, is a life in which all
ideas are suggestive. That is, every idea has many
associates. Every idea suggests familiar associates
and other new associates. Any idea that is followed
or accompanied by feeling suggests other ideas associated with feeling. The psychic sensibility is acute

and comprehensive because suggestion is incessant and multiplying. In the physical world one man submits stolidly to the extraction of a tooth because of a dull set of nerves and a slow mental life, while another is filled to the top of the sky with dire suggestions. The latter should force his sensibility — his suggestibility — down to a low ebb and his courage up to the highest pitch. But the former also feels less happiness in life for the very reason that his psychic suggestibility is small. If the thought-life is poor, ideas accompanied by feeling are inferior and imperfectly conceived, and they have little suggestion-power because there is little "in the mind" to be suggested by anything. If the thought-life is large and rich, all ideas correspond in greatness and intensity, and they are highly prized (which means that they are accompanied by much feeling), and they suggest all sorts of other ideas noted with feeling for the reason that the mind is rich in ideas of every right sort already. Sensibility here is great because suggestibility is active and successful, and the capacity for happiness and suffering is correspondingly large.

Thus we see, when we run the matter down, that the differences that obtain among people in the matter of happiness and suffering are not due to a mysterious entity called sensibility which exists highly in some and scantily in others, but to a plain matter of poverty or wealth of the mental life. Any idea will suggest another if the mind is "up to the level" of that suggested idea — and not otherwise. Suggestibility, and so sensibility, as here referred to, is just a case of psychic culture. Hypnotic suggestibility, though related, is really another matter.

It is understood, of course, that ideas occur in the

subconscious not less than in the conscious self. The former is, then, the main field of the sensibility — the suggestibility referred to above. It is for this reason that in the richest life the ideas mating with feeling and suggesting other ideas so mating are so often vaguely recognized and so confused. When you gaze upon a glorious sunset, or listen to music of the highest order, experiencing the while the most exquisite emotions, you are quite unable to trace out clearly all the ideas suggested by the one thought: "beautiful world," or "heavenly harmony." The realm of description is one of reduced law and order and language, but there is another realm beyond this, the realm of mere wordless appreciation. Nevertheless, your exquisite emotion is a product of all sorts of ideas confusedly massed, or in confused sequence, in your subconscious mind.

The wealth and suggestibility of thought-life follow the *law of compensation*. Better, it obeys a law of being. Such a thought-life necessarily makes for great feeling, emotion, passion. And if there is great capacity for happiness for that reason, this fact means and is great capacity for suffering. But the reverse is equally true. Whoever suffers deeply has the compensation: an equal *capacity* for happiness. You are, therefore, invited to know this: If you suffer deeply and do not find now the equal happiness, the latter awaits you in so far as you are seeking harmony with the Universal System in which we live. *It is law that to every soul ultimately shall come all that his nature demands and is capable of receiving.* And the demand and the capability of your nature are one.

Psychic sensibility, then, is psychic suggestibility, and the latter depends on the thought-life and consequently on the suggestibility to ideas. The application of these truths to fear of the crowd critical is evident. Your mental condition before an audience may indicate your ability to force the interest and to win that audience,— and it may also indicate utter unfitness ever to face any audience.

Observe, now: The latter fact can only be determined by experience, since neither the individual's judgment nor that of others has value before you have tried. The judgment of the individual may coincide with that of other people in the decision of unfitness, yet occasional ways may arise to disprove that judgment. If a man feels sufficiently impelled to speak, and has something to say that is vital to him, he will usually prove the master of the situation. The best evidence of unfitness for public utterance is an absence of passion .for expression of ideas felt to be vital to the self, or lack of ideas — the one or the other, or both.

This question, however, is mostly foreign to the present purpose, as is also training in the art of address. The concern here is courage necessary before an audience, or the fears which must be overcome for such work.

Your mental condition prior to, or in the act of facing an audience, may produce a sense of *physical strain and nervousness* which may indicate intense suggestibility—all sorts of ideas confusedly crowding before your mind; but this is one of the very best evidences of ability to do the thing feared if only the mental and physical conditions can be sufficiently mastered to give you freedom in controlled speech. Excitement of mind and body here indicate some sort of fineness of nature and some degree of active and full thought-

life — provided you have anything vital to yourself
to say and any passion to say it.   One who is "dead"
to his audience may not expect to move his hearers.
People are often bored by one who has thought enough
but is under no physical or psychic strain. The suggestibility of his own ideas is slow, and his suggestions stirred
in the audience lack interest because they think more
quickly than he.   Everyone concedes his thought to be
well enough, yet all wish devoutly that he would go
away.

It is evident, then, that certain states of mind
and body before an audience may be welcomed as signs
of power.   The pain attending such states is the cost
of ability and success.   The causes of this pain should
be valued as among the greatest treasures of life.   It
is worth much to possess a fine nature, to be sensitive
to human presence, to own a thought-life so active
and full that its wealth and movements suggest even
ideas that give rise to suffering, and often, it may be,
to the temptations of fear — if only the objective
consciousness is not overwhelmed and the temptations
do not prove successful.

The fearsomeness of fear before an audience, however, is just this: that it *induces defeat.*   Fear is not
worth troubling about when it is followed by a triumph,
or if experience shows that the fear-actions preceded
victory.   It is the defeat, which is painful in proportion
to sensitiveness of nature, that makes physical strain
and nervous tension so suggestive of fear.   And it is
this suggested fear that is so fearful.   Fear of hurt
to self — to pride — is the fearfully suggestive thing.

Now, all true regimes are outcomes of analyses
of conditions.   Fear for an audience is an emotion
having behind it certain definite ideas.   Were these

ideas not to arise, how could fear be possible? The ideas that spring up in view of public speaking are —

(*a*). The idea of *failure* — an anticipation — an idea held or holding persistently in mind;

(*b*). The idea, therefore, of *danger* — anticipation — an idea similarly held or holding.

This idea of danger refers to: physical and mental *peace or comfort*, the danger being a threat against such agreeable conditions — anticipation again — idea held or holding persistently; and threat against personal *pride* — an anticipation of hurt by public opinion — idea held or holding. These ideas induce the feeling of *suffering* — a present fact, but also an idea held or holding by way of anticipation of suffering conceived as inevitable. The chief result of such ideas, finally, appears from the beginning in a sense of *inadequacy*, a feeling of *weakness*. These ideas breed fears.

Remove the ideas, displace them by their opposites, and fears vanish — inevitably. For, note the following connected hypotheses:

If you anticipate *success* — if you displace the idea of failure by the idea of victory —

If you anticipate high *response by your hearers* — if you displace the idea of discomfort by the idea of inspiration —

If you anticipate the *satisfaction* of a good piece of work — if you displace the idea of hurt pride by the idea of pleased and complimentary hearers —

If you anticipate the *enjoyment* in speech — if you displace the idea of suffering by the idea of pleasure —

If you anticipate a sense of *physical poise* and *mental power* — if you displace the idea of weakness by the idea of ability —

And if you cultivate a reasonable *indifference*

for the adverse opinion of any audience, and hold
steadily in mind the fact that you will neither be ruined
nor come to your death should you actually fail on
this particular occasion —

Persisting in these anticipations and substitutions,
always prior to speaking, always when speaking —
your fears for an audience will infallibly disappear.

This analysis and the consequent hypothetical
propositions may suggest that the overcoming of
fear in public speaking is difficult and demands a
good deal of hard work. It is precisely so. Yet no
ambitious person begrudges the cost of great success.
All true success is worth all it costs, no matter what the
cost may be. True success is to be valued not alone
for itself but more for what it does for the winning soul.
When you really succeed, you go higher "in the class."
Recalling the preceding paragraphs on anticipations,
you are therefore invited to take up and carry on,
courageously and persistently, the regimes now to be
offered.

Regimes for Fear of Crowd Critical.

First Regime for Facing the Crowd Critical:
Hardening in the Work. You are urged to continue
the practice of public speaking before *all kinds* of
audiences. The speaker who loses fear for an accustomed audience often fails to do his best in new and
strange presences, and needs to get used to variations
and surprises — which are indeed fearfully and wonderfully made, and capricious. Getting used to these
things requires practice — practice — practice, with
the variations and surprises. New audiences always
bring the "beast" with them. The regime consists,
therefore, in speaking before new audiences, as often

as possible — to get used to the "beast." In this way comes the hardening by concrete experience. In addition, the regime involves thinking of all sorts of varying and surprising crowds as being successfully addressed. The hardening process is now exclusively mental, making the thinker used to changing and peculiar conditions of the crowd critical before the "beast" has had time to appear.

SECOND REGIME FOR FACING THE CROWD CRITICAL: *Right Valuation of Sensitiveness and Suggestibility.* The usual attitude of the fearful speaker is one of regret for and hostility toward his painful conditions of mind and body when engaged in speaking. This attitude is really an idea —"Hateful disturbance"— which tends to increase the condition and to suggest danger, hurt, flight = fear. You are therefore invited to reverse the attitude. This reversal may be accomplished by habituating yourself to and in the thought: "*My appreciation of what public speaking means, my physical strain, my nervous excitement, my mental suggestibility, my sensitiveness to conditions, to people, to the regard of an audience — all these are values of my nature. I would not part with them if I might. They are signs of something in me worth while.*

> '*Low kinds exist without,*
> *Finished and finite clods, untroubled by a spark.*'

"Now and from henceforth my attitude of mind is and shall be that of welcoming and cherishing such conditions as signs of power. As the vibrations of musical strings touched by wandering winds show what they can do anon if the master handles the bow, so these stirrings, nerve-movements, heart-beats, swift breathings, and the like, reveal my nature, mind, thought-life, inspiration which I also shall awaken, handle, con-

trol and use as I stand before my audience, master of
myself, master of the people."

THIRD REGIME FOR FACING THE CROWD CRITICAL:
Anticipation of Success. You are invited to train the
subconscious self in the habitual thought of success
as surely your victory. This is accomplished by refusing to think of failure at all — anywhere — prior
to speaking and in presence of the audience. The way
not to think of a thing is instantly to think of something else. You tend to think failure. Think now of
success. Whenever you associate yourself with an
audience, think of self as pleasing the people and as
achieving a triumph. By this method you compel the
subconsciousness to embrace that idea only, and so,
to suggest to you all the elements of thought and action
which are essential to success.

FOURTH REGIME FOR FACING THE CROWD CRITICAL:
Anticipation of Enjoyment. Dread of an audience is
always associated with the notion of an unhappy time
in speaking. The idea may not be consciously recognized, but somewhere below the feeling of dread it
surely lurks. So long as thought dwells on this notion,
so long will the feeling of dread continue. The remedy
consists in persistently assuming that the effort will be
enjoyable; in pertinaciously clinging to the idea of a
happy occasion. It is not here intended that this method will guarantee success in speaking; it will, however,
tend to eliminate the element of fear from anticipation of public speaking. And by so much as the idea
of enjoyment occupies the mind, by so much does
that idea, that occupation, suggest courage and various
notions and feelings essential to success. You are
therefore invited to assume and assert that in every
address you make you will feel and reveal the proper

pleasure of the occasion. By so doing you habituate the subconscious self to the anticipation of "a good time," and this prevailing idea and its consequent attitude will come to your service in the time of your public need — provided you incessantly act, mentally and consciously, prior to and during the effort, on the assumption and assertions. Such action is a procedure which expects and demands an agreeable response from your hearers — in anticipation and at the time of speaking. In other words, you are not to rest contented with a barren assertion: "I shall be inspired," a mere mental say-so; you are to conduct your mental activities exactly as if the enjoyment were assured, or were now yours. The invitation, then, is to realize enjoyment of public speaking by anticipation as a right and as in fact now with you. You are, in mind, addressing the people; they are responding finely; you are having the best time in the world.

FIFTH REGIME FOR FACING THE CROWD CRITICAL: *Anticipation of Applause.* However exalted the motive in public address, the speaker cannot cease to be human. Fear may, for the most part, have its root in doubt that the audience will see the truth advanced, or the argument in a certain way — that the address will fail in such respects. That sort of fear is not discussed in this book, since it is a matter of scepticism rather than of feeling. It is idea-fear, mere doubt, not fear-feeling with distress. Yet no speaker is willing to fail in both the respects indicated. One may say: "I care not how these people shall think of me, how my personal pride may be hurt, if only my thought carries with them;" but no one can affirm total indifference toward personal reputation and the outcome of his effort before an audience. In ordinary public address personal pride is present and is legitimate, and fear for an audience springs in part from the idea of failing to win appreciation and applause. If the idea of hurt pride be decreased in its intensity, then, the fear-feeling will be proportionally lessened. If you do n't care much what your hearers may think about your effort, you cannot greatly fear them.

But this indifference may induce conditions in yourself which will actually prevent your doing well. On the other hand, oversensitiveness about reputation may bring to pass the same outcome. The remedy, then, for fear related to personal pride permits a degree of indifference sufficient to quiet disturbing nervousness, and calls for a regard for your hearers sufficient to inspire your best effort. In order to this courage-breeding condition of body and mind you are invited —

To cultivate a due and proper indifference for your pride and for criticism.

But, in the meantime, to hold steadily in mind the anticipation of success and its reward — the commendation of your hearers. A suggestive sentence here would be —

"*I am reasonably indifferent to carping criticism, yet I shall certainly deserve the commendation of people who are really worth while.*"

Sixth Regime for Facing the Crowd Critical: *Anticipation of Poise and Power.* Poise and power for special occasions are merely poise and power habitually asserted and possessed. You cannot summon at some particular time what you have never had, — in its fulness,— and the more habitually you try to possess conscious abilities and qualities, the surer you are of having them in time of need. Poise and power belong preëminently to the realm of the subconscious mind. They are not superficial. Nor are they occasional or spasmodic, in the nature of the case. Poise, as here referred to, means an established equilibrium of feelings and ideas which are commendable. To secure such poise there must be practice, and this means "fit for business." Your ideas and feelings are at poise after practice making them harmoniously "fit for business." In such a condition all the power your nature is capable of at a given time is at your service. The word "power" means just that—coming from the Latin, *pono:* "I am able." Power is poise — established equilibrium of feelings and ideas which are commendable in character. And poise is power — commendable ideas and feelings harmoniously "fit for business."

The regime anticipates poise and power in the hour of address. The only ground on which such anticipation can justify is the persistent cultivation of commendable ideas and feelings harmoniously "fit for business"— poise — and the sense of power — as everyday possessions. Habitual poise and power may be secured by daily regimes in assertion that you *are now* at poise, are now self-controlled, are now able to command ideas and feelings, are now the soul of power. The cultivation may proceed by verbal claims, as follows:

"I am now in a state of poise and self-control."

"I command my ideas and feelings, speaking sanely, as I will."

"I am well in hand for all occasions."

"I have resources of emotion and thought adequate to all demands."

"I am! I am power!"

If you will thus assume and assert daily for long,

you will infallibly find a sense of poise and a feeling of personal ability growing more and more habitual and pronounced. These things will themselves breed courage and stand you in good stead in the hour of public address.

But you are invited, on such occasion, to recall and vigorously repeat the above-quoted sentences because their emphatic and confident repetition will revive the long-continued suggestions to the subconscious self of poise and power and command that self now — at the time of speaking — to be — poise and power.

SEVENTH REGIME FOR FACING THE CROWD CRITICAL: *Assertion of Courage.* One may think fear so long that the thought becomes a habit, the trend of mental activities sets toward the idea and feeling of fear under all conditions, and fear becomes the most easily and readily suggested thing in life. On the contrary, one may think courage until the very idea is habituated in the subconscious self and at every occasion of experience the courageous attitude and feeling leap into consciousness and inspire the whole personality. It is with courage in view of an audience as with poise and power. You are urged to make idea and feeling permanent in mind by incessantly asserting that courage is yours. You practise courage-sense through all your mental activity until these things become established as parts of your inner life and thus "fit for business." But you also assert courage as you confront your audience, thus reinforcing the subconscious self and inspiring it to permeate your entire being with the warmth and glow of courageous confidence.

Practice in public speaking, together with the

above regimes, will infallibly dispel your fears for the crowd critical as an audience and substitute therefor courage adequate to your public opportunities. "I am master of every condition that may come into my life." And observe — *your boundless power.*

Within the limits of the laws of Nature and of your personal endowments, you can train your subconscious self to do any nameable thing. You cannot train it, for example, to put a broken limb straight, yet it does "set" that limb when mechanical manipulation has performed the work required. You cannot train it to win you a vast fortune without regard to your native endowments, yet it has won every fortune man ever earned. The conscious self can only earn day wages, equally in the case of ditch-digging or of high finance. It is for the subconscious self alone to achieve the Suez or Panama Canals and pile up millions of money. You cannot train the subconscious self of a real clod to inspire a world's Congress in time of international crisis, but it did thrill a world when the outward-seeming "clod," Lincoln, gave, at Gettysburg, the fire with which his soul had been consumed for years. Lincoln was always more transliminal than conscious, more infinite than finite — a lotus flower deep-set and a-bloom on the Eternal Nile of Life. Your subconscious self has its limitations — like the Infinite One: it cannot pass them, nor can That. Your nature is its law, and so is the Nature of That *its* Law. Within the Law, That is infinite. And within your law of nature, you also are —boundless, lawfully infinite so far as you are psychic and harmonic life. Herefrom issue some *inspiring principles* — given in one sentence:

All the truth, beauty, power, confidence, courage,

*rightness you shall ever know as your own you already
possess, since you also root and bloom on the Eternal Nile
of all wealth.*

With this conception inspiring you, you are, then,
invited to direct and use your subconscious self as you
would direct and use — That which you call God! For
no man may say where the *Infinite ceases* to be *you*
and *you* begin *to be* you. There is no isthmus discoverable between your personal life and that Infinite
Nile!

Eighth Regime for Facing the Crowd Critical:
Courage-Building During Sleep. The value of sleep
cannot be estimated in physical terms alone. There
are reasons for believing that not only are bodily force
and tissue received and renewed, but that the business
of psychic growth is also carried on, during the hours
of slumber. The conscious self, which is incessantly
engaged while awake with sensations, suggested ideas
and the execution of its own orders in will, has in
sleep opportunity for assimilation of fact, truth, beauty,
law, and the organization of the personal "body of
thought." Always associated in this work, the subconscious self now obtains larger freedom in its own
related activities. When body and conscious mind
are disposed for sleep, and when sensations and their
usual stimulations are vastly less, the whole self becomes amenable to directions imperatively and confidently given it during waking hours. Thus you can
accomplish much for your power-life while you are
seemingly asleep. Hence the present regime:

You are invited, in accord with the above principles, to make it your practice for long to affirm the
substance of the preceding regime-directions, beginning with your preparations for retiring and continuing

each night until lost in sleep. The affirmations should be vigorously and confidently addressed to yourself in the second person singular form. When you find a feeling of courage for public address developing within you, this should inspire you to further effort until the labor becomes unnecessary. Let us here note

Certain Delayed Results. Observe, at this point, the fact so often apparent everywhere in life. Multitudes begin culture-work with enthusiasm, go on admirably for a time, but then, if astonishing results do not soon appear, relax effort and finally drop out of the ranks of the growers.

All students of the Power-Books who persevere, reap most desirable rewards. In this outcome a great law has been manifest. This law, while given various names in science, may here be called the *Law of Delayed Psychic Response.* Sometimes the delay is that of *direct* response, sometimes that of *indirect* response. In the one case you may not succeed in immediately reaching the subconscious self because you have not at first quite gotten at the method. *Always realize as done in the deeper self what you are commanding in the conscious self.* Sometimes you reach the subconscious self, indeed, and this proceeds to obey, but there are intervening things to be accomplished before your command can be directly carried out. In other words, the command has to be obeyed *indirectly.* Frequently it is the case that the conscious self only becomes in earnest and charged with confidence after it has formed the habit of thinking and commanding thus and so. In work like the present, moreover, there goes on more or less of reorganization or reconstruction of the self "down cellar," subconsciously, preparatory but occasioning delay in response to a given command which

you have formulated. Finally, some time may elapse
before you can be conscious of results. All psychic
growth involves this law of delay — more or less.

Students of telegraphy claim that the improvement
in learning to receive messages, while rapid for a time,
ceases at a point just below the required efficiency.
For many weeks there is an improvement which the
student can feel sure of, and which is proved by actual
tests. Then follows a long period when the student
can feel no improvement, and objective tests show
little or none. At the last end of the work — just
prior to a new discovery — the messages in the main
line are, according to the unanimous testimony, a
senseless clatter to the student. But then, suddenly,
within a few days, the change comes, and the senseless clatter becomes intelligible telegraphic speech.

You are invited, in view of this law, to persevere
in all the regimes—as you take them up, of course—
for a long enough time to bring out definite consciousness of the results desired. The results will come.
The regimes are in themselves infallible. "I am
master of every condition that may come into my
life."

IV. FEAR OF CROWD CRITICAL—PUBLIC OPINION.

Preliminary on Freedom. The familiar saying,
Vox populi vox Dei, — "The voice of the people is the
voice of Deity," — cannot be proved. Prophets declare
the contrary in Jewish history, Russia saw no Deity in
the revolt of the Tartars, nor did England in The
Declaration of Independence. The voice of the people
is often vague and is always fickle. Public opinion,
therefore, is passion, prejudice, an unreasoning evidence
of contagion, a baseless hallucination, a well-grounded

fact, a manifesto of reason — one of these things at least always, never all of these things entirely.

Whatever its origin or character, however, public opinion is a fact. Taken all and in all, as a fact, the *long-run intention* of public opinion is human betterment, since it is then an exhibition of the law of (racial or community) self-preservation. Man intends to stay on the earth and to come to his best.

But humanity viewed in the long run must be taken as an individual. No man's mere intention constitutes right. Humanity makes mistakes precisely as does the individual.

This intention of any age or nation or community to stay on the earth and to get to its best estate, expresses itself in public opinion. It is precisely because the intention is the law of self-preservation — as conceived at the time of any particular phase of the intention — that the intention, and so, public opinion, is so strong.

The intention is necessarily tyrannical, and so, public opinion is and has to be a tyranny. If it were not a tyranny, it would have no value, not because tyranny is a value in itself, but because public opinion must be tyrannical to be itself at all. Your physical life, your instinct for happiness, your impulsion to "get on," are all tyrannies in their nature. Make them easy-going, and you find their worth to you little or nothing. These things express in a kind of public opinion in the "communities" of your body and mind — parts, functions, powers, activities — which you call your self. You intend to stay and to get the best (as you certainly should), and so there is a tyranny of "public" opinion for every atom and phase of your personality. This holds you together.

The tyranny of the larger public opinion may inspire these attitudes in the individual man or woman:

It may be *laughed* at — scorned.

It may be regarded with *slavish respect.*

It may be regarded with *reasonable respect.*

It may be *feared.*

This book suggests the third attitude for its readers. The tyranny is unescapable. It is so many parts right, so many parts wrong. But always it is here — to be reckoned with.

The third attitude alone is admissible for any human being, because only individual freedom can be right or best, and such freedom calls for respect for freedom.

Public opinion is a tyranny simply because it expresses for human freedom.

The highest duty of all men and all women is to be absolutely free.

Such absolute freedom, however, can only be realized in the absolute intention. The obligation upon us all is, *to fully intend, all the time, to be fully and all the time free.*

Freedom is very far from being the right to do as one pleases.

Freedom is the right and the power to be and do the best thing known and possible.

To be and do the best thing known and possible is to strive for harmony with the laws of personal being. Harmony with the laws of personal being is harmony with the laws of Universal Nature. Such harmony is to be what the laws of Universal Nature evidently intend one to be. To discover this intention and to strive for its realization in personal life constitute the only reasonable goal of human existence. This intention of Nature for each individual — meaning by "intention" capability of becoming — is a tyranny. It is the Voice of Deity. It is Cosmic Opinion.

You **are** invited to give that phrase, *Cosmic Opinion*, full opportunity in your mind.

It is evident, then, that here are two public opinions, both tyrannies, both age-long and relentless.

In the life of man these tyrannies have sometimes seemed vaguely to agree. For the most part they have been in opposition. Always in the agreement *human* public opinion has *yielded* to *Cosmic Opinion*, and always that agreement by yielding has worked good for man. So it appears to the writer. Always the opposition has shown that *Vox populi non vox Dei* — "The voice of the people is *not* the voice of Deity." History is the record of war between these two tyrannies.

Human opinion, therefore, is to be *weighed by the dictates* of Cosmic Opinion. This weighing can only be done by the individual, since public opinion cannot possibly weigh itself;—it can only *assert* itself. When it pretends to weigh, it is merely asserting itself over again.

The task of weighing public opinion according to the dictates of Cosmic Opinion demands, as its very first principle, as follows:

The individual must wholly intend wholly to be free in the sense of exercising his right and power to be at his discoverable best all the time.

In such freedom the individual will not —

Scorn public opinion as such, since it may seek to express Cosmic Opinion;

Regard public opinion with *slavish respect*, since the free man can know no such respect, and since public opinion may oppose Cosmic Opinion — and the decision must rest with the individual;

Fear public opinion, since this would jeopardize his freedom, and he cannot be at his best and fear that which may itself be in error.

In true freedom the individual will regard public opinion with reasonable respect. A reasonable respect requires that public opinion shall make no demands for its own sake, shall base all demands on facts that have the right to be, shall limit these demands by reason demonstrating in practical life for good, shall stand for no beliefs because they are old simply, or new simply, or present simply, or make for anything short of highest present and ultimate human welfare.

And always a reasonable respect for public opinion *concedes the individual the right* to decide every one of the questions suggested above — for himself alone.

A reasonable respect for public opinion, however, requires that the individual shall not *ignore* public opinion in deciding such questions, but shall give it that weight which seems admissible to him.

The free man must use his two ears: one turned toward public opinion, one turned toward Cosmic Opinion. If he intends so to do, wholly and all the time, he will be free in so far forth. He will indeed make mistakes, but in opposition to this fact must be placed the great truth that honest errors are a part of the cost of freedom itself.

You are, therefore, invited to resolve from henceforth to be as free as your growing soul may from time to time permit. This resolution should be intensely felt and strongly willed, and in such form be repeated for long as a proposition of fact, say, the self-assertion: "*I am, even now, fully and splendidly free, because consciously right, so far as intention is concerned, in all my relations with public opinion*"

This regime, however, is general and preliminary to further important work. In order that such work may be indicated, it is necessary at this point to analyze public opinion more particularly.

Analysis of Public Opinion. The tyranny of public opinion is shown in two ways, as follows:

1. By *criticism* of thought and action in individuals and in groups;

2. By *demands* made which seek to control individuals and groups as regards both thought-life and practical conduct.

The criticism and the demands are to be justly scorned,— or treated with indifference,— if they are in any way unjust. And always may (and must) the individual decide the question involved for himself — provided: he is bent on that freedom which consists in the right and the power to be what the nature of things evidently intended him to be, so far as he can ascertain, through the struggle for harmony with the Universal System of things and worlds.

The criticism and demands are never entitled to any person's slavish respect, nor to any person's feeling of fear.

The criticism and demands merit reasonable regard only on the condition (*a*) that they are not made for their own sake, thoughtlessly, or as the outcome of habit and tradition; (*b*) only as they are based on facts that have the right to be; (*c*) only as they validify in practical good, and are not mere notions and whims; (*d*) only as they represent beliefs which, whether old or new, are capable of the freest examination and universal application to life.

Now, *criticism* by public opinion is really a *demand* in itself. You are, let us say, criticised for an act, a thought, and so on. This means, in any given case, that you are to do, to think, to wear clothing, to build your house, to conduct your business, and so on, in a way pleasing to the critics, under penalty of disapprobation. In other words, it is demanded that you be and do what is agreeable to those who criticise. People are not always aware of this fact, and would often demur to it with the remark: "Why, no; what do I care about it?" Nevertheless, the logic holds. If a man does not want me to resemble him — if he really is indifferent — why does he criticise me? For the common good? Some one must decide that common good. So far as *my* life is concerned, this someone is myself, not the critic — always with the proviso that I am seeking the harmony above indicated. The critics may be right as thus determined (by the standard of freedom and harmony), yet if fear-feeling goes with my concession of that fact, it is evil and useless, and, right or wrong, is evil, since all criticism of another is a demand for conformity to the critic's ideas.

Fear of this critico-demand has its *roots*, again, in *ideas*. The ideas here are: the thought-desire to please others; the idea of hurt to body or soul; and the idea of wounded pride — an injury to reputation. The control of these ideas is the cure for fear of public opinion. Hence the following regimes:

First — Regime of Freedom Claimed. You are invited to resolve from henceforth to be as fully free as your growing soul may from time to time permit. This resolution should be intensely felt and strongly willed, and be repeated for long as a proposition of present fact, say, in this form: "*I am, even now, fully and splendidly free, because I am consciously right by intention in all my relations with public opinion. I respect public*

opinion if evidently correct, but I do not fear it, and I enter-
tain no slavish regard for its decisions or its dictates."

SECOND — REGIME OF INDIFFERENCE AND ASSER-
TION. As in the case of antipathies, so in the present
instance, it is well to cultivate, along with a reasonable
regard for public opinion when evidently right, an
equally reasonable indifference for it when it handles
matters of small importance, or when it is a mere passing notion, or when it is probably wrong. The writer
employed a carpenter to build a small shop, and desired
that the roof should overhang the walls a certain
distance. The workman expressed disapproval, and
said: "Why, nobody does it that way. What will
these people say when they see it?" This was really
a case of pride for himself, and the answer came: "Let
the roof overhang. Why should I care for mere personal notions!" Thus with innumerable matters that
inspire criticism. In many instances the opinions have
no value because the occasions lack importance. But
beyond this, the fear-feeling for public opinion needs
a vigorous treatment of indifference, cultivated until
it is measurably experienced, all round the field of
one's life, even though matters of more or less importance be embraced, because you are entitled to the
feelings of courage and freedom, and these may never
be yours unless you grow in your soul a reasonable independence of human tyranny.

Independence comes of assertion of self. It is
unhealthful to be dominated by any person, friend or
foe. You are invited to assert your selfhood as rightly
free in action, thought, tastes, customs, beliefs, so far
as such items are in harmony with a similar privilege in
others.

Such indifference and assertion may be acquired

by thinking, often and vigorously: *"It is a matter of indifference to me what criticisms I may inspire or what public opinion may hold, for I am now consciously seeking harmony with that higher forum, the opinion of Cosmic Intelligences."*

THIRD — REGIME OF REASONABLE COUNTER-DEMANDS. This regime has already been suggested, but the case will bear further detail instruction. Public opinion is sometimes guilty of criticisms and demands merely for its own sake or merely for the sake of criticising and demanding; is not always based on facts at all or on facts that have a right to be; is not confined always to the limits of reason demonstrating in practical welfare; and it has always insisted on beliefs simply because such beliefs have been held. The invitation now offered concerns these factors, and suggests a personal attitude which constitutes a counter-demand on others or against public opinion itself. The purpose sought is the exhibiltion of courage by assuming the attitude of counter-demand, and the development of courage through assertion of such demand.

When you discover in yourself fear because of the criticisms and demands of others, you are invited to ask the question:

Is this criticism of, this demand for, my thought and conduct, actually based on actual facts? The carpenter above referred to feared criticism of an overhanging roof on the ground that buildings were not so constructed. He was mistaken. Here was criticism without supporting fact. The invitation requires that all expression of public opinion shall justify in some fact-foundation.

Public opinion frequently bases in facts which

have no *right to be*. For example, the fact that every-body observed Sunday in the way of the Puritans, in some communities, had no inherent right to be a fact, since that observance was in various respects harm-ful to the cause which it represented. Public opinion in regard to the subject was, therefore, a tyranny with-out justification. There are millions of facts in this world which are not founded in right, and can furnish no foundation for public opinion.

If, then, you proceed to examine your conformity to customs and opinions, you will find that in many instances you are fearing criticisms and demands that have either no foundation in fact or a foundation in facts which are themselves without right. You are invited to run to cover your fears because of public opinion and to find out exactly what the facts are, whether existing or legitimate. By so much as you dis-cover "no facts," or "facts without right to be," by so much must your fear in the case disappear.

And you are invited to ask the question also: Are these criticisms and demands put forth merely for the sake of criticism and domination, or merely for the sake of asserting public opinion? Criticisms often prevail for no other reason than that they prevail. It has not been considered in certain circles to be "in good form" to go off into " Christian Science," or Spiritualism, or to be identified with what is called the "New-Thought" movement. The critics have not usually stopped to get at facts of any importance. They have criticised from habit, because of a prevailing bent, for the sake of domination. Public opinion in such cases is merely an opportunity presented to you of asserting your utter independence of its senseless tyranny.

You are therefore, invited to accept this proposition: Public opinion has no value whatever in itself; all its values depend on its relation to the freely developing individual life making toward its largest and richest form. When you become saturated with this conviction, your fear of public opinion will vanish. You will still be conscious of a reasonable regard for it, but this regard will displace all fear-feeling in relation to its criticisms and demands.

Thus you are now invited to asked a further question: Are the criticisms and demands of public opinion confined to the limits of reason making for the general welfare? Many people are in bondage to the prevailing modes, fashions, customs, traditions, beliefs — especially in their own class. These things tend always to transcend the limits of reason in any sense — to be overdone. Certain questions indicate the fact so declared. Do you read and admire the going things? Is your style of speech cultured? Do you accept the traditions of your church or party? Have your beliefs been certified to by some one? You may answer these questions in the affirmative as regards a fair degree of conformity, but the tendency of opinion in these matters is always toward some extreme: the height of fashion — affectation in literature and art — the stereotyped in speech — the imitative in society — the moss-back in religion and politics — the mummified belief. None of these extremes is essential to anyone's intellectual and moral development, most of them are foes thereto, and not even the things that thus grow into extremes can be said always to make for human welfare. A dress decollete, a "swallow-tail" coat, the use of a fork, a taste for George Eliot, a conventional house, a belief in a man-God, conformity with a religious ceremony, — matters of such sorts are never surely essential to mental power or moral worth. And so with millions of other things.

Three great factors only are essential to human welfare: Harmony with the Infinite, or, if you prefer, with the laws of the Universe, the Golden Rule in all fields of life, and the right and the power to realize in personal development the highest possibilities of one's nature.

You are therefore, invited to question every criticism and demand of public opinion somewhat as follows:

Do the criticism and demand undoubtedly mean for myself and others better harmony with the laws of the Universe?

Do they mean a more complete fulfilment of the Golden Rule?

Do they signify a larger right and power to realize the best human nature?

If so, they warrant due regard and conformity. If not, they merit no consideration beyond purely personal convenience. In any event they are no just cause for fear on the part of any human being.

And absolutely every criticism and demand which does not clearly make for betterment, individual and social, may justly be ignored as of merely convenient importance or as of no importance in any sense. (Of course these conclusions do not regard the *legal enactment* of public opinion.)

When you attain the attitude here suggested, your good day of courage in the face of public opinion will have arrived. You will value the force of such opinion, whatever that force may be, and will feel that its proper consideration is a virtue, and you will still weigh and credit it for what it is really worth; but you will no longer fear it.

These suggestions apply to *your* individual life in regard to several vital matters:

Your *personal habits:* Do they contribute to the social good as well as your own, or are they harmless in such respects? If not, public opinion may justly be your judge. If so, public opinion may be ignored. For you also are a part of public opinion,— in a way, — and what your personal habits are signifies what you practically would have public opinion to be. You are invited to make good the present claim of the insistence on freedom by being right *yourself*, and so helping to mold public opinion for the welfare of all.

Your *business life:* Is this in harmony with that great maxim which is so indispensable to general and individual financial prosperity — *Every business for the general good?* If so, criticisms and demands of all sorts may be ignored as the passing winds of the passing show. If not, public opinion again may justly be your judge. For you are a part of public opinion in such a sense that when it makes for other than the general welfare you are entitled to ignore it and so reform it; and when it makes for that welfare and opposes you, you become yourself the subject of reform.

In your street, town, state, nation, certain right human relations would, if established, make for the good of all. The outcomes here follow the lines already indicated. Public opinion condemns our relations or not, as the case may be, high or low, as for example, class distinctions or the marriage of divorced persons, and so on, and so on. Always the decisive reference must be to human welfare. If any relation (with its background of thought) makes for the welfare of the one and the many, public opinion contrary is a thing to be ignored. If the opposite is true, criticism and demand of public opinions are just. You are, in reference to these things, also a part of public opinion, and your life, it may be, assists in making opinion exactly what it is — on the one side or the other of every important question.

Your *beliefs.* Do they stand for truth essential to human life, or for tradition merely, or just for a church, or simply for a party? The great majority of beliefs have had no more, necessarily, to do with the matter of harmony with the Infinite, or the laws of the Universe, with the Golden Rule, with the true freedom of the human self, than so many fairy tales have had to do. You can stand for these great essentials and throw overboard nearly the whole furniture of intellectual and religious dogma. The general trend of a man's belief is of importance to him, of course, having much to do with his character and life, but the real truth in this statement is almost always missed because an artificial truth forever gets in its way. A true *tendency* to believe *something*, together with a considerable fund of beliefs which *seem* right — these things are indispensable to any human life. That is the real truth. The artificial truth is the alleged importance of a tendency to believe *certain prescribed* matters and to possess a large fund of *labeled* beliefs demanded by public opinion. Let us illustrate:

It is important that people should tend toward decency and wear some kind of clothing; but this importance does not attach to covering the neck, face, head in some defined way, nor to wearing clothing of a certain cut, color, make, style. The main things are decency and clothes enough to cover the body. Styles change, but let decency abide.

It is important that a human being should decline

to degenerate into a personalized denying machine, but
should keep open house to beauty, truth and goodness.
It is not important that he shall admire *my* or *your*
goodness, accept *our* form of truth, imitate *our* ideals
of beauty. It is important that one be possessed of
a rich and varied store of beliefs about himself, nature,
life, death, the present, the hereafter, the Universe,
and so on. But it is not important that one shall
accumulate a certain definite and named assorted list
of beliefs, social, political, scientific, religious. These
things are like food and clothing. We must have much
in the long run, but the individual items may vary.
Beliefs vary, yet belief abides because it is native and
necessary to the full life. Variation of belief always
obtains if the soul is a growing one. The mind should
maintain psychic decency by donning some sort of
covering and not exposing nude scepticism gone
stark to the skin; and it must have something called
truth, many things deemed true, lest, like hibernating
animals, it fall dead asleep in a wintry life and consume
itself to death. But never may any honest man or
woman prescribe exact and fixed diet for any soul that
lives—beyond the great essentials of all human betterment — as above suggested. Harmony with the laws
of the Universe, or with the Infinite, the Golden Rule,
and true freedom — these gigantic things give rise to
many lesser beliefs, some essential to one person, some
essential to another person, but always it remains true
that the lesser come and go, revive and fade, change,
die in particular forms, while yet the Greater, like the
sea, like the mountains, like the Galactic Circle across
the sky, like the Pole Star, remain, the huge constants
without which life is valueless because animal and
shorn of ideal and eternal law.

Even these three giants wear different aspects as the world climbs on and up, as Polaris drifts in its journey through 50° from the true pole-position, as the configurations of the heavens slowly change during the æons of the years. Yet still the Pole holds, still the constellations abide, and still the Master Beliefs of all time continue immutable amid change, still one reality clings to the moral worth of existence — *Cosmic Opinion.*

You are invited, then, to cultivate a full sense of the unimportance of the lesser subjects of belief and a larger appreciation for the Master Beliefs. By so much as you succeed in so doing will the public opinion of a passing day cease to exercise unjust tyranny over you, and fear of it, its criticisms and demands, vanish out of your life.

YOUTH IS COURAGE.

"The wine of ignorance," affirm wise dullards,
"Intoxicates with courage:
As witness youth, unconsciously proclaiming,
'In me a god Olympian assumes his own.'"

Would we had secret of recovering
This daring, happy egotism!
For, whether our old wisdom, scarred and fighting fear,
Has preferable pretensions
To such sheer know-no-better, glorious faith
In raw self — with high joys pirated from life —
Is question I, for one, cut short
In favor of godship.

The wine of ignorance makes drunk with fear:
Young was the world when man first quaked.

What's youth but life?
Brain-cells submerged in lava-blood,
Muscles a-quiver with energy puissant,
Ideas swarming as locusts in Egypt,—
So, courage to honor first thoughts
Born of sheer satisfaction of being —
Full-conscious being *alive*, from crown to boot?
How, now, can *that* consummate life have fear?

The courage of youth is the fruit,
Not of ignorance — weed of the primal swamp —
But of the Tree of Life in the Garden Edenic of old.
And the fear of wise fools, cursed by the cherubim,
Defeat and Death,
Is that Apple of Knowledge which even That foregoes
Whose first good law decreed:
"*Eat not of the weakness of self.*"

— THE AUTHOR.

CHAPTER XII.

FEAR OF EVENTS — OLD AGE.

"Pleasures are feelings that seem to accompany states in which the organism is being built up, or prevailingly refreshed, so that its vitality is for the moment heightened. Pain or displeasure, on the other hand, is such feeling as is predominant at moments when the organism is breaking down, or is being lowered in vitality." — *Royce.*

COURAGE in regard to events may·spring from two varieties of temperament: that of the animal, incapable of real thought about the future, and that of the consciously superior man who thinks adequacy to meet events because he feels adequate in the present. This type of people may be described thus:

"In their minds the consciousness of power is ever present. Above all things they strive to avoid a show of weakness, whether it takes the form of inefficiency or of a too-easy yielding to passion or emotion. They never sink exhausted into a chair. On the train, when the vulgar try to make themselves comfortable these higher folk avoid reclining. They do not seem to get tired after hours of standing at court. To a provoking speech they reply with politeness and self-possession — and not as if horrified, crushed, abashed, enraged or out of breath, after the manner of plebeians. The aristocrat knows how to preserve the appearance of ever-present physical strength, and he knows, too, how to convey the impres-

sion that his soul and intellect are a match to all dangers
and surprises, by keeping up an unchanging serenity
and civility, even under the most trying circumstances."
You are invited to be that sort of aristocrat — and n⁻
other.

WILL AND THE COURAGE-HABIT.

The voluntary formation of any habit demands
effort in proportion to its need.   This fact is significant.
Our activities, both physical and psychic, run naturally
to the easiest way, and tend to "set" in habits that
resist alteration, especially resist breaking up in any
thorough-going fashion.   The most of our fears disclose
this mental tendency.   Fear-feeling is a race-habit
because man has always entertained fear-thought under
the influence of imagination.   One who is "naturally"
fearful simply takes up and carries on this racial fear-
habit.

If we wish to reverse such habit, we must proceed
to cultivate the courage-habit.   It is useless *merely* to
kill fear — and impossible.   Reversing the fear-habit
is really accomplished by developing courage.

It is evident that habit can only be arrested, or
changed, when some contrary or modifying force is
brought t bear upon the activities of which it is composed.   Such opposition r ay arise in *external circumstances,* or it may spring up *within the individual.*   (a) In
the former case, the result may occur instantly, as in the
event of some great accident, or it may only appear
under long-continued modifying conditions, as in
general education conducted by schools and colleges.

But at the heart of this common run of things in
body and mind, the animal bent of initiative is always
at work to prevent a total "set" of personal activities,
and to inaugurate new activities and tendencies so

essential to human career. Such *initiative* is due to psychic *restlessness*. This factor builds the Universe. The spirit of restlessness, if properly controlled by the self, is the psychic power which ever forsakes settled things, ever pushes out into new territories, ever calls backward to the old and pulls life forever on toward advanced ground. Therein lies its value. Not the control of Sleepy Hollow wins success and breeds courage; rather, bold restlessness curbed by practical sense — building the strenuous soul, forcing a place in the march of events. (*b*) It is chiefly this inner power that must be enlisted boˌh for the overcoming, and for the development, of habits. Oftentimes the mere operations of mind accomplish the results. We form habits because we are restless, and for the same reason we modify them, and form new ones. When the opposition to "set" tendencies is not immediately caused by restlessness, the will has come to the fore. The will is the master power by which we intelligently utilize both habit and restlessness for building soul and winning life's success.

We cannot here go into a discussion of the nature of will, referring the reader to "*Practical Psychology*" for an elaborate analysis of the subject, but take the common conception of the "faculty" as sufficiently correct for these pages. Now, the essence of will, as so conceived, is courage. We may say that will is idea-impulse-pusher and director in our rational life. In fact, the least tincture of fear in will means just so much less will. (This is a contradiction, of course, but that is exactly the point). The very nature of will makes it fearless. Technically speaking — to go into the matter thus much — *will is dynamic idea* — that is, action-idea inducing action. Idea cannot

become dynamic so long as it is fear-idea *of* action —
though the fear-idea does become dynamic *for* action.
But you see, when you fear-act, you do not fear *that*
act. We do not consciously *will* fear-action; the
idea merely becomes dynamic and forces action. If
we assume 100° as the standard of will — here taken
for mind as expressing will — then 10° of will involves
10° of courage, and so on, up to, say, 30°, 50°, 75°, 100°
of each. Always there are in any act as many degrees
of courage as of will — inevitably.

It should be observed, however, that we do not
confuse fear-thought with fear-feeling. In company
with the best of will, fear-*thought* may occur. If we
express this matter as in the above suggested equation, we may say that 50° of fear-*thought* may
accompany 60° of will, courage thus being the real
fact; but that if 50° of fear-*feeling* obtain with 40°
of will (a contradiction, again), defeat is inevitable.
The 60° in the first instance could not be 40°, and the 40°
in the second instance could not be 60°. Will never
contains in itself the smallest degree of fear, for real
fear is always feeling, and fear-feeling induces action
not because we immediately and consciously will that
action, but because we lack will to refuse it. If we
possess will to refuse fear-action, this is because the
courage-idea has become regnant in place of the fear-
feeling.

Remembering, now, that general physical and
psychic activities tend to "set," but that our native
restlessness nevertheless keeps mind open to new
variation of action, we see that conscious will operates
(*a*) both in the overcoming of habit injurious, or the
development of habit beneficial, and also (*b*) in that
psychic restlessness which, no less than habit, is so

characteristic of life. Now, satisfaction of some sort must follow the "set" of mental activity and the initiation of new forms of actions. Hence appear two great laws, and from their operation result two of the most sovereign habits of human life.

CERTAIN LAWS AND HABITS.

These Laws are: 1. The law of satisfaction in habit and initiative;

2. The law that courage obtains so long as such satisfaction holds on, and obtains also the moment conscious will begins to work for some new satisfaction.

The corresponding habits are: 1. The general habit of optimism in normal physical and psychic life.

2. Necessarily, also, the general habit of courage in such normal life. We proceed to discussions.

THE SATISFACTION OF NORMAL LIFE.

FIRST DISCUSSION. Formation of habit along lines of least resistance entails satisfaction, in the very nature of mental processes, whatever the habit's character, though its consequences may entail unhappiness. Similarly, there is satisfaction in initiative, though here, again, consequences may be unsatisfactory, and there is a kind of satisfaction even when initiative requires painful effort. We are braggarts after the dental chair because we had to be braggarts to get there. The mind takes satisfaction in doing what it is capable of doing, whether or no outcomes chance to be pleasing. And, so long as mental operations remain normal and satisfying, a measure of courage must obtain with regard to such operations. Of course, the moment of voluntary initiation is the moment of courage, with regard to the initiation, since it *is* voluntary.

SECOND DISCUSSION. But the satisfaction of habit-forming and of initiative and of courage itself tends to breed hopefulness, for fear and monotony and pessimism breed unhappiness.

Optimism is a habit in the normally working mind, and this habit runs side by side with courage.

DISCUSSION THREE. Evolution has made pessimism impossible to healthy physical and psychic life. The gloomy outlook always means something wrong either in body or in mind, often in both. But when body is sound all through and psychic factors are working harmoniously, alarm in the present and forebodings about the future are by these conditions inevitably prevented. Evolution has brought the law of optimism forth, because evolution is a process of cell-construction and function-building, and body-fashioning by and for the individual animal. The process has *made into man's well-being.* The inevitable accompanying feeling is also that of well-being. Nature could not work in such a manner that nerve-welfare should mean distress-feeling. The feeling must report the fact. (One may feel well and yet be diseased, to be sure; but the feeling here is not the report of disease; it is report of health remaining). Thus, evolution has always worked out the law and the habit of satisfaction in normal existence.

DISCUSSION FOUR. But this satisfaction breeds courage in healthy life. To develop a normal body and mind is to induce therein a feeling of adequacy. A good nervous system feels equal to present conditions and demands. Especially is this the case when will is normal, alert and in right action. The thrill of a sound body, the buoyancy of an inspired mind, these things create a feeling correspondent, and the correspon-

dent feeling cannot be that of weakness— inadequacy—
defeat, but must be that of ability — power — courage.

So, I say, *normal life is optimistic and courageous.*

The reverse conclusion is evident.   The prevalence
of fears in the world reveal universal abnormality, and
they constitute a demand on each of us to return, or
to advance, to the normal condition from which all
good things are expected and all sane things are dared.

Why We Fear Future Events.

When, now, the usual operation of the two laws
noted, and of the habits associated therewith, are
interrupted in one's consciousness, a general feeling of
discomfort arises because there is then opposition to
the "set" of things in personal life.   Speaking by and
large, interference with satisfaction in habit and initiative appears —

1.   In a pronounced recognition of presently unknown or of always unknowable conditions;

2.   In a pronounced feeling of inadequacy.

Satisfaction must be *broken when* you confront:
A — A vast unknown *time;* B — A vast unknown
change in life; C — A vast unknown *ending of life;*
D — And satisfaction disappears in a pronounced
feeling of inadequacy, of inability to cope with things,
known or unknown.

Such interference with satisfaction is an element
of confusion among natural functions and those states
of quiescence and comfort which accompany a nervous
system and a bundle of activities that ought to mean,
"all good," and, therefore, ought to report in a consciousness, "all well."   Before the looming unknown
and the object or condition concerning which you cannot feel able,— adequate,— ordinary satisfaction of
life in itself is disturbed, upset, possibly destroyed.

The raising within us of a recognition of the *now-unknown* or the *always-unknowable* is equivalent to the inducement of a feeling of inability-to-cope-with. The normal body and mind have satisfaction in themselves *because* they are normal, and so, in the common run of things, are usually adequate — carry a feeling of ability-courage. But the huge unknown and the physically or psychically overwhelming run amuck with the habits of satisfaction and courage, so that this opposition begets awe, uneasiness, apprehension, fright, terror,— some phase of the fear-feeling.

An encouraging truth, however, appears at this point. We say that "familiarity breeds contempt." *By so much as you become accustomed to the conditions or objects which set up internal opposition to the laws and habits noted, by so much do the emphasis of recognition of the unknown and the feeling of inadequacy lose more or less in depth and edge.* Thus the adventurer ceases to regard unknown possibilities with concern, and the soldier becomes "case-hardened" to danger and odds and death. Thus, too, the mountaineer learns to look upon lofty heights without excitement, and the sailor holds himself sternly to confronting of tempest and wave. The fact is, here, that life has re-adjusted itself, and, finding itself intact, has resumed the habits of satisfaction and adequacy-feeling or courage.

A GREAT TRUTH thus appears: *You may so accustom yourself to the idea of meeting the unknown and to believing in your ability to cope with great powers, as to acquire, on a higher level, the old habits of satisfaction —. sense of well-being — and assurance of ability, of confidence and of courage.*

Previous experience shows that you have accomplished this readjustment again and again. Some unknown condition or object has lost its power permanently to induce discomfort of mind. The following also has been true in your case. Some great difficulty, danger, reality, has only brought out your unsuspected abilities. You have confronted the Jordan and found it out, the Red Sea and crossed over.

This fact should be used to inspire within you an uplift-feeling before the idea of anything unknown, anything overwhelming.

Nevertheless, we must here modify a little. If the readjustment were *literally* possible in the *full sense*, experience would deprive of all fear all men who have had half a life's existence. The truth is, however, that the age of fear is the noon or afternoon of life, so far as fears concern the unknown and the overwhelming. Youth is not the time of fears — for then the habit of satisfaction in well-being is so active and pronounced that almost invincible courage obtains. The two paragraphs preceding this, then, may stand as invitations and teachers, yet leave much undisposed of in our problem of fear.

The Vital Facts About These Fears.

The vital thing may be brought out in an advancing form. The *power of the ideas of the unknown and the overwhelming* should be overcome and destroyed. The power of such ideas is evolved from three sources :

I — A false conception of Time; II — An unduly active forepicturing of Conditions; III — An abnormal expectation of events. We take up these factors in their order.

I. First Factor: A False Conception of Time. The first source of confusion to normal mental satisfaction, a false conception of time, is twofold.

One phase consists in a *wrong view of time*, the other in an *apprehensive attitude toward time*. The second phase is induced by the first, although the two usually exist as parts of one thought. The first phase demands consideration because of this fact; the matter is practical in bearing, however metaphysical in its nature.

We can best approach the practical element by a brief discussion of the theory of the time idea. Man is the only animal that is capable of this idea, since he alone is able to say, "I am identically myself through all the passing of activities whether within or without," thus rising to the idea of *continuity amid change.* Having the idea *of* identity, man makes action's continuance a measure *for* identity, and then calls that measure, *time*.

The false view of time consists in the fact that we get away, in our thought, from this measure-element of mere thought, and come at last to regard the *measure of internal and external activities* as an external reality in itself.

The idea of space, again, is a a mere-element *in thought* of external action or inaction — properly conceived; but here also we make a *thought-measure* to be an external reality.

In other words, we put a *thought,* "identity-action-continuance," outside ourselves, and call that, *time;* and we put a further *thought,* "external action or inaction," outside ourselves, and call that, *space.*

Now, let us observe certain facts concerning time and space. It is only necessary to compare the origin of various time-words and space-words with this present conception of time and of space, to discover precisely the process of putting the *thought*-thing outside our-

selves and making it an *outside reality-thing.* The
following list of words illustrates the fact that man began his life by really giving names to his own inner
processes of thought, only later making those names
to stand for things as though outside his thought.   That
is, however external things *appeared* to him to be, he
began by naming his *inner* thoughts *about* those things.
Thus, to select at random, we have:

Thing from the Sanscrit, *Tak,* "what is prepared or
made an object."   Prepared *where?*   In *thought about*
a something that acted upon the mind, induced a
final mental action.   You see, the action-upon is
transformed by the responsive mental action into a
thing.

Object, from *Jet,* "to throw" and *ab,* "against"—
"to throw against."   Throw against *what?*   In last
analysis, against *mind,* inducing mental *action* which
is *named,* object.

Subject, "to put under," primarily, in a thought —
necessarily so.

Reality, from Latin, *Res,* "a thing;" "what is prepared or made an object;" "what is thrown against
mind."

Fact, from Latin, *Facere,* "to make, do;" "what
is made, done."   *Do,* from Sanscrit, *Dha,* "to place."
Here, also, a mental action: "to place by thought."
How could the placing be recognized except by
thought?

Existence, from Sanscrit, *Stha,* "to stand," from
As, "to breathe."   The thing is placed in the thought
induced by the thing thrown against mind.

Being, from Sanscrit, *Bhu,* "to grow, become."
The mind perceives a something thrown against it as
becoming or growing.

Life, "what remains;" the remaining seeming at the last simply in mind.

Action, from Latin, *Agere,* "to do;" what is being done as observed by and in mind.

Space, from Sanscrit, *Spa,* "that which is drawn out." But the drawing out must seem in the thinker to take place *outside* because he makes a *thought-object* an *object of thought.* The *thought-seeming* occurs in mind; the objective *fact-seeming* seems outside mind.

Distance, "stand apart." *Where?* In the thinker's inner observation. The stand-apart idea is *there;* not elsewhere; but as object of recognition, it is referred outside its origin.

World, "age of man;" *Age,* "a course;" *Era,* "a calculation." Here, again, we have the fact of inner mental *processes* receiving inner *names,* so that named things appear to have reality in themselves, but have their known reality in mind.

Time, referring to *Tide,* from Sanscrit, *Day (Da,* "to give"), "to allot." It is a measure-idea.

Year, from *Ya,* "that which passes;" the idea of passing being a mental *conclusion,* and the notion, *year,* being a mere mental *measure-naming* in conclusion.

In all this it appears that, however real *things, space, time,* may be as objects of thought, they can only be known *in thought,* so that in naming them man has simply named his own thoughts.

And so, when man tries to find a "thing-in-itself," apart from his thought, he must fail in the effort, since the thing-in-itself, apart from thought, if found (impossible, of course), would then be, not apart, but in thought. And when he tries to find space independent of thought, he must also fail, for a similar reason: the *non-thought* space would then be an *in-thought* space.

What else could it be? Finally, when man tries to find time existent apart from thinking activities that pass in his mind, failure is inevitable, because the activities must first be recognized in mind, the passing must be observed in mind and the time-measurements, hour, day, year, are merely thought-names of units selected *in* mind out of the passing activities *of* mind.

The world of Nature *as you know it* or perceive it is really a *thought-world* which you have built up in your mind. There *is* an external world, but that world is by you perceived *in your* mind. You can never know any world other than your inner reflection (so to speak) of a something outside called the world because you name your thought. Thus with all things, objects, processes, combinations. You cannot get outside of yourself to know; you are compelled to *know* inside yourself the things that are outside yourself.

Space is a word that stands in our thought for *relations of nearness and remoteness* of things-ideas, and, since these things themselves are, as *we know* them, thought-reflections occurring *within* our minds, the word *space* stands for such thought-relations of thought-reflections. For example: you observe in the night sky a star far north and a star far south, and the two stars appear to occupy space. But each star, as you *know* it, is a thought-reflection in your mind, and the two are *related in a thought*, "remoteness-from-one-another." This sort of mental perception we call space because the relation between various thought-reflections of things seems "drawn out"—*Spa.*

Similarly, *time* is a word standing in our thought for *relations of sequence between thought-reflections of activities*. It is not a thing-in-itself; it is a certain

mode of our mental action.   This is also true of space.
None of these considerations, of course, deny the reality of world, or of action, or of sequence.   The conclusion is merely that the world and space and time, as we
know them, are known only in the mind.   "World
known to each," and "space" and "time" are names
which we really give to mental actions.   Such mental
actions are *induced* by activities outside the mind, but
when outside activities become *known in* mind, the
things known are the mental activities — *signs* of the
external facts.

A mirror reflects whatever stands or moves before
it.   Here are two realities: the things and actions that
are not the reflections, and—the reflections.   If the
reflection could be a *knowing*, the mirror would know,
but the knowing could only be *in* the mirror.   When
we make the mirror to represent the mind, we see
that knowing a world, space, time, is reflecting within
mind.

The ancient, Plato, discoursed once in the form of
a dialogue.   He conceived of a man (in a talk between
two speakers) confined in a cave, with his back to the
cave's opening and his face toward the rear wall.
You see, he, one speaker — and so, Plato — said,
that if men, objects and animals outside the cave pass
before the opening, the light of day will cast their
shadows on the rear wall, and the cave-dweller will
perceive and come to know the shadows.   Although,
through the shadows, he will know outside objects,
his knowing will be of the shadows alone.   In this sense
he will know the outside objects, but only as reflected
on the cave's wall.   It is thus with our mind-knowing:
we perceive only with the mind, on the mind's wall,
as it were.   So, a Universe is a complex thought in

man's mind, and space and time are relation-thoughts
which concern things and activities as thought.

When, therefore, the mind understands these
truths, the fact becomes evident that the idea of time
arises from mental perception of sequence in activities.
The activities are the main thing, besides the feeling
of personal identity. Self-identity erects a standard,
a stationary post, so to speak, and the sequence of the
activities makes the latter to seem to pass before us.
Any now-passing is the *present* — our self-identifying
consciousness. Then memory comes in to repeat
mental activities that correspond with the items in
the sequence, and we refer such items to a *past*. But
then, again, reason and imagination enter into the
process, and we believe that activities of some sort will
continue to go right on indefinitely, and we call this
to-be going-on a *future*.

But, of course, activities that merely *have been*,
are *now* no more. They have ceased. What is left
is simply a *thought* —"past." The past cannot be a
thing-in-itself. It is only the *"has-been"* of activities
which now are not.

And a *to-be* going-on of activities is *not-yet*, because
it *is* "to be." Such activities have not occurred.
They are merely *imagined*. This going-on sequence
that is *"to be"* cannot be *now* and *"to be"* at once. The
"to-be" is simply a *thought* —"the future."

There is no past save as thought of a has-been.

There is no future save as thought of a yet-to-be.

Only the present is real, and this is real because
it is perception and knowing in mind of mentally reflected activities.

Having thus disposed of space and time and worlds
(as subjects of thought), the two great remaining

facts are — *Agents* and *Actions*. We now have our
conclusions in regard to Fear. Putting these considerations together for our treatment of fear, we
remark:

If we think of time as a thing-in-itself, how vast,
everlasting, portentious! If we think of space as a
thing-in-itself, this also looms up to overwhelm us.
If we think of a mysterious Universe, apart from our
little mind-world (which alone we can *know*), which
alone need ever concern us, the idea grows on us until
a sense of awe, bewildering and overloading, threatens
to confuse and terrify consciousness.

*But the human mind has no such concern with real-
ities other than those revealed in its own thoughts.*

The Universe is revealed in a System which is just
as vast as a man's thought — your thought — and
no vaster, *so far as you know*. This truth reduces the
Universe you know to activities within your mental
scope.

Space is revealed in the relation-reflections of a
man's mind — your mind — and reduces to your com-
prehension, *your comprehending mental activities*.

Time is revealed in the relation or sense of nearness and remoteness of a man's thoughts — your
thoughts — and reduces to *your mental calibre*.

In the field of the two great remaining facts, agents
and activities, you take your place. Every other
human does the same. To each there remain only
activities — of the self and of the Not-self known by
the self. Each man perceives various activities constituting *his* world, taking place in *his* mind-reflecting
relations of space and time.

To each, then, nothing remains but activities in
the sequence of *his* perceiving.

The idea of time, therefore (to drop the ideas of world and space), concerns a flow of mental activities alone. We come, thus, to our regimes.

REGIMES CORRECTING EFFECTS OF FALSE TIME-NOTION.

GENERAL REGIME — NUMBER ONE: *Minimizing the Time-Notion.* You have shown commendable patience in pursuing this (really brief) discussion, but the reward is at hand. You have no foreboding about *present* time, since this you both have and know. It is only the *future* that seems to invite distress, and this, especially, as it looms afar, as it is conceived as more and more remote from the present — being, let us say, the future of another year, or of a decade hence, or of old age.

The remedy consists in remembering that there *is no* future in fact, and never can be; that all life is contemporaneous — of the "dead," of the living, of other beings in other conditions, — of Deity or of angels. *Life is now only.* The life of the past was *then* only, has ceased as *of* then. Life is now as fact, and forever will be: the now-life of all universes. Only the present is real. The host of intelligences, occupying even an infinite Universe, march abreast in everlasting *now.*

And this now is a now of action and actors. To you, then, the now is a now of activities alone. You are, now, in the midst of these activities. To the now-conditions of things you are invited to hold yourself adequate. The now is an instant — enough in itself. Any now is an instant, and enough for life. You should affirm, with the courage of the normal existence:

"*I am equal to the demands of the Now. Always*

*shall I say this and be so equal. Thus there can be no
imaginary coming "Now" in which I shall not be adequate."*

This is precisely the attitude of normal mind in
healthy body. The satisfaction of well-being involves
courage for the *now*. The well-being inspires a feeling
of now-confidence, which is the only felt need, since
there never can be a real time other than a now-time.

GENERAL REGIME—NUMBER TWO: *Proving Adequacy to the Now.* The condition indispensable to the
preceding regime is that you *make good* the claim of now-
adequacy. And make good *now.* If you maintain normal health of body and mind, and are doing and living
the reasonable best in your relation to the world's now-
activities, you are not apprehensive of any so-called
future — unless you are under the tyranny of sheer
imagination, which is purely a case for resolute will-
power banishing a perfectly causeless notion. In the
condition just above indicated, you are conscious of
well-being and of well-doing, and so are necessarily
optimistic. Optimism concerns the present far more
than the future. Its spirit of hopefulness is vitalized
by present satisfactions. Well-being and well-doing
induce a satisfaction which, because of itself now, *normally* believes that itself shall continue. Hence the
invitation that you assist yourself into normal conditions now, and that you do your reasonable best in
all your relations to the world's activities now. With
the consciousness that you are so doing, you are urged
to combine the clear idea of time — of next year or
of forty years hence—conceived as merely a measur-
ing-thought of the now-activities around you. Life
reduces to proving adequate to the present situation —
more or less—in some satisfactory way. Life can never

and will never be other than precisely that. When you maintain these two activities,— that of well-doing and that which makes time a now-matter,— you find apprehension for the future dying out because nothing remains of the vague unknown something on which apprehensions can feed and fatten. We come, then, to the second factor in thought supporting fear.

II. SECOND FACTOR : AN UNDULY ACTIVE FORE-PICTURING OF CONDITIONS. The second source of confusion to normal life's satisfaction and courage, so far as the future is concerned, is an unduly active fore-picturing of conditions. This book, it should be observed, does not concern methods for insuring satisfactory conditions in the future, except in the development of courage. That work is provided for in the other volumes of this Library. At present we have to do solely with fear that the future may prove unfortunate. This fear is altogether needless. Especially is worry about it totally gratuitous and always harmful. Worry never improves conditions of living, either actual or imagined; it always makes present conditions worse and prepares for other conditions of the same order.

Apprehension concerning future conditions of life infallibly proves two things: *first,* that the *will has shirked,* or been *driven from,* its duty of pushing and directing for personal well-being. When will acts normally in this regard, it asserts well-being, pushes on to well-being, directs for well-being, and by sheer activity and revealing of energy breeds courage and confidence. The appropriate invitation, therefore, is apparent: Banish all ideas save those of *asserting, pushing, directing* for well-being *now.*

GENERAL REGIME—NUMBER THREE: *Will Promising a Good Future.* You are, thus, urged, to arouse the idea of well-being, as present and as to come and continue, to the utmost vividness; that is, to think of yourself as well and prospering and as continuing so, with the greatest mental energy and confidence. This effort will infallibly arouse the will to a high pitch of resolute activity and determination.

The fact proved by apprehension concerning the future is that the imagination has become unduly inventive and has been given liberty in unhealthful directions.

Imagination cannot become too active, or too full of invention if only it is controlled and applied to life in right practical ways, but it is always capable of exercising its powers in wrong directions and on unhealthful objects. The normal mind in a sound body, since it has the feeling of well-being or satisfaction that reports the fact of normality, tends to imagine only on the plane of its satisfaction in itself, and healthy imaginations therefore deal with happy expectations. When imagination sees time and space looming large and forbidding on the idea of a far future, and creates therein the shapes of portent, this is a sign of mind not normal. A cure for this brooding and foreboding imagination will be found in the will to be happy, the will to do one's best in present situations, the will to face all odds courageously. This cure may be presented as follows:

GENERAL REGIME — NUMBER FOUR: *Will Counteracting Imagination.* You are therefore invited to affirm, vigorously, confidently, and daily for long: *"I will to be, and I am, full of good cheer and power now. I am now doing my best reasonably possible in work and life — and such always shall I do. Hence, I now will myself able to face whatever conditions may come to me. I am power now! I am prophet now of success to come!"*

This assertion of will is doubly demanded because forebodings about the future usually spring from unhappy conditions of body or of mind. And one proof of need of the regime will be any feeling of *distaste* for it. If you positively dislike the idea or effort of willing as directed, that fact is imperative call for such willing. The regime will prove hard and unwelcome to the melancholy mood or temperament, of course. We see in different types of mind actual tests of the regimes' value. Said an acute thinker: "On meeting with a disaster, the man of melancholy temperament selects and indulges in the woful aspects of it, the phlegmatic man takes his satisfaction in the thought that such things must happen, the sanguine man his in hopes of repairing it, and the irascible man his in anger with the cause of it." The happiest man is the sanguine, but he needs not the present regime. The phlegmatic man is the most philosophical if he can also be sanguine. The irascible man adds disaster to disaster, for his anger breeds poison in his blood. The melancholy man above all needs to arouse his will just because he is what he is. Precisely the attitudes indicated will these types of men assume in regard to the future. *A man's future in thought is only the reflection of his present.* If he enjoys misery now, he will fill the future with unhappiness. But this tendency is his disease, and he more than others should inspire his will to assert the best to be, as well as select the best that is for his thought — in his thought of himself for all conditions of life.

GENERAL REGIME—NUMBER FIVE: *Substitution of Happy Imagination for Unhappy.* If the future in our thought is but a reflection of the present in our mind, imagination full of possible unhappy events, or imagination running in the direction of such events, is a demand

in itself for substitution of precisely the opposite contents and directions. So long as you dwell on this
trouble-fear, so long do you make unhappy imaginations
the subject of your thoughts — and thus vitalize them.
The tendency and the thoughts should always be suppressed by ideas and pictures of well-being and adequacy and success. You are therefore invited to resolve that when unpleasant anticipations occur in
mind you will instantly banish them. You are urged
to will at the required time, immediately, such forebodings out of mind. And you are invited always
to keep your mind active on plans and pictures of
good work, good results, good fortune — surely coming
welfare.

Had Plato's man in the cave possessed a keyboard
so connected with outside objects that he could man-
ipulate the shadows on the wall, he would certainly
have pressed, or permitted to be pressed, only those
keys which controlled happy scenes before him. Thus
with imaginations about the future. You possess the
keyboard. You may not altogether control events —
that subject is not before us. You can control your
attitude toward the present, and, above all, you can
accustom the mind to respond only to, to throw up on
the imaginary wall of the future only, objects and
events which shall accord with the normal mind's satisfaction in itself. This brings us to the third factor
of confusion —

III. THIRD FACTOR: AN ABNORMAL EXPECTA-
TION OF EVENTS. The two preceding regimes dispose,
in a general way, of the third source of confusion to
normal satisfaction in life — that which is here indicated. Our question is, always, it should be remembered: "How to overcome fear concerning the future."

Events will come to pass, and some of them will be unpleasant. These two facts are certain.

"Into each life some rain must fall."

Nevertheless, in the living world, man tries to be ready for evil and for good, and in a normal state he is conscious of reasonable adequacy and courage concerning the future. Our purpose has to do with mental conditions in which apprehension creates all sorts of possible disastrous happenings. These apprehensions may be displaced by their opposites, which suggests *A Certain Fact and A Certain Law Working Infallibly for Your Assistance.*

(1) The *Fact* is that the word "mind" is merely a name for a "bundle" of regularly established activities (see "*Practical Psychology*"), each expression of which, when it ceases, leaves nothing whatever in mind except its characteristic tendency. You do not "store" thoughts; by thinking you merely develop tendencies toward thoughts. There is nothing in mind save action and its mental meaning. (In fact, the meaning *is* the action). This is the fact referred to.

(2) The *Law* is that the activities and their tendencies, when they become definitely habituated, can only be eliminated by substitution of their opposites. Only optimistic expectations can eliminate forebodings, and they can do so by substitution alone. You cannot will mental activities to cease except by thinking thoughts that drive apprehensions out of mind. If apprehensions, then, are habitual with you, you have a tendency to think in that way, and you must develop a tendency to think in the opposite way. Since mental activities are nothing when they cease,—leave nothing "stored" in mind, — you see that your task is not to throw out fears but to think hope and courage

in terms of actual good fortune *expected.*   The tendency
so to think will infallibly be developed if you will from
now on engage always in happy thoughts about the
future and in nothing contrary whatever.   The method
is simple: *Never think evil; persistently think good
pictured concretely in imaginary experience,* by filling
your mind with scenes in which you are invariably
fortunate and surcharged with the feelings of success.

You are invited, therefore, to cultivate habitual
expectation of a bright future by always calling to
mind and dwelling upon — without exception — ideas
of *your own power,* ideas of *efficient work,* ideas of
fortunate outcomes from whatever you may undertake.

These general regimes introduce us to further considerations of the satisfaction of normal life which are
preliminary to our special regimes to be given in the
next chapter.   We touch, now, some very quick spots
in human nature.

Shall Death Cease on Earth?

It is remarkable that the twin facts, old age and
death, do not overwhelm us all and make impossible
both interest in life and the zest of achievement.
Where is the use of the striving for success, of entertaining hope and seeking inspiration, since the body
must surely decay and death is the inevitable end?
Such would naturally be our thought, it would seem,
in our present age, however confidently we may look
forward to some coming era in which death on the
earth shall have finally ceased. Yet the attitude
indicated by the question is the exception rather than
the rule. Distress concerning the coming of old age
and the certainty of death is always regarded as
abnormal, and we say of the suicide: "He must have

been insane." Life's satisfaction in itself and the optimism that springs therefrom hold the soul steady in spite of the facts — decay and death.

Now, in accordance with the law that *everything in Nature has a meaning,* if only we could discover it, this general condition of immunity to the fears suggested must also be regarded as significant. A hint of purpose or tendency seems thus to appear. (You are invited to disregard the fad of some scientists of to-day that universal law can operate without purpose, and to admit intelligence in Nature when you see that which would be intelligence in your own life, and to concede that when you see *intelligence,* you see *purpose*). Evolution has produced the nervous system and the psychic factor. In doing these things it has overcome ten thousand difficulties and eliminated many impediments to its own advance. The ability to confront old age and death while maintaining the world's present good cheer and courage may be a first step toward the final conquest of both — under certain conditions of development yet to arrive. Youth, and the love of life, and interest in its affairs, these are marvelously powerful factors, and the vital tenacity thus disclosed, the tendency to cling to life, aided by growing intelligence and quenchless faith, may ultimately solve the problem of physical immortality of body refined to fit the triumphant tenant — a soul that itself has grown within itself the endless life.

I believe that the human race will ultimately banish from earth the incidental imperfection called physical death.

If the psychic factor is a product of material activities and conditions, remember that matter is nothing other than spiritual in its evident last analysis.

All its physical qualities, conceived as such, disappear on scientific investigation and thought. Matter is motion of the ether within the ether, it is said, and the ether does not reveal purely physical qualities — does not seem to be matter. The highest realities we know are thought and the thinker. We conclude that matter — which is motion of ether — which is non-physical — is thought. Evolution has produced matter-thought, in which appears psychic thought. The matter-thought is, then, a means to the psychic thought. And since we now know that the psychic thought does mightily influence the matter-thought of the body, the hint emerges of a final reaction of soul upon body to refine it, to especially vitalize it, to infuse the psychic powers of existence throughout all its cells and functions, and thus to give it ability to remain — forever young, forever deathless.

If the soul be not a product of material activities (so-called), but is an essentially independent existence, or if it be an evolution out of material conditions of a something that is not matter in any sense, the above conclusions hold good. Old age and death may indeed be natural in the present history of life on the earth. Many things may have been natural in the long lines of man's ascent which are now entirely unnatural. It has been natural for reptiles to crawl, and for birds to fly, and for apes to stop short of thought, and for man to think — and the naturalness has appeared in one historic line of advance.

The facts that in certain body-cells the living nucleus decreases while cytoplasm increases, and that the cells need to "congugate" for a renewal of energy, finally, however, losing energy entirely — considerations now employed by some to "demonstrate" the naturalness of

decay and death — do not necessarily demand that conclusion. We do not *know* that these facts may *not* mean
a struggle in life to overcome the tendencies noted.
The facts are not *known* to be *final*. The *meaning* of
the facts may as well point to *ascent* as to descent — to
a stage of being possessed of growing powers of continuance, not decreasing powers. Science does not
know to the contrary. Some scientists merely believe
that age and death are natural now. But this belief is
simply the belief of scientific men, some of whom reveal
predilections for the densest sort of materialism in
thought. Science is merely the work of human beings.
Let us have done with mere authority here no less than
in matters of religion. Science has been mistaken in
the past. It is not infallible, and the love of an occasional votary for mud and decay should not disturb us.

The history of evolution is a history of arrivings.
Always a tendency is evident here to arrive on higher
levels of being. The coming of men climaxed physical
and psychic development in the matter of types. We
may not (probably) look for any higher type of body
—in its general form and adaptability,— any higher
type of mind — in its general functions and activities.
Evolution now deals with the improvement of the
human body, the development of mind-powers along
lines of psychic possibilities in man. This limitation
of evolution can mean, if it means anything, only an
arrival of man at a stage of perfecting *physical* expression of perfecting *psychic* life. Thus may our conclusion be, that the later achievement of the human self
shall rescue body from death because the self has "laid
hold" on immortal existence.

Now, such a far-off, divine event, even though
we know it not to be presently realized in any existing

individual, has yet an inspiration for all. We are on the way! The earth-life, figuratively speaking, means not an endless recurrence of day and night, an inevitable closing-down of the shadow on every life so long as earth shall swing through space. It means that some *day* shall hold its own against all night, some individual lives shall ascend out of the cycle-plane and stand triumphant on the plane of deathless being.

The curve of life should not be the circle; it should be the parabola.

How do we know that the Universe moves only in cycle stages? The fact that the Universe is running down, and that earth and sun are losing their conservative forces, is offset by the fact that the Universe is now also building — systems, planets, even matter as we know it here, evolved from known and unknown conditions. There is upbuilding no less than downtearing. The highest expression of the upbuilding process is the psychic factor, and the highest conceivable stage of the psychic factor is immortal existence realizing endless development. Amid the cycles of world-coming and world-going, well may the human self be conceived as passing on triumphant because at last it has arrived where material activities of whatever sort may never reach or influence its functions and growth.

Inspiring to every intelligence conceiving it should be such a thought. The conception breathes courage, and hope, and assurance, and creates indomitable will to catch the higher wisdom and to live the best that may be possible under existing conditions.

But this thought points unerringly toward immortal youth. Mortal youth we now have, and that prophetic gift *each may regain and retain,* if the self will but resolutely enter this divinest of quests. Here the satisfaction of normal life in itself both climaxes and discloses a way to that youth of the spirit which nothing may quench or discourage.

THE SPIRIT OF YOUTH AGAINST FEAR OF OLD AGE.

The purpose of these pages is not to instruct in prevention of disease, the passing of the years, the final exit, but simply to suggest remedies for fear-feeling inspired by the thought of such things. Only courage is our goal, and this involves various other qualities which not only destroy fear but impart to life a priceless zest.

To invite youth into the soul's life is to summon its gracious companions. Thus, in order to work out our regimes (to appear in the next chapter), we need to understand the nature of youth, that the self may suggest to itself incessantly the things that constitute youth and give it value.

When we try to picture youth, we always ignore its clouds, storms and mishaps, and we surround some ideal human with Nature's fairest scenes. Youth means to us the forward look and the assurance: "I shall arrive! I have won! Greater things yet shall I achieve!" This is our thought of boy or girl — and it is the truth. That truth the man and the woman see, each in a different way, but never in a manner to blur the beautiful fact. The "Man in the Moon" forever lures the race: the face is the face of youth — to either woman or man, youth faring immortally on.

> *She* sees the features of a maiden's face
> Upturned to take the kiss of star-eyed Space;
> *He* sees the head of manhood just begun,
> With wind-blown hair and forehead toward the sun;
> Let Love assent, and Fancy add her grace,
> If Truth declare the heavenly visions — one.

Always youth symbolizes the self aflame facing love and good fortune, with the courage-will alert and afire to go on and on, and to win, and to have joy of existence. Therefore we picture youth as overarched by azure skies, and guarded by verdure-clad hills, and invited by green fields and woods, and entranced by the song of birds and streams, and lured by the call of ocean afar — the call of the infinite and of power.

The sounds we hear in such a picture are — laughter, and whispers of love, and words that vibrate with courage and confidence. Youth rides the chariot of the sun. Youth inhales the incense of Religion's Temple till crusades issue forth in every era. Youth guides the vast machinery of world-industry, dictates the turn of fortune's wheel, flashes the sword of war, masters the earth as a gift to sheer love and passion of love. Youth comes — the world thrills. Youth always comes — and dazzles us till we see not age and death. Youth is for every soul once at least, and the divine gift is almost worth failing age and death itself. Youth would be worth all things could we take the splendoring gift as we might take it, instead of permitting, as we do, the cheat of advancing age and ageing experience to rob us of its continuance. If you will hold the youth that is yours, or re-seize the youth that may be yours, the glory of it shall be worth whatever comes to body — for nothing evil comes to youth regained.

The youth-feeling of self-life may be preserved and may be recaptured if only you are resolute in the wooing of it.

An analysis of youth is merely an analysis of things which any human intelligence may achieve. Let us see:

ITEM ONE. Youth means a splendid *interest in life.* This interest involves, for example —

A self that is young: the body's activities; variety; achievements; means and methods thereto; competition and prizes; adventures; new scenes and experiences; amusements; successes; instruments of action; excitements; hazards; triumphs. By the action of certain social instincts youth is interested in other people, selected by temperament, and in their lives, their reverses, their successes.

Youth is stirred by the *vast* and the *wonderful,* and ever does it discover such incitements to interest. In the beginning life thrills at everything; then gradually selects the objects of its special or lasting attention,— but so long as youth holds, the selection holds, or the selecting process runs on and on.

And youth is intensely interested in *life:* just physical being, mental existence,— and so it always tends to optimism and idealism.

Finally comes *love.* It may be of a conventional and mild type, it may be a magnificent passion, for some individual of the opposite sex — who is idealized in dumb ecstacy.

These are some of youth's most excellent qualities and interests. Thus we come to what may be called

A FIRST INTERLUDE REGIME OF YOUTH. This regime falls between the general regimes concerning the normal satisfaction of life and the regimes of the next chapter relating to so-called evil events, because youth has that satisfaction and may guard against those events.

The paragraphs analyzing youth are not mere writing: they are intended as suggestive pointers for practical use. You are invited to read and re-read them, noting their truth, dwelling upon the truth, seeking to feel the inspiration of youth's magical interest in the matters referred to. Take a bath in the thought of youth. You are invited as follows:

1.   Let it be assumed that you are still young. In that case you should resolve always to retain the zest, the interest-urge, which belongs to youth *par excellence.*

2.   Driven to confess that you have passed the mere years of youth and have begun the folly of counting yourself old, and of apprehending weakness and age, resolve to capture this lost kingdom, as surely you may if you will but accept the regimes here offered and employ them in your daily life.

ITEM TWO. Again, youth is characterized by its *perennial enthusiasm.* It is the time of objective superlatives, vivid descriptions. Let not teachers succeed in reducing your language to stereotyped dead excellence. Better wild roses than cut hedges, excess of color than bloodless clays. "Enthusiasm" derives its word-meaning from a Greek word, *enthous*, "to be full of the God," "having a god within," inspired, since *en* signifies "having" and *theos*, "a god." This god within reveals himself in language and action — chosen to express the blazing and abounding interest of life. Youth is enthusiastic, and in the trait it discloses one of its greatest values. Here, again, then, we specialize, and present

A SECOND INTERLUDE REGIME OF YOUTH. 1.   If you are yet young in years and spirit, cling to life's enthusiasms.

2.   If you miss the spirit of young life, proceed to reawaken the dual feeling of enthusiastic interest in self and in the world with which you come in contact.

ITEM THREE. A wonderful trait always discoverable in youth is its *courage*. The exuberant sense of
well-being overflows in action, daring, adventure.
Fear is not native to youth, and if fear spring up now
and then in the young heart, it is quickly downed as
alien and contradiction. Youth does not think of time,
cares not for obstacles in the way of its desires, is apt
to be contemptuous of foes, and holds old age to be
impossible. It is because youth is courageous that it
is impatient and thoughtless. Courage is sense of
power, and the power must needs be used, since the
feeling is intense and imperious. It is natural for
youth to be courageous: *cours* — *cors*, "heart;" "of
good heart"— as it is for "angels" to be lovable.
Remember, and hold fast, and conquer fear.

A THIRD INTERLUDE REGIME OF YOUTH. 1. If
you are young, guard your courage, feed its fires, keep
it clean of ashes, give it the draft of life.

2. Have your years begun to suggest the "melancholy days"? Then discount some of your caution,
put a dash of recklessness into your conservatism, give
the laugh of scorn to all fear-feelings, and, arousing
your mind to a new search for new interests and renewed
enthusiasms of all sorts, bring back to heart and soul
the flying light of courage. Dare to be young; be
young in your daring. All things are yours in the only
world that lasts — the world of thought and imagination — the world of youth. And only the world that
lasts is worth while.

ITEM FOUR. Youth is *confident*. Doddering age
deals out stale counsel, but youth calls for war, invention, conquest, achievement. "Wisdom" has received
undue honor. It settles into its throne and calls for
homage—and falls asleep while youth hints the ever-

right wisdom of the new and the better.   Wisdom puts
its house in order and assumes that this house and this
order are infallible.   Youth searches out a finer building and creates a nobler order — and is all unwitting
of its doing a good thing.   The wisdom of age blinds
the old to the flash of fortune and dulls the aged spirit
to the velvet touch of unseen wings — the wings of
opportunity.   Opportunity comes but once to the
self holding council with its own conviction
holding convictions only so long as they serv
the flash, notes the brushing of pinions ag
blooded cheek, and sees opportunity eve
Youth is alertness: the wild animal vibrant t
influence, the human intelligence so alive wit
that it *intuits* the meaning of things, the call and
and urge of a Universe pressing upon it with the
ness and the stimulation of the flesh on the sou
youth is incessantly moved to action and to ve

Youth is keyed to Nature and toned to life.
est, enthusiasm, courage and confidence thrill it,
· it, make it divinely watchful — watchful to self-
ing and self-thought, watchful to the new and the fre
ly possible, watchful to realities and ideals, watchf
to opportunity and progress, watchful to realities and
ideals, watchful to opportunity and progress, watchful
to the joy and the laugh and the heroism of existence.
This quality itself is priceless, and so, combined with
other facets on the diamond of living, makes a human
defiant of the fear and the canker of age.   It needs
not to pawn the jewel: that possession convinces the
world of its wealth.

A FOURTH INTERLUDE REGIME OF YOUTH. 1. You
are invited to drive your mind out of settlements of
wisdom and the rules of the years and the apathy of

that overpraised state, maturity, and to recover the joy and the power of youth's untiring alertness — if you have begun to think the folly, "I am growing old."

2. And into all life, if you are still young, you are urged to throw alertness of eye, ear, hand, fancy, intuition, talent of discovery, divine knowingness — values which have no price and which you may, if you will, hold forever.

Why must a man or a woman become stale? Why must you assume that the time of lethargy and blindness is bound to arrive? Why must you mummify still further into such conditions if you discover that divine alertness has come less and less to companion with you? There is no reason in the nature of things for the arriving or the continuance of such a state. The essential nature of things is spirit, not dead leaves; and if leaves die and matter falls down the ways of life to inertness, you are spirit, part of that wondrous reality which is forever *climbing* the ways of life, alert always to the "just above."

ITEM FIVE. Youth is *idealistic*. Love is blind, it is said. This is no truth. Love is open-eyed to see the hidden and the undeveloped. Sex-love sees the lovely or the godlike body which the material misfit covers. True sex-love never makes a mistake. Soul-body seeks soul-body, not for creation, but for joy of togetherness. Love's idealism does not imagine: it does not create: it finds. The sex-life phases the psychic magnetism which, when the sex-life works true, never runs falsely. The quality called Beauty is merely the Desirable according to psychic needs. Psychic magnetism pushes together two Desirables. Body visible phases invisible body, and soul desirable rushes to desirable soul. There are few real marriages. Matter, and insane passion, and "wise" conventions throw us together so hurriedly that the heavenly chemistry has scant opportunity to demonstrate the intention of this union. The blindness of love is due not to love, but to false world-life. The idealism at which we laugh is misunderstood: we laugh at our own folly. The real idealism is ideal-realism — the finding in a human body of a body unseen and a self not fully expressed, which our unseen body and our nobler soul must possess, if it would live.

All this belongs to youth. Youth idealizes — carelessly, happily, inconsistently, with flitting attention — but that idealism is the truth. Youth babbles of the "Beauty of Nature." Why, Nature *is* beautiful. Youth elevates some or all Women to high place. Why, the high place *is* every woman's own place. There never has breathed a lost Magdalene some atom or part of whom has not been left there — on the high place of womanhood. In something unwrecked in all men we must believe. The idealism of youth is its true vision of the true real. Youth feels life to be Splendid. Why, life *is* splendid — if its intention has the love of the sun in it. It is splendid to see with eyes, hear with ears, perceive with mind, feel with heart; splendid to breathe, and be, and move about, and create a Universe within, and plan and achieve, and will and carry out. Every flower, field, wood, river, sea, star, is more beautiful than I can see — idealism is *truth*. All music is more lovely than I can hear: idealism is *truth*. Every woman is more adorable than I can recognize: idealism is *truth*. Every man is nobler than I can know: idealism is *truth*. All values are more valuable than I can estimate: idealism is *truth*. All prizes are worth more than I can make out: idealism is *truth*. When the values, prizes, adorablenesses pall on us, the feeling does not belittle the things; it merely proves that *we* have sunk below them or have grown past them.

The alternative is significant. To sink below the ideals is to die. And, to grow past the ideals and set up no other ideals is also to die.

When we call past ideals stale, we either confess decay or we call truth a lie. But to grow past ideals by *finding other* ideals is to live. When we do this — find other ideals succeeding other past ideals — we assist truth in growing into more self-identifying forms.

Always youth does precisely these things. It passes realized ideals, but the fact that it finds new ideals shows that it still reckons the old as ideals in their day — truths, not lies. And so youth lives because it idealizes.

A Fifth Interlude Regime of Youth. 1. Especially, then, I urge that, if you wish to body-live, sex-live, soul-live, you should yield to no deception that an ideal, once an ideal, can ever be other than ideal. Thus you keep sweet and fresh the attitude, the mood, the habit, of idealism. This is to live!

2. Or, if young, you are vehemently urged to remain young by holding deep in your heart the divine plan of idealizing all things. So will you maintain life's satisfaction in itself, and thus, all the qualities of youth; and so will the lure of the ideal preserve its spell in your heart to bring you to achievement and happiness. Also, as must be evident, will you find yourself a stranger to doubt, the sneer, the suspicion, the poison of carping criticism. Do not fear the overdoing of idealism so long as you remain a practical worker in

life. Fear rather the ageing influence of the dry rot
of mere practicality.

The Grand Cañon of the Colorado, in Arizona, no
artist could over-color. Behold in yourself a rift in
the Infinite, and let infinite idealization maintain you
in your place there.

And if you fear age, meet the fear with ideals of
thought and with ideal feeling, so that the truth shall
become more real to you: "Nature and life are indeed
splendid and worth the best that is in me."

ITEM SIX. *Happiness* is the assured heritage of
youth.   Life seems new prior to twenty, and interest
then flares unceasingly.   With renewing zest in action,
enthusiasm of thought and feeling, abounding courage,
confidence always rising Phœnix-like from the ashes of
yesterday, and imagination clothing the world with high
significance, youth is bound to be perennially happy.
Not always is youth cheerful (another matter), but
the opposite mood is superficial unless permitted to
become habitual — which it never can become in true
youth.   Cheerfulness is natural where life is normal,
but the habit of moroseness is a crime because it is a
kind of pleasure due to the perversion of the nature of
things.   Youth does not, as youth, pervert; it merely experiments. The want of cheerfulness in the
young is experimental only.   Nor is youth always
found in a state of pleasure.   It is too many-sided.   It
is too inventive.   It devises new pleasures, discarding
old ones, because the psychic factor must maintain
interest and enthusiasm, and idealism is always on a
quest. But youth is, if normal, fundamentally always
happy.   Life has not yet learned the crime of dissatis-
faction with itself.   Life's inherent self-satisfaction
insures deep and perennial happiness to youth.   The

latter does not try to be happy. The combination
indicated is a contradiction. If you *try* to be happy,
you are *un*happy. There are people who make desperate efforts to be cheerful. The absurdity will be
evident if I print on a large card for every room in my
house — or self — this legend: "I will be cheerful,
d——n it!" The fact is, cheerfulness, pleasures, or
happiness must be sought indirectly. The indirection
runs the way of law. Find the principle of cheer, the
rule of pleasure, the law of happiness — and obey!
Then the nature of things brings the reward. When
you try for a thing, you go straight at it. In this case
you also take to it something not consistent with it,
as seen in the printed card, and thus defeat the pursuit.
But when you harmonize with principle, rule, law, you
leave that inconsistent something behind, you forget it,
and then the prize is yours. Youth tries to be cheerful, and irritates the world; seeks pleasure, and worries
the whole earth. But when youth is just its own
glorious self, it is happy, down to the ground and up
to the skies. Then the world forgets even death.
Youth always is normally happy because it is always
indirect in its dealings with itself. It only deals with
itself through other things. Take love as an example.
We love a woman, a man, and shout: "I will give you
my life — will die for you!" We really mean: "I
want you for my own happiness!" We unconsciously
pretend that we care only for the happiness of the beloved object, but every one knows it is our own happiness we seek. We cultivate our own interest indirectly
through this beautiful deception which the other person
believes because he or she also follows the same method.
Thus everywhere. Youth is really happy because it
does not try to be happy, but flames with interest,

enthusiasm, confidence, courage, alertness and idealism.   And so, in conclusion, I give you an infallible
multiple *Rule for True Happiness:*

Keep life's interests alive!

Be enthusiastic in sheer living!

Fear naught!   Trust destiny confidently!

*Catch opportunity and all her brood of details on
the wing!*

*Idealize clay and worship the beautiful — which is
always true!*

Have a passion for achievement and genuine success.
(You will not then run on any quest for happiness, since
the prize will be yours perennially.)

The happiness of youth is expression.   The expression phases the indirection which does not knock at
heavenly gates, but walks the way of harmony, and
is always opening gates to a heaven that is ever present.

A Sixth Interlude Regime of Youth.   1.   You
are urged to keep well to this highway, if young, by
maintaining the traits which make you young.

2.   If many years are yours, you are invited to
initiate those traits — assuming, asserting, making
good — until they become yours again, never more
to pass from you.

Item Seven.   Youth is passion for *prizes, goals,
achievements.*   When so-called "happiness" walks in
wooden shoes, or dodders before the fire-place of meaty
comfort, we know that it was born with infantile paralysis.   The doctors do not cure infantile paralysis —
nor does the preacher who cozzens bed-ridden respectability.   It is the masseuer who arouses inactive nerves
while the physicians deplore "unprofessional methods."
For bed-ridden respectability no cure is possible.
Happiness never yet fruited from inaction, aimlessness,

fussy running to and fro. Happiness is the Infinite breathing up into a live self. The live self always has purpose burning at the core. Life without passion is worthless. Existence validifies in some immense passion to be or to do. That is youth. The lungs of it crave fire, and the heart of it lava. This is right, because Nature says it is right. Breathing fire and circulating lava constitute running government, business, art, religion, and race-preservation. Civilization is not water. Progress is the push of piston before steam — and steam is matter in a passion. People grow old because they settle down to breathing common air and circulating a pink blood. Youth knows better — and is happy and creative. You remain young so long as you have fire in your lungs and lava in your arteries. Less than these is death or, worse, old age. It is some fine passion: passion to be, to do, to get, to win out splendidly, that makes youth the power it is.

A SEVENTH INTERLUDE REGIME OF YOUTH. Our advices, then, are evident. 1. Let youth hold fast its deep passions for prizes and victories.

> Existence comes to best
> In qualities that give it zest:
>   In intuition swift and passions bold.
> And these are youth's at worst —
> Wines of all years distilling first
>   That man may drink, and know, and ne'er grow old.

2. If you have lost somewhat of your youth, here lies your highway of recovery. Bring back to heart and mind, as you may if you will, the passion that wings the self to success.

FEAR NOT EVENTS.

Fear not events:
Contingencies these, controlled in part by Will;
Necessities these, all signs of the human tangle;
All opportunities these, which a MAN can swing
For betterment — one way, other way, *some* way.

See how the wrestler writhes, twists, lunges, stands!
He modifies the opponent's every act.
Thus far he wins.
The other in turn gives him a hard battle.
But *my* man stoops, erects, dodges —
Tactics transformed by contingency and Will.
Now every feint and thrust and lightning shift
He makes a new advantage, seized with wit and power.
Is he defensive? Defense is wily war,
Waiting to turn the airy chances.
The enemy laughs — and, swift and sudden sequence!
On the flash of deific thought,
Goes down!

In all events is merely a question of ability
To hold the soul ready
For opportunity born of the heat of contest,
Whether you throw or be thrown.
Events are simple circumstances:
They ring my soul in?
I shift the centre without.
To circumstances I adjust — alert and elusive,
And ultimately swing them — one way, other way, *some* way.

It is even so, I say.
With poverty? Farm of the stalwart soul!
With friends fled? The man standing clear by himself!
With position lost? Chance for a better place!
With reputation assailed? Opportunity for sure vindication!
With sickness? Time for rest—time to discover unknown forces—
Time to gear in with the System —
Time to forge faith and the last armor of Courage!
With death? *When the Courage-Man dies, he wins!*

— THE AUTHOR.

CHAPTER XIII.

COURAGE FOR FUTURE EVENTS.

"I am discoursing among philosophers. . . . . Keep yourself strong and fit for the uses of life and initiated by being exercised in action.— *Epictetus*.

MAN'S ability to influence matter and mind in the present guarantees power over the so-called future, since the future is but the logical sequence of the present. This seeming commonplace is like the sea for depth and vastness of suggestion.

In projecting influence upon objects and persons, both in the present and in the future, we pursue two methods:

The *direct method* of ordinary conduct, familiar to all;

The *indirect method* affecting some universal medium so that it shall continue to work out natural sequences beyond the present. Let us examine these methods in their order.

DIRECT AND INDIRECT ACTION ON THE FUTURE.

The *direct method* involves physical contact, the operation of conduct, the use of language, and so on. This method by manipulation of present realities—persons, objects, actions—modifies the relations of such realities and the reactions of the outcomes upon the person employing it. The sentence merely indicates the method of everyday life. We may compare the method to the complex activity involved in manipulating various objects and vessels floating on a sheet of water, where the *now*-effects would be due to *present* action on the part of the manipulator, and the *later* effects to momentum and consequent interaction taking place among the objects, and final *outcome-reaction* upon the person doing the work suggested.   On the "sea of life," of course, these "objects" and "vessels" are material things and human beings.

The *indirect method* involves all the elements of the direct, but is indirect because it modifies, *through* this familiar influence, some *universal medium underlying all life*, or pervading all life, which medium always maintains its integrity and unity, yet is capable of modifications in the present that shall continue and develop character and complexity because of the nature of the medium and the natural interaction of the movements secured within it by such modifications.   We are thinking now, not alone of the surface of the human sea, but of the whole depth and body of it — which is more or less influenced by any movement taking place within or upon it.   All that occurs on the surface influences in some way every part of its vastness, and the final effects are due not only to the direct action of persons and objects on our human surface, but also to ultimate sequences of interaction of all the effects and effects of effects throughout the illimitable mass — so long as the original modifications identically continue.

Two such universal, permanent and unitary existences are present to our thought: the *Universal Ether*, and *the Infinite Life or Reality*.   We proceed now to consideration of these media through which we may influence the future.

1.   THE ETHER AS MEDIUM FOR PSYCHIC DEMAND.

The ether of space may be regarded as the matrix of all material and living forms.   "The assumption is that matter is composed, in some way, of electrons ; which again must be considered to be essentially peculiarities, or singularities, or definite structures, in the ether itself." "The ether of space is a continuous, incompressible, stationary (relatively to the earth), fundamental substance or perfect fluid; matter is composed of modified and electrified specks, or minute structures of ether, which are amenable to mechanical as well as electrical force." The etherial matrix also bears relation to the psychic factor in living forms. "We know that matter has a psychical significance, since it can constitute brain, which links together the physical and the psychical worlds. If any one thinks that the ether, with all its massiveness and energy, has probably no psychical significance, I find myself unable to agree with him" (Lodge). "It is as true as any physical fact can be that every movement of an individual — change of attitude, gesture, or expression of countenance — must produce a corresponding change in his field (the surrounding ether), and tend to bring about in others similar movements." "So far as mental action depends upon brain structure, any changes in the latter must produce corresponding changes in the brain field, and there must be a brain field." Every activity of and among the living and psychic forms of existence affects the boundless etheric ocean, and affects its shifting present state not only directly, but also indirectly through the sequences of the direct influence. When you strike a blow, have a thought, utter a word, put forth a volition, you set in motion the universal ether, that is, induce some sort of change therein, which change can be no other than a mode of motion, and the final outcomes of such movements depend, in the matter of reach and character, upon the degree and quality of the original force employed.

Since we, the actors, *remain,* year after year, and continue on the changing scene (both of matter, mind and ether), we see that the *subsequent* etheric movements must in time react upon ourselves. This statement is evidently true on the surface of things in everyday life. We influence obj cts and persons, and are, therefore, correspondingly influenced ourselves by ultimate outcomes of the activities thus induced. Such a thought is perfectly :amiliar. But the ongoing and interacting movements, coming about by our own action and that of others, react upon us when we *arrive into their midst,* for good or for ill, in a similar way.

All influences which we inaugurate and the outcomes of which react upon us, have their *origin in the present.* Speaking generally, *future* etheric reaction upon us is what *present* etheric action determines.

This proposition is so true that we may formulate practical demands on the future, in rational confidence, by so thinking now and so acting now as to insure logical coming sequences which shall react upon us in a general way very much as we desire — and more and more, if we develop ability, as we particularly desire. We proceed, then, to an analysis of psychic demand.

FIRST ANALYSIS OF PSYCHIC DEMAND: *General Factors.* Psychic demand may be analyzed into the factors of *thought* and *action.* In other words, it is ours to influence the future for good and welfare as follows:

(a) By demand-*thought* which claims *now*-welfare more and more to realize in the future;

(b) By such appropriate present *activity,* incessantly held, incessantly improving, as shall continuously create "channels" or "wires" along which the etheric outcomes may realize in the desired responses to demands.

Observe! This realization or fulfilment of demand is more than outcome of practical ability or activity. The practical activity is indispensable, but the psychic demand is itself a compelling force which multiplies the efficiency of activity many fold. Nevertheless, the demand-responses can only come to you as you create "channels," or erect "wires," for their arrival, by activity of the best and completest character possible in your case.

You cannot sit at ease and indolently wish good fortune with any assurance of influencing the universal medium of stellar spaces. On the other hand, scattering and non-energetic activity has no power to stir the depths of the ether-world-sea and institute movements therein that shall hold on through the years and react in due time upon you according to your wish. The thought must be *intelligent* and *concentrated*, and the activity must be *consistent, unwearied* and *confident*. But if your thinking and your acting harmonize and represent intelligence and concentration, consistency and unwearied confidence, it is law that you may expect fulfilment in welfare and goods of this two-fold demand which you thus set up and maintain — according to the influencing power of your personality at any stage of your life. You cannot get out of a machine more than its nature makes possible, though you can always get out of any machine less than its nature makes possible. You have probably been getting out of yourself, the greatest machine, as man, less than your personality provides for. Moreover, you are a machine of life and psychic factor, capable of development indefinitely. Hence the encouragement that the limits of your ability to influence the future by psychic demand have probably never been reached, and that you may so improve the psychic and physical elements of your personality *now*, always *now*, that these limits may extend, more and more, through all the years of your career.

SECOND ANALYSIS OF PSYCHIC DEMAND : *Particular Qualities.* Psychic demand requires further definition by way both of *inclusion* and of *exclusion*. Let us observe:

1.   Psychic demand must *not* be *vague* and *indefinite*. In fact, there is no true demand if the objects of demand are unclear, kaleidoscopic and confused in thought.

(z)   Psychic demand must be *clear* and *definite*. Your thought should embrace precisely *what* you want and *why* and (approximately) *when* you want it.

Substitute (z) for 1.

2.   Psychic demand must *not* be *negative:* doubtful, associated with uncertainty of desire, modified by questions, such as, "Is it best?"   "Is it right?" and the like.

(y)   Psychic demand must be *positive:* emphatic, believing, self-satisfying, self-filling, unmodified by any consideration whatever.

Substitute (y) f r 2.

3.   Psychic demand must *not* be *alternative:* carrying the double intention of a first choice "if possible," but a second choice "if the first fails." The idea of failure is foreign to psychic demand. Such a demand violates (y) and is a mere wish.

(x)   Psychic demand must be *exclusive*, at the time, of every alternative. Moreover, the demand should never be, "*This or nothing*," because "nothing" needs no demanding. Let the demand always be, "*This definite thing!*"

Substitute (x) for 3.

4. Psychic demand must *not* be composed of *variables and mixtures*. One can demand one thing to-day, forget it to-morrow, and another thing then. This sort of thinking merely constructs a *chain of wishes*, the chain being no stronger than its weakest element. And one can wish many things all at once, and thus construct a mere *fagot of mind-stuff*, lacking in continuity, self-convincing power, and so "pulsating" all sorts of impulses into the ether, none of which is effective.

(w) Psychic demand should refer to *one definite thing at once a time*, and should call for that with the entire power of the self. Do not permit your demands to "cross" one another, nor to coalesce, nor to become "tangled up." Of course one may demand many things, taking the matter by and large, but this should mean simply that you concentrate on one of the desires at a time while demanding that, then passing on to another, and so on.

Substitute (w) for 4.

5. Psychic demand must *not* be *unreasonable*. What the unreasonable is with any person must be intuited by that person in the process of psychic growth and practical experience interpreted by good sense. As the self unfolds, and as practical affairs bring common sense to bear upon the desires, the reasonable demand will appear as a conviction, "This is for me to claim."

(v) Psychic demand must be *courageous in interpreting the reasonable*. The reasonable is not merely your present notion of unfitness or inability to bring the desire to pass. Here is the point where courage must be assumed and maintained. It will be well, when a desire seems unreasonable for your life, to look around you and ask the questions: "Other people seem to possess goods and welfare of certain kinds and degrees; why should not I? Why are such benefits unreasonable for me when others have them?" There is surely enough for all; therefore, these things are perfectly reasonable as objects of your demand.

Substitute (v) for 5.

6. Psychic demand must *not* be *irrational in the nature of things*. You cannot rationally demand what your conduct naturally makes impossible. You cannot rationally demand, say, all-round business ability in ten days. And so on. It will not do to imagine that we can do anything we like with the laws of the Universe, as it does not do to reduce life to mere material grind in harmony with man-made laws. Yourself is power, but all power manifests through harmony with the nature of things.

(u) Psychic demand must be *rationally based on the elements, Nature, time, space, growth, power of self, and human relation*. Psychic demand properly relates you to the Universal System and its contents and laws. True demand will not seek to violate real natural law, to ignore time, to act regardless of space, to expect results independently of personal growth, nor to leap beyond the present power of self (nor deny future power as possible merely because of lack of present power), nor to contradict relations which necessarily obtain among human beings.

Substitute (u) for 6.

7. Psychic demand must *not* be made in *mere mental statements* — must not be confined to propositions of the intellect. People often assume that if they mentally speak a demand, in the top of the head, as

it were, they have made a psychic demand. And because results do not follow as wished, efforts are discontinued in disbelief. We have here a case of manipulation of telegraphic keys with no electric current in connection. There is really no power in such mental propositions. It is at this point, for one thing, that the whole subject of demand is misunderstood. One interprets words in terms of one's own thought; if that thought has no room for the very idea of psychic demand, the statements made in relation to it are conceived in terms of the person's present understanding: that is, misconceived. It is common experience that we live with propositions for years, putting our own interpretation upon them, and finally, in some moment of inspiration, suddenly discover a new meaning which now seems as plain as anything could possibly be — that is, discover that what we have supposed we understood we did *not* understand at all. Precisely so with psychic demand. The power is one which must be acquired through psychic understanding of the law and reality of demand itself. When such understanding comes about, you will see that there is no demand-power in mere mental propositions concerning goods or welfare.

(t) Psychic demand is a *subconscious affair:* begun in the ordinary conscious thinking, put there into words, but then projected into the deeper "within" by an effort to *feel* the thought no less than to think it, and to *believe for results,* so that in time the demand becomes an *assured conviction* influencing all the personal contemporaneous life.

Substitute (t) for 7.

To summarize the analysis, we see that psychic demand is (with *consistent, unwearied and confident*

action) *intelligent* and *concentrated thought-claim* (for
goods and welfare) which is *clear, definite, positive, exclusive, single, reasonable, courageous, rational,* a matter
of *conviction,* and *subconsciously maintained.* Such
a demand might be formulated, for example, as
follows:

"*I demand* (name the thing desired clearly and distinctly), *singly, exclusively,* without *alternative* or *doubt,*
and I emphatically *expect* the fulfilment of this demand
within such a time because I am *living* for it, because
it is surely *for me,* and because my best life *requires* precisely that."

II.   The Infinite Reality as Medium for Psychic Demand.

Science assumes the existence of the universal
ether as a ground for the explanation of matter and
various natural forces. The doctrines of the conservation of energy and the correlation of force involve
such a medium. There is a sum-total of physical
energy in our Universe which holds on, under innumerable forms or manifestations, from eon to eon of its
history, and the "deepest" medium in which such
energy "abides" is the ether that reveals in heat, light,
electricity, and so on. This energy reveals in force,
and hence exhibition of force is result of transformation merely, never is a new-creation, in the form of
energy's expression. Every display of physical force
is but a manifestation of etheric conditions.

Similarly, seeking a ground for explanation of
ether, matter, force, life, mind, we assume the existence
of one *Infinite and Eternal Reality.* This is the Central
Energy, the Universal Source of force, whose Thoughts
are Universes and their contents, Nature, the human

self, and other supposable beings. "In Him we live
and move and have our being."

In practical life we always appeal to — make demands on — this Infinite Reality: in farming, by sow-
ing, planting, cultivating; in invention, by investigating, molding matter, combining parts, adjusting forms,
observing laws; and so on. Here we see that thought
and action constitute the common phases of psychic
demand on the Infinite Reality.

Now and then an individual has arisen who has
passed beyond common human venture and made the
most extraordinary demands on this august Universal
Medium. By psychic demand Joseph frustrated his
brothers and became lord of Egypt. By psychic demand Abram acquired greatness of soul and founded
a deathless race. By psychic demand Moses received
the great fundamentals of religion. By psychic demand Plato uncovered the divine "Ideas" and Jesus
deified the human as the goal of evolution. By psychic
demand Phidias coerced the beauty of Venus to live
in marble and Raphael fixed upon canvas the world's
ideal of Motherhood. By psychic demand Shakespeare
achieved the impossible in the mind of a poacher and
held the mirror of Nature up to the astonished soul of
man. By psychic demand was Art created, Music discovered, Industry fashioned, Government builded,
Religion brought forth, Wealth accumulated, Progress
conceived, Power seized, Civilization unfolded.

By psychic demand the animal came to be man,
and man followed on to conscious self, and conscious
self realized in mind, and mind arrived at lordship over
all. The Infinite has forced nothing upon man, yet
all that man has achieved has the Infinite vouchsafed
to human demand — to common toil and to psychic

faith. This is not because the Infinite has arbitrarily given or withholden. It is because the Infinite Reality is the Infinite Medium for human expression, and is in such relation to the human, as underlying Ground of all existences, that the right psychic demand of man as truly calls to his aid the Infinite Reality itself as the right psychic demand calls to his aid the universal ether. We do not assume that science utilizes the etheric medium by guesswork, nor that, when its adjustments are made, the outcomes depend upon arbitrary caprice lurking somewhere in the Universe. The outcomes are matters of law. Similarly, utilization of the Infinite Reality, because of its established relation to man as Ground and Source of all things, need be no affair of guessing on our part. When right adjustments are made, the outcomes here also are surely subjects of immutable law.

Adjustment to the Infinite Reality Required in Psychic Demand.

The right adjustments of physical science are familiar to all. The right adjustment which man must make to the Infinite Reality is Harmony of thought and action with the Reality conceived as Source of all values — which is equivalent to Harmony with the best possibilities of the self and others who are also in such harmony. This is the ideal. And the instrument by which that harmony is lawfully made effective in human life — your life — is psychic demand.

For, observe! The infinite *means* to and for you: health, prosperity, unfoldment, psychic power. The only limits to these outcomes in your case are your sanity and your ability to establish the harmony indicated and to develop and maintain all-conquering demand — of course, within the laws of the nature of things.

The Founder of the Christian religion said: *"Whatsoever things ye desire when ye pray, believe that ye receive them, and ye shall have them."* This states the law of psychic demand. *"Whatsoever things ye desire"*— desire clearly, definitely, positively, singly, exclusively —*"when ye pray,"*— when ye intelligently, concentratedly, reasonably and rationally demand or claim,— *"believe"*— demand feelingly and confidently —*"that ye receive them,"*— not may, might, could, shall, receive in some uncertain future, but, — *"receive them,"*— are even now entering upon the realization,—*"and ye shall receive them"*— shall *then, during* adjustment, *during* demand, *during* the assurance, *have* them.

This is a stupendous proposition. In the realm of religion, it has a personal guaranty. But in the realm of human and Infinite inter-relations, it has the guaranty of the law-nature of the Universe.

APPLICATION OF PYSCHIC DEMAND.

So far as the ultimate progress of man is concerned, the application of psychic demand needs in our thought no modification. Ultimately, man will receive whatever his rightly-unfolded nature claims of the Infinite Reality.

So far as any individual life is concerned, the outworking of the law is limited by three factors: the individual's practical sanity or common sense, his ability to make his demands intelligently, reasonably, concentratedly, and so on as stated in our analysis, and his ability to believe, that is, feel, the demand as assured — and so to actually draw to his aid Infinite Reality.

While no man can achieve the impossible, and each of us will always have much to learn and more and more of the self to unfold, yet we may rest assured of the truth as follows:

1. You can discover your psychic power only through a lifetime of effort;

2. The more you strive to utilize the Infinite Reality, the more will the power develop through response realized;

3. The more experience instructs, the more will your life infallibly exhibit the effectiveness of psychic demand.

The importance of these considerations induces

A PRELIMINARY INVITATION: The discussions thus closed should be read and pondered many times. As you come completely to understand the truth, humanly speaking, and especially as you continue to apply it to your life, you will find growing up within you a great confidence and a deep and brilliant courage to cope with the present and to face the future.

And above all, the life which will thus be induced in thought and action will continually so affect the two media of existence, the Universal Ether and the Infinite Reality, that the logical future sequences and their interactions will infallibly react upon you, both for happiness and for welfare.

Were I not absolutely convinced of the truth of this conception, I could not venture it in these pages. I know nothing truer, saner, surer or more practical for dispelling the fears that relate to the future or for the culture of courage in regard to events. We come, then, to the event-fears, so long held over from the preceding chapter, fear of accident and illness, fear of poverty, fear of final failure, fear of the loss of friends. We take up these fears in the order named.

FEAR OF ACCIDENT AND ILLNESS.

First, the Fear of Accidents will be considered. Many people are haunted by vague foreboding that some accident may yet, or surely will, befall them. Such foreboding is, of course, wholly useless, but, what is more to the point, it is also wholly a psychic evil. The psychic state involved may finally operate as a *cause* of accident feared. Your apprehension of physical mishap cannot *in itself directly* induce accident, but it may *indirectly* do so by bringing about bodily or mental conditions which shall work against you in the time of danger. This operation of psychic factor may tend either to prevent right action in avoidance of danger, or to prevent recovery from injury when sustained. Fear breeds expectation, and expectation provides fear's conditions.

In the meantime, and whether or no, this fear is doing you subtle harm in many possible ways. Primarily, such fear interferes with life's normal satisfaction in itself, and this interference cannot fail to disturb your deeper self, both physical and mental — that is, unsettle your personal equilibrium, poise, sense of power. Moreover, the idea may act as a suggestion to the subconscious self, and the suggestion may actually control your action, thus bringing you all unaware into the presence of danger which you otherwise would never confront. This brings us to our

REGIME AGAINST FEAR OF ACCIDENT. *First Phase*: *Optimism.* You should, therefore, throttle the notion instantly, at its every appearance, and also habituate yourself to the strong feeling of all-wellness, now and to be. The purpose of these directions, of course, is not your protection, but is solely the dissipation of the idea of accident and the fear-feeling arising therefrom. By exercise of will and occupation of the mind with the confident idea of wellbeing, this double end may be accomplished. If you fill your imagination with pictures of yourself as injured, you feed fear and make it a habit. Similarly, you feed courage and make that a habit by occupying the imagination with thoughts of yourself as always in a condition of safety and happiness.

Second Phase: Psychic Demand. You are invited now to have constant recourse to your power of faith-claim for perfect self-handling against all personal mishap. If you persistently make use of true psychic demand that all shall be well with you, you will not only banish fear, but also actually suggest to the subconscious self alertness and adequacy against unseen contingencies and unforeseen events — that is, you will thus train subconscious activities in personal protection.

The *Fear of Illness* naturally follows the preceding fear. In the last paragraph sickness may well be substituted for accident. The former, however, is emphatically subject to suggestion. To forebode illness is very likely to induce illness. The subconscious self, grown accustomed to the notion of trouble in the body, operates often to throw physical functions out of order, so that illness may either be self-induced or be made possible because the physical tone has been lowered in resisting power. The limit of recovery from physical equilibrium in health, or what may conveniently be termed the *index of resistance* (otherwise called the *opsonic index*), varies somewhat for each individual. When the index is high we speak of such a man as strong or robust; when, on the other hand, it is low, (we speak of it) as weak or delicate. Unquestionably fear modifies the opsonic index of the human body.

Thus, it is evil morbidly to dwell upon one's bodily feelings — except to take the warning of evident distress, in which case a physician should be summoned because he may discover avoidable trouble and the fact of his treatment may be just the suggestion that you need, regardless of any other efficiency obtaining in his drugs. The drugs are probably worthless,— in almost a majority of cases,— but the physician's knowledge and his presence are often worth immensely more than you will be willing to pay for. Let us look at the matter thus brought up.

I am for the doctor, not for his own sake, not for the sake of his profession, but for the sake of my subconscious self, without reference to the physical action of medicine, and for the sake of his surplus of knowledge over mine. Medicine is almost wholly a matter of education on my part (this is written representatively for you or for any other person). When ill, my (your— all men's) subconscious self wants a first-class physician, and when I am ill, that self shall have a physician, although, in nearly every instance, my (your) conscious mind feels that the medicine is, in itself, mere useless superfluity. I (representatively speaking) have only lived on the earth a few hundred thousand years, and my (our) ancestral self has come to lean on a set of men many of whom are immensely crude, notwithstanding the fact that they also have ancestrally lived so many centuries. After a time I (man) shall learn the secret of immortality — but thousands of years hence. Meantime, then, I (you) must yield to the ancestral self until he in me (you) becomes wiser. I (we) have no brief doctor, but I have a brief for myself in good health. I have no brief for any other healing profession of the mental or religious sort. What are all these sects and professional divisions to me when they are placed up against the august laws governing personal welfare? The success of mental suggestion and of faith are alike due to law, which is of no school, "science," or religion — is of the nature of things alone, and as impersonal toward you and me as are wind and tide. Imagine a "christian science" tide-mill, or a "mental-healing" tide-mill, or an "old-school" tide-mill, or a "homeo-pathic" tide-mill, or a "suggestive-therapeutics" tide-mill, erected within the flood of law and force that obtain across the diameter of the Universe! I call the physician when I believe I need one, and I call in my infinite psychic resources, in myself or in some men-tal healer, when I desire. If these will not coöperate, both may depart. I am for myself!

He who coddles his symptoms nurses an illness into being. Except as above suggested, therefore, it is wise to ignore the slight variations in one's daily feel-ings and to assert and assume that one is in good or improving health and will so continue. This assump-tion-assertion is suggested to the subconscious self to right-up matters that may be wrong, and to maintain among functions good order now existing or to be surely brought about. It is also one of the finest of psychic tonics operative for wellbeing throughout the entire system.

And if the physician you employ deals in questions about your symptoms, you are invited to decline the interview. He is not skilled if he cannot by indirection uncover more than you may have disclosed to him at the first. He is grossly antiquated if he asks you a large number of leading questions, such as, "Ever fever up? Have any backache?" and the like (questions put to a real patient in actual life). Why must this dealer in dead matter put evil into my subconscious thought? When the doctor begins this unscientific course he accentuates the fundamental trouble for which you have consulted him. We conclude that always is it better to think health as yours, and at least, not to entertain symptoms and ideas of ill-health. Thus we have our

REGIME AGAINST FEAR OF ILLNESS. *First Phase: Pictured Health.* You are urged, therefore, to cease entertaining your symptoms and to eliminate, by will and substitution, the thought of yourself as ill or to be ill in the future. Fix in mind, rather, the confident idea and expectation of a good old age, hale, hearty and happy. And the way in which to accomplish this substitution is simply to think of yourself in pictures representing the desired factors, charging the pictures, as it were, with energy and covering them with an atmosphere of sunlight and good cheer.

SECOND PHASE: *Psychic Demand.* In the manner indicated for the corresponding phase of the preceding regime, you are invited to formulate confident demand that good health shall be yours, now and in the future. Always begin and conduct such demand about as follows: *"I am now in full harmony with the whole Universe and with all right-minded intelligences, and on this basis I demand and claim my own normal order of health."*

FEARS OF POVERTY.

Our discussion now proceeds by a series of observations.

The Culture of Courage.

Poverty a Crime. I hold that poverty is a social crime.

Poverty is a crime, not of the many against the one, but of the many against the many.

Poverty is the one universal sign of incompetence, the sign that points to the prosperous multitude rather than to the unfortunate individual. The individual's incompetence may be enforced, but that of the prosperous many is self-chosen. The people can have anything on which they can agree and for which they will persistently stand. But the people permit poverty because they do not know how to get rid of it, and this incompetence is a crime because the people do not sufficiently desire that every man, woman and child on earth shall have enough for health of body and growth of soul.

It is for such reasons that many are haunted by the fear of poverty in the future. The idea is preposterous and monstrous that any human being should go into old age dependent upon charity for food, clothing, shelter and books. The earth is so big,— and so beautiful,— and so rich! Yet this fear hides in the heart of thousands.

It is not the present object to instruct in the prevention of poverty. You will find much to the point in *"Power For Success"* and *"Business Power,"* on that subject. It may be ventured, however, even if seemingly commonplace, that two certain methods will infallibly work wonders in the directions of prosperity, to-wit:

Love your work, and yourself as workman, and *multiply* yourself valiantly into your work; and

Save a good percentage of your wage or salary.

Nevertheless, such suggestions do not reckon with "bad luck" and disasters, and so the fear of poverty clings to heart and thought throughout the years. Now, these last words are important for they tell the main story.

2. *"Luck" is Real.* The factors of the "lucky" and the "unlucky" should be reckoned with. It is the habit of "wise" people who have never met with mishap to insist sturdily and with scientific accuracy that "there is no such thing as luck," since all events are results of operation of laws. The statement is true, but it has significance only when you are "lucky." When you are "unlucky," the "wise" remark means nothing, and after a time you discover that "luck" is a provision of the law itself, and that the consequences of the law are as hard to bear as they would be were the law a mere fiction. Practically speaking, "luck" is actual enough. Many people believe that they are "down on their luck," and correctly, for so they are. For this unhappy fact they are never *alone* at fault. Some other person is always in *part* to blame when any human being goes "unlucky"— some other person, thing, or event. Yet for the fact, again, the "unlucky" people are themselves always more or less at fault. Let us observe in this matter:

Every man and woman in this world gets in the long run, after childhood, and excepting some awful handicaps of birth — *about what he or she deserves.* But let us again observe:

3. *Desert is a Matter of Law.* The deserving is not what you and I see or believe; it goes down to the very roots and the last shred of our being, action and thought. The "going down" is so thorough that at the last it loses personality and becomes merely a matter of harmony or of disharmony somehow with law.

In the large responsibility thus uncovered, other people must share, so that the most unforunate often

gets somewhat more than he morally and seemingly
deserves, perhaps, but more, also, because he is or has
been somewhere out of gear with the laws of his being.
In the complex equation thus laid bare emerges, now,
a vast compensatory fact,— to-wit:

*The individual power to balance up against all mis-
fortune the product and power of his own thought.* Let
us see about that:

4. *Compensation is for Each.* Jean Valjean is the
most "unlucky" of all fiction heroes, the fact being due
partly to his own violations of law, partly to the evil
in others who come in contact with him. Yet Jean
Valjean's inner world and power of thought grew
through all the terrible history until the man's soul-
wealth and soul-achievements more than compensated
the huge-bulking tragedy of his life.

This is where the Eternal enters the equation.

"Bad luck" is a fact. But thought is also a fact.
As a fact thought is a force. As a force it is a world-
builder. As a world-builder it is Compensation.

We begin, then, with the mere power of thought,
just as one might begin with the mere power of gravity.
Let us see about this :

5. *Thought is Power.* We are dealing with the
vast power of your thought. When you engage in
thinking, you *create* thought. The Universe is the complex Thought of an Infinite Thinker. Nothing exists
outside the Universe of Thought. The only possible
power of creating, then, is that of thinking. Nothing
exists that is not thought into existence. An infinite
space containing nothing would be an infinite nonentity.
Infinite space containing matter and force would be an
infinite closed system. Eternal matter could not exist
without eternal force. The assumed eternal matter

is eternal force.   But, since force and space are not identical, and since space can do nothing, the closed system of infinite force assumes that that force is introduced into infinite space.   In asking how this could be effected we must think in terms of our highest selves, that is, in terms of thought.   When we do this so as to conceive of an Infinite Thinker, we see that the Thinker's Thought *is* space and that the system can come into existence only *within* the Infinite Thinker.   That is to say, the Universe is a Thought-Expression of the Infinite.   So far as our thoughts are concerned, these things are as true of the human self as of the Infinite. For you, all that exists *in* your knowing exists *by* your thinking.   You think into the existence which you know: your world, your Nature, your body, your own mind.   (The mind is not you; it is a product of your activity).   You *create for* your knowing self all that you *know.*   Being exists, of course, independently of your knowing, but you thought-create all that you *know,* because you only know what you *think.*

Ideally considered, then, it is for you to create the kind of body, mind, world that you will — within the limits of your human nature.   This power to create, however, has been corrupted and weakened by thousands of years of false living, so that man practically is unable both to will and to create in all cases ideally. The goal of our development is a far-off psychic state of the human self in which it can create for itself a body, a mind, and a world that shall be perfect relatively to finite individuality.   At present, however, we can only will and thought-create according to what we are, which "what we are" is in part due to ancestral living, in part due to our entertained ideals.   And now, observe:

6.   *Some of the Detail Achievements of Your Thought.*
It is yet the privilege of every human to accomplish
several important things.

(a)   We can make it our business to think only
health, happiness, courage, confidence, truth and goodness.   As we think these things we create them in our
thought-world.

(b)   The influence of this creative thought upon
body, mind and our personal world is immeasurable.
Such thought tends to make more and more our own
the elements health, development, success and a world
beautiful.   The natural outcome is the destruction of
fear through elimination of its conditions.

(c)   You have here the finest possible breeder of
courage.   The conclusion from this and all preceding
pages is that you can directly and indirectly create
courage, since that attitude and that feeling are perfectly natural with thoughts of happiness, success and
personal development.   And so we observe, again:

(d)   This action of your creative thought-power
will infallibly influence external conditions of your
life.   You cannot carry out these suggestions without
bringing things to pass which will insure you against
poverty in old age.   I do not mean, however, that you
will thus compel great wealth.   Let us see about this.

It is only a part of our social crime that men nurse
the notion of the desirability of great wealth.   *Great
individual wealth is never really desirable.*   On the contrary, it is as *undesirable as death*.   It is undesirable
for the *individual* because it limits his best development and robs him of the best success in living.   We
should establish asylums for excusively rich people
who have achieved their own wealth.   *The passion
for excessive riches is insanity;* the great money-getters

who achieve nothing else are *all insane.* Huge individual wealth is also undesirable for *society,* since it means the absurdity and crime of wide-spread poverty. This book has no interest whatever in your future wealth. It advises you to cultivate decency and reasonably limited means. Our goal — in the interest of your courage — is precisely that: the expectation of reasonably limited means for health of body and culture of mind. This induces a further observation:

(e) The limitation of personal means should be purely personal. One man or woman needs — just enough with which to make the most of himself or herself and life — no more, no less. Hence, *our individual needs differ.* You cannot get a twelve-ounce life out of an eight-ounce brain. The twelve-ounce brain, however, has no greater right to make the most of itself than has the eight-ounce brain. The needs of the small personality are as imperative as are those of the larger one. One man needs less than another, but his needs are just as emphatic and true. The Universe is for all, and it provides for all the goal of a fine career of happiness and full development. It does not compel the achievement, but it makes the achievement possible.

(f) Courage before the picture of yourself portrayed in your mind as happy, active, successful according to your needs — this is our present ideal. You can create a self for yourself, a world for and in that self, both of which shall forefend against an old age of poverty and dependence,— barring the one thing, "bad luck,"— if you will masterfully think yourself as adequate now to the work before you and as always to be adequate, and so self-provided for in the days to come. It is necessary, however, to observe:

7. *The Accidents of True "Bad Luck" Do Occur.*
What then? It is essential do define "bad luck" down
to the truth.

A man in the West saw the need of a parcel delivery
system in a southern California city. He instituted
such a system, and later sold his business for ten thousand dollars. Then he built and furnished a good
home for himself, and proceeded to "take comfort."
Here was no "luck," but all law. Then he permitted
his insurance to lapse one day, and his neighbor's house
went to ashes the next night, and his own followed.
Had this man's insurance been kept up, and had
the company carrying his risk, ordinarily sound, been
sent into bankruptcy by the San Francisco disaster,
that would have been a case of *bona fide* "bad luck"—
according to unforeseen and uncontrollable law. The
laws which you cannot control sometimes go against
you, notwithstanding all reasonable precautions that
you have taken, and the outcome is a real "bad luck."
The laws which you can control are always for you *if
you control them.* When you fail to do this, your "luck"
may be bad, but it is not true "luck." The suggestion,
therefore, is that you intelligently control the laws
related to your life so far as that is possible, humanly
speaking. Hence we come to our regime.

REGIME AGAINST FEAR OF FINAL POVERTY. *First
Phase: Now Adequacy.* In the failure to handle
reasonably controllable laws is where your fear of
poverty, perhaps, finds its inspiration. If you feel
adequate to life now, yet feel the vague fear of possible poverty later on, this is purely a case of feverish
imagination, and the present regime should dispel the
fear. You are invited, therefore, to practise intense
and vigorous thinking in some such form as this: *"I*

am adequate now, and ever shall be, to all demands on my ability and courage."

Second Phase: Psychic Demand. You are urged to put into operation the law of demand discussed at the beginning of this chapter, by formulating demands for adequacy and for ample provision for old age, observing the instructions given in the discussion.

Third Phase: Building for Compensation. If you still confront the fact that "bad luck" may strike you in the future, this is your main trouble. For that trouble you are urged to cultivate confidence and courage by the persistent use of the present regime, and you are invited now to observe the still deeper and more beneficent law:

The human self may win compensation against all disaster.

Poor wisdom to conceive
Experience alone may weave
　Fine tapestry of mind, of heart, rare lace:
How work the gods in men —
With brush or chisel, score or pen —
　Ere school of years might claim to give them grace?

And must experience mean
Defeat and pain — the builder's lien —
　Exacted to the full in coin of age,
And not the nobler store
Of youth's perfections brought to more,
　And joy of growth assured, our finest wage?

Thought-creative power is every soul's possession. If you create a wealthy self to-day, no old age can rob you of that. Do not try to gauge the value in old age of such possession. No mood or state of to-day can accurately judge the attractions of to-morrow. When you are ill, food is tasteless, the ticking of the clock is preternaturally loud, and all the wall-figures take fantastic shapes. Will these things turn out exactly as they now seem when boundless health is again your own? Thus with the compensations of creative thought. To-day you desire for old age sufficient means for comfort. That is assured you if you observe the regimes of this book — barring a true "bad luck." But if actual "bad luck" comes and leaves you poverty-stricken in old age — (there is not one chance for that in ten thousand, for you are already on the way to adequacy and success)— yours then, if now you create them, the compensations of a self and an inner world that will be rich in content, happy in growth, full of the memories of a well-spent life.

For, *observe these pictures.* Note the contrasts. The first picture reveals a wrecked, undeveloped, unhonored, memory-blasted old man, alone in a garret, at eighty years of age. I bid you heroically to *create against* that condition.

The second picture reveals a physically feeble but mentally developed, honored, memory-blessed old man, alone in a garret, at eighty years of age. He will not be alone in a garret: thousands to one against such an outcome. But, if so, he has still the vast compensations of the true self, the courageous self: the full-grown mind, the splendid recollections of life. And all values possessed this man has *created* — just as the Almighty has created suns and constellations.

You are invited, then, to remember our insistence that in such a case old age will not find you in a state of poverty, and you are invited to develop and maintain a full sense of adequacy and courage for the now — holding the sense over from day to day until it becomes the permanent possession of your entire being.

Fear of Final Failure.

The fear of failure has its roots in two misconceptions which are everywhere prevalent. You are invited steadily to examine these misconceptions until you fully perceive and feel their utter falsity.

First Misconception: *That Success Means Wealth and Visible Power.* This is the error into which magazine and newspaper literature commonly drifts. The successful people are the moneyed people, it is often supposed, or the leaders of great industries, notable art, politics or society. This conception is untrue and absolutely groundless.

The error is based on the false notions that money is property and that publicity is power.

Money is not property, except in the bare material, and the right to use the material in a certain way. And money is not wealth, except in its material, at all. Money is a substitute for property and a token of material wealth.

A dying man caused all his ownership in property to be converted into money, and then gathering his relations about him, threw the money into the fire, remarking that he thus relieved them from all trouble concerning it. The act was detestable, of course. Yet all the wealth his money had represented still remained in the world. The property that he had surrendered in the exchange for money still remained. Fire merely destroyed the token.

It is error to regard money as evidence of success, in itself. Money represents a *kind* of success when it *stands for* material values created by individual effort. Many possessors of money are unable to point to values behind it as their own creation. Unless your money represents some values which *you* have created, it is not a symbol of *your* success. *Your* success, as indicated by money, consists, then, not in accumulation of money, but in creation of values. Money is not a value: it is a medium of exchange of values. There are multitudes of values in the world which have brought their creators no money. Stolen inventions and the application of scientific discoveries may be cited. No man's success, therefore, is necessarily represented by the amount of money he owns.

Money symbolizes the *superficial* in life, but *success strikes away down into life's very heart.*

Similar truths obtain with reference to power. *Power is ability to create, transform or move values.*

Values are the things that are indispensable to progress.

This power to create, transform or move things that are indispensable to progress cannot reside in publicity nor consist of office or position, since it is often unseen and without the leverages usually employed. Always, at the last, we discover that power is solely a matter of thought and action directed by will.

The only *wealth* man knows is value indispensable to progress.

The only power man knows is ability to create such value.

The only creator of real value man knows is will-directed thought-action.

Success is the development of ability to create values indispensable to progress, and the creation of such values through will-directed thought-action.

We conclude, then: You possess this ability to some degree; if you have made the reasonable most of that ability, you are so far a success.

If you have created some values indispensable to

progress, as, reasonably speaking, you surely may have done, you are a success.

You possess a will and the power of thought: if you have developed and used will and thought to your reasonable best, you are a success.

Let us understand that the average man and woman has it in his or her power to achieve, for him or her, just as great and genuine a success as any man or woman of wealth, position, fame or genius.

It is, therefore, a mistake to look to any other human being for a standard of your success. *You alone can furnish that standard.* The only legitimate standard of an individual's success is what that individual, reasonably speaking, can or ought to be and do according to his endowments — with environment or circumstances merely considered as stimulus to achievement. Thus we come to the

SECOND MISCONCEPTION: *That Success is Ever a Matter Involving Things External to the Individual.* Success is absolutely personal, and has no necessary connection with external matters.

When we measure success by externals, we invariably set up as a standard some other personality or some other person's achievements. Thus we judge individuals, and ourselves, by mere notions. If the individuals fail to realize our notion, they have failed, we thoughtlessly decide. If their life does not take on certain external signs, they are, again, failures, we conclude. Hence, when *we* fail to resemble a given individual in personality or in achievement, we judge ourselves to have failed. But all this is error, which we seek now to remove by the regime:

REGIME AGAINST FEAR OF FINAL FAILURE. *First Phase: Real Success Now.* No man's or woman's

success depends on his resembling a given individual
or upon his duplicating another's achievements. The
juniper bush or ground cedar is not a failure merely
because it may not grow to be as tall as the oak and
bear acorns. The possibility of a given kind or degree
of success is born into every human being. That is his
right and his responsibility. If he wins that, no failure
is he. The real question, then, is this—and it is enough:
"What can I, any human, be and do to create, transform, or move values indispensable to progress?" Your
success is your practical answer to that question.

The fear of failure has, therefore, no ground in
which to thrive, if —

First, you make practically your own the principles of this chapter;

Secondly, you resolve to make good, and, reasonably speaking, do make good, the practical answer to
the question above given. You can never fear failure
while you are so engaged. The resolve and the action
will infallibly breed the courage-feeling that you are
and shall be equal to all the entertainable demands
that may come into your life. As you now read, that
feeling arises in your consciousness: make the feeling
habit by will and by incessantly recalling the idea.

Second Phase: Psychic Demand. In the meantime, you are invited to continue in deepest action the
demand-thought that all success possible to you shall
assuredly be forthcoming from year to year through
all your life. "Whatsoever things ye desire—believe!"

Fear of Loss of Friends.

Your friends are born, not made. Physically
explained, friendship is due to a certain closeness of
harmony between two individuals.

This harmony obtains fundamentally in the etheric movements of the personal atmospheres. If the harmony etheric tends to merging of movements because all movements in one person fit perfectly those of another person, the friendship will be that of love. A looser complementing, so to speak, is the harmony of ordinary friendship. As we are born with a definite number of brain-cells, which may develop, but the multitude of which never in life can be increased, a certain limited range of nature is determined for us by our birth. These and other facts constitute the basis of the conclusion that we are born friends, not manufactured.

In terms of matter, the last analysis of each person's nature leads to the idea of a given arrangement and number of movements in the etheric matrix as ground of physical body and parts. With such an endowment we are also born.

In terms of psychics, the individual nature is definitely endowed for development with powers and traits which may be symbolized by such etheric movements, but which really express within them.

In mechanics, some varieties of motion will not harmonize with others. So, in the ether-ground and the psychic system of any individual, harmony with other systems (persons) may require greater ingenuity of skill in adjustment — often obtaining not very satisfactorily, failing to secure certain friendships, or even proving utterly impossible.

Your real friends, then, are given you when you come into the world. Somewhere they await you, as you await them; sometime they will come to you as you will go to them. You need not seek them: the nature of things will in due time bring them to you.

Then you will know the one who has come: not, perhaps, instantly, but sooner or later — surely know.

The measure in which these propositions are sanely
true depends on the measure of your steadfast fidelity
to your truest and highest self.   By so much as you
are splendidly and growingly YOU at the best (reasonably speaking), by so much will you have true friends to
the very last.   This is an infallible method for winning
friends.   If you *try* to make them, you will fail.   You
can only *create* friends, and this you accomplish by
growing friendships, and this you achieve by being
always, freely, with idealism and aspiration as your
motive powers, your whole true and highest self.

When you catch and feel the certainty of the truth
here presented, your fears for future loneliness must
vanish — provided you accept the regime:

REGIME AGAINST FEAR OF THE LOSS OF FRIENDS.
First Phase: The True Self Now.   You are, therefore,
urged now to resolve and always to make good the resolution: *"I am now and from henceforth I freely shall be,
in idealism and aspiration, my whole highest true self."*

If you will look back upon your life, you will see
that always your deepest friendships have sprung up
without search, effort or planning.   You have for a
time, now and then, felt that this or that person was
surely your friend.   But time, space, work, have inter-
vened, and the so-solid seeming bonds have faded away.
Yet here and there bonds have somehow held — your
relations of friendship have been kept up, and you know
now that nothing can dissolve the ties that bind,
nothing can destroy the few friendships which remain
to you.   These values are yours forever.

Second Phase: Self as Resource.   It is the loss of
the ephemeral friendships that suggests some final day

of loneliness to you, and inspires the fear now before us. We observe:

No human being should ever permit himself to depend on any other human being for happiness. The happiness which springs from friendships is legitimate and desirable, with a reservation — that self and God's world still hold good and are enough, whatever become of this friendship or that companionship. Thus appears the foundation-truth of real friendship.

Your value to your friend, and his value to you, is in each case measured precisely by your ability to companion and be alone with your own soul. You enjoy your friend by giving and receiving values, and the values depend on the depth and wealth of the self. If you can find happiness and wealth in self, you will make a true friend for some other self. But when you *depend* on your friend, you by so much leave yourself unmined, undiscovered, undeveloped, and you thus rob yourself and your friend.

You are therefore, urged to be your whole true and highest self, and to cultivate ability to find there happiness, and power and comradeship. By so much as one observes such a principle, by so much must the fear of future loneliness vanish from his thought.

Third Phase: *Psychic Demand.* You are invited to bring psychic demand upon the present for true friends now and thus to develop within the subconscious self an attitude and quality which shall in the future always secure you the now-friends you need, both for happiness and for welfare and success. Psychic demand alone will infallibly banish the fear here discussed.

THE ROCK OF COURAGE.

When fails the august Law of Laws
That each effect must have its cause,—
When self, the I, from Self Supreme
Divides, as life from death's dull dream,
    Then is all courage dear.

But lo, I am! image as soul
Of Cause Uncaused — the Living Whole:
But lo, my life 's the sure effect
Of all my thoughts and will elect;
But lo, as God attracts but Good,
So I, in equal masterhood:
    How, now, shall fears appear?

While reigns the changeless Law of Laws
That each effect reveals its cause,—
While I, the self, and Self Supreme
Share will and thought,— as bank and stream,—
Mine is the courage of the soul
Harmonic with the Perfect Whole:
    Immune as God to fear.—

                    —THE AUTHOR.

CHAPTER XIV

A Perpetual Tonic.

"Fear hinders the free vibration of the life through the body by paralyzing the life-force which is in it. To fear is to lessen your spirit's hold on its godhood. To fear is to lose confidence in the power of your own spirit to hold you and to keep you in perfect harmony. To fear is to weaken your spirit's hold on its supply — God. To fear is to place yourself as a servant to all those things that are beneath you.

"There is no cause for fear, as man is made with the possibility of *generating all power within himself*. He masters every condition by *keeping himself so positive* that he can *attract* to himself *only* the *best* of all knowledge, all power and all harmony. He can then mould all circumstances to his desire. He does this by his knowledge of the law of attraction, like attracting like. If he holds within himself *only supreme desire*, or godlike desire, he can attract to himself *only superior* powers and *supreme* gifts. But he must constantly hold himself as supreme, never forgetting for one moment that he is one with God." — *Elizabeth Deuress.*

WE have discovered long ere this that the treatment of fear and the development of courage, to be successful, demand far more than the mere reading of a book. Doubtless, even a rapid journey through these pages has revealed the possibility of high courage in all, has even inspired, now and then, genuine if temporary moods of real fearlessness; but the courage that surely justifies our work is a growth within the deeper self, is therefore permanent, and is always all-round for all occasions. Such a psychic power demands two things, speaking generally:

Instruction in *exactly what to do and how to do exactly that* — the standing motto of the Power-Book Library.

A consciousness of adequacy that is really vital, since *vital education is the evolution of consciousness* — the foundation-principle of all the Power-Books.

The instruction given in preceding chapters meets the first requirement. Vital consciousness of courage can only result from work in the regimes set forth — according, of course, to personal needs. By constant practised thought and iteration of ideas and inspirational sentences, day after day, month after month, a personal spirit and a mental attitude are developed which more and more *realize* the *opposite* of every sentence in the first paragraph of the quotation preceding this chapter, and the full *affirmative* of every statement in the second paragraph of that quotation. Thus we come to our

Final Affirmations.

You are invited to repeat the affirmations given below, in their order, daily for long, until they represent your real mood, deep and permanent:

Section One. 1. "My courage induces free vibration (or action) of the life throughout my body by inspiring the life-force within it."

2. "My courage strengthens my spirit's hold on its godhood."

3. "My courage inspires within me confidence in the power of my own spirit to hold me and to keep me in perfect harmony."

4. "My courage strengthens my spirit's hold on its supply — the Infinite."

5. "My courage makes me master of all those things that are beneath me."

Section Two. 1. "I, as human, possess the practical possibility of generating all power within myself."

2. "I master every condition by keeping myself *so positive* that I attract to myself *only the best* of all knowledge, all power and all harmony."